Frommer's®
Beijing

My Beijing
by Jen Lin-Liu

BEIJING, A CAPITAL AS HUGE AND SPRAWLING AS LOS ANGELES,

doesn't blow you away with its beauty. Hazy smog hovers over the city, and in spring it is engulfed by sandstorms from the Gobi Desert. I lived here for a year and then left, dismayed by the traffic, pollution, and weather. But a few years later I returned, and I've called Beijing home ever since. What brought me back? The chance to witness the world's next superpower in the making. I've watched clusters of skyscrapers spring up before my eyes. Fusion restaurants open by the week. If I ignore the bar scene for a month, I'm clueless about the new hot spots.

Beijing is also a study in contrasts. Tian'anmen Square and the Forbidden City have a grandness that few other attractions possess. But I find solace in the *hutongs,* the old alleys of single-level courtyard dwellings in which I live. The human-scale *hutongs* are rapidly being bulldozed; the ones that remain often feel like a quaint village lane, where vendors sell everything from toilet paper to beer from wagons pulled behind their bicycles.

That Beijing has managed to keep me as a longtime resident is a testimony to the city's energy, quirks, and, yes, beauty. Read on and discover a few of my favorite things.

The sky begins to light up a few days before the **CHINESE NEW YEAR (left)** and reaches a fiery crescendo by midnight, when Beijing's residents launch fireworks from every patch of outdoor space in the city. Find a high floor or a roof for a prime view of the world's biggest fireworks show. The cacophony is not to everyone's liking, and it can be dangerous, but the display is stunning in its breadth and length. The Chinese continue to fire rockets for 15 days.

My favorite way of getting around Beijing is **ON BICYCLE (above).** On two wheels, I pass cars and buses stuck in traffic, coast through the narrow *hutongs,* and pause for any particularly appealing streetside snacks. Bicycle rentals are cheap and easy. I suffered from bike rage until I realized the rules of the Beijing road: 1) Might Is Right— yield to any vehicle bigger than you; and 2) keep your eyes trained on what's ahead of you.

The **DRUM TOWER (left)**, originally built in the 13th century, provides an unobstructed view of the crowded, old labyrinth of alleys in central Beijing. Drumming performances such as this one echo down Beijing's wide avenues and start every other hour. My friends and I sometimes take over the square behind the tower for an impromptu game of ultimate frisbee; it's also a great place to launch a kite. At night, the tower is stunning and lights up like a beacon.

Beijing sits on a patch of desert, which makes the man-made wonder of **HOUHAI LAKE (above)** all the more spectacular. A sunset ramble on the pedestrian path always clears my mind after a long day of writing. In the dead of winter, middle-aged and elderly Beijingers strip down to their Speedos and plunge into icy pools cut out of the frozen lake. In the warmer months, locals and tourists alike gather en masse, riding kayaks, gondolas, and boats shaped like swans.

Starting around eight o'clock on weekend mornings, Tibetans in bright robes, elderly men in Mao suits, long-haired urban artists, and other vendors set up stands at the **PANJIAYUAN OUTDOOR MARKET (left)**. Among the items for sale are 1960s-era posters of Mao Utopian scenes, black-and-white photographs of now-destroyed Beijing neighborhoods, and replicas of antique Chinese furniture. (Be prepared to bargain down to half-price.) Even when I'm not actively shopping, I enjoy visiting the market to absorb the carnival-like atmosphere.

The practitioners of **WATER CALLIGRAPHY (below)** are elderly men who hang out at Beihai Park and the Temple of Heaven. They wield 4-foot-long calligraphy brushes that look more like mops than writing instruments. The characters they scrawl disappear within minutes into the dry Beijing air, but practitioners appear unfazed by the ephemeral nature of their hobby. They sometimes let me hold their brushes to practice my own strokes—so don't be shy to ask if you'd like to try.

Contemporary Chinese art fetches sky-high prices at international auctions, and much of it was created in the sprawling neighborhood of 798 Dashanzi, once a military factory zone. Studios and galleries like 798 Space and **CHINA ART 110 (above)** feature airy Bauhaus architecture and Communist slogans. In between galleries, duck into one of the funky cafes serving lattes and French crepes or the fashion boutiques selling modern Chinese designs.

The Beijing food scene is as diverse as New York's or London's, but it has one defining dish: Peking Duck. Wrapped in chewy paper-thin pancakes with plum sauce, the thin slices of duck have a crisp skin and are only slightly fatty. At more sophisticated establishments, like **MADE IN CHINA (right),** you can dip your duck skin in sugar (for a treat that tastes like candy) or minced garlic (for a hearty bite).

The **GREAT WALL OF CHINA** (below) stretches from the eastern coast to the far desert interior, and some of its most dramatic sections meander along mountain passes just north of Beijing. If you're a hiker like me, hire a private vehicle to take you to more remote sections like Jiankou and Jinshanling, where you can hike and even camp on unrestored, several-hundred-years-old parts of the Wall.

© Chu Yong/AGE Fotostock

Beijing

6th Edition

by Jen Lin-Liu & Sherisse Pham

Wiley Publishing, Inc.

Published by:

WILEY PUBLISHING, INC.

111 River St.
Hoboken, NJ 07030-5774

ISBN 978-0-470-52566-1

Editor: Melinda Quintero
Production Editor: M. Faunette Johnston
Cartographer: Roberta Stockwell
Photo Editor: Richard Fox
Production by Wiley Indianapolis Composition Services

Front cover photo: The Forbidden City © Best View Stock / AGE Fotostock, Inc.
Back cover photo: Beijing band Brain Failure at MAO Livehouse © Lou Linwei / Alamy Images.

For information on our other products and services or to obtain technical support, please contact our Customer Care Department within the U.S. at 877/762-2974, outside the U.S. at 317/572-3993 or fax 317/572-4002.

Wiley also publishes its books in a variety of electronic formats. Some content that appears in print may not be available in electronic formats.

Manufactured in the United States of America

5   4   3   2   1

CONTENTS

9 SHOPPING 165

10 BEIJING AFTER DARK 182

11 THE GREAT WALL & OTHER SIDE TRIPS 195

12 FAST FACTS 216

13 THE CHINESE LANGUAGE 221

14 THE BEIJING MENU 230

INDEX 239

LIST OF MAPS

ABOUT THE AUTHORS

Jen Lin-Liu is a food and travel writer based in Beijing and Cambridge, MA. She is the author of *Serve the People: A Stir-Fried Journey Through China* and the founder of the cooking school Black Sesame Kitchen in Beijing.

Sherisse Pham was a Beijing-based freelance journalist for over four years, but recently relocated to New York to study journalism at Columbia University. She has contributed to several Frommer's guides and has written for *WWD, The South China Morning Post, People Magazine, CNN.com,* and *Zagat Survey* among others. She hopes to return to Asia to continue reporting upon graduation.

ACKNOWLEDGMENTS

Jen would like to thank Candice Lee and Sherisse Pham for their assistance with this book. She is also grateful for the help and suggestions of her husband, Craig, parents-in-law Caroline and Dave, and her mother Sen.

Sherisse would like to thank Karen Xiaolin Wang for her fantastic work as a fact-checker and translator. She would also like to thank her editor, Melinda Quintero, for her patience and support in putting this guide together.

HOW TO CONTACT US

In researching this book, we discovered many wonderful places—hotels, restaurants, shops, and more. We're sure you'll find others. Please tell us about them, so we can share the information with your fellow travelers in upcoming editions. If you were disappointed with a recommendation, we'd love to know that, too. Please write to:

Frommer's Beijing, 6th Edition
Wiley Publishing, Inc. • 111 River St. • Hoboken, NJ 07030-5774

AN ADDITIONAL NOTE

Please be advised that travel information is subject to change at any time—and this is especially true of prices. We therefore suggest that you write or call ahead for confirmation when making your travel plans. The authors, editors, and publisher cannot be held responsible for the experiences of readers while traveling. Your safety is important to us, however, so we encourage you to stay alert and be aware of your surroundings. Keep a close eye on cameras, purses, and wallets, all favorite targets of thieves and pickpockets.

FROMMER'S STAR RATINGS, ICONS & ABBREVIATIONS

Every hotel, restaurant, and attraction listing in this guide has been ranked for quality, value, service, amenities, and special features using a **star-rating system.** In country, state, and regional guides, we also rate towns and regions to help you narrow down your choices and budget your time accordingly. Hotels and restaurants are rated on a scale of zero (recommended) to three stars (exceptional). Attractions, shopping, nightlife, towns, and regions are rated according to the following scale: zero stars (recommended), one star (highly recommended), two stars (very highly recommended), and three stars (must-see).

In addition to the star-rating system, we also use **eight feature icons** that point you to the great deals, in-the-know advice, and unique experiences that separate travelers from tourists. Throughout the book, look for:

(**Finds**)	Special finds—those places only insiders know about
(**Fun Facts**)	Fun facts—details that make travelers more informed and their trips more fun
(**Kids**)	Best bets for kids, and advice for the whole family
(**Moments**)	Special moments—those experiences that memories are made of
(**Overrated**)	Places or experiences not worth your time or money
(**Tips**)	Insider tips—great ways to save time and money
(**Value**)	Great values—where to get the best deals
(**Warning!**)	Warning—traveler's advisories are usually in effect

The following **abbreviations** are used for credit cards:

AE	American Express	**DISC**	Discover	**V**	Visa
DC	Diners Club	**MC**	MasterCard		

TRAVEL RESOURCES AT FROMMERS.COM

Frommer's travel resources don't end with this guide. Frommer's website, **www.frommers.com**, has travel information on more than 4,000 destinations. We update features regularly, giving you access to the most current trip-planning information and the best airfare, lodging, and car-rental bargains. You can also listen to podcasts, connect with other Frommers.com members through our active-reader forums, share your travel photos, read blogs from guidebook editors and fellow travelers, and much more.

The Best of Beijing

by Jen Lin-Liu

The best of Beijing is a study in contrasts—from the ritzy elegance of restaurants located in the snazziest of hotels to the humble yet lively fare available in local dining rooms. We give you a healthy dose of traditional Beijing life, which is rapidly disappearing as the city is bulldozed to make room for skyscrapers. We recommend that you take in a local punk band to get a glimpse of the capital's vibrant youth culture, but also visit an antiquated Peking opera hall, and fraternize with seniors at the city's numerous gardens and parks. For all its big-city development, Beijing's lakes and parks provide solace—a place where you can go to ponder the contradictions that make up this fascinating capital.

1 THE MOST UNFORGETTABLE BEIJING EXPERIENCES

- **Strolling Around the Back Lakes:** You'll find everything around these man-made lakes, from historic courtyard homes, to tranquil spots, to amusing entertainment. Speedo-clad elders dive into the lake year-round—including the chilly winter months—and ducks congregate on a small man-made island on the western end of the lake. Visit around sunset for a particularly romantic experience, and stroll to the nearby restaurants and bars for dinner and drinks. See "Walking Tour 2: Back Lakes Ramble," p. 155.

- **Sinking Your Teeth into Crisp, Juicy Peking Duck at Made in China:** A hotel restaurant it is, but this is the best place to enjoy the capital's most famous dish, and the dining room—set in the middle of an open kitchen—is the best place to see chefs perform their magic. See p. 86.

- **Investigating the Northeast Corner of the Forbidden City:** Away from the main north-south axis on which the former palace's grander halls stand, there's a more human scale similar to that of the rapidly disappearing *hutong* beyond the palace's walls, although with much greater luxury. Venturing far from the main arteries is well worth the effort—you'll find treasures like the ornate theater building where the Empress Dowager Cixi watched her favorite operas on demand and the well in which she ended the life of her nephew's favorite concubine. See p. 123.

- **Praying for a Smog-Free Day with the Monks at Beijing Temples:** Many of the capital's temples have once again become genuine places of worship, as well as tourist attractions. The **Yonghe Gong** (p. 134) has an active and approachable community of Tibetan monks (although under careful scrutiny by the authorities), while the leafy **Fayuan Si** (p. 132) houses amicable Chinese Buddhist monks in Beijing's most venerable temple. **Baiyun Guan** (p. 130) is the Daoist alternative, where blue-frocked monks wear their hair in the rarely seen traditional manner—

long and tied in a bun at the top of the head.

- **Bargaining for Fakes:** At **Panjiayuan Jiuhuo Shichang** (p. 167), the first asking prices for foreigners are at least 10 to 15 times those asked of Chinese, but don't let that deter you from visiting. This weekend market has the city's best selection of bric-a-brac, including row upon crowded row of calligraphy, jewelry, ceramics, teapots, ethnic clothing, Buddha statues, paper lanterns, Cultural Revolution memorabilia, army belts, little wooden boxes, Ming- and Qing-style furniture, old pipes, opium scales, painted human skulls, and more conventional souvenirs. A whole other genre of fakes can be found at the **Ri Tan Shangwu Lou** (p. 174) where samples of Marc Jacobs jackets and Diane von Furstenberg dresses cram the racks.
- **Haggling for Tea at Malian Dao:** If you're a real tea lover, it's worth the jaunt to this far-flung tea street, which features several shopping complexes' worth of tea shops, each individually owned and selling leaves from all over the country. You can try pricey pu'er, the lovely smoked lapsang souchong, and delicate green dragon well tea. Most vendors offer free samples, so pull up a chair and feel free to bargain. See p. 180.
- **Getting Behind a Wok and Leaping Fire in Cooking School:** Several establishments offer Chinese cuisine lessons, including **Black Sesame Kitchen, Hutong Cuisine,** and the **Hutong.** See p. 88.

- **Unwinding at a Traditional Teahouse:** Several quiet teahouses offer you the chance to remove yourself temporarily from the tourist rush. The teahouse in the **Sanwei Bookstore** (p. 170) offers live traditional music with its bottomless cups of jasmine. For a little extra, the **Teahouse of Family Fu** (p. 194) in the Back Lakes area brews your oolong *(wulong)* in the Chinese version of the tea ceremony. Both teahouses are furnished with replica Ming dynasty tables and chairs and make ideal spots for reading, writing, or doing absolutely nothing.
- **Seeing a Band at Yugong Yishan:** The owners of the now-defunct Loup Chante have created what Beijing lacked for years: an atmospheric venue showcasing an eclectic range of musical styles, from Mongolian mouth music to acid jazz. It's stuffy, smoky, housed in a historic building, and run by serious and talented musicians. See chapter 2 for more about Beijing music.
- **Hiking Along the Great Wall at Jiankou:** Our favorite part of the wall is so untouristed that there isn't a tacky postcard tout in sight. The 5-hour hike meanders along a vertigo-inducing stretch of wall that isn't for the faint of heart—but it's an unforgettable experience. See p. 202.
- **Bicycling Through the Hutong Neighborhoods:** We can't get enough of the *hutong*. After taking a stroll, hop on a bike for a completely different experience in the capital's old neighborhoods. See p. 144.

2 THE BEST SPLURGE HOTELS

- **Aman Beijing** (Gongmenqian Lu 15; *©* **010/5987-9999**): If you've ever wondered what it'd be like to live like a Chinese emperor or empress, head straight to the Aman Beijing, a luxurious resort in a private corner of the Summer Palace. Housed in a historic imperial series of courtyards, the resort features luxurious rooms with grand bathrooms, a world-class spa, and a top-notch steakhouse with a Bible-sized wine list. See p. 75.

- **Park Hyatt** (Jianguomenwai Dajie 2; ☏ **010/8567-1234**): This new 66-story hotel impresses with expansive views of the city, top-notch gym and spa facilities, and stylish, unconventional room layouts. See p. 68.
- **Opposite House** (Sanlitun Lu 11; ☏ **010/6417-6688**): The best of a bunch of boutique hotels that have opened in Beijing, the Opposite House features minimalist white and blond wood rooms with floor-to-ceiling windows in the center of Sanlitun, one of Beijing's liveliest bar and shopping districts. The food and drink outlets are all stunning, featuring fresh sushi, Mediterranean fare, and creative cocktails. See p. 68.

3 THE BEST MODERATELY PRICED HOTELS

- **Gu Xiang 20** (Nanluoguxiang 20; ☏ **010/6400-5566**): This lovely three-star hotel is smack in the middle of one of old Beijing's gentrifying neighborhoods. The stylish rooms are decorated with Chinese antiques and flatscreen TVs, and third-floor rooms have picturesque views of the *hutong*. See p. 67.
- **Shi Jia House** (Shijia Hutong 42; ☏ **010/5219-0288**): A boutique hotel down a narrow alley in a central Beijing neighborhood, Shi Jia House has chic rooms with dark wood floors and antique Chinese furniture—and a spacious courtyard perfect for relaxing, complete with a koi pond and a mini-waterfall. See p. 64.
- **Hotel G** (Gongti Xi Lu A7; ☏ **010/6552-3600**): Stylish rooms done up in a 1960s Hollywood glamour theme come with whimsical touches like toy motorcycles on the nightstand and rubber duckies in the bathroom, plus all the modern technology you'll need, including an iPod dock and flatscreen television. See p. 71.

4 THE MOST UNFORGETTABLE DINING EXPERIENCES

- **Beijing Da Dong Kaoya Dian** (1-2/F Nanxincang International Plaza; ☏ **010/5169-0329**): Chef Dong of Beijing Da Dong Kaoya Dian has made a name for himself with his light, crisp, and flavorful duck, which comes with an array of condiments, including sugar and garlic, and new fusion dishes that don't lose sight of the fundamentals of Chinese cooking. See p. 94.
- **Chuan Jing Ban Canting** (Gongyuan Tou Tiao 5; ☏ **010/6512-2277**): Sichuan food has conquered the capital, and this ubiquitous cuisine, loved by Beijingers and Sichuanese alike, is best enjoyed in this chaotic, crowded restaurant owned by the Sichuan Provincial Government. It will also be one of the cheapest meals you can have in Beijing, with the price of an entire meal averaging no more than ¥40 per person. See p. 90.
- **Maison Boulud** (Qianmen Dong Da Jie 23; ☏ **010/6559-9200**): Housed in the former pre-1949 American embassy, the restaurant's refined "soul" food—brought by New York celebrity chef Daniel Boulud—brilliantly gleams amid a landscape of mediocre French restaurants in Beijing. Everything from the food to the wine list to the service to the atmosphere is top-notch. See p. 85.

- **Black Sesame Kitchen** (Heizhima Hutong 3; ℭ **0/1369-147-4408**): A cooking school that also takes dinner reservations, Black Sesame Kitchen will give you a front-seat view of the inner workings of a Chinese kitchen in a century-old courtyard—and a delicious home-style meal with favorites like pork-and-pumpkin pan-fried dumplings. See p. 87.

5 THE BEST THINGS TO DO FOR FREE (OR ALMOST)

- **Go Bohemian at Factory 798:** We left Factory 798 out of the previous edition, reasoning that an ad hoc gathering of performance artists, painters, and sculptors in a former military complex wasn't something the regime would tolerate. We were wrong. Market rents are now charged, so don't expect to pick up a bargain, but there's no need to make a purchase: The Dashanzi art district makes for a thoroughly enjoyable afternoon of gallery and cafe hopping. See p. 141.

- **Pay Your Respects to the Chairman:** While Jung Chang's *Mao: The Untold Story* subjects the Great Helmsman to a Cultural Revolution–style denunciation, you'll find no trace of such disrespect inside **Chairman Mao's Mausoleum,** set to the south side of Tian'an Men Square. While there are souvenir vendors, this is far from the kitsch experience you may expect. See p. 111.

- **Exercise with Elders:** At the break of dawn each day, retired Beijingers flock to numerous local parks. Aside from *taijiquan* and ballroom dancing, you may spy master calligraphers practicing their art with oversize sponge-tipped brushes, or amateur troupes performing Beijing Opera or revolutionary airs from the 1950s. See section 6, "Parks & Gardens," in chapter 7.

2

Beijing in Depth

by Sherisse Pham

Beijing is a frenetic city. The people-watching opportunities here are endless: On any given day you are likely to run into migrant workers on their way to work, carrying their own tools over their shoulders and sporting yellow construction helmets; the newly moneyed clogging the streets with shiny new cars and bad fashion sense; and international expatriates, some equipped with impressive Chinese language skills, who are either in love with the city's cultural charm or lusting after its economic opportunities, or both. Yet despite the vast social, economic, and even cultural differences of the people who inhabit this sprawling city, each represents modern Beijing in some fundamental way. The migrant workers pretty much built "new Beijing," the newly moneyed represent the social mobility of the last few decades, and the expatriates are proof of Beijing's increasing attractiveness to the international community.

Of course the city would be nothing without its storied past. Beijing, which at times feels both newer and older than any place on the planet, prides itself on its rich cultural heritage. Unfortunately, that didn't stop urban planners from tearing down historical architecture to make way for shiny new skyscrapers. In this chapter, we'll take a look at where Beijing is today, where it has been, and where it's likely heading as it catapults its way into the 21st century.

1 BEIJING TODAY

One of my first Beijing shopping trips was to Wangfujing Street, back in 2004. The pedestrian-only avenue offered a rare reprieve from the city traffic, and the wide lane was clean and orderly. As I was sidling up to one of the gleaming new retailers, I spied a young woman in front of me scoop up her toddler and walk him over to a trash can a few feet away from where I was standing. She balanced him over the top of it with his legs held forward to reveal pants split down the middle and a bare bottom. I then watched in equal parts shock and amusement as the pint-sized child began to pee steadily into the bin. An occasional splash arched out onto the street and dribbled onto the sidewalk. When all was said and done, the woman placed him back on his feet, and the kid resumed tee-tering down the modern shopping district, his bare bum peeking out now and again.

Modern China

Twenty years ago, my parents could barely afford to buy me a $1 toy horse for my first Christmas present in London. Today, Chinese tourists flock to Louis Vuitton on the Champs-Elysées.

–Jiajia Liu, a communications professional

It would be the first of many jarring juxtapositions that often define Beijing, a city both modern and backward, money-loving and staunchly communist, sophisticated and yet rough around the edges. It is a place you can love and hate in equal measures. In recent years, I've seen fewer and fewer split-pants-babies around town. The city's crackdown on "embarrassing" social behavior in the run up to the Olympics was partially responsible for the shift, but the real reason is the rising demand for diapers among modern, well-paid Beijing parents. Indeed the growing middle class appears more and more Western with each step up the social ladder. Fewer and fewer cyclists are on Beijing streets. The traditional courtyard home and neighborhood is being abandoned in droves for modern apartments. There is even a growing trend of drinking wine with dinner, rather than steaming cups of green tea.

Meanwhile, the new generation of Beijing youth, raised by doting parents and mostly only-children thanks to China's one-child policy, have grown up in a world of monetary privilege. They are often spoiled and apathetic. Unlike their counterparts in the late '80s, who rallied for democracy and freedom of speech, today's university-age students spend their free hours stuffing themselves with fast food and shopping for new cellphones.

This overall content and disinterested generation, however, can be rallied for a worthy cause—like restriction on its Internet access. In mid-2009, netizens across the country protested the government's mandatory installment of Web-filtering software on all computers sold in China. Labeled the Green Dam-Youth Escort, the software caused a torrent of protests and eventually sent the government in Beijing backtracking on its rule. At the time of writing, it was unclear whether the government would continue to pursue its cause or quietly drop it in the face of such public and commercial condemnation. But while pushing back the Green Dam-Youth Escort was a small victory for Chinese Internet users, Beijing and the rest of China are still subject to strict censorship. Social networking sites like Facebook and Twitter and user-generated-content sites like YouTube are regularly blocked in Beijing and elsewhere in China. Occasionally, service to CNN or the BBC is blacked out when those stations air sensitive stories.

Meanwhile, there is the growing divide in urban Beijing among the social classes. The average annual salary in 2008 was ¥44,715, or roughly US$6,545, according to the Beijing Statistics Bureau; low-skilled workers' annual salaries were less than half that, roughly ¥20,000 (US$2,928). The growing disparity between the haves and the have-nots is a big concern for the Chinese government, which wants to keep the local populace content. The droves of migrant workers that contribute widely to

Driving in Beijing

Spoken Chinese is tonal, which means that a single syllable can have different meanings depending on whether it is flat, rising, falling and rising, or falling sharply. Similarly, a Chinese [car] horn is capable of at least 10 distinct meanings. A solid hoooooonnnnnk is intended to attract attention. A double sound—hoooonnnnnk, hoooonnnnnk—indicates irritation. There's a particularly long hoooooooooonnnnnnnnnnnk that means the driver is stuck in traffic, has exhausted curb-sneaking options, and would like everybody else on the road to disappear. A responding hoooooooooooooonnnnnnnnnnnnnnnnk proves that they aren't going anywhere.

–Peter Hessler, *New Yorker* correspondent

80 后 Bashi hou or the Post-1980 Generation

Boutiques in hip shopping districts often sell T-shirts with Chinese characters that blast "我是 80后" (Wo shi 80 hou, I'm post-80) or simply "80后." The reference is to youngsters born after 1980—individuals who, unlike the generation before them, have known little political upheaval in their lives. The 80 hou often find themselves at odds with trite social expectations—a government survey conducted in Beijing last year found that "post-80" individuals in the workplace "lack the will to endure hardship and work hard," "change jobs frequently," and view their jobs as "beneath them." They may be lousy contributors to the workforce, but this generation is in fact asserting its independence and free spirit in ways that their parents could have only dreamed of doing. One of the most visible ways is through fashion: the 80 hou generation is the driving force behind a resurgent local style. The cheeky I'm post-80 T-shirts are just the tip of the iceberg. This generation has sparked a love for independent Chinese designs, notably the return of Huili, a Shanghai casual footwear and clothing brand older than adidas, and Feiyue, a simple canvas shoe that retails for 55€ in Europe but can be had for about ¥150 a pair in Beijing at places like NLGX on Nanluoguxiang (p. 174).

the city's economic boom find themselves outcasts in this urban landscape, often looked down upon by locals who blame them for petty theft and crime.

Most unfortunately, Beijing remains locked in an ongoing battle with pollution and congestion. During the Olympics, the government ordered several factories moved to the outskirts of Beijing, but pollution levels in the city remain hazardous. The population stands at a staggering 16.95 million—or about the same number of people as in the U.S. state of Nebraska, corralled into an area 11 times smaller. A sizeable chunk of the populace harbors materialistic aspirations, which includes trading up from a bicycle to a CO_2-emitting car. A survey in early 2009 revealed that about 1,500 new cars are added to Beijing roads every day. The new vehicles add to the already headache-inducing traffic as well as the unhealthy pollution levels.

2 LOOKING BACK AT BEIJING

UNDER MONGOLIAN RULE

Modern Beijing stands on the site of the capital founded in 1271 by the Mongols, when the territory of modern-day China was merely a part of a far larger Mongol empire. Known to the Mongols as Khanbalik and to their Chinese subjects as Da Du or "Great Capital," it lay on a plain with limited and bitter water supplies, handy for the steppe from which the Mongols had emerged, but well away from the heartlands of the Han, as the main ethnic Chinese group still call themselves. When, in 1368, the Mongol Yuan dynasty was expelled, the foreigner-founded capital was abandoned for Nanjing, the "Southern Capital." The third Ming emperor, who had formerly been in charge of resisting fresh Mongol advances from the north, returned the city to capital status in 1420, renaming it Beijing, or "Northern Capital."

Although retaining much of the plan and grid of the Mongol founders, the emperor remodeled the city extensively, creating a secondary, broader walled extension to the south of the Mongol original. Many of the capital's major monuments date from this period, and its most extensive, the Forbidden City, right at the city's heart, is the one around which the remainder of the capital is still more or less arranged. The key ceremonial halls lie on a nearly north-south axis (actually aligned on the Pole Star), which bisects the city. Most north-south streets parallel this, and main east-west routes cross them at right angles. Very few major streets run diagonally. The grid created was originally filled in with a maze of lanes peculiar to Beijing and to a handful of other northern cities, called *hutong* (both singular and plural), derived from a Mongol word. But most of these narrow streets have now been destroyed.

In 1644 the Ming dynasty was overthrown by a peasant rebellion, and the peasants were driven out shortly afterward by invading Manchu forces from beyond the Great Wall to the northeast. China was absorbed into the Qing empire, and foreign-

ers ruled from Beijing until the Qing abdication of 1912. Including occupation by foreign forces in 1860 and from 1900 to 1901, and Japanese occupation during World War II, Beijing has been under foreign control for more than half of its existence.

Beijing was once a series of walls within walls. The Qing took over the walled Forbidden City and the walled Imperial City within which it sat, and their followers took over the remainder of the northern section of the walled city. This area was known to other foreigners as the Tartar City, while the broader but separate walled section to the south of the Qian Men (Front Gate) became the Chinese City— the Chinese quarter of Beijing.

The enemy was now within the gates, and the outer city walls were neglected, but the Qing built many temples and palaces, leaving the city's basic grid largely unchanged while building extensive gardens to the northwest.

CLASH WITH THE WEST

With the exception of a limited number of Russians and small groups of missionaries, some of whom were allowed to erect churches, Beijing remained free of Western influence or a Western presence until 1860, when emissaries sent to complete ratification of a treaty forced on the Qing at the end of the Second Opium War by

DATELINE

- **930–1122** A provincial town roughly on the site of modern Beijing becomes the southern capital of the Khitan Mongol Liao dynasty, thousands of kilometers from the ancient centers of early Han Chinese empires.
- **1122–1215** The city is taken over by the Jurchen Tartar Jin dynasty, first as Southern Capital, then Central Capital, as its empire expands.

- **1267–1367** The Mongol Yuan dynasty, having conquered most of Asia and eastern Europe, rebuilds the city on the modern site as the capital Khanbalik; Da Du (Great Capital) in Mandarin; Cambulac in Marco Polo's account of the city.
- **1273–92** Marco Polo, his father, and his uncle are in China, much of the time in Khanbalik. Polo's ghostwritten account of the capital

captures the imagination of European readers for several centuries afterward.

- **1368** The Ming dynasty, having driven out the Mongols, establishes its capital at Nanjing. Da Du becomes Beiping (The Pacified North).
- **1420** The Yongle emperor, third of the Ming, returns the city to capital status, the better to repel attacks by the Mongols from the north. He becomes the first Chinese

On Governance

He who exercises government by means of his virtue may be compared to the north polar star, which keeps its place and all the stars turn towards it.

—Kongzi, The Confucian Analects

the British and French were put to death or imprisoned. British troops, led by Lord Elgin, torched the vast area of palaces and gardens to the northwest of the city, of which now only fragments remain at the Summer Palace and Old Summer Palace. French troops opposed razing such magnificent buildings, and were content simply to loot them.

For the first time, Western powers were allowed to station ministers in Beijing, and accommodation was allocated to them just inside the Tartar City, east of the Qian Men and what is now Tian'an Men Square. At the end of the 19th century, resentment at the expansion of foreign influence in China led to attacks on Chinese who had converted to Christianity, destruction of railway lines and foreign property, and eventually to a siege of the Legation Quarter during which the attackers razed much of the surrounding housing, a fabulous library of ancient learning, and part of the Qian Men. The siege was only lifted 2 months and many deaths later by the forces of eight allied powers

that marched from the coast. Imperial troops, Boxers, Beijing residents, and foreign troops indulged in an orgy of looting and destruction, which supplemented the burning of shops selling foreign goods and the destruction of churches already accomplished by the Boxers. The Legation Quarter subsequently became a further walled enclave, with many foreign banks, offices, and legation (embassy) buildings. In the early 20th century it was still the only area with paved roads and proper drainage and sewerage in an otherwise notably malodorous city.

The churches were rebuilt (and still stand), but the temples that had been collateral damage were mostly left in ruins. The Qing were in decline, and after their fall in 1912, much else went into decline, too, ancient buildings being the victims of neglect or casual destruction. This process continued during the 1911–12 to 1949 Republic and accelerated following the Communist Party victory and the creation of the People's Republic of China.

emperor to reign from Beijing, and the first to give it that name: "Northern Capital." Ming dynasty Beijing is overlaid on the Yuan foundations, and the Forbidden City and Temple of Heaven are constructed.

■ **1549** Mongol horsemen fire a message-bearing arrow into a Chinese general's camp saying that they will attack Beijing the following year. Despite this advance

announcement, they duly make their way up to the city walls as promised. So much for the Great Wall.

■ **1550** In response to Mongol attacks, a lower southern extension to the city wall is begun, eventually enclosing the commercial district, the important ceremonial sites of the Temple (Altar) of Heaven and Altar of Agriculture, and a broad swath of countryside (which remains

free of buildings well into the 20th c.). The whole system of walls is clad in brick. Beijing remains largely the same for the next 400 years, when casual and organized destruction begins with the Republic and is hastened under the People's Republic.

■ **1601–10** After years of campaigning, Italian Jesuit Matteo Ricci finally receives permission to reside in

continues

TRANSFORMATIONS BY THE PEOPLE'S REPUBLIC OF CHINA

Signs at the Old Summer Palace and elsewhere harp on foreign destruction in 1860 and 1900, but since 1949 the Chinese themselves have almost completely demolished their city. Temples have been turned into housing, warehouses, industrial units, offices, and police stations. The slender, walled space south of the Tian'an Men was smashed open to create the vast expanse of the modern square, lined by hideous Soviet-influenced halls of rapidly down-at-heel grandeur. The city walls and most gate towers were pulled down to allow the construction of the Second Ring Road and the first metro line. Areas of traditional courtyard houses were pulverized for the construction of shabby six-story concrete dormitory blocks. Political campaigns against all traditional culture led to the defacing, damage, or destruction of many ancient buildings and their contents, particularly during the 1966 to 1976 Cultural Revolution.

The *hutong,* once "numberless as the hairs on an ox," will soon be no harder to count than your fingers and toes, because China's increasing wealth has seen the government trying to turn the capital from a sleepy backwater into a city of international standing. The broad boulevards apparently required by Marxist theory have become ever more numerous, and the last few years have seen several new routes blasted across the city. An assortment of often hideous towers representing no particular style or culture but sometimes with cheesy Chinese toppings have sprung up within the vanished city walls, dwarfing the Forbidden City and the few older buildings which remain.

The awarding of the 2008 Olympics to Beijing delivered the coup de grâce. Whole blocks of housing disappeared every few weeks as developers, hand-in-glove with the government, expelled residents. Even today, developers race to destroy the remaining halls of ancient and largely forgotten temples before those charged with preserving them can catch up, although a few are given ham-fisted restoration and reopened to the public for a fee. A third, fourth, fifth, and now a sixth ring road have dropped like nooses around the neck of the old city center, inevitably leading to road-widening schemes through the heart of the remaining *hutong.* Demolition of the ancient Da Zhalan district is well advanced, and the latest scheme is to widen De Sheng Men Nei Dajie into a 50m-wide (164-ft.) road, which will plunge right through the heart of the Back Lakes area. All but the basic grid of the Yuan and Ming plan have been swept away for shiny towers and gridlock. The most noticeable buildings are those most alien to China—a three-venue National Grand Theatre resembling a flying saucer which has landed in a lake, occupying space in the heart of the city just west of Tian'an Men Square and designed by Frenchman Paul Andreu and the interlocking Z-like buildings of the new CCTV Broadcast Centre. Culturally, several venues built for the Beijing Olympics hit closer to home: a bird's nest (the National Stadium), a folding Chinese fan (the National Indoor Stadium), and a fiery red and gold dragon (Beijing Capital Airport T3).

3 BEIJING'S ART & ARCHITECTURE

TRADITIONAL ARCHITECTURE

Yes, a lot of Beijing's traditional architecture was lost or razed in the rush to modernize. But the ultimate symbols of this city are indelibly Chinese structures that date back hundreds or thousands of years—the Temple of Heaven, the Forbidden City, the Summer Palace, to name a few. In these temples and palaces, the emphasis is on symmetry; the main structure is the axis, and secondary structures are positioned as mirrored wings on either side to form an open courtyard. And thus you have your basic *siheyuan:* an empty space surrounded on all four sides by buildings connected to one another either directly or through covered archways or verandas. The Forbidden City is essentially one gigantic *siheyuan,* consisting of a series of self-contained courtyards.

Gabled roofs are another marker of traditional Chinese architecture. In the past, common dwellings often had roofs with one straightforward incline, while the wealthier classes enjoyed roofs with multiple sections of incline. Sweeping, curved roofs that rise at the corners were, and are, typically reserved for temples and palaces. Royal palaces and temples usually have decorations along the ridges, typical of imperial construction.

Certain architectural designs were in fact reserved for the use of imperial buildings. Only gates used by the emperor were permitted to have five arches, the center one being reserved for the emperor himself. Yellow is the royal color, so yellow tile roofs are found only on imperial structures. And although it was not an exclusively imperial color, traditional palaces and temples tend to use a lot of red.

government is terminally corrupt and in decline.

- **1858** The Second Opium War sees the Qing and their Chinese subjects capitulating in the face of the superior military technology of "barbarians" (principally the British) for the second time in 16 years. Under the terms of the Treaty of Nanjing, China is forced to permit the permanent residence of foreign diplomats and trade representatives in the capital.

- **1860** The Qing imprison and murder foreign representatives sent for the treaty's ratification. British and French rescue forces occupy Beijing and destroy a vast area of parks and palaces to the northwest, some of the remnants of which form the modern Summer Palace. The Chinese loot what little the foreigners leave and put most of the area back under the plow. Foreign powers begin to construct diplomatic legation buildings just inside the Tartar City's wall east of the Qian Men.

- **1900** The Harmonious Fists, nicknamed the Boxers, a superstitious anti–foreign peasant movement, besieges the foreign residents of the Legation Quarter, with the initially covert

continues

On Beijing Hutong

There are living neighborhoods around Beijing's central development, and the city should help to sustain them. They are, after all, what make Beijing uniquely Beijing.
—Michael Meyer, author

MODERN ARCHITECTURE

For many architects, Beijing is *the* place to be. The Beijing government still seems to have money to commission new projects throughout the city, and it is keen to explore unconventional designs. At times it feels like architects are given free reign to explore the zaniest ideas they can draw up on paper, the crazier the better. The result is a continually evolving city skyline that is undeniably modern, but lacks a cohesive look. For example, if you walk west of Tian'an Men Square on Chang'an Jie, you'll pass the majestic sweeping roofs of the Forbidden City, the boxy Communist architecture of the Great Hall of the People, and the spaceship-like architecture of the newly built National Grand Theatre—all in the span of 3 blocks.

When the People's Republic of China was founded in 1949, its leaders made sweeping changes to the city architecture, installing many chunky, Communist-style buildings of vast proportions. The *Shi Da Jianzhu,* or the **Ten Great Buildings,** of 1959 drastically changed the look of Beijing,

most notably its main artery, Chang'an Jie. The 10 public buildings were built in 10 months to commemorate the 10th anniversary of the founding of the People's Republic of China. The most famous among them are the Great Hall of the People, the National Museum of China, the Beijing Railway Station, the Military Museum, and the Worker's Stadium. It was also during this time that Mao's orders to expand Tian'an Men Square were finally carried out. In October 1949, when Mao declared the creation of the People's Republic of China from Tian'an Men, he was frustrated at the small crowd of 70,000 for the momentous event. He wanted a square large enough to hold all of China, but would have to settle for the current size, which reportedly holds 600,000. The Ten Great Buildings were part of the wave of changes decreed by the Great Leap Forward. In keeping with Zhou Enlai's principle of adopting "all things, both ancient and modern, Chinese and foreign," the design of these buildings was supposed to be open. For the most

and finally open assistance of imperial troops. The siege begins on June 19 and is only lifted, after extensive destruction and many deaths, by the forces of Eight Allied Powers (several European nations, Japanese, and Americans) on August 14. Boxers, imperial troops, Chinese, foreign survivors, and allied soldiers take to looting the city. Payments on a vast indemnity take the Qing a

further 39 years to pay in full, although the British and Americans use much of the income to help found Yanching (now Peking) University and other institutions, and to pay for young Chinese to study overseas.

■ **1911** The Qing dynasty's downfall is brought about by an almost accidental revolution, and betrayal by Yuan Shikai, the man the Qing trusted to crush it. He negotiates with

both sides and extracts an abdication agreement from the infant emperor's regent and an agreement from the rebels that he will become the first president of the new republic.

■ **1915** Yuan Shikai revives annual ceremonies at the Temple of Heaven, and prepares to install himself as first emperor of a new dynasty, but widespread demonstrations and the fomenting of a

Then & Now

Beijing's neighborhoods used to be very quiet. Residents lived simple lives mostly in walled courtyards. A seven- or eight-story building was considered unusually high. Now they are dwarfed by skyscrapers which house fancy shopping malls and outlets like McDonald's, KFC, and Starbucks.

—Jaime FlorCruz, CNN Beijing Bureau Chief

part, however, the styles of the *Shi Da Jianzhu* lean heavily on Stalinist architecture. There are also hints of Chinese style, such as in the pitched roof of the National Agricultural Exhibition Center.

The last few years have seen an explosion of new buildings that, again, are changing the look of central Beijing. Most of the new architecture in Beijing is also completely foreign. The most famous new structures have all been designed and in some cases built by foreign architects and their firms: The aforementioned **National Grand Theatre** by Paul Andreu, the geometric interlocking buildings of the **CCTV (China Central Television) Headquarters** by Rem Koolhaas and Ole Scheeren, the **Beijing**

National Stadium (aka the Bird's Nest) by Herzog & de Meuron, the dragon-inspired **Beijing Capital Airport** (Terminal 3) by Norman Foster, and the list goes on. Even the hippest shopping district in Beijing, the **Village at Sanlitun,** was designed by a team of international architects spearheaded by Japanese wonder Kengo Kuma. And while the impressive glass-and-steel skyscrapers and gravity-defying buildings are undeniably world-class designs, it does leave us feeling like this city, in a quest to prove itself as an ultramodern, ultrachic destination, has forgotten to build itself a sense of identity along with all those shiny new buildings.

4 RELIGION

Freedom to practice religion is enshrined in the Chinese constitution. In reality, of course, this right is subject to frequent and occasionally violent suspension—during times of political upheaval like the Cultural Revolution (1966–76) or, as in the

new rebellion in the south lead him to cancel his plans. He dies the following year.
- **1917** In July a pro-monarchist warlord puts Puyi back on the throne, but he is driven out by another who drops three bombs on the Forbidden City, only one of which actually explodes on target. The imperial restoration lasts exactly 12 days.
- **1919** Students and citizens gather on May 4 in Tian'an

Men Square to protest the government's agreement that Chinese territory formerly under German control be handed to the Japanese.
- **1924** The "Articles Providing for the Favourable Treatment of the Great Ch'ing [Qing] Emperor after his Abdication" provide for the emperor to continue to live in the Forbidden City pending an eventual move to the Summer Palace. But in November he is

removed by a hostile warlord and put under house arrest, later escaping to the Legation Quarter with the help of his Scottish former tutor.
- **1928** Despite fighting among warlords, many of whom are only nominally loyal to the Republic, the Nationalist Party forces in the south declare Nanjing the capital, and Beijing reverts to the name of

continues

case of Tibetan Buddhism and the banned spiritual movement Falun Gong, when specific groups are thought to pose a threat to Communist rule. Despite this, China has maintained what must rank among the world's most eclectic collection of religious traditions, encompassing not only native belief systems—Confucianism and Daoism—but Buddhism, Islam, and several strains of Christianity as well.

Those on tours of Chinese temples, churches, and mosques in the 1980s and early 1990s were wise to exercise a robust skepticism. The monks and nuns you encountered were invariably a specially selected bunch, likely to bombard foreigners with tales of how wonderfully supportive the government was. And the prettiest and best-restored temples were often barely more than showpieces, where it seemed incense was burned only to cover the sour smell of an Epcot-style cultural commodification.

But as faith in Communism wanes (to the point where some Chinese use the greeting *tongzhi*, or comrade, with thinly veiled sarcasm), religious buildings are slowly recovering their vitality as places of genuine worship, sources of guidance in the moral vacuum of a new market-driven society.

Maps of pre-Communist Beijing show an astoundingly large number of religious structures, from the grandest of glazed-tile complexes in the city's imperial quarter to hundreds of tiny shrines nestled in the maze of *hutong*. Most were destroyed or converted to other uses immediately following the Communist victory in 1949 and during the Cultural Revolution. Several dozen more have been bulldozed as part of modern reconstruction efforts, and all but the most prestigious will probably disappear in the future.

China has always been a secular state, but as in European capitals prior to the 20th century, the line between religion and government in Ming- and Qing-era Beijing was usually blurred. The most direct example is the **Lama Temple** (**Yonghe Gong;** p. 134), an immense imperial residence-turned-temple that houses a ritual urn used during the reign of the Qing Qianlong emperor to determine reincarnations of the Dalai Lama, leader of the dominant Buddhist sect in distant Tibet.

The tradition continues today, with Communist leaders playing a controversial role in selecting the most recent Panchen Lama (second from the top in the Tibetan Buddhist hierarchy) and threatening to do the same after the death of the current Dalai Lama, the exiled Tenzin Gyatso.

CONFUCIANISM

The moral philosophy said to have originated with Kongzi—a 5th-century-B.C. figure also known as Kong Fuzi (Latinized

Beiping. In the following years many ancient buildings are vandalized or covered in political slogans.

■ **1933** With Japanese armies seemingly poised to occupy Beiping, the most important pieces of the imperial collection of antiquities in the Forbidden City are packed into 19,557 crates and moved to Shanghai. They move again when the Japanese take Shanghai in 1937, and after

an incredible journey around the country in the thick of civil war, 13,484 crates end up with the Nationalist government in Taiwan in 1949.

■ **1937** Japanese forces, long in occupation of Manchuria and patrolling far beyond what the treaty permits them, pretend to have come under attack near the Marco Polo Bridge, occupy Beiping, and stay until the end of World War II ("The War

Against Japanese Aggression" to the Chinese).

■ **1949** Mao Zedong proclaims the creation of the People's Republic of China from atop the Tian'an Men on October 1. A vast flood of refugees from the countryside takes over the courtyard houses commandeered from their owners, and those houses which once held a single family now house a dozen. Temples are turned into army to "Confucius" by Jesuit supporters enthusiastic about his "family values")—is not really a religion or even a well-defined thought system. Indeed, there is no word in Chinese for Confucianism but only *ru,* a rather vague term that connotes scholarship and refinement. The ideas about proper conduct and government as remembered by Kongzi's disciples in works like the *Lunyu (Analects)* have nevertheless exerted more influence on China than either Buddhism or Daoism and have proven more resilient than anything written by Marx or Mao.

The *Analects* offer pithy observations on dozens of topics ("Those who make virtue their profession are the ruin of virtue," "The noble person is not a pot," and so on), but the three most important concepts are filial piety, proper execution of ritual, and humanity toward others. Kongzi had little trust in Heaven or nature. The ultimate concern is with tangible human relationships: those of the son with the father, the subject with the emperor, and friends with each other. These relationships are rigidly defined, and acknowledgment of them is the highest virtue. Chinese rulers recognized early on that this philosophy was perfectly suited to governing their vast empire. Mastery of Confucian classics, proven through a series of increasingly difficult Imperial Examinations, was a prerequisite for all government officials up until the very end of the 19th century.

Confucian ideas were denounced as "feudal thought" after the Communists took over, but visitors to Beijing need only go as far as a restaurant to realize how little this has meant. At any large table, diners will take seats according to their relationship with the host, toasts will be carried out with ritual precision, and forms of address will vary depending on who is speaking to whom. The Imperial Examinations, too, have been resurrected in the nationwide College Entrance Exam, success in which is considered vital to any young person's future. Some students even study for the exam at **Guo Zi Jian** (the old Imperial College; p. 132) in northeast Beijing while their parents burn incense for them next door at the **Kong Miao,** the second-largest Confucian temple after the one in Kongzi's hometown of Qufu in Shandong Province.

Although even the most modern Chinese display an attachment to family and ritual, cynical observers note that the emphasis on humanity seems to have disappeared. It is debatable, however, whether this was ever as forceful an idea in China as Kongzi wanted it to be.

DAOISM

China's only native-born religion, Daoism (Taoism) began, like Confucianism, as a

barracks, storehouses, and light industrial units.
- **1958–59** In a series of major projects to mark 10 years of Communist rule, the old ministries lining what will be Tian'an Men Square and its surrounding walls are all flattened for the construction of the Great Hall of the People and the vast museums opposite. These and Beijing Railway Station are built with Soviet help, which shows in the design. The city walls, which have survived for 400 years, are pulled down by "volunteers," to be replaced with a metro line and a ring road for an almost completely carless society. The stone from the walls goes to line a system of tunnels into which the entire city population can supposedly be evacuated in case of attack.
- **1966–76** The destruction of old things reaches its peak as bands of Red Guards, fanatically loyal to Mao, roam around fighting each other, ransacking ancient buildings, burning books, and smashing art. Even the tree from which the last Ming emperor supposedly hanged himself is cut down. Intellectuals are bullied, imprisoned, tortured, and murdered, as is anyone with a history of links to foreigners. Scores are settled,

continues

philosophical response to the chaos and bloodshed prevalent in China during the Warring States period (403–221 B.C.). It later split into several schools, certain of which absorbed elements of folk religion and concentrated on alchemy and other practices it was hoped would lead to immortality. With its emphasis on change and general distrust of authority, Daoism was the antithesis of Confucianism and remained largely on the fringes of Chinese civil society, more at home in the mountains than in the cities.

The oldest Daoist texts are the esoteric *Dao De Jing* (or *Tao Te Ching,* "Classic of the Way and Virtue") and the *Zhuangzi,* a prose book sometimes compared in its sly playfulness with the work of Nietzsche. Both deal with the Way *(Dao),* a broad philosophical concept also mentioned by Kongzi but described in a wholly different manner.

The Daoists' dismissal of language, their habit of asking absurd questions, and their frequent self-contradictions are attempts to shake readers free of reason, which is said to obscure an understanding of the Way because it seeks to impose a rigid framework on a universe that is constantly changing.

There has been a revival of interest in both folk Daoism (particularly in the countryside) and the philosophical side of Daoism in recent years, but this is largely

invisible. Daoist complexes like Beijing's immense **Baiyun Guan** (p. 130) are garish and loud, reflecting the religious branch's fondness for magic potions and spells, with little of the contemplative feel most Westerners expect.

BUDDHISM

Buddhism traveled from India through Central Asia and along the Silk Routes to China sometime in the 1st century and began to flourish after a crisis of confidence in Confucianism caused by the fall of the Later Han dynasty (A.D. 25–220). But it would never achieve the same dominance as Confucianism, in large part because of the Buddhists' insistence that they exist beyond the power of the state, the monks' rejection of traditional family relationships, and the populace's xenophobic wariness of a foreign philosophy. Buddhism did become sufficiently pervasive during the Tang dynasty (618–907) to merit its own department in the government, but a neo-Confucian backlash under the succeeding Song dynasty (960–1279) saw it lose influence again. Although it never fully recovered the power it held under the Tang, Buddhism continued to have wide popular appeal and is still China's most prevalent organized religion.

All Buddhists believe human suffering can be stopped by eliminating attachment. But where the older Buddhism of India

and millions die. The education system largely comes to a halt. Many antiquities impounded from their owners are sold to foreign dealers by weight to provide funds for the government, which later decries foreign theft of Chinese antiquities.
■ **1976** The death of Zhou Enlai, who is credited with mitigating some of the worst excesses of the Cultural Revolution, leads to over

100,000 demonstrating against the government in Tian'an Men Square. The demonstrations are labeled counterrevolutionary, and hundreds are arrested. The death of Mao Zedong, himself thought to be responsible for an estimated 38 million deaths, effectively brings the Cultural Revolution to an end. Blame for the Cultural Revolution is put on the "Gang of Four"—Mao's wife and three

other hard-line officials, who are arrested. The 450-year-old Da Ming Men in the center of Tian'an Men Square is pulled down to make way for Mao's mausoleum. Leaders put their backing behind Deng Xiaoping, who returns from disgrace to take power and launch a program of openness and economic reform. His own toleration for public criticism also turns out to be zero, however.

was a sparse atheistic tradition concerned with little more than the individual's achievement of Nirvana (enlightened detachment and extinction), Buddhism in China gradually absorbed elements of Daoism and local folk religion to become an incredibly complex belief system with various gods and demons, an intricately conceived heaven, several hells, and dozens of bodhisattvas (beings who have attained enlightenment but delay entry into Nirvana out of a desire to help others overcome suffering).

Buddhist temples in Beijing often contain large images of Milefo (Maitreya, the Future Buddha) depicted in both Chinese (fat and jolly) and Tibetan (thinner and more somber) guises, and of Guanyin (Avalokitesvara, the Bodhisattva of Compassion), a lithe woman in the Chinese style and a multiarmed, multiheaded man in the Tibetan pantheon, now incarnated as the Dalai Lama. The Manchu rulers of China's final dynasty, the Qing (1644–1911), tried to maintain cultural ties with several ethnic groups on the fringes of the Chinese empire, which explains the unusual prevalence of Tibetan Buddhist architecture in Beijing. Most noticeable are the two *dagobas* (Tibetan-style stupas), towering white structures like upside-down ice-cream cones, at **Bei Hai Gongyuan** (p. 136) and **Bai Ta Si** (p. 130).

ISLAM & CHRISTIANITY

Islam entered China through Central Asia in the 7th century, staying mostly in the northwestern corner of the empire, in what is now the Xinjiang Autonomous Region. It was introduced to more central regions through the occasional eastward migration of Xinjiang's Uighur people, and through the arrival of Arab trading vessels in southeastern ports like Quanzhou during the Song dynasty (960–1270), but it failed to catch on with Han Chinese the way Buddhism did. Those Han who did convert are now lumped into a separate ethnic group, the Hui. Beijing's Hui and Uighur populations don't mix as much as their shared religious beliefs might lead you to expect, the former dominating southeastern Beijing around the **Niu Jie Libai Si** (p. 133) and the latter kept mostly in a series of constantly shifting ghettos. A visit to the mosque on Niu Jie reveals Chinese Islam to be pretty much the same as Islam anywhere else; the glazed-tile roofs and basic layout resemble those of Buddhist or Daoist temples, but the main hall faces west (toward Mecca) rather than south, women and men pray separately, and there are absolutely no idols anywhere.

The first Christian missionary push to make much headway in China came in the 17th century, when Jesuits, led by Italian

■ **1989** The death of the moderate but disgraced official Hu Yaobang causes public displays of mourning in Tian'an Men Square, which turn into a mass occupation of the square protesting government corruption. Its hands initially tied by the presence on a state visit of the Soviet Union's Mikhail Gorbachev, the Party sends in the tanks live on TV on the night of June 3. Estimates of

the number of deaths vary wildly, but the number is thought to run to several hundred unarmed students and their supporters.
■ **2001** Beijing is awarded the 2008 Summer Olympics, and as a result the destruction and complete redevelopment of the city accelerates, to the immense personal profit of the developers. That some are related to the top

members of the administration is common knowledge.
■ **2003** Severe Acute Respiratory Syndrome (SARS) strikes Beijing, with more than 1,000 infected and around 100 dead. Millions of Beijingers stay indoors, while thousands of others are involuntarily quarantined in hospitals and dorm rooms. The epidemic subsides in July, and the government

continues

Matteo Ricci, sought to convert the country by first converting the imperial court. Ricci and his cohorts wowed the Qing rulers with their knowledge of science, art, and architecture (see Jonathan Spence's *The Memory Palace of Matteo Ricci* for more about this) but ultimately failed to make Catholics of the Manchus. Subsequent missionaries, both Catholic and Protestant, continued the war on Chinese superstition and met with some success, but they were also seen as a nuisance. Christianity was linked with both major popular uprisings in the Qing period—the Taiping Rebellion, led by a man named Hong Xiuquan, who claimed to be Jesus' younger brother; and the Boxer Rebellion, a violent reaction to the aggressive tactics of missionaries in northern China which led to the siege of Beijing's Legation Quarter.

Beijing is particularly leery of Catholics, many of whom refused to join Protestants in pledging first allegiance to the state after 1949 and instead remained loyal to the Pope. Missionaries, it goes without saying, are not allowed in China anymore, but many sneak in as English teachers (a favorite tactic of the Mormons in particular). Separate churches in Beijing for foreigners are off-limits to Chinese, although foreigners are allowed to attend Chinese services. The Gothic-style church built in 1904 on the site of Ricci's house still stands near the Xuanwu Men metro stop, and replicas of the Jesuits' bronze astronomical devices can be seen at the Ancient Observatory northeast of the main railway station.

RELIGION & SPIRITUALITY TODAY

Outside of monks and nuns, few Chinese people limit their devotion to a single tradition, instead choosing elements from each as they suit their particular circumstances. "Every Chinese," a popular saying goes, "is a Confucian when things are going well, a Daoist when things are going badly, and a Buddhist just before they die." But even this is a relatively rigid formulation—a Chinese person will often cross religious boundaries in the space of a single day if he thinks his problems merit the effort.

This pragmatic approach to beliefs allows not just individuals but also groups to create new religious systems with bits stolen from older traditions. Despite the government insistence that it is a cult, the Falun Gong's combination of Buddhism with *qigong* exercises and Daoist-like claims to impossible physical feats is very much in keeping with the Chinese tradition of religious collage. Unfortunately, its success has put Chinese leaders in mind of another tradition—the violent overthrow of dynasties by popular religious movements.

and the tourism industry complain of overblown media attention to the disease.

■ **2008** Beijing hosts the Olympic Games. The months leading up to the big event are marred with protests during international legs of the Olympic torch relay, and incredibly high pollution levels in Beijing. The Games themselves are well organized and go off with few hitches. Although Beijing officials designated legal protesting zones throughout the city during the Olympics, many who submitted applications to protest were punished and several disappeared, at least for the duration of the Games.

Despite the rise in religious participation, most visitors to Beijing still complain of a made-for-tourists feel in most of the city's temples. Given the tidal wave of foreigners' cash that flows into places like the **Lama Temple** (p. 134), this will probably never change, or at least not in Beijing proper. For those willing to make the trip, however, the seldom-visited areas just outside Beijing are home to several temples, such as **Tanzhe Si** (p. 207) and **Jietai Si** (p. 207), where tourism plays a secondary role to genuine religious practice. It is in places like these that you're most likely to witness the reawakening of China's older belief systems.

5 BEIJING IN POPULAR CULTURE: BOOKS, FILM, TV, MUSIC

BOOKS

The best single-volume introduction to the people of China and their world is **Jasper Becker**'s *The Chinese.* Longtime resident of Beijing and former Beijing bureau chief for the *South China Morning Post,* Becker delivers an immensely readable account of how the Chinese got to be who they are today; their preoccupations, thoughts, and fears; and the ludicrous posturings of their leaders. *The Search for Modern China* by acclaimed historian **Jonathan Spence** is a hefty account of China from the late Ming Dynasty to the mid-1980s. Do not confuse this well-written and highly accessible book with the drab styles found in high-school history textbooks. This is a fine and well-researched account of this country's past 400 years.

Old Beijing can now be found only in literature. The origins of many Western fantasies of the capital, then called Khanbalik, lie in the ghostwritten work of **Marco Polo,** *The Travels of Marco Polo.* Dover Publications' two-volume reprint (1993) of the Yule-Cordier edition is a splendid read (although only part of Polo's time was spent in Beijing) because of its entertaining introduction and footnotes by famous explorers attempting to follow his route. **Ray Huang**'s ironically titled *1587, A Year of No Significance* is an account of the Ming dynasty in decline; written in the first person, it paints a compelling picture of the well-intentioned Wanli emperor trapped by a vast, impersonal bureaucracy. The parallels with the present regime are striking. **Lord Macartney**'s *An Embassy to China* gives a detailed account of Qing China and particularly Beijing at the end of the 18th century. This should be compulsory reading for modern businesspeople, as it prefigures WTO negotiations. Macartney's prediction that the Chinese would all soon be using forks and spoons is particularly relevant. **Hugh Trevor-Roper**'s *Hermit of Peking,* part history, part detective story, uncovers the life of Sir Edmund Backhouse, resident of Beijing from the end of the Qing dynasty into the Republic, who knew everyone in the city at the beginning of the century, and who deceived them all, along with a generation of China scholars, with his fake diary of a Manchu official at the time of the Boxer Rebellion. A serviceably translated bilingual edition of **Lao She**'s *Teahouse* succinctly captures the flavor of life in Beijing during the first half of the 20th century. The helplessness of the characters in the face of political movements is both moving and prophetic. **John Blofeld**'s *City of Lingering Splendour: A Frank Account of Old Peking's Exotic Pleasures* describes the seamier side of Beijing in the 1930s, by someone who took frank enjoyment in its pleasures, including adventures in "the lanes of flowers and willows"— the Qian Men brothel quarter. In the same period, **George Kates,** an American, lived more decorously in the style of a Chinese gentleman-scholar in an old courtyard house of the kind now rapidly vanishing, and gives a sensitive and very appealing portrait of the city in *The Years That Were Fat.* **Ann Bridge,** the wife of a British diplomat in Beijing, wrote novels of life in the capital's Legation Quarter in the 1930s (cocktail parties, horse racing, problems with servants, love affairs—spicy stuff in its day, and best-selling, if now largely forgotten). *Peking Picnic* features a disastrous trip to the outlying temples of Tanzhe Si and Jietai Si (but one well worth undertaking yourself). *The Ginger Griffin* offers the adventures of a young woman newly arrived in the city, who attends the horse races and who has a happier ending.

David Kidd, another American, lived in Beijing for a few years before and shortly after the Communist victory of 1949, and gives an account of the beginning of the city's destruction in *Peking Story: The Last Days of Old China* (originally *All the Emperor's Horses*). Perhaps the best example of the "hooligan literature" of the late 1980s is *Please Don't Call Me Human* by **Wang Shuo.** There's little plot to speak of, but it's a devastating and surreal parody of Chinese nationalism, all the more poignant in the wake of the Olympics. *Red China Blues,* by **Jan Wong,** is one of our all-time favorite memoirs. Wong initially came to Beijing as a young and fervent Maoist in 1972 and became one of only two international students allowed to study at Beijing University during the height of the Cultural Revolution. Years later, she returned, older and wiser, as an international correspondent for the *Globe and Mail* in 1988, just in time to witness and report on the Tian'an Men protests of 1989. *Black Hands of Beijing,* by **George Black and Robin Munro,** is the most balanced and least hysterical account of the Tian'an Men protests of 1989, putting them in the context of other, better-planned movements for social change, all

of which suffered in the fallout from the chaotic student demonstrations and their bloody suppression. **Frances Wood**'s *Forbidden City* is a short and thoroughly entertaining introduction to Beijing's main attraction.

The past few years have produced many fine books and memoirs from some seasoned Beijing hands. **Michael Meyer**'s *The Last Days of Old Beijing: Life in the Vanishing Backstreets of a City Transformed* is a thoughtful memoir of the author's experience living and working in one of the city's famed *hutong.* **Peter Hessler** was the Beijing-based *New Yorker* correspondent for several years. His second book, *Oracle Bones,* is an insightful look into the lives of young Chinese migrants and colorful personalities from old and new Beijing. And finally, my delightful co-author **Jen Lin-Liu** tells a mouthwatering tale of modern China as viewed through the country's rich cuisine in her memoir *Serve the People: A Stir-Fried Journey Through China.*

FILM

It is a source of frustration to some Chinese filmmakers that foreign audiences are easily duped. The most internationally successful films about China—Ang Lee's *Crouching Tiger, Hidden Dragon,* Zhang Yimou's *Raise the Red Lantern,* Bernardo Bertolucci's *The Last Emperor*—wallow in marketable clichés. The China presented by these films exists almost solely in the simplified past tense, a mélange of incense, bound feet, and silk brocade designed to appeal to foreign notions of the country as unfathomably brutal and beautiful with an interminably long history.

Up until the late 1990s, much of the blame for this belonged to the government, which allowed the export of only those movies unlikely to provoke criticism of the present state of things, regardless of what they said about the past. Recently, however, films that deal with modern China, complex and often comic stories about everything from politics to relationships to harebrained attempts at money-making, have found their way to foreign viewers.

Beijing sits at the center of the Chinese film world and serves as the setting for most of the best films now being produced in China. Many of these cannot be seen even in Beijing itself except at small screenings unlikely to attract the attention of state censors. But those with access to a decent video rental shop will find a few.

Even Blockbuster carries copies of *Shower*, Zhang Yang's at times sappy but ultimately enjoyable story of a Beijing bathhouse owner and his two sons (one of them mentally handicapped) struggling to maintain a sense of family despite pressures of modernization. The film's depiction of a doomed *hutong* neighborhood and the comic old characters who inhabit it won smatterings of praise in limited U.S. release and criticism from the Chinese authorities, who claimed it was anti-progress. Director Feng Xiaogang tried and failed to make it big in the U.S. with *Big Shot's Funeral (Da Wan)*, featuring a (figuratively and literally) catatonic Donald Sutherland. But in a previous film set in and around Beijing, *Sorry Baby (Mei Wan Mei Liao)*, Feng displays a defter touch in a romantic comedy featuring bald-headed comic Ge You at his brilliant best.

Among the earlier generation of films, two that deal specifically with Beijing were big hits at Cannes, and you should have no trouble finding them. *Farewell My Concubine (Ba Wang Bie Ji)*, directed by Chen Kaige and starring the talented Gong Li, is a long bit of lushness about a pair of Beijing opera stars more dramatic in their alleged rivalry over a woman than they are onstage. Zhang Yimou's unrelenting primer on modern Chinese history, *To Live (Huozhe)*, also with Gong Li, traces the unbelievable tragedies of a single Beijing family as it bumbles through the upheavals of 20th-century China, from the civil war through the Great Leap Forward and Cultural Revolution and into the post-Mao reform period. More difficult to find (particularly with English subtitles), but very much worth the effort, are 1980s productions of Lao She's darkly satirical works, *The Teahouse (Cha Guan)* and *Rickshaw Boy (Luotuo Xiangzi)*.

Only specialty shops will carry *In the Heat of the Sun (Yangguang Canlan de Rizi)*, a smart and deceptively nostalgic coming-of-age film about a pack of mischievous boys left to their own devices in Cultural Revolution–era Beijing. Penned with help from celebrity rebel writer Wang Shuo, it was one of the first pictures to break free of the ponderous melodrama that dominated Chinese cinema through most of the 1990s. Life for migrant workers on the margins of Beijing is captured in the bleak but dryly witty *The World (Shijie)*, set in The World Park in the southwestern suburbs of Beijing. At times it borders on melodrama, and much of the subtlety is lost in translation, but Jia Zhangke's film craft delivers a satisfying reverie on alienation, fantasy, and trust. If the film inspires you to "see the world without leaving Beijing," take bus no. 744 from opposite Beijing Railway Station to the terminus.

The documentary *Gate of Heavenly Peace* is obligatory viewing for anyone hoping to understand what transpired in 1989. If all you recall is a statue of liberty and talk of democracy, you're in for a shock.

MUSIC

The vapid, factory-produced syrup of **Mandopop** (think Céline Dion by way of Britney Spears sung in Mandarin) blares out of barber shops and retail stores throughout Beijing, as elsewhere in China. But like Washington, D.C., and London, China's capital is ultimately a rock-'n'-roll town.

Godfather of Chinese rock **Cui Jian,** somewhat of a joke now as he clings to fading fame, got his start here in the early 1980s. A decade later, Chinese-American Kaiser Kuo, frontman for the no-longer-existent headbanger outfit **Tang Dynasty (Tang Chao),** helped kick off a pretentious and fairly derivative heavy metal scene. (Kuo now plays guitar for original, local Beijing band **Spring & Autumn,** or **Chunqiu**). But it wasn't until a shipment of Nirvana CDs found its way into local record shops in the late 1990s that Beijing finally developed a genuine musical voice.

Nirvana's *Nevermind* inspired nearly every Chinese kid who heard it to pick up a guitar and start a band. Investigations into Kurt Cobain's roots led to punk, which made its first major appearance in Beijing in late 1997 at the Scream Club, a sweaty dive in the Wudaokou neighborhood. It was a natural response to Beijing's swaths of urban decay and post–Tian'an Men political disillusionment, and American pop-culture magazines as big as *Details* quickly tapped the snarling, mohawked youth—most better at posing with their instruments than playing them—as easy symbols of China's new lost generation.

Beijing's punks were probably never as concerned with political protest as they were made out to be, and are even less so now as they enjoy the fruits of small-scale fame. But they continue to draw relatively large foreign audiences, and a handful have actually begun to produce music worthy of all the attention. The vulgar but talented **Brain Failure (Nao Zhuo)** and ska-influenced **Reflector (Fanguang Jing)**—both born at the now-defunct Scream Club—have each recorded listenable songs and evolved beyond just spitting beer in their live shows (though you can still expect the occasional shower). Also on Scream Records, the all-girl pop

punk group **Hang on the Box (Gua Zai Hezi Shang)** sings in charmingly accented English.

Chinese musicians wanting to produce significant popular music suffer from the same dreadful self-consciousness of working in a foreign idiom as do artists in other imported media. Some try desperately (and without much success) to create "rock with Chinese characteristics," while others opt to simply lay Chinese lyrics over melodies lifted, sometimes note for note, from Western CDs. Even the most creative of efforts will sound suspiciously derivative, and those that don't usually appeal only to Mandarin-speaking foreigners who delight primarily in their ability to understand the lyrics. The other major barrier to the local music industry is piracy, particularly the ready availability of music downloads. Most band members still have day jobs.

Second Hand Rose (Ershou Meigui) has an eponymous full-length CD (available only in Beijing), an excellent effort that stitches together Chili Peppers guitar, folk instrumentals, and sardonic *errenzhuan* opera–influenced lyrics ("I'm a name brand cigarette / I've been stuffed in the mouth of a poor man") into one of the very few uniquely Chinese sounds you'd actually want to hear. The band's live performances, built around the raised-eyebrow theatricality of cross-dressing singer Liang Long, are among the most entertaining musical experiences not just in China, but anywhere.

For information on when and where the above bands might be playing, check music listings in *Time Out, the Beijinger,* or *City Weekend,* available free in hotels, bars, and cafes where foreigners gather. Currently, **Yugong Yishan** (p. 188) is the best live music venue in Beijing, hands down.

Planning Your Trip to Beijing

by Jen Lin-Liu

Whether you plan to travel at random, with a prebooked route, or with a fully escorted tour, it's *vital* that you read this chapter carefully to understand how the way you travel, even in many other developing nations, doesn't apply here. Much supposed wisdom on China travel is far from wise, and what's good advice in the rest of the world is often the worst advice in China. If you haven't absorbed what's below, some of the rest of this guide may seem inscrutable. So put down your preconceptions, and read on . . .

---

1 WHEN TO GO

The biggest factor in your calculations on when to visit Beijing should be the movement of domestic tourists, who during the longer public holidays take to the road in tens or even hundreds of millions, flooding transportation, booking out hotels, and turning even the quieter tourist sights into litter-strewn bedlam.

PEAK TRAVEL SEASONS

CHINESE NEW YEAR (SPRING FESTIVAL) Like many Chinese festivals, this one operates on the lunar calendar. Solar equivalents for the next few years are February 14, 2010; February 3, 2011; January 23, 2012; and February 10, 2013. The effects of this holiday are felt from 2 weeks before the date until 2 weeks after, when anyone who's away from home attempts to get back, including an estimated 225 million migrant workers. If you are flying from overseas to Beijing, this won't affect you, but a land approach may be difficult, except in the few days immediately surrounding the holiday. Banks, as well as smaller restaurants and businesses, may be shut for a week. But main attractions are mostly open.

LABOR DAY & NATIONAL DAY In a policy known as "holiday economics," the May 1 and October 1 holidays have been reduced to 3 days each (including 1 weekend—most people are expected to work through the weekend prior to the holiday in exchange for 2 weekdays, which are added to the official 3 days of holiday). These two holidays now mark the beginning and end of the domestic travel season, and mark the twin peaks of leisure travel, with the remainder of May, early June, and September also busy. The exact dates of each holiday are not announced until around 2 weeks before each takes place.

CLIMATE

For the best weather, visit Beijing in September or October when warm, dry, sunny days with clear skies and pleasantly cool evenings are the norm. The second-best time is spring, late March to mid-May, when winds blow away the pollution but also sometimes bring clouds of scouring sand for a day or two, turning the sky a livid yellow. Winters can be bitter, but the city is much improved visually under a fresh blanket of snow: The gaudy colors of

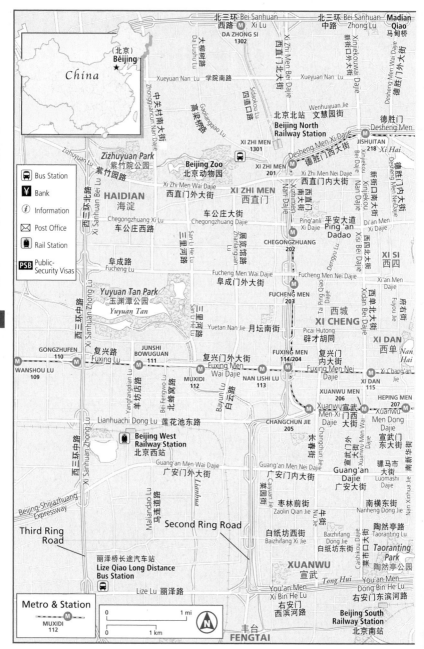

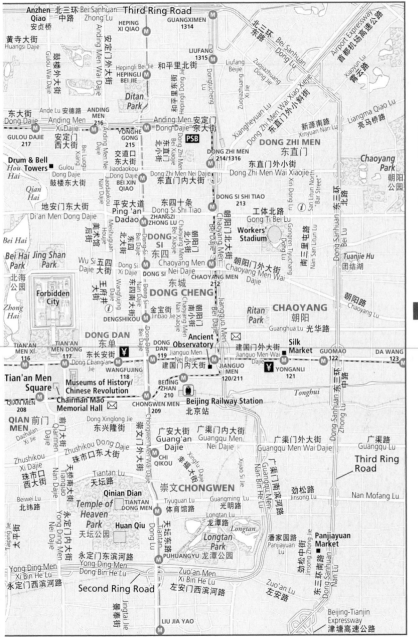

the Forbidden City's palaces are emphasized, as is the Great Wall's bleakness. Summers are humid and hot, but air-conditioning makes them tolerable. The number of foreign visitors is high during summer, but the Chinese themselves mostly wait until the weather cools before traveling.

Beijing's Average Temperatures & Rainfall

	Jan	Feb	Mar	Apr	May	June	July	Aug	Sept	Oct	Nov	Dec
Temp. (°C)	-3	-1	6	14	20	24	26	25	21	14	5	-1
Temp. (°F)	26	31	43	57	68	76	79	77	69	57	41	30
Days of Rain	2.1	3.1	4.5	5.1	6.4	9.7	14.5	14.1	6.9	5.0	3.6	1.6

HOLIDAYS

A few years ago the Chinese were finally granted a 2-day weekend, but while offices close, shops, restaurants, post offices, transportation, and sights all operate the same services 7 days a week. Most sights, shops, and restaurants are open on public holidays, too, but offices and anything government-related close for as much time as possible. Although China switched to the Gregorian calendar in 1911, some public holidays (and many festivals—see the following "Beijing Calendar of Events") are on a lunar cycle, with solar dates varying from year to year. Holidays are **New Year's Day** (Jan 1), **Spring Festival** (Chinese New Year's day and the following 2 days—see "Peak Travel Seasons" above, for exact dates in coming years), **Labor Day** (May 1 plus up to 4 more weekdays and a weekend), and **National Day** (Oct 1 plus extra days, as for Labor Day).

BEIJING CALENDAR OF EVENTS

Festivals are more family affairs in Beijing, which doesn't have much of a calendar of public events compared with some other parts of China.

For an exhaustive list of events beyond those listed here, check http://events. frommers.com, where you'll find a searchable, up-to-the-minute roster of what's happening in cities all over the world.

WINTER

Spring Festival (Chun Jie), or Chinese New Year, is still the occasion for large lion dances and other celebrations in Chinatowns worldwide, but in mainland China it's mainly a time for everyone to return to his or her ancestral home and feast. Fireworks are now banned in Beijing; however, temple fairs have been revived but are mostly fairly low-key shopping opportunities without much of the color or professional entertainers of old. But in the countryside, there's been a gradual revival of stilt walking and masked processions. New Year is on the day of the first new moon after January 21, and can be no later than February 20.

Lantern Festival (Deng Jie) perhaps reached its peak in the late Qing dynasty, when temples, stores, and other public places were hung with fantastically shaped and decorated lanterns. Many people paraded through the streets with lightweight lanterns in the shapes of fish, sheep, or other animals, and hung others, often decorated with riddles, outside their houses. There are modest signs of a revival. This festival always falls 15 days after Spring Festival.

SPRING

Tomb-Sweeping Festival (Qingming) is frequently observed in Chinese communities overseas, and more often in rural areas of China, as a family outing on a free day near the festival date. It's a day for honoring ancestors by visiting and tidying their gravesites, and making offerings of snacks and alcohol, which often turns into a picnic. It is now an official holiday and people usually get a long weekend. April 4.

AUTUMN

The last remnant of the **Mid-Autumn Festival (Tuanyuan Jie),** except among literary-minded students, is the giving and eating of *yuebing* (moon cakes), circular pies with sweet and extremely fattening fillings. Traditionally it's a time to sit and read poetry under the full moon, but pollution has made the moon largely invisible. Like the Tomb-Sweeping Festival, this is now an official holiday and companies usually grant a 3-day weekend. Takes place the 15th day of the 8th lunar month (usually Sept).

National Day itself is for avoiding Tian'an Men Square, especially if the government considers the anniversary important enough for one of its military parades, when the square may be blocked to you anyway. October 1.

---

2 ENTRY REQUIREMENTS

PASSPORTS

Visitors must have a valid **passport** with at least 6 months' validity from time of entry into the country, and two blank pages remaining (you *may* get away with just one blank page).

VISAS

All visitors to **mainland China** (as opposed to Special Administrative Regions of Hong Kong and Macau) must acquire a visa in advance. Visa applications typically take 3 to 5 working days to process, although this can be shortened to as little as 1 day if you apply in person and pay extra fees. "L" (tourist) visas are valid for between 1 and 3 months. Usually 1 month is granted unless you request more, which you may or may not get according to events in China at the time. Double-entry tourist visas are also available. It varies, but typically your visit must *begin* within 90 days of the date of issue.

You should apply for a visa in person at your nearest **consulate,** although it's possible to obtain Chinese visas in other countries while you're on an extended trip. To apply for a visa, you must complete an **application form,** which can be downloaded from many consular websites or acquired by mail. Visas are valid for the whole country, although some small areas require an extra permit from the local police. Temporary restrictions, sometimes for years at a time, may be placed on areas where there is unrest, and a further permit may be required to enter them. This is currently the case with Tibet, where travelers are required to book a tour with guide and driver to secure a permit. In general, do not mention Tibet or Xinjiang on your visa application, or it may be turned down flat.

Some consulates request that you show them an airline ticket, an itinerary, or proof of sufficient funds, or they claim to issue visas only to those traveling in groups (while happily carrying on business with individuals who have none of the supporting documentation). Such guidelines provide consulates with a face-saving excuse for refusing a visa should there be unrest or political difficulties, or should Tibet or Xinjiang appear on the application.

Children must have their own passport and visa.

A complete list of all Chinese embassies and consulates, including addresses and contact information, can be found at the Chinese foreign ministry's website: www. fmprc.gov.cn/eng (or various mirror sites around the world). Click on "Missions Overseas." Many consulates (including all those in the U.S. and Canada) will accept applications only in person; applications by post or courier must go through an agent, who will charge additional fees. Contacting some embassies can be very difficult: Many telephone systems are automated, and reaching a human can be next to impossible; faxes and e-mails usually don't receive a reply; and websites are often out-of-date.

What follows are visa fees and requirements for some countries:

- **Australia:** Single-entry visas are A$40; double-entry, A$60. Add A$50 per package dealt with by mail or courier, and a prepaid return envelope. Visit http://au.china-embassy.org/eng for an application. The **Chinese Embassy Canberra** is at 15 Coronation Dr., Yarralumla, ACT 2600 (② 02/6273-4780).
- **Canada:** Single-entry visas are C$50; double-entry, C$75. Visit www.china embassycanada.org for an application form. Applications must be delivered and collected by hand, or sent via a visa agency. The **Chinese Embassy** in Canada is at 515 St. Patrick St., Ottawa, Ontario (② 613/789-3434).
- **New Zealand:** Single-entry visas are NZ$140; double-entry, NZ$210. Add NZ$15 per package dealt with by mail or courier, and a prepaid return envelope. Visit www.chinaembassy.org.nz or www.chinaconsulate.org.nz for an application. The **Chinese Embassy** in New Zealand is at 2–6 Glenmore St., Wellington (② 644/472-1382).
- **United Kingdom:** Single-entry visas are £30; double-entry, £45. There's a supplementary charge of £35 for each package dealt with by mail. Visit www.chinese-embassy.org.uk for an application or call the **Chinese Visa Application Center** (② 0207/842-0960).
- **United States:** Single-, double-, and multiple-entry visas are US$130. Visit

www.china-embassy.org, which has links to all U.S. consular sites and a downloadable application form. Applications must be delivered and collected by hand, or sent via a visa agency. The **Chinese Embassy** can be reached at ② 202/328-2500.

Note: The visa **fees** quoted above for each country are the current rates for *nationals of that country,* and can change at any time. In addition to the visa fees quoted, there may be supplementary fees for postage. Payment must always be in cash or by money order.

VISA EXTENSIONS   Single-entry tourist visas may be extended twice for a maximum of 30 days each time at the PSB Exit/Entry Division offices in most cities. The office in Beijing (② 010/8402-0101) is on the south side of the eastern North Second Ring Road, just east of the Lama Temple metro stop (Mon–Sat 8:30am–4:30pm). You will also need your Registration Form of Temporary Residence (your hotel should have a copy) and a certificate of deposit issued by a Chinese bank (ICBC, Bank of China, and so on) proving you have at least US$100 per day for the duration of your stay; for example, if you are requesting a 30-day extension, you need to show US$3,000 in a certificate of deposit. Applications take 5 working days to process. Bring your passport and two passport photos (these can be taken at the office for ¥30). Extension fees vary by nationality: Australians and Canadians pay ¥160, U.K. citizens ¥469, and U.S. citizens ¥940.

GETTING A VISA IN HONG KONG Nationals of most developed nations do not require a visa to enter Hong Kong, and visas for mainland China are more easily obtainable there than anywhere else.

The cheapest tourist visas are available at the **Visa Office of the PRC,** 7th Floor, Lower Block, China Resources Building, 26 Harbour Rd., Wanchai (② 852/3413-2424; www.fmcoprc.gov.hk; Mon–Fri 9am–noon and 2–5pm). Here a single-entry tourist visa costs HK$210 for Australians and Canadians, HK$500 for citizens of the U.K., and HK$1,080 for U.S. citizens. Same-day service costs at least double. For urgent departures, or 6-month "F" *(fan-gwen)* visas, go to **Grand Profit International Travel Agency,** 705AA, 7th Floor, New East Ocean Centre, 9 Science Museum Rd., Tsimshatsui (about a 15-min. walk east of Nathan Rd.; © **852/ 2723-3288**).

CUSTOMS
What You Can Bring into China

In general terms, you can bring anything into China for personal use that you plan to take back with you, with the usual exceptions of arms and drugs, or plant materials, animals, and foods from diseased areas. There are no problems with cameras or video recorders, GPS equipment, laptops, or any other standard electronic equipment. Two unusual prohibitions are "old/ used garments" and "printed matter, magnetic media, films, or photographs which are deemed to be detrimental to the political, economic, cultural, and moral interests of China," as the regulations put it. Large quantities of religious literature, overtly political materials, or books on Tibet might cause you difficulties but, in general, small amounts of personal reading matter in non-Chinese languages do not present problems. Customs officers are for the most part easygoing, and foreign visitors are rarely searched. Customs declaration forms have now vanished from all major points of entry, but if you are importing more than US$5,000 in cash, you should declare it, or theoretically you could face difficulties at the time of departure—although, again, this is highly unlikely.

What You Can Take Home from China

An official seal must be attached to any item created between 1795 and 1949 that is taken out of China; older items cannot be exported. But, in fact, you are highly unlikely to find any genuine antiques, so this is moot (however, a genuine antiques dealer would know how to obtain the seal).

For information on what you're allowed to bring home, contact one of the following agencies:

Australian Citizens: Australian Customs Service at © **1300/363-263,** or log on to www.customs.gov.au.

Canadian Citizens: Canada Border Services Agency (© **800/461-9999** in Canada, or 204/983-3500; www.cbsa-asfc. gc.ca).

New Zealand Citizens: New Zealand Customs, The Customhouse, 17–21 Whitmore St., Box 2218, Wellington (© **04/ 473-6099** or 0800/428-786; www.customs. govt.nz).

U.K. Citizens: HM Customs & Excise at © **0845/010-9000** (from outside the U.K., 020/8929-0152), or consult their website at www.hmce.gov.uk.

U.S. Citizens: U.S. Customs & Border Protection (CBP; © **877/287-8667;** www.cbp.gov).

MEDICAL REQUIREMENTS

Unless you're arriving from an area known to be suffering from an epidemic (particularly cholera or yellow fever), inoculations or vaccinations are not required for entry into Beijing. In the recent past, China has been known to go overboard in its reaction to media-fanned epidemics and pandemics. In mid-2009, the H1N1 flu pandemic caused headaches for many Beijing travelers. At China's international airports, quarantine officials targeted aircraft from countries where the virus had been detected (including the United States and Canada). Disembarking passengers had their temperatures measured and filled in questionnaires disclosing where they were staying and how they could be contacted. Some travelers found themselves immediately quarantined after showing signs of the virus; others were allowed to leave the airport only to be quarantined later (after health officials tracked them down at hotels or private residences) because they sat too close to another passenger with a fever or other flu symptoms.

3 GETTING THERE & GETTING AROUND

GETTING TO BEIJING
By Plane

On direct, nonstop flights, China's own international airlines always offer rates slightly lower than those of foreign carriers. Cabin staff try to be helpful but are never quite sure how. Air China only recently suffered its first and only fatal accident and should not be confused with China Airlines from Taiwan, at quite the other end of the scale. **Departure tax** is now included in the price of your ticket.

Beijing's international airport (PEK) is about 20km (12 miles) north of downtown. A new terminal, T3, was added in 2008 to handle the extra traffic during the Olympics. Several major airlines moved their operations to the shinier new building, including Air China, British Airways, Singapore Airlines, and Dragon Air.

To find out which airlines travel to Beijing, see "Airline Websites," p. 219.

Getting into Town from the Airport

Taxi   You will be pestered by **taxi** touts as soon as you emerge from Customs. *Never* go with these people. The signposted taxi rank is straight ahead and has a line that mostly works, although a few people will always try to cut in front of you. Line up at the two-lane rank, and a marshal will direct you to the next available vehicle as you reach the front of the line. Rates are clearly posted on the side of each cab. All cabs are ¥2 per kilometer. After 15km (9⅓ miles), rates increase by 50%. If you only want to go to the hotels (such as the Westin, Kempinski, Hilton, or Sheraton) in the San Yuan Qiao area, where the Airport Expressway meets the Third Ring Road,

your taxi driver may be a bit grumpy, but that's his bad luck.

Expect to pay around ¥80 to the eastern part of the city and around ¥100 to the central hotels. These estimates include the meter rate and a ¥10 expressway toll, which you'll see the driver pay en route. Fares to the central hotels will increase significantly if you travel during rush hours (8–9am and 3:30–7pm). For most of the day, you can reach hotels on the Third Ring Road within about 30 minutes, and central hotels in about 45 minutes—the latter trip may rise to more than an hour during rush hours. Make sure you read the box "Ten Tips for Taking Taxis around Town," in this chapter.

Airport Buses   Air-conditioned services, run by two different companies, leave from in front of the domestic arrivals area. The Airport Shuttle Bus (¥16) runs five routes; the most useful, Line 2 to Xidan, runs every 10 minutes from 7am to last arrival. Destinations include San Yuan Qiao (near the Hilton and Sheraton hotels), the Dong Zhi Men and Dong Si Shi Tiao metro stations, and the CAAC ticket office in Xidan. Lines 1 through 5 all pass through San Yuan Qiao, but only Line 2 lets off passengers at a location convenient for picking up taxis to continue to other destinations. Most hotels in the center of the city can be reached by taxi for under ¥30 from there. If you're staying in the university district, save yourself a bundle and take Line 5 to Zhongguancun Bridge. From there it is a ¥10 to ¥20 taxi ride to most of the major universities. For more detail on the airport buses and where they stop, check out the airport's website, **www.bcia.com.cn.**

There is also a Kong Gang Bus for ¥1 to ¥3 available at the exit of both terminal buildings. It stops at destinations very close to the airport (Ying Hua Yuan, Guo Tai Guang Chang, and the Airport Hotel).

Express Train The new airport express train to **Dong Zhi Men** is a mixed blessing. For ¥25, you'll get yourself to downtown Beijing in about 20 minutes. You can use regular metro cards (see "Getting Around," below) for the journey. Unfortunately, the logistics of taking the train can be incredibly annoying. The mandatory X-ray machine at the airport station often means waiting in line and then heaving your heavy suitcases onto the conveyor belt. Getting to street level at Dong Zhi Men involves a short escalator and then a steep set of stairs (there's an elevator after the escalator but it doesn't take you all the way to street level). Then there's the madness of hailing down a cab around the hordes of public buses just outside the station. Passengers are funneled into the northeast exit of Dong Zhi Men, and if you want to get to any of the other three corner exits, you will have to pay the ¥2 subway fare to walk through the subway station. If you want to switch to the subway, expect more stairs and yet another X-ray machine. The express train also stops at **San Yuan Qiao,** a short cab ride away from the hotels on Third Ring.

By Car

Foreign visitors are not permitted to drive their own vehicles into China, unless arrangements are made far in advance with a state-recognized travel agency for a specific itinerary. The agency will provide a guide who will travel in your vehicle, or in a second vehicle with a driver, and make sure you stick to the planned route. You will have to cover all the (marked-up) costs of guide, driver, and extra vehicle if needed, and of Chinese plates for your vehicle. The agency will book and overcharge you for all your hotels and for as many excursions as it can. Forget it.

By Train

From Hung Hom station in Kowloon (Hong Kong), expresses run directly to Beijing's West Station on alternate days (see the Intercity Passenger Services section on www.kcr.com.hk for schedules and fares). From Moscow weekly trains arrive via Ulaan Baatar in Mongolia, and weekly via a more easterly route directly to Harbin in China's northeast and down to the capital. There's also a separate weekly run from Ulaan Baatar to Beijing. Trains run twice weekly from Hanoi in Vietnam to Beijing West via Guilin. There's also a service between Beijing and Pyongyang in North Korea, but you'll be on that only if you've joined an organized tour.

By Boat

Ferries connect from Incheon in South Korea (http://english.visitkorea.or.kr) and from Shimonoseki and Kobe in Japan (www.celkobe.co.jp) to Tianjin, a couple of hours from Beijing.

GETTING AROUND
By Metro

The Beijing metro system *(ditie)* is undergoing a process of rapid expansion. This is leading to traffic snarls at ground level, which make using the existing lines essential. The Olympics ushered in a host of new lines, brand-new trains, and modern electronic ticket-reading gates.

Eventually there will be 15 metro and light-rail lines, but for now the system consists of 7 lines. The **Loop Line** (sometimes known as **Line 2**), which follows the upper portion of the Second Ring Road, cutting across under Qian Men, effectively follows the line of the Tartar City walls that were demolished to make its construction possible (the Dongnan Jiaolou, home to the Red Gate Gallery, was spared because the metro takes a turn at that point). **Line 1** runs from Pingguo Yuan in the west, the site of Capital Iron and Steel and other heavy industry which are the sources of much of Beijing's pollution, right across town beneath Chang'an Jie and its extensions to Si Hui Dong in the east. The **Baotong Line** extends Line 1 into the eastern suburbs. The light-rail **Line 13** swings in a suburban loop to the north, from the Loop Line's Xi Zhi Men to Dong Zhi Men stations. New to this book are lines 5, 8, and 10. **Line 5** runs north-south, cutting through the Loop Line and lines 1, 10, and 13. **Line 8** is just three stops that run to the Olympic sites and venues. **Line 10** traces the northeast perimeter of Third Ring Road (eventually it will trace the southwest portion as well). Stations are numbered (see the Beijing metro map, on the inside front cover of this book), signs on platforms tell you which station is the next in each direction, and English announcements are made on trains, so navigation is not difficult.

Ticket booths are below ground, and a ticket costs ¥2 for a ride anywhere with unlimited transfers. The metro card, officially known as the "Municipal Administration and Communication Card" (Shizheng Jiaotong Yikatong, or Yikatong for short) can be bought for a ¥40 minimum, including the ¥20 refundable deposit. You can buy and return cards at any station. Single-ride tickets are available from the cashier or from the new electronic ticketing machines that have service in English.

Entrances are not always clearly marked. Find them on maps, marked with a D (for *ditie*) in a circle, and look for the same sign at entrances. Escalators are up only, staircases are long, and there are no elevators. Some stops have installed wheelchair stair lifts, but not all. Those with limited mobility should stay on the surface.

By Taxi

Beijing's rapid conversion from a city for bicycles to one for cars has brought the inevitable traffic jams. Get on the road well before 7:30am to beat the rush, or forget it until about 10am. The city's arteries start to clog again about 3pm, and cir-

culation slows to a crawl until 7:30pm. Take the metro to the point nearest your destination and jump in a cab from there.

The red **Fukang**, a Citroën joint venture built in Wuhan on the Yangzi River, are slightly older than the colorful **Xiandai** (Hyundai, a Beijing-based joint venture) taxis. The Xiandai have better air-conditioning and are much roomier. Both have an initial charge of ¥10, which includes 2km (1.2 miles), and each subsequent kilometer is ¥2, or ¥3 after 15km (9⅓ miles).

There is a mix of old and new **Santana** and **Jetta** cabs built in various Volkswagen joint ventures around China. They're similar to popular Volkswagen models in the West and are equally solid. A joint venture between **LXI** (London Taxis International) and Shanghai-based Geely Automobile produced spacious, London-style hansom cabs specifically for limited-mobility travelers (same price as the sedans). They were seen widely around town during the Paralympic Games, but are now few and far between. Beijing does have taxis with dodgy meters that hang around larger hotels where corrupt bellhops call them for you. Always follow the advice in the box "Ten Tips for Taking Taxis around Town."

All taxis are metered. But on the front of the meter they also have a button, for one-way trips out of town, which is pushed regardless of the type of trip to be taken. This causes the per-kilometer rate to increase by 50% after 15km (9⅓ miles). If you hire the vehicle to take you somewhere, wait, and bring you back, or to run you around town all day, then insist that the button not be pushed. As elsewhere in the world, the meter also ticks over slowly when the vehicle is stationary or moving very slowly.

Between 11pm and 5am the meter starts at ¥11 and rates increase to ¥2.40 per kilometer, or ¥3.40 after 15km (9⅓ miles).

(Tips) Ten Tips for Taking Taxis around Town

1. **Never** go with a driver who approaches you at the airport (or railway stations). Leave the building and head for the rank. As with everywhere else in the world, airport taxis are the most likely to cause trouble. Drivers who approach you are usually *hei che*—illegal and meterless "black cabs."

2. Cabs waiting for business outside major tourist sights, especially those whose drivers call out to foreigners, should be avoided, as should cabs whose drivers ask you where you want to go before you even get in. Always flag down a passing cab, and 9 times in 10 the precautions listed here will be unnecessary.

3. Better hotels give you a piece of paper with the taxi registration number on it as you board or alight, so that you can complain if something goes wrong. Often you won't know if it has, of course, and there's no guarantee that anything will happen if you complain to the hotel, but hang onto it anyway.

4. Look to see if the supervision card, usually with a photo of the driver and a telephone number, is prominently displayed, as regulations require. If it isn't, you may have problems. Choose another cab.

5. Can you clearly see the meter? If it's recessed behind the gear stick, or partly hidden by an artfully folded towel, for example, choose another cab.

6. Always make sure you see the meter reset. If you didn't see the flag pushed down, which shouldn't happen until you actually move off, then you may end up paying for the time the cab was in the rank. This is a particularly popular scam outside better hotels.

7. If you are by yourself, sit in the front seat. Have a map with you and look as if you know where you are going (even if you don't).

8. Rates per kilometer are clearly posted on the side of the cab. The flag drop of ¥10 includes 2km (1¼ miles), after which the standard ¥2 kilometer rate begins. But in Beijing, after 15km (9⅓ miles), the rate jumps by 50% if the driver has pushed the "one-way" button on the front of the meter. This button is for one-way trips out of town and usually should not be pushed, but always is. As a result, it's rarely worthwhile to have a cab wait for you with the meter running and take you back.

9. Pay what's on the meter, and don't tip—the driver will insist on giving change. Always ask for a receipt *(fa piao)*. Should you leave something in a cab, there's a remarkably high success rate at getting even valuable items back if you call the number on the receipt and provide the details. You'll need the assistance of a Mandarin speaker.

10. If you'd like to have one cab driver for your entire stay, you can arrange a day rate. These are subject to negotiation, but expect to pay ¥400 to ¥500 per day if you are staying within the city.

By Bicycle

There used to be considerable charm in being one fish in a vast shoal of bicycles, but cycling is now ill-advised for the timid (or sensibly cautious). But enthusiasts for two-wheeled travel will certainly find that at some times of day they can get around more quickly than anyone else. Many upmarket hotels will rent you a bicycle for around ¥500 for the day; however, a *new* bike may be purchased for as little as ¥250, so if you're going to be using a bike for a few days, buying one is a better deal. Don't expect sophisticated accessories such as gears on rental bikes or bikes purchased for these prices—flat Beijing does not require them anyway. Budget accommodations and some bike enclosures next to metro stops charge a more appropriate ¥20 per hour. Check the bike's condition carefully, especially the brakes and tires. Sidewalk bicycle-repair operations are everywhere and will make repairs for a few yuan, if worst comes to worst. Always park the bike in marked and supervised enclosures, using the lock, which is built in or provided, or expect the bike to be gone when you get back. The parking fee is usually ¥.20.

By Car

The rule of the road is "me first," regardless of signs, traffic lights, road markings, safety considerations, or common sense, unless someone with an ability to fine or demand a bribe is watching. In general, the bigger your vehicle, the more authority you have. Maximum selfishness in the face of common sense characterizes driving in general, and there is no maneuver so ludicrous or unexpected that someone will not attempt it. Residents have time to adapt—visitors do not. Our strong advice is to forget it, and take a taxi. If you are intent on driving in Beijing, keep in mind that foreign driver's licenses are not recognized in China and you will have to take a driving exam to obtain the proper permits.

By Bus

Unless you are on the tightest of back-packer budgets and are traveling alone, your first choice for getting around town is the metro, your second choice is taxi, and your last resort should be the bus. There are dedicated bus lanes during rush hours, but everyone gets bottlenecked during those times. Regular bus fares start at

¥1, while air-conditioned buses charge ¥2 and up. Fares are slightly cheaper with metro cards. Entrance and exit doors are marked with the *shang* ("up" or "get on") and *xia* ("down" or "get off") characters, respectively (see chapter 13).

TRAVELING BEYOND BEIJING
By Plane

Daily **direct flights** connect Capital Airport to nearly every major Chinese city, including Shanghai for around ¥1,130, Guangzhou for ¥1,700, Xi'an for ¥1,050, Chengdu for ¥1,440, and Lhasa for ¥2,430. Prices vary widely, according to the season and your bargaining skills, and may be reduced to half the amounts quoted here. Much Chinese domestic flying is done on a walk-up basis, but the best discount is never available at the airport. The aviation authority officially permits the airlines to discount to a maximum of 40% on domestic flights, but discounts of 50%, sometimes even more, are not uncommon at ticket agencies.

Tickets for domestic flights (and international flights) on Chinese airlines are best purchased through a travel agent, such as **Airtrans,** C12 Guang Hua Lu, opposite Kerry Centre (© **010/6595-2255**), or in one of two main ticketing halls: the Aviation Building (Minhang Dalou; © **010/6656-9988;** fax 010/6656-9333; 24 hr.) at Xi Chang'an Jie 15, just east of the Xidan metro station; or the Airlines Ticketing Hall (© **010/8402-8198;** fax 010/6401-5307; 9am–7pm), at 6/F Building B, Zhong Ding Da Sha, Bei San Huan Xilu A18 (subway line 13, at Da Zhong Si stop). You can use a credit card at the ticketing hall. **Ctrip** and **eLong** are two companies that offer excellent prices on domestic and international tickets through their online websites **www.english.ctrip.com** and **www.elong.net**. You can book flights online and pay for tickets in cash upon delivery. You can also

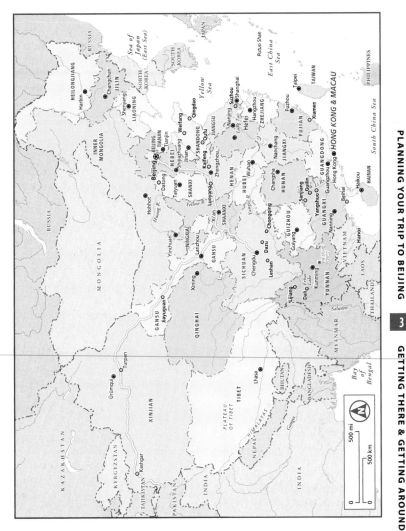

pay by credit card (expect a 3–5% sur-charge) after faxing through a credit card authorization form. If you hate the Internet, both companies have English-speaking agents that can walk you through the booking and payment process.

Booking from overseas via websites offering tickets for Chinese domestic flights, most of which do not appear on international ticketing systems, is *always* a mistake. You'll nearly always be charged the full price (which is generally paid by only a handful of people traveling at peak times at the last minute), and probably a booking fee, too.

Most hotels can arrange tickets for flights on **foreign airlines,** but they tend to levy hefty service fees. The airline offices themselves do not usually attempt to match the prices offered by agents, but are merely a source of the price to beat elsewhere. Special offers are often published in the monthly expat magazines *The Beijinger* and *Time Out,* but sometimes agents undercut even these, or they bend the rules on advance booking requirements to give an advance-purchase price at the last minute.

By Train

The main railway stations are **Beijing Railway Station (Beijing Zhan;** (C) **010/ 5101-9999)** and **West Station (Xi Ke Zhan;** schedule information (C) **010/5182-4233).** Tickets can be purchased at these stations for any train leaving Beijing up to 4 days in advance, and during the busiest seasons up to 10 days in advance. It is possible to buy **round-trip tickets** *(fancheng piao)* to major destinations like Shanghai or Xi'an up to 12 days in advance, subject to availability. Nineteen new **Z trains,** which depart at night and arrive early the following morning, directly connect with other cities. Cities served are Changchun, Changsha, Hangzhou, Harbin, Hefei, Nanjing, Shanghai (five trains), Suzhou, Wuhan (four trains), Xi'an, and the newly opened railway station in Yangzhou. All compartments are spanking new, and staff is more enthusiastic than on other services. Television screens have been installed in soft-sleeper compartments, which may disturb your night's rest. Tickets for Z trains may be purchased 20 days in advance.

Satellite ticket offices *(tielu shoupiao chu)* scattered throughout the city charge a negligible ¥5 service fee; convenient branches are just inside the main entrance of the Sanhe Baihuo (department store), south of the Xin (Sun) Dong An Plaza on Wangfujing Dajie (9am–9pm); at the Shatan Shoupiao Chu farther north at Ping'an Dadao 45, west of Jiaodaokou

Nan Dajie ((C) **010/6403-6803;** 8am–6pm); and at the Gongti Dong Lu Shoupiao Chu ((C) **010/6509-3783)** in Sanlitun, opposite and slightly south of the Workers' Stadium east gate. Tickets for all trains from Beijing can also be booked free of charge at Beijing South Station (Beijing Nan Zhan; (C) **010/5186-7999)** and at Beijing North Station (Beijing Bei Zhan, (C) **010/5186-6223),** which is more conveniently located just north of the Xi Zhi Men metro station. Ordinary travel agents without computers on the railway system will usually also handle rail-ticket bookings. The fee per ticket should be no more than ¥20, including delivery to your hotel, although some agencies like to take foreign visitors for a ride in more than one sense. Ticket desks in hotels may charge up to ¥50 per ticket.

At **Beijing Railway Station,** the best place to pick up tickets is the "ticket office for foreigners" inside the soft-berth waiting room on the ground floor of the main hall, in the far-left corner (5:30am–11pm). Tickets for both versions of the **Trans-Siberian,** the Russian K19 via Manchuria (Sat 10:56pm) and the Chinese K3 via Mongolia (Wed 7:40am), must be purchased from the CITS international railway ticket office inside the International Hotel ((C) **010/6512-0507** or 6512-0507; Mon–Fri 8:30am–noon and 1:30–5pm, weekends 9am–noon and 1:30–4pm) 10 minutes' walk north of the station on Jianguo Men Nei Dajie (metro: Dong Dan). Both trains travel to Moscow for ¥2,512 soft sleeper, but only the K3 passes through Mongolia and stops in Ulaan Baatar for ¥845. There is a separate train, the K23, which goes to Ulaan Baatar (Sat 7:40am).

At the **West Station,** the best ticket outlet is not the main ticket hall but a second office inside the main building, on the second floor to the left of the elevators (signposted in English); this is also where you go to purchase tickets for the **Q97** express to **Kowloon/Jiulong** (departs daily at noon; 25 hr.; ¥738 soft sleeper, ¥465 hard). The West Station is also the starting point for **trains to Hanoi,** but you have to buy tickets (departs at 4:08pm Thurs and Sun; 34 hr.; ¥2,204 soft sleeper only) at a China Railway Travel Service, 1st Floor, Building 20 of Tie Dong Compound, Bei Feng Wo Lu

(© 010/5182-6541; 9am–4:30pm). The nearest **airport shuttle** stops at the Aviation Building in Xidan (see above), reachable by bus no. 52 from the station's east side. The taxi rank is on the second floor.

Warning: Larger baggage is X-rayed at the entrances to most Chinese railway and bus stations. Keep film in your hand baggage.

4 MONEY & COSTS

The Value of the Renminbi vs. Other Popular Currencies

¥	US$	Can$	UK£	Euro (€)	Aus$	NZ$
1	$0.15	C$0.17	£0.09	€0.11	A$0.18	NZ$0.23

Frommer's lists exact prices in the local currency. The currency conversions quoted above were correct at press time. However, rates fluctuate, so before departing consult a currency exchange website such as **www. xe.com/ucc** to check up-to-the-minute rates.

CURRENCY

While for most destinations it's usually a good idea to exchange at least some money before you leave home so you can avoid the less-favorable rates at airport currency-exchange desks, mainland China is different. Renminbi (RMB) yuan are not easily obtainable overseas, and rates are worse when they can be found.

There is no legal private money-changing in mainland China. Nationwide outlets offer the same rates on a daily basis. You can exchange currency at the airport when you arrive, at larger branches of the Bank of China, at a bank desk in your hotel, or at major department stores. Shops that offer to exchange money at other than formal Bank of China exchange counters do so illegally, and are known for rate shenanigans and passing fake bills, which are fairly common. *Do not deal with black market money-changers.*

Keep receipts when you exchange money, and you can **reconvert** excess RMB yuan into hard currency when you leave China, although sometimes not more than half the total sum for which you can produce receipts, and sometimes these receipts must be not more than 3 months old.

Hotel exchange desks will change money only for their guests but are open very long hours, 7 days a week. **Banking hours** vary from branch to branch but are limited on Saturday, and banks are closed on Sunday. For more information, see "Banks, Currency Exchanges & ATMs," in chapter 12.

YUAN NOTES There are notes for ¥100, ¥50, ¥20, ¥10, ¥5, ¥2, and ¥1, which also appears as a coin. The word *yuan* is rarely spoken, and sums are referred to as *kuai qian,* "pieces of money," usually shortened to just *kuai. San kuai* is ¥3. Notes carry Arabic numerals as well as numbers in Chinese characters, so there's no fear of confusion. The next unit down, the *jiao* (¥.10), is spoken of as the *mao.* There are notes of a smaller size for ¥.50, ¥.20, and ¥.10, as well as coins for these values. The smallest and almost worthless unit is the *fen* (both written and spoken),

3

Exchange Rates: the Yuan, the Dollar, the Pound & the "Crawling Peg"

In a bid to avert a trade war with the U.S., China allowed a 2% appreciation of the yuan in 2005. It is no longer pegged solely to the U.S. dollar, but rather to a basket of currencies, in an arrangement known as a "crawling peg." The U.S. dollar has recently been trading around ¥6.8, the pound sterling at ¥11, and the euro at ¥9.4. The latest rates can be found at www.xe.com/ucc.

or cent. Unbelievably, when you change money you may be given tiny notes or lightweight coins for ¥.05, ¥.02, and ¥.01, but this is the only time you'll see them except in the bowls of beggars or donation boxes in temples. The most useful note is the ¥10, so keep a good stock. Street stalls, convenience stores, and taxis are often unhappy to receive ¥100 notes.

ATMS

There are many ATMs in China. Bank of China, ICBC, and China Construction Bank machines are reliable and accept foreign cards. Bank of America members can withdraw from China Construction Bank ATMs without a fee. Check the back of your ATM card for the logos of the **Cirrus** (www.mastercard.com), **PLUS** (www.visa.com), and **Aeon** (www.americanexpress.com) systems, and then contact the relevant company for a list of working ATM locations in Beijing, which is fairly well served. The capital also has seven Citibank branches (the most convenient being at Oriental Plaza) and eight branches of HSBC. These banks have ATMs that take just about any card ever invented. Bank of China machines have a limit of ¥2,500 per transaction, while HSBC and Citibank machines have a limit of ¥3,500 to ¥4,000. These banks often allow a second transaction the same day. Call © **95533** within China for locations. *Note:* If you have memorized your PIN as a word, be sure to learn it as a number.

TRAVELER'S CHECKS

Traveler's checks are accepted only at selected branches of the Bank of China, at foreign exchange desks in hotels, and at the exchange desks of some department stores. In bigger bank branches, checks in any hard currency and from any major company are welcome, but at department store exchange desks, currencies of the larger economies are preferred. You can exchange U.S. dollars in cash at most branches of almost any Chinese bank, so even if you plan to bring checks, having a few U.S. dollars in cash (in good condition) for emergencies is a good idea. Checks attract a marginally better exchange rate than cash, but the commission (generally 1%) to cash checks makes the result slightly worse (worse still if you paid the general 1–4% commission when buying them).

CREDIT CARDS

Although Visa and MasterCard signs abound, credit cards are of limited usefulness—in many cases only the Chinese versions of the cards are accepted. You can use foreign cards at most hotels, but they are accepted only at relatively upmarket restaurants outside hotels, and at those souvenir shops where you are paying well over the odds—in fact, if a shop accepts foreign credit cards, you might consider looking elsewhere.

You can also obtain cash advances on your MasterCard, Visa, Diners Club, or

What Things Cost in Beijing	Yuan ¥
Taxi from airport to city center (use meter!)	64.00–96.00
Up to 2km (2¼ miles) by taxi	10.00
Metro ride	2.00
Local telephone call	0.48
Hearty bowl of beef noodles at a basic restaurant	5.00
Regular coffee at Starbucks	15.00
McDonald's set meal for one	23.00
Tasty dinner for two at a simple home-style restaurant	30.00
Dinner for two in restaurants around foreigner-frequented bar areas	100.00
Dinner for two in top hotel restaurants	640.00
Bottle of beer at an ordinary restaurant or store	3.00
Bottle of beer in a foreigner-frequented bar district	30.00
Admission to the Forbidden City	60.00
Admission to the Summer Palace	60.00

Amex cards at major branches of the Bank of China, with a minimum withdrawal of ¥1,200 and 4% commission, plus whatever your card issuer charges you—this expensive way to withdraw cash makes sense only for emergencies. If you do plan to use your card while in China, it's a good idea to call your issuer in advance to let them know that you'll do so.

EMERGENCY CASH

American Express runs an **emergency check-cashing system,** which allows you to use one of your own checks or a counter check (more expensively) to draw money in the currency of your choice from selected banks. Consult American Express for a list of participating banks before leaving home.

You can also have money wired from **Western Union** (☎ **800/820-8668;** www.westernunion.com) to you at many post offices and branches of the Agricultural Bank of China across China, including 50 in Beijing. Western Union charges a $14 service fee for money transfers of up to $1,000 to China from the U.S. You must present a valid ID to pick up the cash at the Western Union office.

5 HEALTH

STAYING HEALTHY

Should you begin to feel unwell in China, your first contact should be your hotel reception. Many major hotels have doctors on staff who will give a first diagnosis and treatment for minor problems, and who will be aware of the best places to send foreigners for further treatment.

Be very cautious about what is prescribed for you. Doctors are poorly paid, and many earn kickbacks from pharmaceutical companies for prescribing expensive medicines. Antibiotics are handed out like candy; indeed, dangerous and powerful drugs of all kinds can be bought over the counter at pharmacies. In general, the best policy is to stay as far away from Chinese healthcare as possible.

See the "Fast Facts," p. 217, for a list of reliable (and very expensive) clinics with up-to-date equipment and English-speaking foreign-trained doctors.

COMMON AILMENTS

TUMMY TROUBLES The greatest risk to the enjoyment of a holiday in China is an **upset stomach** or a more serious illness arising from low hygiene standards. Keep your hands frequently washed and away from your mouth. Only eat freshly cooked hot food, and fruit you can peel yourself—avoid touching the part to be eaten once it's been peeled. The CDC's advice *"boil it, cook it, peel it, or forget it"* is a golden rule while traveling in Beijing. We highly recommend drinking only bottled water, though most stomachs can handle the boiled water that is used to brew tea in Chinese restaurants. *Never* drink from the tap. Use bottled water for brushing your teeth.

RESPIRATORY ILLNESSES The second most common cause of discomfort in Beijing is an **upper respiratory tract infection,** or **common cold,** which is caused by **heavy pollution.** Many standard Western remedies or sources of relief (and occasionally fake versions of these) are available over the counter, but bring a supply of whatever you are used to. If you have sensitive eyes, you may wish to bring an eye bath and solution.

SUN/ELEMENTS/EXTREME WEATHER EXPOSURE Standard precautions should be taken against exposure to **strong summer sun.** Its brightness may be dimmed by Beijing's pollution, but the sun's power to burn is undiminished.

BUGS, BITES & OTHER WILDLIFE CONCERNS Mosquito-borne **malaria** comes in various forms, and you may need to take two different prophylactic drugs, depending upon the time you travel, whether you venture into rural areas, and where you go. You must begin to take these drugs 1 week *before* you enter an affected area and *for 4 weeks after you leave it, sometimes longer.* For a visit to Beijing and other major cities only, prophylaxis is usually unnecessary.

6 SAFETY

China is one of Asia's safest destinations. As anywhere else, though, you should be cautious of theft in places such as crowded markets, popular tourist sites, bus and railway stations, and airports. Take standard precautions against pickpockets (distribute your valuables around your person and wear a money belt inside your clothes). The main danger of walking the ill-lit streets at night is of falling down an uncovered manhole. There's no need to be concerned about dressing down or not flashing valuables—it's automatically assumed that all foreigners, even the scruffiest backpackers, are astonishingly rich, and the average Chinese cannot tell a Cartier from any other shiny watch.

Visitors should be cautious of various **scams,** especially in areas of high tourist traffic, and of Chinese who approach and say in English, "Hello, friend! Welcome to China!" or something similar. Scam artists who want to practice their English and suggest moving to some local haunt may leave you with a bill which has two zeros more than it should, and with trouble should you decline to pay. "Art students" are a pest, approaching you with a story about raising funds for a show overseas, but in fact enticing you into a shop where you will be lied to extravagantly about the authenticity, uniqueness, originality, and true cost of various paintings you will be pressured into buying. The man who is foolish enough to accept an invitation from pretty girls to sing karaoke deserves all the hot water in which he will find himself, up to being forced by large, well-muscled gentlemen to visit an ATM and withdraw large sums to pay for services not actually provided.

If you are a **victim of theft,** make a police report (go to the same addresses given for visa extensions, p. 28; you are most likely to find an English-speaking policeman there). But don't expect sympathy, cooperation, or action. The purpose is to get a theft report to give to your insurers for compensation.

Harassment of **solo female travelers** is very rare, but slightly more likely if the traveler appears to be of Chinese descent.

Traffic is a major hazard for the cautious and incautious alike. In mainland China, driving is on the right, at least occasionally. The rules of the road are routinely ignored for the one overriding rule, "I'm bigger than you so get out of my way," and pedestrians are at the bottom of the pecking order. Cyclists come along the sidewalk, and cars mount it right in front of you and park across your path as if you don't exist. Cyclists go in both directions along the bike lane at the side of the road, which is also invaded by cars looking to mount the sidewalk to park. The edges of the main road also usually have cyclists going in both directions. The vehicle drivers are gladiators, competing for any way to move into space ahead, constantly changing lanes and crossing each other's paths. Pedestrians are like matadors pausing between lanes as cars sweep by to either side of them. Pedestrians often edge out into traffic together, causing cars to swerve away from them, often into the paths of oncoming vehicles, until one lane

of traffic parts and flows to either side, and the process is repeated for the next lane.

In mainland China, in casual encounters, non-Chinese are treated as something between a cute pet and a bull in a china shop, and sometimes with pitying condescension because they are too stupid to speak Chinese. At sights, Chinese tourists from out of town may ask to have their picture taken with you, which will be fun to show friends in their foreigner-free hometowns. ("Look! Here's me with the Elephant Man!") Unless you are of Chinese (or even Asian) descent, your foreignness is constantly thrust in your face with catcalls of *"laowai,"* a not particularly courteous term for foreigner, and a bit like shouting "Chinky" at a Chinese you encounter at home. Mocking, and usually falsetto, calls of "Helloooooo" are not greetings but are similar to saying "Pretty Polly!" to a parrot. Whether acknowledged or not (and all this is best ignored), these calls are usually followed by giggles. But there's little other overt discrimination, other than persistent overcharging wherever it can possibly be arranged. In general, however, once some sort of communication is established, foreigners get better treatment from Chinese, both officials and the general public, than the Chinese give each other. People with darker skin do have a harder time than whites—some cab drivers will outright refuse or ignore black passengers—but those who do not speak Mandarin will probably not notice.

7 SPECIALIZED TRAVEL RESOURCES

In addition to the destination-specific resources listed below, please visit Frommers.com for additional specialized travel resources.

GAY & LESBIAN TRAVELERS

Homosexuality was removed from an official list of mental illnesses only in 2001, but the situation (while still grim) has improved in recent years. In 2009, China had its first ever representative at the World Outgames and held its first gay-pride event in Shanghai. Beijing has a few gay bars of note, and the expatriate magazine *Time Out* recently broke the long-standing taboo against using the words "gay" and "lesbian" with its monthly "G&L" column. **The International Gay & Lesbian Travel Association (IGLTA)** (© 954/630-1637; www.iglta.org) lists three gay-friendly organizations dealing with in-bound visitors to China. See p. 184 for a description of the gradually improving scene.

TRAVELERS WITH DISABILITIES

For a city that recently hosted the Paralympics, Beijing remains shockingly inaccessible for travelers with disabilities. If you do choose to come here, travel with a specialist group (although such tours to Beijing and China are rare) or with someone fully familiar with your particular needs. The Chinese hide people with disabilities, who are rarely seen unless reduced to begging, when they may even be subjected to taunting (although this won't happen to foreigners).

Beijing is difficult for those with limited mobility. The sidewalks are very uneven, and public buildings, sights, and hotels almost always have stairs with no alternative ramps. There are tactile guided paths in certain areas of the city, but they are often blocked by parked cars or simply unfinished. Accessibility in metro stations is a mixed bag (some stations have wheelchair rail staircases, others do not); any escalators usually run up only; and elevators are few and far between. Wheelchair-accessible cabs hit Beijing's roads during the 2008 Paralympic Games, but they are extremely scarce these days.

In theory, some major hotels in the largest cities have wheelchair-accessible rooms, but rarely are they properly executed.

FAMILY TRAVEL

Beijing is not the place to make your first experiment in traveling with small children, although it's a better choice than anywhere else in China. Your biggest challenges will be the lack of services or entertainment aimed at children, the lack of familiar foods outside the bigger hotels and fast-food chains (unless your children have been brought up with Chinese/Asian food), and hygiene.

Some children find Chinese strangers a little too hands-on, and may tire of forced encounters (and photo sessions) with Chinese children met on the street. But the Chinese put their children firmly first, and stand up on buses while the young ones sit.

China is grubby at best, and for children who still have a tendency to put their hands in their mouths, constant vigilance will be necessary, or constant toilet visits will result. Older children should be instructed on frequent hand washing and special caution with food.

Some familiar Western brands of disposable diapers, along with familiar creams and lotions, are available in Beijing.

Beijing **hotels** generally don't charge for children 12 and under who share a room with their parents. Almost all hotels will add a bed, turning a double room into a triple, for an extra ¥80 to ¥100, which you can often bargain down.

Although **babysitting** services are not uncommon in the best hotels (the Sino-foreign joint ventures with familiar names, in particular), in most cases the babysitters will speak very little English or none at all, will have no qualifications in child-care, and will simply be members of the housekeeping staff.

All **restaurants** welcome children, but outside the Western fast-food outlets, some Chinese copies of those, and major hotels, don't expect highchairs or special equipment except very occasionally. The general Chinese eating method of ordering several dishes to share will at least allow your child to order whatever he or she deems acceptable (although it will not taste the same in any two restaurants), while allowing you to try new dishes at each meal.

Although Chinese food in Beijing is different from (and mostly vastly superior to) Chinese food served in the West, it would still be wise to acclimate children as much as possible before leaving by making trips to the local Chinese restaurant. In many cases only chopsticks will be available, so consider taking forks and spoons with you to China. You can now find McDonald's (complete with play areas), KFC, and Pizza Hut in Beijing, and almost all hotels of four stars or up have coffee shops which deliver poor attempts at Western standards.

Keep in mind that although Western cooking is available at many excellent Beijing restaurants, authenticity comes at a price. Cheap bakeries, however, often sell buttery cakes and close relatives of the

muffin containing raisins and chopped walnuts.

In general, **attractions** for children are few, and exploring temples may quickly pall. Success here will depend upon your ability to provide amusement from nothing, and the sensitivity of your antennae to what captures your child's imagination.

Discounts for children on travel tickets and entrance fees are based on height, not age. There are variations, but typically children below 1.1m (3 ft., 7 in.) enter free and travel free if they do not occupy a seat on trains and buses. Children between 1.1m and 1.4m (4 ft., 7 in.) pay half-price. Many ticket offices have marks on the wall at the relevant heights so that staff can quickly determine the appropriate price.

To locate accommodations, restaurants, and attractions that are particularly kid-friendly, refer to the "Kids" icon throughout this guide.

8 SUSTAINABLE TOURISM

Sadly, the environment remains a rather low priority in Beijing. The city suffers from incredible levels of pollution, has a staggering population of 17.4 million (though many people believe this to be much higher given the influx of unregistered migrant workers), and has a growing middle class eager to buy private cars and contribute to the CO_2 emissions. As a visitor here, you will have to make a very conscious effort to travel green.

Taxis are plentiful and cheap, but this is the original city of bicycles! Beijing is a sprawling landscape, but it is flat as a pancake and larger boulevards—Chang'an Jie, for example—have excellent bicycle lanes. During rush hour, biking is often faster than taking a cab. Most hotels rent bicycles at affordable day rates. You'll also find entrepreneurial *xiaomaibu,* or convenience

stalls/newspaper stands, renting bicycles. Several *xiaomaibu* beside popular subway stops (Jian Guo Men, exit A; Liangmaqiao, exit B, among others) rent reliable wheels for ¥2 per hour or ¥20 per day, plus a ¥200 deposit. Be sure to try the bike and test the lock first.

A great way to cut down on your own emissions is to fiddle with the temperature control in your hotel room. High-end chains often have the central-air units turned down to a chilly temperature (19°C/66°F?!) during the hot summer months. Ceiling fans are much greener options, or a more energy-efficient temperature between 21°C and 23°C (70°F–73°F).

Street bins with dual containers for recyclables and trash are starting to show up on Beijing's major streets. The underground recycling trade here is prolific, however, so there's no need to hang on to empty water bottles in an attempt to find the appropriate recycling bin—just leave it on top of a trash can or (I know, it's hard) on the street and a bottle collector will pounce upon it soon enough.

9 SPECIAL-INTEREST TRIPS & ESCORTED GENERAL-INTEREST TOURS

ACADEMIC TRIPS & LANGUAGE CLASSES

Despite what everyone says, Chinese is *not* an impossible language—20% of this planet speaks it, for Pete's sake! You can pick up some survival phrases while also exploring the city at the **China Culture Center,** Room 101, Kent Center, Anjialou, Liangmaqiao Lu 29 (© **10/6432-9341**). The CCC, as it is colloquially known about town, also hosts classes and lectures on Chinese culture, martial arts, history, and traditional Chinese medicine, and does day trips around town.

Local boutique travel service **VariArts** (© **010/8532-4808**) organizes tailormade special-interest trips. They can arrange everything from a stay on an organic farm in Beijing to a special rickshaw tour through the city's *hutong* with an expert from the Beijing Cultural Heritage Protection Center serving as your personal guide.

ESCORTED GENERAL-INTEREST TOURS

Escorted tours are structured group tours with a group leader. The price usually includes everything from airfare to hotels, meals, tours, admission costs, and local transportation. Almost all include a visit to Beijing, but very few tackle Beijing alone, or in any depth. For that you'll need to ask the companies below to organize an independent tour for you (but you'd be better off just to jump on a plane and be completely at liberty once you arrive).

Again, due to the distorted nature of the Chinese tourism industry, escorted tours do not usually represent savings, but rather a significant increase in costs over what you can arrange for yourself. Foreign tour companies are for now required to work with state-owned ground handlers, although some book as much as they can directly or work discreetly with private operators they trust. But even as markets become more open, most arrangements will continue to be made with the official state operators, if only for convenience. Read the brochures skeptically (one man's "scenic splendor" is another's "heavily polluted"), and carefully read the advice in this section.

As with package tours, the arrangements within China itself are managed by a handful of local companies, whose cupidity often induces them to lead both you and your tour company astray. Various costs, which should be in the tour fee, can appear as extras; itineraries are altered to suit the pocket of the local operator; and there are all sorts of shenanigans to separate the hapless tourist from extra cash at every turn, usually at whatever point the tour staff appear to be most helpful. (The driver has bottles of water for sale on the bus each day? You're paying three times the shop price.)

Evaluating Tours

When choosing a tour company for China, you must, of course, consider cost, what's included, the itinerary, the likely age and interests of other tour group members, physical ability required, and the payment and cancellation policies, as you would for any other destination. But you should also investigate:

SHOPPING STOPS These are the bane of any tour in China, designed to line the pockets of tour guides, drivers, and sometimes the ground-handling company itself. A stop at the Great Wall may be limited to only an hour so as to allow an hour at a cloisonné factory. The better foreign tour operators design their own itineraries and have instituted strict contractual controls to keep these stops to a minimum, but they are often unable to do away with them altogether, and tour guides will introduce extra stops whenever they think they can get away with it. Other companies, particularly those companies that do not specialize in China, just take the package from the Chinese ground handler, put it together with flights, and pass it on uncritically. At shopping stops, you should never ask or accept your tour guide's advice on what is the "right price." You are shopping in the wrong place to start with, where prices will often be 10 to 15 times higher than they should be. Your driver gets a tip, and your guide gets 40% of sales. The "discount" card you are given marks you for yet higher initial prices and tells the seller to which guide commission is owed. So ask your tour company how many of these stops are included, and simply sit out those you cannot avoid.

TIPPING   There is *no* tipping in mainland China. If your tour company advises you to bring payments for guides and drivers, costs that should be included in your total tour cost are being passed on to you through the back door. Ask what the company's tipping policy is and add that sum to the tour price to make true comparisons. Some tour guides are making as much as *400 times* what an ordinary factory worker or shop assistant makes, mostly through kickbacks from sights, restaurants, and shops, all at your expense, and from misguided tipping. Some tour operators say that if they cut out the shopping stops, then they have to find other ways to cover the tour guides' income or there'll be no tour guide. Shopping-free trips are nearly always accompanied by a higher price or a higher tip recommendation (which is the same thing). The guides are doing so well that now, in many cases, rather than receive a salary from the ground-handling company, they have to *pay* for the privilege of fleecing you. The best tour companies know how China works, make what arrangements they find unavoidable, and leave you out of it. A middle path is to put a small sum from each tour member into a central kitty and disburse tips as needed, but only for truly exceptional service and at a proper local scale which short-time visitors from developed nations are incapable of assessing. Foreign tour leaders can be tipped according to the customs of their country of origin, and most companies issue guidelines for this.

GUIDES   Mainland guides rarely know what they are talking about, although they won't miss a beat while answering your questions. What they will have on the tip of their tongue is an impressive array of unverifiable statistics, amusing little stories of dubious authenticity, and a detailed knowledge of the official history of a place which may bear only the faintest resemblance to the truth. Their main concerns are to tell foreigners what they want to hear, and to impress them with the greatness of China. So you may be told that the Great Wall can be seen from outer space (silly), that China has 5,000 years of culture (what does this actually mean?), and that one million people worked on building the Forbidden City (it was only 100,000 on last year's trip). Guides are shortchanged by China's shoddy and politically distorted education system, and also tend to put the potential profit from the relationship first.

Ask your tour company if it will be sending a guide and/or tour manager from home to accompany the trip and to supplement local guides. This is worth paying more for, as this person's presence ensures a smoother trip and more authoritative information.

TOUR COMPANIES

Between them, the following tour companies (a tiny selection of what's available) serve just about all budgets and interests. The companies are from Australia, Canada, China, the United Kingdom, and the United States, but many have representatives around the globe. Plus you can often just buy the ground portion of the trip and fly in from wherever you like.

- **Abercrombie and Kent** (U.S.): Top-of-the-range small group tours, with the very best accommodations and transport. ✆ **800/554-7016;** fax 630/954-3324; www.abercrombiekent.com. ✆ 0845/618-2200; www.abercrombie kent.co.uk. ✆ 1300/851-800; www. abercrombiekent.com.au (Australia). ✆ 0800/441-638 (New Zealand).

- **Academic Travel Abroad** (U.S.): Tours in China for the Smithsonian (educational, cultural) and National Geographic Expeditions (natural history, soft adventure). ✆ **877/338-8687;** fax 202/633-6088; www.smithsonianjourneys. org.; ✆ 888/966-8687; www.national geographicexpeditions.com.

- **Adventure Center** (U.S.): Small group tours aimed at those who are usually independent travelers; one tour includes the Eastern Qing Tombs and walking on several stretches of the Great Wall. ✆ **800/228-8747** or 800/227-8747; www.adventurecenter.com.

- **China Focus** (U.S.): Larger groups at budget prices, but with additional costs to cover extras. ✆ **800/868-7244** or 415/788-8660; fax 415/788-8665; www.chinafocustravel.com.

- **Exploritas** (U.S.): Educational tours for seniors. ✆ **800/454-5768** or 877/426-8056; www.exploritas.org.

- **Gecko's Adventures** (Australia): Down-to-earth budget tours for small group tours of 20- to 40-year-olds, using smaller guesthouses, local restaurants, and public transport. ✆ **03/8601-**

4444; fax 03/8601-4422; www.geckos adventures.com.

- **Intrepid Travel** (Australia): Slightly more adventurous tours with small groups, following itineraries that are a deft mix of popular destinations and the less-visited. One trip includes 4 days of trekking on the Great Wall. ✆ **1300/364-512** (in Australia), 3/9473-2626 (outside Australia); fax 03/9419-4426; www.intrepidtravel.com.

- **Laurus Travel** (Canada): Small group tours from a Vancouver-based China-only specialist, run by a former CITS guide. ✆ **877/507-1177** or 604/438-7718; fax 694/438-7715; www.laurus travel.com.

- **Monkey Business** (China): Beijing-based outfit specializing in organizing onward travel on the Trans-Siberian express. ✆ **010/6591-6519;** fax 010/6591-6517; www.monkeyshrine.com.

- **Pacific Delight** (U.S.): A large variety of mainstream trips for a wide range of group sizes, with endless permutations for different time scales and budgets. Watch for extra costs. ✆ **800/221-7179;** www.pacificdelighttours.com.

- **Peregrine Adventures** (Australia): Sister company of Gecko's Adventures (see above), Peregrine offers small group trips with good quality centrally located accommodations; trips include visits to private houses and smaller restaurants frequented by local people and, possibly, walks and bike rides. ✆ **03/8601-4444;** fax 03/8601-4422; www.peregrine adventures.com. ✆ 800/227-8747 (U.S.).

- **R. Crusoe & Son** (U.S.): Small group tours include extras such as a visit to areas of the Forbidden City usually closed to the public. ✆ **800/585-8555;** fax 312/980-8100; www.rcrusoe.com.

- **Ritz Tours** (U.S.): Groups range in size from 10 to 40 people, and ages range widely; parents often bring children. Ritz is the foremost U.S. tour operator to China in terms of volume. ✆ **800/ 900-2446;** www.ritztours.com.

- **Steppes East** (U.K.): Tours organized to very high standards. Its itineraries are merely suggestions that can be adapted to your specifications. ✆ **01285/ 880980;** fax 01285/885888; www. steppeseast.co.uk.
- **VariArts** (China): Beijing-based boutique tour company offering tailor-made tours. All tours incorporate sustainable travel practices. ✆ **010/ 8532-4808;** fax 010/8532-4809; www. variarts.com.

- **Wild China** (China): Founder Mei Zhang started this company for many reasons, one of them being that she wanted to explore China's lesser known paths and still have a good cup of coffee in the morning! Beijing-based Wild China offers highly specialized tours that focus on sustainable travel. ✆ **010/ 6465-6602;** fax 010/6465-6602; www. wildchina.com.

For more information on escorted general-interest tours, including questions to ask before booking your trip, see www.frommers. com/planning.

10 STAYING CONNECTED

INTERNET PHONE

Voice over Internet Protocol, or VoIP, is a popular and affordable way to stay connected while overseas. **Skype** (www.skype. com) is a well-known application that allows fellow Skype users to talk and/or videoconference for free, and also connects to landlines for affordable rates. Whatever VoIP you chose, I recommend downloading the software onto your computer in advance; that way you can familiarize yourself with it before you travel abroad.

TELEPHONES

To call China:

1. Dial the international access code: 011 in the U.S. and Canada, 00 in the U.K., Ireland, and New Zealand, or 0011 from Australia.
2. Dial the country code: 86 for China.
3. Dial the city code, omitting the leading zero, and then dial the number. To reach Beijing from the U.S., you would dial 011-86-10-plus the 8-digit number.

To call within China: For calls within the same city, omit the city code, which always begins with a zero when used (010 for Beijing, 020 for Guangzhou, for example).

All hotel phones have direct dialing, and most have international dialing. Hotels are only allowed to add a service charge of up to 15% to the cost of the call, and even long-distance rates within China are very low. To use a public telephone you'll need an IC (integrated circuit) card *(aicei ka),* available from post offices, convenience stores, and street stalls, available in values beginning at ¥20 (wherever you can make out the letters *IC* among the Chinese characters). A brief local call is typically ¥.30 to ¥.50. Phones show you the value remaining on the card when you insert it, and count down as you talk.

To make international calls: First dial 00 and then dial the country code (U.S. or Canada 1, U.K. 44, Ireland 353, Australia 61, New Zealand 64). Next dial the area or city code, omitting any leading zero, and then dial the number. For example, if you want to call the British Embassy in Washington, D.C., you would dial 00-1-202-588-7800. Forget bringing access numbers for your local phone company—you can call internationally for a fraction of the cost by using an IP (Internet Protocol) card *(aipi ka),* available wherever you see the letters *IP.* You should bargain to pay less than the face value of the card—usually ¥40 for a ¥100 card from street vendors. Instructions for use are on the back, but you simply dial the access number given, choose English from the menu, and follow the instructions to dial in the number behind a scratch-off panel. Depending on where you call, ¥50 can give you an hour of talking. If using a public phone, you'll need an IC card (see above) to make the call. In emergencies, dial 108 to negotiate a collect call, but again, you'll need help from a Mandarin speaker.

For directory assistance dial 114. No English is spoken, and only local numbers are available. If you want numbers for other cities, dial the city code followed by 114—a long-distance call. You can text the name of the establishment you are looking for (in English) to a service called "Guanxi" at 010/669-588-2929, and for a small fee, the address will return in English. For an additional ¥1 you can get the address in Chinese, ready to show to your taxi driver.

For operator assistance: Just ask for help at your hotel.

Toll-free numbers: Numbers beginning with 800 within China are toll-free, but calling a 1-800 number in the States from China is a full-tariff international call, as is calling one in Hong Kong from mainland China, or vice versa.

CELLPHONES

All Europeans, most Australians, and many North Americans use GSM (Global System for Mobiles). But while everyone else can take a regular GSM phone to China, North Americans, who operate on a different frequency, need a more expensive tri-band model.

International roaming charges can be horrendously expensive. Buying a prepaid chip in China with a new number is far cheaper. You may need to call up your

cellular operator to "unlock" your phone in order to use it with a local provider.

For Beijing, **buying a phone** is the best option. Last year's now unfashionable model can be bought, with a chip (quanqiutong) and ¥100 of prepaid airtime, for about ¥800; you pay less if a Chinese model is chosen. Europeans taking their GSM phones, and North Americans with tri-band phones, can buy chips for about ¥100. Recharge cards (chongzhi ka) are available at post offices, newspaper stands, and mobile-phone shops. Calling rates are low, although those receiving calls pay part of the cost.

INTERNET & E-MAIL

Despite highly publicized clampdowns on cybercafes, monitoring of traffic, and blocking of websites, China remains one of the easiest countries in the world in which to get online.

Without Your Own Computer

In central Beijing, government clampdowns have significantly reduced the number of Internet cafes (wangba). Those still in operation tend to charge from ¥4 to ¥20 per hour. Keep your eyes open for the wangba characters; see "Internet bar," chapter 13.

Many media websites, and those with financial information or any data whatsoever on China which disagrees with the Party line, are blocked from mainland China, as are even some search engines and social networking sites.

With Your Own Computer

Many cafes and hotels in Beijing offer wireless connectivity in public areas. Most hotels also offer free in-room Wi-Fi connections.

Mainland China uses the standard U.S.-style RJ11 telephone jack also used as the port for laptops worldwide. Cables with RJ11 jacks at both ends can be picked up for around ¥10 in Beijing department stores and electrical shops. Standard electrical voltage across China is 220v, 50Hz, which most laptops can handle, but North American users in particular should check. For power socket information see "Fast Facts," p. 216.

Those with onboard Ethernet can take advantage of broadband services, which are sometimes free in major hotels. Ethernet cables are often provided, but it's best to bring your own.

Suggested Itineraries

by Jen Lin-Liu

Seeing Beijing in a day? You must be kidding. It is technically possible to see the big-name attractions—the **Forbidden City, Temple of Heaven, Summer Palace,** and **Great Wall**—in as little as 3 days, but you'll need at least a week to get any sort of feel for the city. But if a day is all you have, we want to help you make the most of it by providing a ready-made itinerary that allows you to have a satisfying trip.

We've left the Great Wall out of the itineraries below, as it requires a full day in itself, or better yet, an overnight stay to allow for spectacular late-afternoon and early-morning photography (see chapter 11 for details). The traffic in Beijing means that the only sensible way to tour the city is to tackle the sights in groups. We take you to the central sights on the first day, to the north of town on the following day, and to the less-visited south of town on the third day.

1 BEIJING LAYOUT

MAIN STREETS

The main west-to-east artery of interest to visitors runs across the top of Tian'an Men Square, past the Tian'an Men (Gate of Heavenly Peace) itself. It changes names several times, but is most importantly Xi Chang'an Jie to the west of the square, Dong Chang'an Jie to the east, then Jianguo Men Nei Dajie until it crosses the Second Ring Road, when it becomes Jianguo Men Wai Dajie. Compass points such as *xi* (west) and *dong* (east) turn up very frequently in street names, as do words such as *men* (gate), *nei* (inside), and *wai* (outside). Metro Line 1 runs under this route, passing several major hotels and shopping areas. The Xi Dan Bei Dajie and Wangfujing Dajie shopping streets run north from this route. The Second Ring Road runs around the combined outer perimeter of the old city walls they replaced, still showing the bulge of the wider Chinese City to the south and, depending on the time of day, usually provides a quicker route around the city center than going though it. Farther out and quicker still, the Third Ring Road, which links with the airport expressway and routes to the Summer Palace, is the site of several major long-distance bus stations, numerous upmarket joint-venture hotels, and important restaurants. Beware the taxi driver who suggests using the Fourth or Fifth ring roads. Speeds on these routes are higher, but the kilometer count for getting round the city will also be significantly greater, and so will the cost.

FINDING AN ADDRESS

Maps of Beijing are rarely accurate—the cartographers don't seem to feel it necessary to do more than sketch the main roads—and the smashing of new routes across and around the city is so rapid they can't keep up. Although some claim to issue half a dozen editions a year, the presence of *zui xin* or "newest" on the map cover is only an indication that the characters *zui xin* have been put on the cover. Bilingual maps, or maps with Romanized Chinese, tend to be less accurate to start with, and are printed less often. Regardless of this, **always buy a map,** available from vendors at all arrival points and at all bookstores, for around ¥5. The small pages of this book cannot give you a detailed picture of any area, but the characters on the maps, the map keys, and in the text of chapters 5 and 6 can be used to help you find your way around the Chinese map. The staff at your hotel can mark where you are and where you want to go, and you can compare the street-name characters with those on the road signs so you can keep track of your route. There's no question of really getting lost, and you can always flag down a cab and show the driver the characters for where you want to go. Street numbers are given in this book: Odd numbers indicate the north or west side of the street, while an even-numbered residence will be on the south or east side, but otherwise no one uses them. Navigation is by street name and landmark.

NEIGHBORHOODS IN BRIEF

Citywide architectural uniformity makes the boundaries of Beijing's official districts rather arbitrary, so we've avoided them in favor of maps showing in more detail the areas of most interest to visitors for their clusters of accommodations, restaurants, and attractions. Beyond the districts listed below, the metropolitan area stretches far into the countryside, adding perhaps another 5 million people to the urban population of around 12 million.

DONG CHENG Dong Cheng (East City) occupies the eastern half of the city center, spreading north and east from the southwest corner of Tian'an Men Square until it reaches the Second Ring Road, and occasionally spills over it. It includes the square itself, the Forbidden City, major temples such as the Yonghe Gong (Lama Temple) and Confucius Temple, and the major shopping streets of Wangfujing and Dong Dan. It's essentially the eastern half of the Qing-era Tartar City, north of the wall separating it from the Chinese City, of which the twin towers of the Qian Men (Front Gate) are the most significant remaining fragments.

XI CHENG The western half of the old Tartar City, Xi Cheng spreads farther west beyond the line of the original city wall at the Second Ring Road. It is home to Zhong Nan Hai, the off-limits central government compound otherwise known as the new Forbidden City, Bei Hai Gongyuan, and the Bai Ta Si (White Dagoba Temple). The Shicha Hai (Back Lakes) and Di'an Men area within Xi Cheng, with its string of lakes and relatively well-preserved *hutong,* is where the last fading ghosts of (pre-1949) Old Beijing reside. It's popular among writers, musicians, foreigners teaching in Beijing, and other younger expatriates who haunt a collection of trendy bars and cafes at the waters' edge. Several minor sights here provide the excuse for a day's wandering.

CHAOYANG Part urban, part suburban, Chaoyang sprawls in a huge arc around the northeast and eastern sides of the city, housing the three main diplomatic compounds, the Sanlitun and Chaoyang drinking districts, and the so-called CBD (Central Business District) around the China World Trade Center. This is the richest district in Beijing, the result, according to some, of the district's good feng shui.

THE SOUTH If Chaoyang has Beijing's best feng shui, the old Chinese City south of the Qian Men, made up of Chongwen (east) and Xuanwu (west), both enclosed by the suburban sprawl of Fengtai to the south and southwest, has the worst. Squalid since its construction in the Ming dynasty, this is where you'll find the city's grittiest *hutong* and some of its best bargains on fake antiques, as well as Ming architectural jewels such as the Temple of Heaven (Tian Tan).

HAIDIAN & YAYUN CUN   Sprawling to the northwest, Haidian is the university and high-tech district, referred to hopefully in local media as "China's Silicon Valley" and home to the Summer Palace. Directly north of town is Yayun Cun (Asia Games Village), home to Beijing's best new Chinese restaurants, and site of many Olympic venues.

2 THE BEST OF BEIJING IN 1 DAY

Fortunately for the harried tourist, when the Mongol founders laid down the Beijing (then Khanbalik) city grid, it was on a north-south axis, making navigation straightforward and grouping the key landmarks in a central location. The main downside, for which Kublai Khan cannot be blamed, is that there are few dining options en route, so we recommend that you eat a hearty breakfast at your hotel. ***Start:*** *Tian Tan Dongmen (Temples of Heaven East Gate) metro.*

❶ Temple of Heaven (Tian Tan Gongyuan) ★★

Just after dawn you'll find regular park goers practicing *taijiquan,* kung fu, group dancing, or giant calligraphy on this huge park's greenery and paved walkways. As you walk through the grounds, in addition to the music providing background tunes for the dancers, you'll probably hear birds and crickets chirping happily through their cages as their owners (mostly retired elderly men) take them out for walks. Don't miss **Qinian Dian (Hall of Prayer for Good Harvests).** Its history dates back to 1420, but the current structure is a replica built in 1889 when the original burned to the ground. The circular wooden hall, with its triple-layered cylindrical blue-tiled roof, is perhaps the most recognizable emblem of Chinese imperial architecture outside of the Forbidden City. The main hall is 38m (125 ft.) high and 30m (98 ft.) in diameter and—here's the kicker—it was constructed without a single nail. See p. 126.

Ride the metro to:

❷ Tian'an Men Square (Tian'an Men Guangchang) ★

Set on the site of the former Imperial Way, the broad square is also a recent creation, dating from the 1950s when Mao, encouraged by his Soviet advisors, ordered the clearing away of the old government ministries. There were plans to "press down" the "feudal" Forbidden City by surrounding it with high-rise buildings and smokestacks, but the fledgling republic lacked the resources to carry out the plan.

To your left looms the **Great Hall of the People,** to your right is the **National Museum**—neither worth a visit if you're pressed for time. Impressive in its vastness, there's little to do in the Square unless you plan to cut short your tour by unfurling a protest banner. See p. 105.

Walk to the southern end of the Square to:

❸ Chairman Mao's Mausoleum (Mao Zhuxi Jinian Guan) ★

Built on the site of Da Qing Men (Great Qing Gate), this hastily constructed building is unimpressive in itself, but what makes this site compelling is the genuine reverence of local visitors for The Great

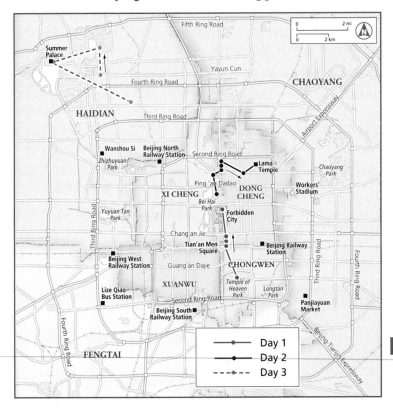

Helmsman. It makes for a memorable 15 minutes of people-watching. ***Note:*** The Mausoleum is closed Sundays. See p. 111.

Walk north, taking the underpass to:

❹ Tian'an Men (Gate of Heavenly Peace)

Climb to the dais above Mao's portrait for a view south along the former Imperial Way. Beyond **Qian Men (Front Gate)** you may spy the newly reconstructed **Yongding Men.** It's not in the same spot as the original, but it is one of the first steps in a plan to revamp the north-south axis. A boulevard connecting to Olympic Park in the north of town is underway, with input from Albert Speer, Jr., who also happens to be the son of Hitler's personal architect.

A less traditional structure is apparent to your right: The National Centre for Performing Arts resembles a UFO that made an emergency landing in a pond. See p. 185. Continue north, through the gate to:

❺ Forbidden City (Gu Gong) ★★★

The majority of visitors to Beijing's main attraction rent their audio tour and rush through the central route without ducking into the eastern and western axes. This is a mistake. The most charming and intriguing parts of the Forbidden City are located away from the main tourist route. Allow at least 3 hours, and do not miss newly opened sights, particularly the **Wuying Dian** (west side) and **Juanqin Zhai** (northeast side). See p. 121.

SUGGESTED ITINERARIES

4

THE BEST OF BEIJING IN 1 DAY

> **TAKE A BREAK**
> After battling the crowds at all the sites, retreat to **Ch'ien Men 23** (𝒞 010/6522-4848), a set of restaurants located in historic buildings that once housed the American embassy. You can take your pick from Chinese, French, or Spanish cuisine at Zen 1903, Maison Boulud, or Agua (see chapter 6 for more details). From the Forbidden City, walk south along the eastern edge of Tian'an Men Square. When you reach the south

end of the square, turn left, cross the street, and Ch'ien Men 23 will be on your left.

If you wish to also get an aerial view of the Forbidden City, proceed to the rooftop bar of The Emperor hotel (p. 62). From the eastern gate (Donghua Men) of the Forbidden City, turn left on Beichizhi Dajie, then right on Qihelou Jie. The low-rise hotel will be on your left.

3 THE BEST OF BEIJING IN 2 DAYS

If you've survived "The Best of Beijing in 1 Day," you'll find that your second full-day tour takes in a different side of Beijing. Today we'll take you to the Lake district, our favorite city retreat, and a couple of impressive temples for good measure. *Start: Bei Hai Gongyuan.*

❶ Bei Hai Gongyuan (Bei Hai Park) ★

After all the grandeur you've just sampled, you'll find that this park, set around a lake carved out in the 12th century, provides a welcome change. On the south side of the park, **Qiong Dao,** an islet topped by a white *dagoba* built to commemorate the visit of the first Dalai Lama to the capital in 1651, is worth a quick look.

The north side of the park is more interesting, so catch a boat from the islet to the opposite side of the lake. Don't miss **Daci Zhenru Bao Dian,** one of the most impressive structures in Beijing. See p. 136.

Emerging from the north of the park, turn right and cross at the first set of lights to:

❷ Qian Hai Hou Hai (The Lake District) ★★★

Qian Hai and Hou Hai's banks, now overflowing with alfresco bars, cafes, and the odd curio shop, were once exclusive areas for nobles and merchants. Prior to 1911, only people with connections to the imperial family were permitted to maintain houses and conduct business here. The

present-day commercial fare on the main banks can be wearying, but the area's back alleys are still ripe for exploration. Walk northeast along Qian Hai Nanyan until you come to Yinding Qiao (Silver Ingot Bridge), the bridge that marks the boundary between Qian Hai and Hou Hai. From here you can watch the boats drifting along below, several of which come complete with zither players strumming out classics such as "Moon River" for foreign passengers. If you want your own Sino-Western serenade, you can rent boats with musicians from the small dock near the Lotus Lane entrance.

Cross Yinding Qiao, walk straight for 2 minutes, turn right on:

❸ Tobacco Alley (Yandai Xiejie)

This little street is packed with cafes and small stores selling various trinkets, clothing from minority regions, and reproductions of Cultural Revolution memorabilia. Street vendors set up shop on the already narrow pathway and often sell fresh lollipops blown into animal shapes, or candied fruit kebabs.

Follow the alley until it ends at the main road. Walk ½ block directly north (left) to:

④ Drum Tower (Gulou)

The Drum and Bell towers lie on the northern part of the north-south axis that runs the length of central Beijing, through the center of the Forbidden City. You need to climb up only one tower's steep set of stairs, and your best bet is the Drum Tower. The upper chamber has replicas of traditional drums, which are showcased in performances several times per hour. Outside, a clear day provides a fantastic view of Hou Hai Lake to the west. See p. 158.

> **TAKE A BREAK**
> Just across the street from the Drum Tower, on the right, is Excuse Café (68 Zhonglou Wan Hutong; ℗ 010/6401-9867; daily 7:30am–10pm), serving terrific coffee and sandwiches.

Take a ¥10 cab east to:

⑤ Yonghe Gong (Lama Temple) ★★★

Though often referred to as the Lama Temple, Yonghe Gong actually translates as "The Palace of Peace and Harmony." But being one of Beijing's top tourist attractions, this temple is rarely peaceful. Try to ignore the crowds and roam around the many courtyards at a leisurely pace, exploring the temple's impressive offerings, such as a 6m (20-ft.) bronze statue of Tsongkapa (1357–1419), founder of the now dominant school of Tibetan Buddhism, housed in **Falun Dian (Hall of the Wheel of Law).** You'll find the temple's most prized possession in the last of the

major halls, **Wanfu Ge (Tower of Ten Thousand Happiness).** There, standing 18m (59 ft.) tall, is the ominous Tibetan-style statue of Maitreya (the future Buddha), which was carved from a single piece of white sandalwood and was transported all the way from Tibet as a gift to Qianlong from the seventh Dalai Lama. See p. 134.

Exit Yonghe Gong, cross the street, and walk south for less than half a block. Turn right onto the street marked by a traditional Chinese arch. Walk for about 5 minutes to:

⑥ Confucius Temple (Kong Miao) ★

On a tree-shaded street lies China's second-largest Confucius Temple. Two stelae at the front instruct you in six different languages to park your horse. The Temple is the busiest before national university entrance examinations, when students and parents descend in droves to seek out the Great Sage's assistance. Students make a beeline for the main hall, **Dacheng Dian.** They throw their incense on the shrine rather than burn it because of fire regulations. See p. 132.

> **TAKE A BREAK**
> Turn right when you exit Confucius Temple, and make a right down the next alley (Jianchang Hutong). At the end of the alley, make a right on Wudaoying Hutong and walk 183m (600 ft.) to **Vineyard Café** (℗ 010/6402-7961), on your left, which has excellent all-day dining, from healthy breakfasts and coffee to a good selection of Western pastas and pizzas, along with wines by the glass.

4 THE BEST OF BEIJING IN 3 DAYS

It's time to get away from the city center. For the third full-day tour, we take you to the far-northwest corner of Beijing. The district is home to China's top two universities, the self-styled Harvard and M.I.T. of China, as well as the Beijing Foreign Language and Culture University (BLCU), where you can find foreign students from all over the world learning Chinese. Nestled among all the student bars and Wi-Fi cafes are a couple of imperial playgrounds. *Start: Take a cab to the east gate of Peking University (Beida Dong Men).*

❶ Peking University (Beijing Daxue or "Beida")

This is China's most famous university and its campus has seen plenty of action in its hundred-odd years. Beida, as the university is commonly known, was traditionally home to student activists, including some of the leaders of the infamous Tian'an Men demonstrations of 1989 (ironically, the campus has a road called Minzhu Lu, Democracy Road). You can ponder the campus's historical significance from the rocky seats surrounding Weiming Lake. Better yet, if you're visiting in winter, rent some skates and take a spin around the frozen lake.

Exit from the east gate and walk 800m (½ mile) north to the major T-intersection marked by the west gate of Tsinghua University (gaggles of Chinese tourists will be taking their photos here). Turn left and walk 400m (¼ mile) to:

❷ The Old Summer Palace (Yuan Ming Yuan) ★★

If pushed for time, just visit the northeast side of the park, which is home to the remnants of the **Xi Yang Lou (Western Mansions).** These buildings were razed by British and French forces in 1860, a year before Cixi rose to Empress Dowager status. They featured spectacular fountains and housed magnificent European art, but it could have been worse—the Anglo-French forces considered destroying the Forbidden City. See p. 138.

Head to the park's east gate, beside the parking lot, to find:

> ☕ **TAKE A BREAK**
> The **Aman** resort ★★★ (☎ **010/5987-9999**), on the eastern side street of the Summer Palace, serves a delectable afternoon tea, served next to a koi pond in a historic series of courtyard buildings.

Give your feet a rest and take a cab to:

❸ Summer Palace (Yi He Yuan) ★★★

Later in her rule, Cixi spent a considerable amount of time in this watery imperial playground, even setting up her own photographic studio. Modeled on Hangzhou's West Lake, the complex was ransacked by foreign troops in 1860 and 1900, and restored under Cixi's orders, on the first occasion with funds earmarked for the navy. The lake is the gem of the palace: Escape the crowds for an hour or so by hiring a boat, or in winter a pair of skates. On land, allow 3 hours for a cursory look around.

Proceed to the south exit to join a rusty "imperial yacht." See p. 127.

Take a cab to the Wudaokou metro stop.

> ☕ **TAKE A BREAK**
> You are now in Wudaokou, a coffee shop/bar/bookstore area that has sprung up around the metro stop of the same name. It is a veritable hub of intellectual activity where all the foreign students come to hang out, study, and party. **Sculpting in Time,** Building 12, Huaqing Jiayuan, Chengfu Lu (south of the metro on the street that runs parallel to the tracks; ☎ **010/8286-7026**) is a cafe in the heart of this youthful area. It serves some excellent coffee with free Wi-Fi to boot.

Take the metro one stop to Da Zhong Si and explore:

❹ Da Zhong Si

This Qing temple now houses the Ancient Bell Museum (Gu Zhong Bowuguan). It was once known as Juesheng Si (Awakened Life Temple), but clearly there wasn't enough awakening going on, so a 47-ton bell was transported here on ice sleds in 1743. The third hall on the right houses clangers garnered from around Beijing. Some were donated by eunuchs wishing the relevant emperor long life, with hundreds of donors' names scrawled on their sides. But, frustratingly, none of this is fleshed out in the museum. The main attraction is in the rear hall—a big bell carved inside and out with 230,000 Chinese and Sanskrit characters. It tolls once a year, on New Year's Eve. Visitors rub the handles of Emperor Qianlong's old washbasin, and climb up narrow steps to make a wish while throwing coins through a hole in the top of the bell.

Navigate the confusion of the metro system by changing trains twice to get to the Wangfujing stop. Get out here to explore:

❺ Wangfujing Dajie

In contrast to today's first destination, this pedestrian mall is "new China," the side the regime is desperate for you to see. Those with weary legs may wish to duck into **Oriental Plaza** for coffee and air-conditioned comfort, while the energetic can sample part of our Walking Tour of Wangfujing (p. 158).

Be sure to reach your final destination before sunset.

TAKE A BREAK
With nothing but air between you and the Forbidden City, the rooftop bar **Palace View Bar (Guan Jing Jiuba)** ★★ offers a magical spot to view Beijing's pollution-enhanced sunset. Open June through October. In the Beijing Grand Hotel (© 010/6513-7788, ext. 458).

5

Where to Stay

by Jen Lin-Liu

Fortunately for you, Beijing has emerged from its Communist era of drab government-owned hotels and motels characterized by horrendous service, dim lighting, and rock-hard beds, which were often accompanied by pillows stuffed with beans. In the old days, hotel attendants let you in and out of your room, keeping control over your keys. Toilets were smelly. The breakfast buffet consisted of leftovers from last night's stir-fries and fake Wonder bread.

Nowadays, booking a room in the capital has never been easier, and a glut of new privately owned guesthouses and hotels—spurred by development for the 2008 Olympics—means that fun options exist for every budget. In fact, with dozens of five-star hotels having opened in the capital in the last decade, Beijing has become one of the best values in the world for a luxury hotel stay: in the off season, you may be able to pay as low as ¥800 for a sparkling, new room with all the modern amenities (flatscreen TV with satellite service, iPod dock, DVD player) at branded hotels like the Hilton. Creative types will be drawn to the plentiful boutique hotels hidden down the alleys of new and old Beijing decorated with antique Chinese furniture and contemporary art.

As with hotels and guesthouses in most cities, the rack rate for Beijing accommodations is set high—sometimes double or triple what guests usually end up paying. The key is to bargain directly with the hotel—in Mandarin, preferably. (If you don't speak Mandarin, perhaps you can find a friend to do the bargaining for you.) Make sure to ask what the rate includes—if you're willing to forgo breakfast and airport transfer, you can often save a few hundred yuan. Or you may want to bargain by asking for a room upgrade—many hotels in Beijing offer executive rooms, which come with lounge privileges that provide complimentary Wi-Fi, breakfast, and drinks. Most hotels are also willing to offer better rates for longer stays. When booking your room, make sure to specify if you want a double bed; otherwise, you may wind up with two very unsexy twin beds. Many hotels these days have non-smoking floors or rooms as well.

When arriving at the hotel, check out the room to make sure you've gotten what you've bargained for. These days, most hotels take credit cards, though the infrequent cash-only establishment may ask you for their full fee plus a deposit upfront—the best way to negotiate is to pay for the first night, plus deposit, and then pay daily for each additional night's stay.

While service has become more chipper in Beijing, it still lags behind that of other international cities. With the competition fierce between hotels to retain quality staff, you may find that hotel employees lack proper communication skills (like English fluency) to get simple tasks completed. The proper response is patience and to remember that China is still a developing country. Also remember that tipping is never expected, but is appreciated for staff who may make less than the price of one night's stay in most luxury hotels.

On the other hand, you may be offered services that you simply don't want or need—prostitutes disguised to varying degrees pop up in hotel bars or massage rooms, and may make phone calls to your room in the evening hours asking if you'd like a "massage." If you do receive such a call, make a complaint to the front desk and if need be, unplug your phone. Prostitutes usually work in large, lower-end hotels; the hotels we've chosen in this guide are generally safe from unsavory elements, but even some quality establishments turn a blind eye to the practice, so you should beware.

All establishments still need to report your presence to the local police station (a procedure from the Communist era that still exists), so be sure to have your passport with you when you check in. Many places will refuse to check you in unless you have proper identification, though they may accept a copy or fax of your passport. As for what to do with your passport during your stay, my husband and I are divided on this: He insists on placing his in the safe, while I hide mine in my luggage. (Nowadays, there's no reason to carry your passport with you at all times, though it is wise to have a copy of it with you.)

We've picked our favorite accommodations in Beijing and hope you'll enjoy your stay—there are so many new establishments in the capital that it's been difficult to narrow down the list. Each of the places we feature offers something special, whether it is a prime location to Beijing's tourist sites, a historic Imperial setting, or a rooftop Jacuzzi!

HOW TO CHOOSE THE LOCATION THAT'S RIGHT FOR YOU

For the most atmosphere and proximity to tourist sites, you should choose the **Back Lakes (Hou Hai)** area. Plenty of hotels and guesthouses have blossomed in the alleys to meet every budget. Another nearby option is the **city center,** within walking distance of the Forbidden City and Tian'an Men Square, on Wangfujing Dajie or nearby. The range of accommodations in this area—from superluxury to rock-bottom—is unmatched.

The greatest luxury and highest standards of service can be found in **Chaoyang,** near the two main diplomatic areas just outside the East Second Ring Road. The district's southern half, also known as the **CBD** (Central Business District), is filled almost exclusively with high-end hotels and is the city's glitziest shopping area. The north has proximity to the airport and the dining and nightlife options of Sanlitun.

A good option if you're planning on spending time near the universities and the western tourist sites (like the Summer Palace, the Olympic Green, and the Fragrant Hills) is the **western district,** with the new superluxe Aman resort and some decent budget options. The **southern districts** of Xuanwu (southwest) and Chongwen (southeast) are the least desirable but offer convenient access to the Beijing Railway Station, and Beijing West Railway Station.

1 BEST HOTEL BETS

- **Best Newcomer:** With the glut of hotels that opened in time for the Olympics, there are plenty of places to choose from, but the definite winner in this category is the **Opposite House,** a stylish Japanese-designed boutique hotel on Sanlitun Bar Street. With modern minimalist rooms, great restaurants and bars, and impressive service, it would be difficult to go wrong here—except that it comes with a hefty price. See p. 68.

- **Best City Getaway:** Tired of the noise and pollution of central Beijing? Head north to the **Aman Beijing,** a new Southeast Asian managed property that sits on the edge of the Summer Palace, with a private entry to the imperial quarters, gorgeous rooms in traditional courtyard structures, and a top-notch steakhouse. See p. 75.

- **Best Whiff of Old Beijing: Han's Royal Garden Hotel** offers luxurious courtyard-style accommodations with a distinct historical touch just off a bustling alley in central Beijing. The five sets of buildings situated around Chinese courtyards, painstakingly restored, provide a glimpse of how wealthy Chinese lived a century ago. See p. 65.

- **Best Hotel Garden:** The **Bamboo Garden Hotel**'s three courtyards are filled with rockeries, stands of bamboo, and other green leafiness. A traditional Chinese garden stretches away behind the otherwise modern **Shangri-La Beijing Hotel** to its tennis courts at the rear. See p. 67 and 76, respectively.

- **Best Business Hotel:** Despite being a relatively "old" hotel, having been around for a decade, the **Grand Hyatt** is still the most popular hotel for business travelers, with professional service, a great location, and excellent dining venues, including Made in China. See below.

- **Best Design: Opposite House,** our pick for best newcomer, also gets this award for stylish details from the stainless-steel-bottomed pool to the Chinese modern art installations in the sedate atrium lobby. Not far behind is **Hotel G,** which blends a 1960s Hollywood feel with a modern Chinese aesthetic. See p. 68 and 71, respectively.

- **Best Health & Fitness Facilities:** The **Park Hyatt** has not one, but two, gorgeous pools and fitness facilities, one located on an upper level exclusively for hotel guests and a second one on a lower level with aerobics classes and state-of-the-art Technogym equipment. See p. 68.

- **Best Pool:** If you're looking for a novelty pool, head to the **Grand Hyatt,** which looks like a lagoon buried among mock-tropical decor beneath a ceiling of electric stars. **The Regent** has a much more understated pool that is perfect for lap swimming and a great Jacuzzi for a post-workout plunge. See below and p. 62, respectively.

- **Best for Children:** The **Westin Beijing, Financial Street** pays special attention to young kids, with cribs available in rooms and highchairs (rare in China) in the restaurants; a kids' center offers babysitting. The **Kerry Centre Hotel** also has a supervised play area for children, a wide range of sports facilities, and a pool for the older ones. See p. 70 and 71, respectively.

2 BEIJING CITY CENTER, AROUND WANGFUJING DAJIE

VERY EXPENSIVE

Grand Hyatt Beijing (Beijing Dongfang Junyue Dajiudian) 北京东方君悦大酒店 ★★   The Grand Hyatt is unrivaled for location: directly over the Wangfujing metro station, attached to one of the city's best indoor malls, at the foot of the capital's most famous shopping street, and within walking distance of the Forbidden City. Standard rooms are spacious, with soft carpets and desks equipped with buttery leather chairs. Bathrooms are a bit on the small side, but do have separate shower units. They recently extended the reception area, which is a good thing because check-in time can be hectic. Thankfully, service is fantastic and reception staff are quick to make eye contact, apologize for the wait, or quickly wave you over when they are free. The palatial lobby is a popular meeting place, with live music in the evenings and Beijing's best chocolate shop at one end. The vast swimming pool has a mock-tropical decor, with rock caves and a ceiling of electric stars—it's very kitsch and un-Hyatt but worth a visit even if you have no plans to swim. Some of Beijing's best restaurants—including Noble Court and **Made in China** (p. 86)—are scattered throughout.

Dong Chang'an Jie 1 东长安街1号 (within the Oriental Plaza complex at the foot of Wangfujing Dajie); see map p. 106. ⓒ 800/633-7313 in the U.S. and Canada, 0845/888-1226 in the U.K., 1800/13-1234 in Australia, 0800/44-1234 in New Zealand, or 010/8518-1234. Fax 010/8518-0000. www.beijing.grand. hyatt.com. 825 units. ¥3,800 standard room (discounts up to 60% during the low season), plus 15% service charge. AE, DC, MC, V. Metro: Wangfujing. **Amenities:** 5 restaurants; cafe; bar; fitness center with latest equipment; Jacuzzi; indoor resort-style pool (50m/164 ft.) and children's pool; room service; sauna; solarium. *In room:* A/C, satellite TV, hair dryer, Internet, minibar, scale.

The Peninsula Beijing (Wangfu Bandao Fandian) 王府半岛饭店 ★★ The

Peninsula, well-known for its flagship in Hong Kong, has a rather unappealing white bathroom-tile exterior and is one of the city's older hotels, but the hotel still has a certain cachet in Beijing, for good reason. English-speaking service staff is some of the best in the capital, and while rooms are slightly smaller than those at Beijing's newer hotels, they have shiny marble bathrooms, flatscreen televisions, and plush beds. The hotel also has a great location and a terrific spa, managed by an outside group called Espa. It's well worth a visit for a treatment, which begins with a visit to a well-outfitted sauna, steam room, and relaxation room, and is followed with pampering from an experienced therapist.

Jinyu Hutong 8 金鱼胡同8号 (1 block east of Wangfujing Dajie); see map p. 106. ⓒ 866/382-8388 (toll-free from U.S.) or 010/8516-2888. Fax 010/6510-6311. www.peninsula.com. 525 units. ¥2,850 standard room (discounts up to 50% during the low season), plus 15% service charge. AE, DC, MC, V. Metro: Dengshikou. **Amenities:** 2 restaurants; cafe; ATM and bank; babysitting; concierge; fully equipped fitness center; Rolls-Royce and Mercedes limousines; indoor pool; room service; saunas and steam rooms; spa. *In room:* A/C, 42-in. plasma TV/DVD, silent fax, hair dryer, minibar, Wi-Fi.

Raffles Beijing (Beijing Fandian Laifushi) 北京饭店莱佛士 ★ If you're look-

ing for a slice of old-world charm, look no further than Raffles Beijing. The hotel took over management of this historic building and lovingly restored it with wood paneled floors and sparkling chandeliers. Rooms also feature marble entrances and Oriental rugs. All rooms in the historic building are decorated differently. Personality suites are named for famous historical characters. The Li Zongren (a former general for Chiang Kai-shek and later a Communist sympathizer) suite has a four-poster bed on a raised platform, Chinese bric-a-brac, and a huge bathroom that has two separate entrances. Mounted black-and-white photos of old Beijing adorn the walls. The huge plasma TV is a bit out of place, and cheekily encased in an early-20th-century-esque gold frame. Rooms facing south look out onto Chang'an Jie, one of Beijing's main thoroughfares. Sadly, none of the rooms has a balcony. Certain amenities are also inconveniently located in a separate building—you have to walk by a Japanese restaurant and a vaulted atrium to get to the pool and health club. Business travelers who don't need the historic decor might want to check out the contemporary executive suites housed in the same building as the pool and gym.

Dong Chang'an Jie 33 东长安街 33号 (1 block west of Oriental Plaza); see map p. 106. ⓒ 800/768-9009 (toll-free from U.S.) or 010/6526-3388. Fax 010/8500-4380. www.beijing.raffles.com. 171 units. ¥3,800–¥4,700 standard room (discounts up to 40% during the low season), plus 15% service charge. AE, DC, MC, V. Metro: Wangfujing. **Amenities:** 3 restaurants; bar; babysitting; concierge; fully equipped fitness center; indoor pool; room service; saunas and steam rooms. *In room:* A/C, LCD TV, fax and DVD upon request, hair dryer, minibar, Wi-Fi.

EXPENSIVE

The Emperor (Huangjia Yizhan) 皇家驿栈 ★ Down a shady lane right next to the Forbidden City, this four-story boutique hotel offers a fabulous location for tourists and unique rooms. Beds and sofas are built into each room's white walls streaked with bright textured fabric in a single color of turquoise blue, lime green, or bright orange, giving the rooms a futuristic, stylish feel. While modern, the rooms also pay respect to Chinese culture: Each comes with a Chinese seal that guests can take with them when they leave, and rooms are named after China's various emperors. The rooftop bar and spa have one of the best views in town—guests can gaze straight into the maze of rooms at the Forbidden City. The bar is often filled with expats until the early-morning hours during the summer, while the spa comes with a decadent alfresco Jacuzzi.

Qihelou Lu 33 骑河楼街33号; see map p. 106. ☏ **10/800-3746-8357** or 010/6526-5566. Fax **010/6523-8786.** www.theemperorbeijing.cn. 55 units. ¥840–¥1,120 superior/deluxe room. Rates include service charge and breakfast. AE, DC, MC, V. Metro: Tian'an Men East. **Amenities:** Restaurant; rooftop bar; concierge; forex; health club; meeting rooms; indoor pool; room service/butler service; all smoke-free rooms; spa. *In room:* A/C, satellite TV, hair dryer, Internet, free minibar.

Hilton Beijing Wangfujing (Beijing Wangfujing Xierdun Jiudian) 北京王府井希尔顿酒店 ★★ This new hotel is an excellent addition to the city center: It's right beside the shopping paradise of Wangfujing, a block away from two major metro stops and within walking distance of the Forbidden City and Tian'an Men Square. Regular rooms here are larger than those at the nearby Regent or Grand Hyatt, and come with amenities (free shoeshines, MP3 docking stations, and so on) that other five-stars would reserve for suites. Deluxe Plus rooms and suites have sexy black-and-white claw-foot tubs inside gigantic shower cubicles, while regular Deluxe rooms come with standard tubs that are rather awkwardly placed in the middle of the room (there's a sliding door if you're shy). For my money, I'd skip the suites and book myself into the Deluxe Plus room, which has bigger windows and the layout—long entranceways from which shoot off walk-in closets and spacious bathrooms—really maximizes space. All rooms are equipped with big, cozy beds, 42-inch flatscreen TVs embedded into light wood paneled walls, and sleek office desks. The breakfast spread is excellent, but avoid the in-house restaurants for lunch and dinner—both serve disappointing, lackluster fare.

Wangfujing Dong Jie 8 王府井东街8号; see map p. 106. ☏ **010/5812-8888.** Fax 010/5812-8886. www.wangfujing.hilton.com. 255 units. ¥1,500–¥2,000 deluxe; ¥2,500–¥3,000 suites; ¥3,000–¥3,500 executive deluxe; ¥3,500–¥4,000 executive suite. AE, DC, MC, V. Metro: Wangfujing or Dongsi. **Amenities:** 2 restaurants; cafe; bar; babysitting; small fitness center with latest equipment; library; glass-enclosed indoor pool (80m/262 ft.); room service; top-notch spa. *In room:* A/C, satellite TV, hair dryer, Internet, minibar, scale.

The Regent Beijing (Beijing Li Jing Jiu Dian) 北京丽晶酒店 ★ The Regent is sparkly and grand, with an excellent location and fine amenities to boot. But bang for buck, it falls short of the brand-new Hilton Wangfujing a mere block away, which has bigger rooms and better amenities. The rooms here are still spacious and have an understated elegance with nice Chinese antique accessories. The beige marble bathrooms have free-standing bathtubs that are some of the most comfortable in Beijing and separate shower stalls. The Regent's health club is the best in the Wangfujing area, with multiple workout rooms and a gorgeous 32m (105-ft.) swimming pool that laps along its edges like a tide. Skip dining in the lobby lounge. Sure, it looks impressive, with floor-to-ceiling glass walls, a vaulted atrium, and the modern waterfall centerpiece, but the service is consistently abominable.

Jin Bao Jie 99 金宝街99号; see map p. 106. ☎ **800/545-4000** or 800/610-8888 toll free in the U.S., 010/8522-1888 from China. Fax 010/8522-1818. www.regenthotels.com. 499 units. ¥1,800 standard room (discounts up to 40% during the low season); ¥1,950–¥2,750 suite, plus 15% service charge. AE, DC, MC, V. Metro: Dengshikou. **Amenities:** 5 restaurants; cafe; bar; babysitting; executive-level rooms; forex; health club; indoor pool; room service; smoke-free floor; spa. *In room:* A/C, satellite TV, hair dryer, Internet, minibar.

MODERATE

Crowne Plaza Hotel (Guoji Yiyuan Huangguan Fandian) 国际艺苑皇冠饭店

The location of this popular sleeping ground for American tour groups is pretty well near perfect—being so close to the Forbidden City, Tian'an Men Square, and the Wangfujing shopping area. Rooms are pleasant, with flatscreen TVs, decent bathrooms, and nice images of old Beijing silk-screened on the walls, but beware: Some of the rooms have windows that face only an inner atrium. The public atrium, with a large lobby lounge, is a popular meeting place for Chinese, and amenities include a decent pool and gym. The rooms here are also far more affordable than at The Peninsula hotel around the corner.

Wangfujing Dajie 48 王府井大街48号 (corner of Dengshi Kou Dajie); see map p. 106. ☎ **877/932-4112** in the U.S. and Canada, 1800/830-8998 in Australia, 0800/80-1111 in New Zealand, 0800/917-1587 in the U.K., or 010/5911-9999. Fax 010/5911-9998. www.beijinghotels.crowneplaza.com. 395 units. ¥1,180 standard room, plus 15% service charge. AE, DC, MC, V. Metro: Wangfujing or Dengshikou. **Amenities:** 2 restaurants; bar; babysitting; concierge; small health club with old equipment; underwhelming Jacuzzi; tiny indoor pool; room service; sauna; solarium. *In room:* A/C, satellite plasma TV, hair dryer, Internet, minibar.

Haoyuan Binguan 好园宾馆 ★

Located down a lane just off one of Beijing's trendiest shopping streets, the 19-room Haoyuan is among the most exclusive of the city's popular courtyard-style hotels. Red doors hung with lanterns and flanked on either side by stone lions mark the entrance. Inside is a neatly restored Qing-era house, with a small unadorned courtyard in front and a sublime larger courtyard at the back, decorated with flowers and tree-shaded, stone chess tables. Larger rooms in the rear courtyard are furnished with canopy beds and custom-made Ming reproduction furniture. A bonus for fans of Communist Party history: The house once belonged to Hua Guofeng, Party chair after Mao, who aped the Great Helmsman's coiffure but didn't gain his stature.

Shijia Hutong 53 史家胡同53号 (blue sign points way on Dong Dan Bei Dajie); see map p. 106. ☎ **010/6512-5557.** Fax 010/6525-3179. 19 units. ¥668 standard room (discounts rare, even in winter). AE, DC, MC, V. Metro: Dengshikou. **Amenities:** Restaurant; bike rental; Wi-Fi. *In room:* A/C, satellite TV, fridge, hair dryer.

Park Plaza Beijing (Beijing Li Ting Jiu Dian) 北京丽亭酒店 ★ (Value)

Sitting next to its sister hotel, The Regent, the Chinese four-star Park Plaza is one notch below in price and grandeur, but it's a good value for the business or leisure guests looking for comfortable rooms in a great location without the opulent amenities. Rooms, decorated in wood and beige tones, are a bit cramped but do the job just fine. The hotel is often booked to capacity and is popular with Western business travelers. (Another incentive for staying here: This hotel often overbooks and upgrades its bumped guests to the luxurious Regent next door.)

Jin Bao Jie 97 金宝街97号; see map p. 106. ☎ **010/8522-1999.** Fax 010/8522-1919. 216 units. ¥850–¥1,150 standard room; ¥1,700 suite (discounts up to 50% in the low season), plus 15% service charge. AE, DC, MC, V. Metro: Dengshikou. **Amenities:** 2 restaurants; bar; babysitting; executive-level rooms; fitness center; forex; room service; sauna; smoke-free floor. *In room:* A/C, satellite TV, hair dryer, Internet, minibar.

Shi Jia House 史家会馆 ★★ (Finds) Beijing's boutique hotel scene is getting chicer and chicer. This new addition, housed in a *hutong* just west of Wangfujing, is one of our favorites. Spacious rooms have dark wood floors and are decorated with refurbished antique Chinese furniture. Colors are rich and warm, with silk pillows and bed throws mixed in to lighten the mood. Wooden doors that look like Chinese armoires reveal large, well-appointed bathrooms equipped with rain showers. Exposed wooden beams line the sloping ceilings and every room comes with skylight windows that open at the flick of a wall switch. The spacious courtyard is a wonderful retreat from the city chaos—a place to relax under a sun umbrella and enjoy the feng shui vibes of the small koi pond and mini-waterfall. The one annoyance is negotiating a cab into the narrow *hutong*. **Note:** Shijia Hutong is a one-way street from 7am to 10pm, so you can travel only east to west during those hours.

Shijia Hutong 42 史家胡同42号; see map p. 106. ☎ **010/5219-0288.** Fax 010/5219-0119. www.shijia house.com. 8 units. ¥1,100–¥2,000 suite. AE, DC, MC, V. Metro: Dengshikou. **Amenities:** Restaurant; bar. *In room:* A/C, TV, hair dryer, Wi-Fi.

INEXPENSIVE

Days Inn Forbidden City (Beijing Xiangjiang Daisi Jiudian) 北京香江戴斯 酒店 ★ A terrific budget choice and a brand familiar to westerners, the Days Inn is just a few minutes' walk in either direction to the Forbidden City and Wangfujing. Rooms are small and don't have much character, but come with all the necessary amenities, including satellite TV; a bright, clean bathroom; and Wi-Fi. The staff at reception is fluent in English, something that's hard to come by at other three-star hotels. This is a great value for the neighborhood, where five-star hotels often command triple or quadruple the price of this motel. If you're planning on staying for 3 nights or more, apply for a VIP card for ¥38, which gives you perks from complimentary lunch to an extra night free, depending on how long you stay.

Nanwanzi 1, Nanheyan St. 南湾子1号进南河沿大街; see map p. 106. ☎ **010/6512-7788.** Fax 010/65265229. www.daysinn.com. 164 units. ¥448–¥558 standard/superior rooms. Rates include service charge. AE, DC, MC, V. Metro: Tian'an Men Dong. Amenities: Restaurant; concierge; forex; room service; smoke-free floors. *In room:* A/C, satellite TV, hair dryer, Internet, minibar.

Saga Youth Hostel (Shijia Guoji Qingnian Lushe) 实佳国际青年旅社 ★ Housed in one of Beijing's most famous *hutong*, the Saga is a favorite among savvy backpackers. The decade-old hostel just underwent a long-overdue renovation and looks fresh and lively. The second-floor hallway has been painted a sunny yellow on top of which stylish Chinese calligraphy in heavy gold paint has been added. The ceiling is brightly painted with scenes from Chinese folklore. Spacious standard rooms come with their own wet bathrooms (the kind with no divider between the toilet and the shower); some rooms have separate sitting areas. The third floor, home to clean and functional dorm rooms, is much more utilitarian hostel in style and decoration. Past visitors have scribbled their thoughts in kaleidoscopic ink and paint on the hallway's white walls. The ratty public bathrooms have thankfully been replaced with clean blue tile, separate cubicles, and showerheads offering decent pressure. The biggest bonus of top-floor accommodations is proximity to the third-floor balcony; the fantastic view west across well-preserved old courtyard houses is a joy, especially at sunrise. There's also a central courtyard on the main floor with cozy patio furniture and sun umbrellas.

Shijia Hutong 9 史家胡同9号 (west of intersection with Chaoyang Men Nan Xiao Jie); see map p. 106. ☎ 010/6527-2773. Fax 010/6524-9098. www.hostelworld.com. 24 units, 12 with in-room shower. ¥288 twin; ¥65 dorm bed. No credit cards. Metro: Dengshikou. **Amenities:** Cafe; cheap Internet access; kitchen; table soccer. *In room:* A/C, no phone.

3 BACK LAKES & DONG CHENG

VERY EXPENSIVE

Du Ge Hotel (Duge Siheyuan Yishu Jingpin Jiudian) 杜革四合院艺术精品酒店 ★ **Kids**   This posh, cozy 10-room boutique hotel sitting right off of the popular alley of Nan Luogu Xiang is a sign of Beijing's rapidly gentrifying times. Each room is decorated with a different theme and name, ranging from "The Tibetan Kingdom" to "The Peony Pavilion." Lacquered furniture in bright colors has been custom-made and fitted, while fancy touches like crystal chandeliers and antique carpets round out the polished, flashy feel of the rooms. Though definitely grand—it was once part of the home of a Qing dynasty finance minister—the hotel feels a little cramped with a minuscule lobby and small outdoor space which doubles as a bar and restaurant. The hotel is less willing to bargain than other places in the area, but for those who appreciate style and fashion, a stay here will feel worthwhile. One nice touch is two small, intimate rooms which are designed for single travelers or to give parents relief from their children. A range of complimentary services includes transfers to and from the airport, use of cellphones and bicycles, and around-the-clock refreshments, coffee, and tea.

Qianyuan'ensi Hutong 26 前圆恩寺胡同26号; see map p. 106. ✆ **010/6406 0686.** Fax 010/6406-0628. www.dugecourtyard.com. 10 units. ¥1,200–¥3,000 standard/suite, plus 15% service charge. AE, DC, MC, V. Metro: Beixinqiao. **Amenities:** Restaurant; bar; airport transfers; bike rentals; cellphone rental; concierge; cooking demos; heating and A/C; room service; spa; translator/tour guides; Wi-Fi. *In room:* A/C, satellite TV, hair dryer, Internet, minibar.

Han's Royal Garden Hotel (Hanzhen Yuan Guoji Jiudian) 涵珍园国际酒店 ★★ **Finds**   A collaboration between a wealthy Chinese American and the grandson of a Qing Dynasty chef, this painstakingly restored series of five courtyards has been turned into a luxurious hotel with an emphasis on preserving China's history and culture. The courtyards feature goldfish ponds, hawthorn trees, and stone carvings. Most rooms are decorated comfortably with expensive yet understated dark wood furniture with a Western feel, while the more lavish rooms have been filled with antique Chinese rosewood furniture. The hotel houses an Imperial cuisine restaurant with private rooms on two floors, while a third floor features a stage for the same sort of after-dinner performances that royal families used to indulge in. A basement houses a bar with a stage for dancing and a small spa with Thai, Chinese, and Western massage. The location is fantastic, just off the busy alley of Nan Luogu Xiang, yet on a very quiet, low-key alley where you'd least expect to find such a gem.

Bei Bingmasi Hutong 7 北兵马司胡同7号; see map p. 106. ✆ **010/8402-5588.** Fax 010/6401-5556. www.hansroyalgarden.com. 33 units. ¥1,290 deluxe room, plus 15% service charge; ¥ 6,800 Rosewood suite, plus 15% service charge. AE, DC, MC, V. Metro: Zhangzizhong Lu. **Amenities:** 2 restaurants; bar; forex; Internet. *In room:* A/C, satellite TV, hair dryer, minibar, Wi-Fi.

EXPENSIVE

Courtyard 7 (Qihao Yuan) 七号院 ★   Located just off the very popular alley Nan Luogu Xiang, this boutique hotel in a traditional courtyard dwelling offers cozy rooms decorated with Chinese antiques and white curtained windows overlooking one of several central gardens. The hotel has taken an environmental approach in its design: Many bricks have been reused from former dwellings and old stone stelae with faded engraved calligraphy decorate the outer walls. Rooms come with central air conditioning and heating,

The Best Hotel Spas

The glut of new luxury hotels also means that there's a glut of luxury hotel spas in Beijing. The city's new spas feature state-of-the-art treatment and relaxation rooms and masseuses who excel in Asian treatments. Prices tend to be on par with what you'd pay in other international cities—but it doesn't hurt to bargain. One of our favorites is the Tian spa at the new **Park Hyatt** (p. 68), which offers a range of treatments based on traditional Chinese medicine, plus access to the hotel's gorgeous pool and gym. For a completely sedate experience, visit the **Espa at the Peninsula** (p. 61), where you'll first go to the sauna and steam room and de-stress in a plush reclining armchair before finally sinking into a heated massage bed in a darkened treatment room. Both of the **Ritz-Carltons** (p. 69 and p. 75) offer luxurious treatments, while if you're looking to get away for an entire day, try the **Aman Beijing** (p. 75) near the **Summer Palace** or **Chi at the Shangri-La** (p. 76), with calming Tibetan-themed rooms.

rather than the typical individual cooling and heating units in most buildings in the neighborhood.

Qian Gulou Yuan Hutong 7 前鼓楼苑胡同 7 号 (near Nanluoguxiang); see map p. 106. ℂ **010/6406-0777.** Fax 010/8402-6867. www.courtyard7.com. 19 units. ¥1,180–¥1,900 standard room/suite. AE, DC, MC, V. Metro: Beixinqiao. **Amenities:** Restaurant; bar; concierge; room service, smoke-free. *In room:* A/C, TV, hair dryer, Internet.

Hotel Côté Cour S.L. ★   This courtyard hotel, down an unassuming alley, is the best of the bunch of a crop of courtyard accommodations that have flooded the Beijing market. Lime green walls, Chinese antiques, and funky tiled bathrooms make this a charming boutique experience. The outdoor garden is a great place to unwind and read if you happen to be staying in Beijing's more pleasant months; otherwise, head to the airy lounge decorated with contemporary art, where free breakfast and cappuccinos are served.

Yanyue Hutong 70 演乐胡同70号; see map p. 106. ℂ **010/6512-8020.** Fax 010/6512-7295. www.hotel cotecoursl.com. 14 units. ¥1,295 standard room; ¥ 2,668 suite. AE, DC, MC, V. Metro: Dongsi. **Amenities:** Restaurant; bar; lounge; smoke-free floors. *In room:* A/C, satellite TV, hair dryer, Wi-Fi.

Red Capital Residence (Xin Hong Zi Julebu) 新红资俱乐部 ★   It was once one of the few boutique hotels in town, but the Red Capital Residence has been overtaken by a number of new entries in the back alleys of Beijing. Still, Art Deco furnishings steal the show at this Cultural Revolution–themed *siheyuan,* set around a tiny central courtyard which conceals a homemade bomb shelter, now converted into a somewhat claustrophobic wine bar. It may be a tad museum-like, pretentious even, but if you can't resist the chance to curl up with a book in stuffed armchairs once used by Marshal Peng Dehuai and Premier Zhou Enlai, then this boutique hotel is worth the outlay. The two Concubine's Private Courtyards, fitted with ornate Qing dynasty beds, are the most romantic rooms in the capital. Service can be a little spotty.

Dong Si Liu Tiao 9 东四六条9号 (walk a long block west from metro, turn left into Chao Nei Bei Xiao Jie, and take 4th turn on right); see map p. 106. ℂ **010/8403-5308.** Fax 010/8403-5303. www.redcapitalclub.com. cn. 5 units, shower only. ¥1,188 single room; ¥1,480 standard room, plus 15% service charge. AE, DC, MC, V. Metro: Dong Si Shi Tiao. **Amenities:** Cigar lounge; underground wine bar. *In room:* A/C, satellite TV.

MODERATE

Bamboo Garden Hotel (Zhu Yuan Binguan) 竹园宾馆 ★　Said to be the former residence of the infamous Qing dynasty eunuch, Li Lianying, Bamboo Garden was the first major courtyard-style hotel in Beijing and is among the most beautiful. Rooms border three courtyards filled with rock gardens, clusters of bamboo, and covered corridors. Standard rooms in two multistory buildings at opposite ends of the complex are decorated with Ming-style furniture and traditional lamps that cast pleasant shadows on the high ceilings. A restaurant looks out over the rear courtyard.

Xiaoshi Qiao Hutong 24 小石桥胡同24号 (3rd *hutong* on right walking south from metro stop); see map p. 106. ☎ 010/6403-2229. Fax 010/6401-2633. www.bbgh.com.cn. 44 units. ¥580–¥680 standard room (discounts rare). AE, DC, MC, V. Metro: Gulou. **Amenities:** Restaurant; bar; concierge; forex. *In room:* A/C, satellite TV, fridge.

Gu Xiang 20 (Gu Xiang Er Shi) 古巷20 ★　This intimate hotel located on a bar-lined alley in the *hutong* has modern rooms decorated with Chinese antiques and flatscreen TVs. Beds are dark wood, and long, emperor-style calligraphy tables serve as desks. Rooms on the third floor are larger and some come with their own balconies with views overlooking the rooftops of traditional courtyard houses nearby. They're well worth the upgrade. The English service is uneven, but everyone is superfriendly.

Nanluoguxiang 20 南锣鼓巷20号 (about 200m/656 ft. south of north entrance of Nanluoguxiang); see map p. 106. ☎ 010/6400-5566. Fax 010/6400-3658. www.guxiang20.com. 28 units. ¥500–¥1,280 standard room. AE, DC, MC, V. Metro: Beixinqiao. **Amenities:** Restaurant; bar; room service; rooftop tennis court. *In room:* A/C, satellite TV, fridge, minibar, Wi-Fi.

Qomolangma Hotel (Zhumulangma Binguan) 珠穆朗玛宾馆 ★　At the rear of the Qomolangma Hotel is a vast courtyard containing four other separate and private courtyards. Make sure to request a room here, rather than in the street-facing building, which is a completely unimpressive hotel. Courtyard rooms are furnished with traditional Chinese furniture, and the deluxe suites come with big bathtubs. The restaurant hosts free Tibetan song and dance performances Friday nights from 7 to 8pm.

Gulou Xi Dajie 149 古楼西大街149号 (northwest of Drum Tower); see map p. 106. ☎ 010/6401-8822. Fax 010/6401-1330. www.qomolangmahotel.com. 65 units. ¥518–¥1,000 standard room. AE, MC, V. Metro: Gulou. **Amenities:** Restaurant; exercise room (currently being renovated, should be done by the time you read this). *In room:* AC, satellite TV, fridge, hair dryer, Internet.

INEXPENSIVE

Beijing Downtown Backpackers Accommodation (Dong Tang Qingnian Lushe) 东堂青年旅社★　This is one of the most popular hostels in Beijing, and it's in a fabulous location. They have bargain-basement dorm rooms as well as private singles and standard rooms. The bathroom has that annoying layout with a toilet placed smack in the middle of the shower area, but it is very clean and the folks manning the reception desk speak excellent English.

Nanluoguxiang 85 南锣鼓巷85号; see map p. 106. ☎ 010/8400-2429. Fax 010/6404-9677. downtown@ backpackingchina.com. 20 units. ¥150–¥190 standard room. Rates include breakfast. No credit cards. Metro: Beixinqiao. **Amenities:** Restaurant; Internet; free airport pickup if you're staying over 4 days (you pay the ¥20 toll fees). *In room:* AC.

Confucius International Youth Hostel (Beijing Yong Sheng Xuan Qingnian Jiudia) 北京拥圣轩酒店 ★　This hostel is right in the thick of things on up-and-coming Wudaoying Hutong, a lively alley that has seen a slew of cafes, restaurants, and boutiques open in the past year. Rooms are basic but a good size (bigger than at nearby

Beijing Downtown Backpackers Accommodation). They come with squeaky-clean tile or faux-wood floors and separate wet bathrooms—the kind with no official division between shower and toilet, though there is a shower curtain in place. There's little decor to speak of in-room, just crisp white duvets and plain walls, but the sunshine streaming in during the day and the daily sounds of *hutong* life make for cozy environs. The hostel itself is a two-story converted courtyard. Public spaces are done in traditional Chinese fashion: Eaves on the central walkway are painted with Chinese scenes or flowers, and wooden beams and pillars have shiny coats of red paint. The best rooms are on the second floor. They may be a bit cramped for taller guests, but the sloping roofs with exposed natural wood beams are a step up from the bare walls and ceilings in first-floor rooms. The hostel doesn't have an outdoor balcony, but indoor verandas on the second floor look down into the central courtyard. Pick this place and you'll be a stone's throw from the Lama Temple and the Beijing subway (Loop Line).

Wudaoying Hutong 38 五道营胡同38号; see map p. 106. ℂ 010/6402-2082 or 0/13910769159. 16 units. ¥200 standard room. No credit cards. Metro: Yonghegong Lama Temple. **Amenities:** Restaurant; cafe. *In room:* A/C, TV, Wi-Fi.

4 CHAOYANG

VERY EXPENSIVE

Opposite House (Yu She) 瑜舍 ★★   Located on the Sanlitun bar street, this classy boutique hotel represents how far this once-scummy area (and Beijing as a whole) has come. You won't expect much from the boring glass exterior, but inside, everything is stylish, from the open atrium lobby featuring Chinese modern-art installations to the stainless steel–bottomed pool in the basement. Rooms are decorated in minimalist white with floor-to-ceiling windows and are anchored with pale wood floors. Bathrooms are separated by a glass partition and feature wooden tubs redolent of the Japanese designer Kengo Kuma's ethnic heritage. Hotel staff, in hooded beige vests and appropriately gelled hair, are extremely helpful and courteous. What's also a draw are the food and beverage outlets, including the very popular Mediterranean restaurant **Sureño** (p. 93) and **Bei** (p. 92) for some of the city's finest sushi, plus the twin lounge and nightclub **Mesh** and **Punk** (p. 192). Great venues plus stylish rooms equals the most happening hotel in town.

Sanlitun Lu 11, The Village, building 1三里屯路11号院1号楼,三里屯Village; see map p. 110. ℂ 010/6417-6688. Fax 010/6417-7799. www.theoppositehouse.com. 99 units. ¥5,000–¥6,500 studio/studio suite, plus 15% service charge. Pets allowed (for free). AE, DC, MC, V. Metro: Tuanjiehu. **Amenities:** 3 restaurants; 2 bars; fitness center; forex; heating and A/C; indoor pool; room service smoke-free floors; complimentary culture tour; Wi-Fi. *In room:* A/C, satellite TV, hair dryer, Internet, free minibar.

Park Hyatt (Beijing Baiyue Jiudian) 北京柏悦酒店 ★★   Rising above the area known as the CBD (the Central Business District), this new 66-story hotel impresses with expansive views of the city, top-notch gym and spa facilities, and unconventional room layouts decorated in beige tones. Most rooms open into an airy bathroom, outfitted with marble tubs next to an open shower, a free-standing his-and-hers sink and mirror, and a sliding door that separates the bathroom from the sleeping quarters beyond. It's sexy, if you're staying with a romantic partner, but inconvenient if you happen to be traveling with your grandmother. There are plenty of fun in-room amenities, including Japanese toilets with bidets and automatic-opening lids, fragrant soaps, and a beautiful

The Mandarin Oriental Fire

Images of fireballs engulfing the yet-to-open Mandarin Oriental hotel made international news in early 2009, after the property was set ablaze by illegal fireworks during the Chinese New Year holiday. The hotel, one of the most highly anticipated luxury property openings, was part of a larger development that included the iconic Rem Koolhaas–designed CCTV tower, consisting of two sloping towers connected by a platform in the sky. Fortunately, the fire resulted in only one fatality since the hotel was unoccupied, but the blaze caused 4 billion yuan ($588 million) in damages—and plenty of embarrassment to the Chinese Communist government, since it illustrated the lack of safety controls for even the most prestigious of addresses. As of press time, the gutted structure still stands and rumors have been circulating that the hotel serves as a counterbalancing weight to the main CCTV tower and thus can't be demolished.

collection of complimentary teas. The food and beverage venues are highly popular among business travelers and expatriates: The 66th-floor China Grill offers delicious, if pricey, steaks and raw seafood, while the 6th floor Xiu on a terrace offers reasonably priced cocktails and live entertainment. But flaws abound as well: Located within a luxury apartment and office complex that was in a rush to be completed by the 2008 Olympics, the hotel suffers from shoddy finishing touches, like faucets with loose handles (we even ripped a faucet handle out of its socket by simply twisting it). We found the Internet spotty—a deal breaker at a five-star business hotel. But if you're looking for a convenient location in the CBD, impressive views, and stylish rooms, this may be it. If you can get a deal for under $250, it's worthwhile.

Jianguomenwai Dajie 2 建国门外大街2号; see map p. 110. © **010/8567-1234.** Fax 010/8567-1000. www.beijing.park.hyatt.com. 237 units. ¥2,000–¥2,500 standard/deluxe, plus 15% service charge. AE, DC, MC, V. Metro: Guomao. **Amenities:** 3 restaurants; bar; airport limousine transfers; concierge; fitness center; forex; indoor pool; room service/butler service; spa; Wi-Fi. *In room:* A/C, satellite TV, hair dryer, minibar, MP3 docking station, newspaper.

Ritz-Carlton Beijing (Beijing Lisi Kaerdun Jiudian) 北京丽思卡尔顿酒店 ★★

Not to be confused with the *other* new Ritz-Carlton on the other side of town, this new five-star hotel sits just east of Beijing's CBD (Central Business District) and comes with impressive service and a distinctly old-world, European feel. While rooms have a classic look with flowery throw pillows and dark wood furniture, they're also outfitted with modern technology like iPod docks, flatscreen televisions, and Wi-Fi (but, strangely, no DVD players). The gym, spa, and pool are located on the top floor, giving guests great views of the city. The hotel offers stellar restaurants, including Yu, serving Cantonese cuisine and decorated with celadon green ceramics and Buddhist stone sculptures and jade pieces in the private-room wing, and Barolo, which offers traditional Italian cuisine with wines by the glass. If you can, try to upgrade to an executive room, which comes with access to the private club room, where a complimentary buffet and drinks are served throughout the day.

Jianguo Road 83A 建国路83A号; see map p. 110. © **010/5908-8888.** Fax 010/5908-8899. www.ritzcarlton. com. 305 units. ¥4,800–¥5,800 deluxe/executive, plus 15% service charge. AE, DC, MC, V. Metro: Dawang Lu. **Amenities:** 3 restaurants; bar; club lounge; ballroom; fitness center; forex; health club; free Internet for club rooms or higher price; indoor pool; meeting rooms; smoke-free floors; spa; Wi-Fi. *In room:* A/C, satellite TV, hair dryer, Internet, newspaper, minibar.

St. Regis Beijing (Beijing Guoji Julebu Fandian) 北京国际俱乐部饭店 ★

It was once the best hotel in town, but the St. Regis no longer stands out as the front-runner with so many new five-star hotels vying for attention. Still, rooms are homey and comfortable, with Chinese touches, modern Bose speakers, big flatscreen televisions, and DVD players. Beds are plush and feature high-thread-count sheets, and bathrooms have been made fancy with white marble. One unique touch is the complimentary tea and coffee service, offered throughout the day and brought by a butler in coattails. Service is professional and unobtrusive. The health club and pool is popular with expatriates, as is the Sunday Champagne brunch. The central location, near embassies, the CBD (Central Business District), and the Forbidden City, makes this a good choice for business and leisure travelers alike.

Jianguo Men Wai Dajie 21 建国门外大街21号 (southwest of Ri Tan Park); see map p. 110. ℂ **010/6460-6688.** Fax 010/6460-3299. www.stregis.com/beijing. 273 units. ¥4,100–¥4,200 standard room; ¥4,500–¥5,000 suite, plus 15% service charge. AE, DC, MC, V. Metro: Jianguo Men. **Amenities:** 5 restaurants; bar; billiards room; butler service; cigar and wine-tasting rooms; concierge; forex; well-equipped exercise room; gorgeous indoor pool (25m/82 ft.); putting green and driving area; room service; smoke-free rooms; spa; squash courts. *In room:* A/C, satellite TV/DVD, hair dryer, Internet, minibar.

Westin Beijing Chaoyang (Jin Mao Beijing Weisiting Da Fandian) 金茂北京威斯汀大饭店 ★★

One of Beijing's newest five-star hotels, this second Westin to open in the capital offers stylish, modern rooms in a fairly central location with quick access to the airport. It was Hillary Clinton's choice when she made her first visit to China as secretary of state (the U.S. embassy is located just a few blocks away). Like most Westin hotels, the feel is overwhelmingly corporate in the public spaces, but the rooms have a nice homey touch with white orchids, Chinese artwork, and furniture accents, and bathrooms are spacious with separate tubs and showers. Some rooms have terrific views of downtown Beijing—try to book a south-facing one. A luxurious spa, along with a well-equipped gym and large swimming pool, make for standout amenities. Grange, the hotel's steakhouse, serves fine cuts of meat with delicious side orders, and the Sunday brunch is popular with expatriates.

Xinyuan Nan Lu 1 新源南路 1号; see map p. 110. ℂ **010/5922-8888.** Fax 010/5922-8999. www.westin. com/chaoyang. 550 units. ¥3,500–¥4,800 standard room/presidential suite, plus 15% service charge. AE, MC, V. Metro: Liangmaqiao. **Amenities:** 3 restaurants; bar; concierge; executive-level rooms; forex; health club; IP telephone; indoor pool; room service; smoke-free floors; spa. *In room:* A/C, satellite TV, hair dryer, minibar, Wi-Fi (for a fee).

EXPENSIVE

China World Hotel (Zhongguo Dafandian) 中国大饭店

It has a great location for business travelers and was one of the first five-star hotels in Beijing, but nowadays, after more than a decade of business, the rooms feel outdated compared to those at newer luxury hotels in town (particularly the flashy Park Hyatt, across the street). Still, the China World remains a landmark in Beijing, with a gorgeous lobby decorated with crystal chandeliers and Chinese artwork and an extensive shopping mall on the basement level. The hotel is very popular for foreign businessmen and hosts many conventions, and it sits above a major connection point for two subways, making it convenient to access other points of the city. For wine lovers, in-house restaurant Aria has about 450 bottles and sommeliers are on hand to help out with choices.

Jianguo Men Wai Dajie 1 建国门外大街1号 (at intersection with E. Third Ring Rd.); see map p. 110. ℂ **010/6505-2266.** Fax 010/6505-0828. www.shangri-la.com. 716 units. ¥2,800–¥3,000 standard room (discounts up to 60% during the low season); ¥3,300–¥3,900 suite, plus 15% service charge. AE, DC, MC, V. Metro: Guomao. **Amenities:** 4 restaurants plus several more in attached mall; concierge; executive-level rooms; forex; golf simulator; full-service health club; indoor pool (25m/82 ft.); room service; smoke-free rooms; spa with aromatherapy; 3 indoor tennis courts. *In room:* A/C, satellite TV, hair dryer, Internet, minibar, Wi-Fi (in executive rooms).

Hotel G ★ Ⓥalue   Part of the growing boutique hotel trend in Beijing, Hotel G offers stylish rooms done up in a "1960's Hollywood" glamour theme in a central location right near much of Beijing's pulsating nightlife. There's a whimsical touch, with rubber duckies near the tub and toy motorcycles decorating the rooms, which also come with all the modern technology you'll need, including an iPod dock and a flatscreen television. There's no pool, unfortunately, but a cozy gym makes up for it with extensive Technogym workout equipment, and the bar downstairs, Scarlett, features a large cheese bar with selections from Europe and many bargain-priced wines. The hotel is priced lower than many of its competitors, making it an overall value, especially if you appreciate the irreverent style over the feel of corporate hotel chains.

Gongti Xi Lu A7 工体西路A7号; see map p. 110. ℂ **010/6552-3600.** Fax 010/65523606. www.hotel-g.com. 110 units. ¥1,088–¥1,288 standard room/suite, plus 15% service charge. AE, DC, MC, V. Metro: Chaoyangmen. **Amenities:** 2 restaurants; fitness center; room service; smoke-free floors; Wi-Fi. *In room:,* A/C, satellite TV, hair dryer, minibar, MP3 docking station.

Kerry Centre Hotel (Beijing Jiali Zhongxin Fandian) 北京嘉里中心饭店 ★★ Ⓚids   Like its sister hotel, the China World, the Kerry Centre is showing signs of age, especially compared to the newer players in town. Still, it's well-regarded for its service and remains a popular choice with business travelers. Standard rooms are decorated in textured, solid colors of gold and dark green, with maroon accent pillows. Bathrooms are small and rather awkwardly laid out, with tubs jammed into the corner and toilets tucked behind the door. Executive floors have far roomier bathrooms and added luxuries like free Internet (broadband or Wi-Fi), Bose CD players, huge plasma TVs, and DVD players. They also have a great health club, including a spacious gym with the latest equipment, a 35m (115-ft.) indoor lap pool and two Jacuzzis, two indoor tennis courts, and even a short outdoor jogging path. Their restaurant Horizon is popular for its scrumptious ¥168 dim sum lunch buffet for two, and Centro has been a long-running favorite watering hole for expatriates.

Guanghua Lu 1 光华路1号 (on west side of Kerry Centre complex, north of Guomao metro); see map p. 110. ℂ **010/6561-8833.** Fax 010/6561-2626. www.shangri-la.com. 487 units. ¥1,300–¥1,450 standard room; ¥1,700–¥2,150 suite (discounts up to 50% during the low season), plus 15% service charge. AE, DC, MC, V. Metro: Guomao. **Amenities:** 2 restaurants; bar; concierge; executive-level rooms; indoor basketball/tennis/badminton courts; fitness center; forex; children's play area; indoor pool; roof-top track for running and in-line skating; room service; smoke-free floors; sun deck. *In room:* A/C, satellite TV, hair dryer, Internet, minibar.

MODERATE

A.hotel   This is a modern, minimalist hotel and a cheap alternative to nearby Hotel G or The Opposite House. The dim lighting, black-and-white curlicue wallpaper, and ambient music in the curved hallways (following the architecture of the Worker's Stadium, where the hotel is located) remind us of a hip bar lounge—soothing and mildly stimulating at the same time. Bathrooms are a bit on the small side, but they come with sleek rain showers. Rooms have big windows and are decorated in neutral tones of beige, cream, and white with maroon accents here and there and chic monochrome photos on the walls. The location is excellent, a quick walk from Sanlitun and literally around the corner from the Worker's Stadium's bars and restaurants, but because the hotel is actually *in* the stadium complex, you may have to deal with the pain of uptight security during soccer matches and concerts. During such times, head straight for the east gate and the hotel should have a staff member waiting at the ready to escort you in past stadium security.

East Gate of Worker's Stadium 6 Tai 工人体育场6台; see map p. 110. ✆ **010/6586-5858.** Fax 010/6507-8468. www.a-hotel.com.cn. 116 units. ¥400–¥650 standard room; ¥1,788 suite. AE, MC, V. Metro: Tuanjiehu, 3 long blocks west, or Dongsi Shitiao, 3 long blocks east. **Amenities:** Restaurant. *In room:* A/C, TV, fridge, hair dryer, Internet, minibar.

Traders Hotel Beijing (Guomao Fandian) 国贸饭店   The greatest advantage to staying in this efficient and well-run Shangri-La four-star hotel is access to the five-star health club facilities in the China World Hotel next door. (These two sister hotels are joined by an underground shopping center.) Otherwise, Traders is a straightforward business hotel, with slightly cramped and plain but nicely outfitted rooms, unobtrusive service, and easy access to the metro. The only major drawback is the tiny bathrooms. The West Wing has the slightly nicer (and more expensive) rooms.

Jianguo Men Wai Dajie 1 建国门外大街1号 (behind China World Hotel); see map p. 110. ✆ **010/6505-2277.** Fax 010/6505-0838. www.shangri-la.com. 560 units. ¥1,250–¥1,350 standard room; ¥1,550–¥1,970 suite, plus 15% service charge. AE, DC, MC, V. Metro: Guomao. **Amenities:** 2 restaurants; bar; concierge; executive-level rooms; forex; small exercise room; Jacuzzi; room service; sauna; smoke-free rooms. *In room:* A/C, satellite TV, hair dryer, Internet, minibar.

INEXPENSIVE

Zhaolong Qingnian Lǚguan 兆龙青年旅馆   The Zhaolong, despite its location in the Sanlitun bar area, is a quiet alternative to the madness of its better-known cousin, Poacher's. Most guests are Chinese backpackers or foreigners conversant in Chinese. Doors close at 1am to discourage revelers. Twins and dorms are simple and clean; neither has an in-room bathroom, but common showers are adequate. Facilities are minimal. Proximity to the East Third Ring Road means convenient bus access to all parts of town.

Gongti Bei Lu 2 工体北路2号 (behind Great Dragon Hotel); see map p. 110. ✆ **010/6597-2299,** ext. 6111. Fax 010/6597-2288. www.hihostels.com. 50 units. ¥60 dorm beds; ¥160–¥180 standard room; ¥300 2-bed suite. AE, DC, MC, V. Bus: no. 115 from Dong Si Shi Tiao metro to Nongzhanguan. **Amenities:** Bar; access to indoor pool and sauna. *In room:* A/C, no phone.

---

5 BEIJING SOUTH

EXPENSIVE

The Grand Mercure (Xidan Meijue Jiudian) 西单美爵酒店 ★ Ⓥalue   Although not among the main clusters of foreign hotels, this hotel is as close to the center of things as any of them, and is quieter and better connected than most. (The location—just south of the no. 1 Line's Xi Dan station and north of the Circle Line's Xuanwu Men station—enables guests to get in and out during the worst of rush hour.) The lobby, sumptuously decorated with white marble and gold friezes, is stylish yet of a modest enough scale to suggest the atmosphere of a discreet boutique hotel. The medium-size rooms are well-appointed, although bathrooms are somewhat cramped. Cafe Marco features buffet or a la carte dishes from the Mediterranean, Middle East, Southeast Asia, and China in honor of the routes the great traveler took himself.

Xuanwu Men Nei Dajie 6 宣武门内大街6号 (south of Xi Dan metro stop); see map p. 114. ☎ **010/6603-6688.** Fax 010/6603-1481. www.accorhotels.com. 296 units. ¥2,080 standard room (discounts up to 70% during the low season), plus 15% service charge. AE, DC, MC, V. Metro: Xi Dan. **Amenities:** 2 restaurants; bar; concierge; executive-level rooms; fitness center; forex; indoor pool; room service. *In room:* A/C, satellite TV, hair dryer, Internet (for a high fee), minibar.

Holiday Inn Central Plaza (Zhonghuan Jiari Jiudian) 中环假日酒店 ★★ ⓥ Value

This site was right in the middle of things during the Jin dynasty (1122–1215), but there's nothing central nowadays about the location of this stylish hotel. However, if you're visiting Beijing to be among Chinese people, rather than pampered expatriates, we strongly recommend this hotel. InterContinental Hotels in China often present a bland, cut-price version of luxury (such as the Downtown and Lido Holiday Inns), but this Zen-like hotel is a startling exception. Credit must be given to the local designer, who has achieved the architectural Holy Grail: minimalism without coldness. Service is equally to the point. Set in a residential area, Beijing's Muslim quarter is a short walk to the east, a lively strip of restaurants near Baoguo Si lie to the north, and it's also handy to both of Beijing's main railway stations.

Caiyuan Jie 1 菜园街1号; see map p. 114. ☎ **800/830-6368** or 010/8397-0088. Fax 010/8355-6688. www.holidayinn.com.cn. 322 units. ¥1,660 standard room, plus 15% service charge (discounts up to 50% during the low season). AE, DC, MC, V. Bus: no. 395 from Changchun Jie metro. **Amenities:** 2 restaurants; cafe; bar; concierge; executive-level rooms; forex; well-equipped exercise room; indoor pool; room service; yoga room. *In room:* A/C, satellite TV, hair dryer, Internet, minibar.

MODERATE

City Central Youth Hostel (Chengshi Qingnian Jiudian) 城市青年酒店 ★★ ⓥ Value

Housed in the old post office building, this newly opened hostel-cum-hotel has an unbeatable location directly opposite Beijing railway station. The manager was inspired by a visit to Sydney Central YHA, and has attempted to create a replica here. Standard rooms on the fifth and sixth floor are minimalist and clean, with none of the sleaze associated with other railway hotels (such as the nearby Howard Johnson, whose rooms now sport point-and-choose menus of massage girls), and at a fraction of the expense. Ask for a room on the north side, facing away from the railway station square. Dorm rooms on the fourth floor have double-glazed windows and comfortable bunk beds, but squat toilets are a surprise for the less limber.

Beijing Zhan Qian Jie 1 北京站前街1号; see map p. 114. ☎ **010/6525-8066.** Fax 010/6525-9066. www.centralhostel.com. ¥288 standard room; dorm beds from ¥110. Discounts on dorm beds for YHA members. No credit cards. Metro: Beijing Zhan. **Amenities:** Bar; bike rental; billiards and movie room; Internet; kitchen; supermarket. *In room:* A/C, TV, Internet.

Harmony Hotel (Huameilun Jiudian) 华美伦酒店

A stone's throw from Beijing Railway Station, this small and slightly tattered three-star is ideal for those arriving late from the station or looking to catch an early train. Rooms are small for the price and renovations long overdue; however, staff is friendly, and after years of struggling to comprehend the broad accents of Intrepid Tours groups, their English is passable. "Luxury" rooms *(haohua jian)* are nearly double the size of standard rooms and come with bathtubs—well worth the extra ¥100. Ask for a quieter room on an upper floor facing the west side, as the railway area is predictably rowdy.

(Finds) In the Red Lantern District

Southwest of Qian Men, beyond the mercantile madness of Da Zhalan, is where you'll find the remains of Beijing's once-thriving brothel district, **Ba Da Hutong** (eight great lanes). Prior to the Communists' elimination of prostitution in the 1950s (and its rapid reemergence since the 1980s), government officials, foreign diplomats, and other men of means would come here to pay for the pleasures of "clouds and rain."

The transaction was not always lurid. The women were closer to courtesans, akin to Japanese geishas, and their customers often paid simply for conversation and cultured entertainment. Popular guidebooks were published advising on the etiquette for wooing courtesans. Although the promise of another brand of entertainment always lurked in the background, and many of the women who worked south of Qian Men were kidnapped from other provinces, the dynamic was not half as base as its modern counterpart's.

Many wonderful old bordellos still stand, although local tour groups are forbidden to take tourists to the area or even mention it. Most buildings were converted into apartments or stores, but a few were restored and turned into cheap hotels. While those who can afford it will prefer to stay in a more luxurious hotel farther north, travelers on a budget would be hard-pressed to find affordable accommodations with so much character.

Among the best restored of the old brothels is **Shanxi Xiang Di'er Binguan** 陕西巷第二宾馆 (© **010/6303-4609**), at the north end of Shanxi Xiang (once home to the most upmarket bordellos), a poorly marked and malodorous lane a few minutes' walk south of Da Zhalan. As with most buildings of its kind, it is recognizable by its multistory height (rare in a neighborhood made up of single-floor houses) and by the glass that divides its roof, designed to let light into the central courtyard while blocking an outsider's view of the activities taking place inside. Far nicer than the late-night barber shops and karaoke parlors where Beijing's working girls now do business, the hotel is spacious and lavishly decorated, with red columns and walls supporting colorfully painted banisters and roof beams, the latter hung with traditional lanterns. The rooms, arranged on two floors around the courtyard, are tiny and windowless, as befit their original purpose, but now have air-conditioning, TVs, and bathrooms for ¥100 per night. From the Hepingmen subway station, walk south on Nan Xinhua Jie for 1km (less than 1 mile), turn left on Zhu Shikou Xi Dajie, and then make a left at the second alley, Shanxi Xiang.

WHERE TO STAY

5

BEIJING SOUTH

Suzhou Hutong 59苏州胡同59号 (from Beijing Zhan metro walk west, taking the 1st right onto Youtong Jie and continuing for 100m/328 ft. northwest); see map p. 114. © **010/6528-5566.** www.harmony hotelbeijing.cn. Fax 010/6559-9011. 122 units. ¥788 standard room (discounts up to 25% during the low season). AE, DC, MC, V. Metro: Beijing Zhan. **Amenities:** Restaurant; cafe; bike rental; concierge; forex. *In room:* A/C, TV, fridge, minibar.

INEXPENSIVE

Far East Youth Hostel (Yuandong Qingnian Lǜshe) 远东青年旅社 ★ (Finds)

Buried deep inside one of the city's most interesting *hutong* neighborhoods, but only a 10-minute walk from both the Heping Men and Qian Men metro stations, the Far East offers comfortable rooms at competitive rates. Even the hallways—partly adorned with faux brick and latticed, dark wood panels—are pleasant. The hostel maintains cheaper dorms behind a courtyard house across the street, but those in the main building are far better. The Far East makes a good choice even if you usually stay at midrange places.

Tieshu Xie Jie 113铁树斜街113号 (south of Liulichang); see map p. 114. © **010/5195-8561,** ext. 3118. Fax 010/6301-8233. 110 units. ¥328 standard room (often discounted to ¥200); ¥45–¥70 dorm bed. AE, DC, MC, V. Metro: Heping Men. **Amenities:** Restaurant; bike rental; Internet; kitchen. *In room:* AC, TV, fridge.

Feiying Binguan 飞鹰宾馆

The Feiying became one of the top budget options in the city after completing a top-to-bottom refurbishment in 2002 and joining Youth Hostelling International. It's the most "hotel-like" YHA you'll find. Standard rooms are bright and well equipped with low, slightly hard twin beds; bathrooms have proper tubs. Dorms are also nice, with in-room bathrooms and brand-new floors. The hotel's best feature is its location, just east of the Changchun Jie metro stop and next to several useful bus stops.

Xuanwu Men Xi Dajie 10 宣武门西大街10号 (down alley east of Guohua Market); see map p. 114. © **010/6317-1116.** Fax 010/6315-1165. www.yhachina.com. 46 units. ¥158–¥488 standard room; ¥60 dorm bed. Discounts for YHA members. No credit cards. Metro: Changchun Jie. **Amenities:** Bar; Internet; kitchen; small convenience store. *In room:* A/C, TV.

6 BEIJING WEST, HAIDIAN & YAYUN CUN

VERY EXPENSIVE

Aman Beijing (Beijing Anman Wenhua Jiudian) 北京安曼文化酒店 ★★★

Known as one of the most luxurious resort chains in Asia, the Aman has arrived in Beijing in style. Abutting the Summer Palace on the outskirts of Beijing, the resort is the perfect place to relax and unwind while absorbing many of the historical sites in the area. Traditional courtyard structures which once housed the imperial kitchen of the Summer Palace have been converted into gorgeous, spacious rooms with wood floors, three-story-high ceilings, and classic Ming-style furniture. The resort makes good use of its location next to the palace where Qing emperors summered; not only are morning tai chi classes offered in the Summer Palace, but guests can access the historical site anytime through a private backdoor entrance. The resort also features a world-class spa, a movie theater with plush armchairs, and a Pilates studio. Foodies will enjoy the choice cuts of meat offered at the **Grill** (p. 101) and the Japanese *kaiseki* (multi-course) cuisine restaurant, both of which feature outstanding wine selections from the resident "cellar master."

Gongmenqian Lu 15宫门前路15号; see map p. 116. © **010/5987-9999.** Fax 010/5987-9900. www. amanresorts.com. 51 rooms. ¥3,740–¥4,420 guest room/courtyard, plus 15% service charge. AE, DC, MC, V. **Amenities:** 3 restaurants; bar; cinema; concierge; executive-level rooms; forex; health club; indoor pool; room service; smoke-free floors; spa; Wi-Fi. *In room:* A/C, satellite TV, hair dryer, minibar.

Ritz-Carlton, Financial Street (Jinrong Jie Lijia Jiudian) 金融街丽嘉酒店 ★★

Though this hotel caters to a corporate clientele, the place is decorated with homey touches, as if run by a Chinese version of Martha Stewart. The beds are the comfiest in town, and spacious marble bathrooms come with his-and-her sinks and televisions anchored in front of the bathtub. The basement health club and spa are top-notch, with a luxurious swimming pool that features a giant television screen on one wall and lounge chairs imbedded in the pool that deliver water jet massages. Upgrading to an executive room gives you access to a 24-hour club lounge that serves a steady stream of delicious bites and drinks throughout the day, plus free Wi-Fi. Be sure to dine in **Cepe** (p. 102), which serves the city's best upscale Italian fare. The only drawback is the location, which isn't particularly central, even though it's an up-and-coming business district. The hotel is attached to a chic new shopping center.

Jinchengfang Dong Jie 1 金城坊东街1号 (next to the National Security Council Building); see map p. 116. ✆ 010/6601-6666. Fax 010/6601-6029. www.ritzcarlton.com. 253 units. ¥4,500–¥5,000 standard room; ¥7,500–¥8,000 suite (discounts up to 60% during the low season), plus 15% service charge. AE, MC, V. Metro: Fuxing Men. Amenities: 3 restaurants; bar; babysitting; concierge; executive-level rooms; fitness center; forex; Jacuzzi; indoor pool; room service; sauna; spa. *In room:* A/C, satellite TV, hair dryer, minibar, scale, Wi-Fi.

The Westin Beijing, Financial Street (Wei Si Ting Da Jiu Dian) 威斯汀大酒店 ★ (Kids)

The Westin caters to business travelers and families, who will find a resortlike atmosphere smack in the middle of Beijing's financial district. The Westin's standard rooms are decorated plainly in wood, gray, and beige tones but come with luxurious amenities, complete with marble bathrooms with large tubs, flatscreen TVs, Bose radios, and beds so comfortable they're trademarked "The Heavenly Bed." Upgrade to a "relaxation" room, and a bathologist will come to your room to draw you a personalized bath. There's also a spa on the premises that features Chinese reflexology treatments. The hotel has one of Beijing's few poolside bars. A kids' center with babysitting entertains the little ones and gives parents a break.

Jin Rong Dajie Yi 9 金融大街乙9号; see map p. 116. ✆ 010/6606-8866. Fax 010/6606-8899. www.starwood hotels.com. 486 units. ¥2,900 standard room (discounts up to 55% during the low season), plus 15% service charge. AE, DC, MC, V. Metro: Fuxing Men. **Amenities:** 3 restaurants; bar; executive-level rooms; fitness center; forex; indoor pool; room service; sauna; smoke-free floor; Wi-Fi. *In room:* A/C, satellite TV, hair dryer, Internet, minibar.

EXPENSIVE

Crowne Plaza Park View Wuzhou (Wuzhou Huangguan Jiari Jiudian) 五洲皇冠假日酒店 (Kids)

From a feng shui perspective, the Wuzhou is unbeatable. It lies close to the north-south axis that runs through the Forbidden City. Far from the expatriate ghettos, the surrounding area has considerable appeal: Yayun Cun is a (relatively) pedestrian-friendly residential area with some of Beijing's best Chinese restaurants (see chapter 6). Within the striking white edifice, you'll find a very North American brand of luxury: *USA Today* delivered to your door and the inevitable Brazilian restaurant. It's all comfortable enough, but we find it a bit bland. Little luxuries are lacking, and service can be indifferent. It's worth upgrading to a "luxury" *(haohua)* room, as bathrooms in the "superior" *(gaoji)* rooms are a bit poky.

Bei Si Huan Lu 4 北四环路4号 (northwest of Anhui Qiao on the N. Fourth Ring Rd.); see map p. 116. ✆ 800/830-8998 or 010/8498-2288. Fax 010/8499-2933. www.crowneplaza.com. 478 units. ¥1,900 luxury rooms (discounts up to 25% during the low season), plus 15% service charge. AE, DC, MC, V. Bus: no. 803 from Anding Men metro. **Amenities:** 3 restaurants; bar; concierge; executive-level rooms; exercise room; forex; Jacuzzi; indoor pool; room service; sauna. *In room:* A/C, satellite TV, hair dryer, Internet, minibar.

Shangri-La Beijing (Xianggelila Fandian) 香格里拉饭店 ★★

It looks like a pair of drab office towers from the outside, but the Shangri-La is one of the most well-regarded hotel chains in China. Standard rooms in the older tower are comfortable, but slightly worn—for an extra ¥500, it's worthwhile to upgrade to the Valley Wing, a luxurious tower of new executive rooms decorated in elegant muted beige tones, with access to an indulgent lounge with free breakfast, afternoon cocktails, and canapés. The bathrooms feature large his-and-hers sinks, marble bathrooms, and L'Occitane products. The Chi Spa, one of the most luxurious in the city, offers pricey massages and facials in a calming Tibetan atmosphere. Although off by itself in the northwest, the hotel benefits by having space for a large and lush garden (which includes an outdoor bar and pond), easy access to the Summer Palaces and the Western Hills, and quick routes around Beijing via the Third and Fourth ring roads.

Zizhuyuan Lu 29 紫竹院路29号 (northwest corner of Third Ring Rd.); see map p. 116. ℂ **010/6841-2211.** Fax 010/6841-8002. www.shangri-la.com. 657 units. ¥1,050–¥1,150 standard room (discounts up to 25% during the low season); ¥1,480–¥1,800 Valley Wing rooms, plus 15% service charge. AE, DC, MC, V. **Amenities:** 3 restaurants (including Blu Lobster, p. 102); bar; concierge; executive-level rooms; forex; health club with sauna; indoor pool; room service; smoke-free rooms; solarium. *In room:* A/C, satellite TV, hair dryer, minibar, Wi-Fi .

MODERATE

Beijing Marriott West (Beijing Jinyu Wanhao Jiudian) 北京金域万豪酒店 ★
The first full-fledged Marriott in Beijing, this hotel offers good value after the discount, although the location is far from the major sights. The structure was originally an apartment building before Marriott took over, so rooms are immense. Eighty percent have Jacuzzi tubs and all include sumptuous beds and overstuffed chairs. Guests have free access to the attached Bally fitness center.

Xi San Huan Bei Lu 98 西三环北路98号 (in Jinyu Dasha, at intersection with Fucheng Lu); see map p. 116. ℂ **010/5993-6699.** Fax 010/5993-6560. www.marriotthotels.com/bjsmc. 155 units. ¥950–¥1,150 standard room; ¥1,450–¥1,750 suite, plus 15% service charge. AE, DC, MC, V. **Amenities:** Restaurant; bar; bowling center; concierge; executive-level rooms; forex; health club with indoor pool; room service; smoke-free rooms; tennis courts. *In room:* A/C, satellite TV, hair dryer, minibar.

Marco Polo Parkside (Zhongao Mage Boluo Jiudian) 中奥孛罗酒店 ★★
The Olympics National Stadium is about a 5-minute walk away from this swank new hotel. Marble entranceways lead the way to plush carpets, generous-sized bathrooms with separate shower units, and chic dark wood furniture. Even the decor is slick, with chocolate brown textured velour bed throws and subtle silk-screens. In deluxe rooms, an almond-shaped bathtub sits next to a huge glass window marking the boundary between the bedroom and the bathroom. Too scandalous? Don't worry, the press of a button sends down an electronic curtain. Get a room facing west to see the National Stadium just visible beyond the neighboring high-rises. Staff are overeager, though still a little unsure of themselves.

Anli Lu 78安立路78号 (next to Olympic Green, 1km/²/₃ mile from the National Stadium). ℂ **010/5963-6688.** Fax 010/5963-6500. www.marcopolohotels.com. 315 units. ¥800–¥1,500 superior/deluxe room, plus 15% service charge. AE, DC, MC, V. Metro: Olympic Park. **Amenities:** 3 restaurants; bar; concierge; executive-level rooms; forex; health club; indoor pool; room service; smoke-free floors; spa. *In room:* A/C, satellite TV, hair dryer, Internet, minibar.

INEXPENSIVE

Red Lantern House 红灯笼客栈西院 ★
Though technically on the west side of town, this sprawling backpacker's hotel, located in a traditional courtyard dwelling, is still quite central to many of Beijing's main sites. Another draw is that it's in a local neighborhood, away from most touristy or expatriate areas, giving it an authentic feel. Rooms vary

Airport Hotels

Plenty of hotels, all with free shuttle services, are located near the airport. The most pleasant choice is the new **Hilton Hotel (Xierdun Jiudian)** 希尔顿酒店 (✆ **010/6448-8888;** fax 010/6458-8889; www.hilton.com), right next to Beijing's sparkling Terminal 3 Airport, where most international flights arrive and depart. The **Sino-Swiss Hotel (Guodu Dafandian)** 北京国都大饭店 ★ (✆ **010/6456-5588;** fax 010/6456-1588; www.sino-swisshotel.com) contains large rooms with two queen-size beds for around ¥856 after discount. It has a pleasant resort-style pool complex, and regular shuttles go to the airport (every 30 min. 6:15am–10:45pm) and downtown. Farther from the airport, in northern Chaoyang, the **Holiday Inn Lido (Lidu Jiari Fandian)** 丽都假日饭店 (✆ **010/6437-6688;** fax 010/6437-6237; http://beijing-lido.holiday-inn.com) is part of an extensive complex with foreign restaurants and shops. Standard rooms are large but in dire need of refurbishment (¥1,300 after discount), and the coffee served with breakfast is vile. Right near the Lido, and a 20-minute drive away from the airport, is the new **Traders Upper East Hotel (Shangdong Chengmao Fandian)** 上东盛贸饭店 ★ (✆ **010/5907-8888;** fax 010/5907-8808; www.shangri-la.com), part of the well-respected Shangri-La hotel chain. The hotel has a good restaurant, Wu Li Xiang, offering regional Chinese dishes.

in size, with the smallest being very small and cramped—be sure to check out the room before you put down your money. However, there is plenty of space in the central garden and in the dining area to laze about and take advantage of the complimentary Wi-Fi. Guests are mostly young and friendly Americans and Europeans. Be sure to specify if you want an en-suite bathroom; otherwise, you'll be using the communal toilets.

Zhengjue Hutong 5, Xinjiekou Nan Dajie. 新街口南大街正觉胡同; see map p. 116. ✆ **010/8328-5771.** Fax 010/8322-9477. www.redlanternhouse.com. 68 units. ¥50–¥330 dorm rooms; ¥140–¥280 private rooms. No credit cards. Metro: Jishuitan or Ping'anli. **Amenities:** 3 restaurants; airport transfers; bike rentals; Internet-ready computers; large lounge; luggage storage; TV/DVD; Wi-Fi. *In room:* A/C, lockers.

Where to Dine

by Jen Lin-Liu

When I first moved to Beijing in 2000, I approached each meal with caution. Menus were a minefield—dishes with beautiful, literary names would arrive at the table in the form of duck tongues, fungus, and offal. Chefs, after being deprived of basic staples for decades, were newly liberated to douse dishes with as much oil and MSG as they wanted. During my first Sichuanese meal, I bit into a Sichuan peppercorn, which numbed my mouth like a shot of Novocain at a dentist's office.

Thankfully, the dining scene in Beijing—along with my taste buds—have changed dramatically in the past decade. I've gradually come to appreciate all kinds of new textures and flavors after living in Beijing for the past nine years; meanwhile, the dining scene has become more sophisticated and upscale. (If you're interested in reading more about my eating adventures, you can pick up my food memoir, *Serve the People: A Stir-Fried Journey Through China.*)

As the capital of China and a growing international city, Beijing these days offers a huge range of cuisines to satisfy a wide range of budgets, whether you want to spend ¥5 or ¥5,000—and whether you're craving dim sum, Persian cuisine, or world-class French fare. A typical dinner for two at a nice restaurant costs under ¥200, but prices can go much lower with little to no drop in quality.

Plenty of hole-in-the-wall eateries still exist, which serve top-notch home-style Chinese cuisine, as well, and I recommend you visit these places in addition to dining at the city's more celebrated restaurants. Hygiene standards are improving, and so

long as you take care to eat hot dishes that have just come off the wok, it's unlikely that you'll get sick. (Though it's always a good idea to make sure your Hepatitis A shots are up-to-date.)

Beijing has a few local dishes that are worth trying: dumplings, hot pot, and Peking duck. While these mainstays remain popular, it seems that every few years, a new "hot" regional cuisine trend sweeps the city. A decade ago, it was Cultural Revolution nostalgia dishes, then yuppified minority food from Yunnan, and now it's fiery Sichuanese dishes served in upscale dining rooms. Each leaves its mark on the culinary landscape after it has passed, making it possible for visitors to sample authentic dishes from nearly every corner of the country. (For a summary of the most popular cuisines, see the box "The Cuisines," below.)

You don't need to feel guilty about eating non-Chinese cuisine in Beijing these days—there's much more to choose from other than McDonald's and KFC. (And, actually, KFC serves a pretty decent Peking duck wrap.) Vietnamese cuisine has become very trendy, along with upscale French cuisine, Spanish tapas, and Japanese sushi bars. And if you're feeling like a homesick American, there is always Subway, Sizzler, and even Outback Steakhouse.

Main courses in almost every non-Western restaurant are placed in the middle of the table and shared between two or more people. The "meal for two" price estimates in this chapter include two individual bowls of rice and between two and four dishes, depending on the size of the portions, which tends to decrease as prices rise.

The Cuisines

China has between 4 and 10 seminal cooking styles, depending on whom you ask, but regional permutations, minority contributions, and specialty cuisines like Buddhist-influenced vegetarian and medicinal dishes push the number into the dozens. Most of these have at least passed through Beijing since privately owned restaurants really took off in the 1980s. Below are summaries of the most consistently popular styles, as well as the cuisines du jour, which may or may not be around the next time you visit:

Beijing   This ill-defined cuisine was influenced over the centuries by the different eating habits of successive rulers. Emphasis is on lamb and pork, with strong, salty, and sometimes musky flavors. Staples are heavy noodles and breads rather than rice. *Jiaozi*, little morsels of meat and vegetables wrapped in dough and usually boiled, are a favorite local snack.

Cantonese   The most famous Chinese cooking style, Cantonese tends to be light and crisp, with pleasing combinations of salty and sweet, elaborate presentations, and a fondness for rare animal ingredients at the high end. As with Sichuanese food, real Cantonese puts its American version to shame. It's available in swanky and proletarian permutations.

Home-Style (Jiachang Cai)   The most pervasive style in Beijing, home-style food consists of simplified dishes from a variety of regions, primarily Sichuan. It is cheap, fast, and gloriously filling, with straightforward flavors that run the gamut. This is the Chinese equivalent of down-home American cooking, but far healthier and more colorful.

Huaiyang   This ancient style from the lower reaches of the Yangtze River (Chang Jiang) is celebrated for delicate knife work and light, slightly sweet fish dishes. Vegetarian dishes often make interesting use of fruit. The tendency here is to braise and stew rather than stir-fry.

Credit cards are generally accepted in most restaurants above the moderately priced level. Hotels frequently levy a 15% service charge, but free-standing restaurants seldom do. Tips are not necessary; waitresses will often come running out into the street to give your money back if you try to leave one.

Restaurants in this chapter are a mix of established favorites and new, exciting restaurants mostly located in the core of the city. Beijing's enthusiasm for the wrecking ball can sometimes take down even the most venerable of eating establishments,

but new worthies inevitably rise to fill the gap. Most restaurants that cater to foreign clientele are located in Chaoyang, but excellent establishments exist all over the city. The most picturesque spot to dine in Beijing is around the Back Lakes, north of Bei Hai Park, an area of well-preserved *hutong* (narrow lanes) and idyllic man-made lake promenades that is home to several of the city's most compelling eateries.

Note: For more tips and a menu guide to the city's most popular dishes, see chapter 14.

Shanghai These richly sweet, oil-heavy dishes are no longer as trendy as they were a few years ago, but are still easy to find. Shanghainese food tends to be more expensive than fare from Sichuan or Beijing, but affordable Shanghai-style snack shops dot the city. Best are the varieties of *baozi,* or bread dumplings.

Sichuan The most popular of the pure cuisines in Beijing, real Sichuanese is far more flavorful than the "Szechuan" food found in the United States. Main ingredients are vividly hot peppers, numbing black peppercorns, and garlic, as found in classics like *gongbao jiding* (diced chicken with chilies and peanuts). Spicy Sichuan-style hot pot is the city's best interactive food experience.

Southern Minority Cuisine and rare ingredients from Naxi-dominated regions of Yunnan Province are especially fashionable, but Hakka, Dai, Miao, and other ethnic traditions are also well represented. This is some of the city's most interesting food right now, but also its most inconsistent and overpriced.

Uighur Uighur cooking is the more distinctive of Beijing's two Muslim styles (the other being Hui), with origins in remote Xinjiang Province. The cuisine is heavy on lamb and chicken and is justly adored for its variety of thick noodles in spiced tomato-based sauces. Uighurs produce the city's favorite street snack: *yangrou chuan,* roasted lamb skewers with cumin and chili powder.

Vegetarian An increasingly diverse style, the Beijing version of vegetarian cuisine is moving away from its previous obsession with soy- and taro-based fake meat dishes. Decor and quality vary from restaurant to restaurant, but none allows smoking or booze.

The price ranges in the reviews below reflect the following equivalents, in terms of price per person: Very Expensive ($$$$) = ¥400 and up; Expensive ($$$) = ¥200–¥400; Moderate ($$) = ¥100–¥200; Inexpensive ($) = under ¥100.

1 BEST DINING BETS

- **Best Peking Duck:** Chef Dong of **Beijing Da Dong Kaoya Dian** has made a name for himself with his light, crisp, and flavorful duck, which comes with an array of condiments, including sugar and garlic, and new fusion dishes that don't lose sight of the fundamentals of Chinese cooking. See p. 94.
- **Best Sichuan:** Chaotic and crowded, **Chuan Jing Ban Canting,** a restaurant owned by the Sichuan Provincial Government, is the most authentic place for spicy, numbing Sichuanese cuisine in the capital. There's usually a 30-minute wait for dinner, so come

either early or late and be sure to order plenty of beer with your meal to cool your tongue. If you prefer a more sedate and intimate atmosphere, try **Black Sesame Kitchen,** which serves the city's best kung pao chicken. See p. 90 and 87, respectively.

- **Best Inventive Cuisine:** Beijing's dining scene is on the whole conservative by international standards, and the experimental restaurants veer into truly weird and undesirable territory (for instance, Whale Inside, which serves food in a pitch-black dining room). For inventive cuisine that's actually appetizing, your best bets are **Agua,** serving Spanish tapas with an array of textures and temperatures, and **Beijing Da Dong Kaoya Dian,** which features stellar Peking duck and artfully presented Chinese dishes. See p. 84 and 94, respectively.
- **Best Hot Pot:** Classy hot pot can be found at **Ding Ding Xiang,** where the Chinese fondue comes in individual-serving pots for diners who'd rather not take the family-style route. Fresh vegetables, an addictive dipping sauce, and yummy steamed buns make this the best hot pot place in town. See p. 98.
- **Best Noodles:** Available in dozens of shapes and sauces, Shanxi-style noodles at the fashionable and aptly named **Noodle Loft** are among the most satisfying in Beijing, and without the crimes of hygiene perpetrated by the more typical noodle joints. See p. 98.
- **Best Karma** (Vegetarian): **Pure Lotus** offers delicious veggie fare in a stylish environment—visit the Holiday Inn Lido location for a particularly meditative, dimmed atmosphere that's perfect for dinner. See p. 96.
- **Best European: Maison Boulud,** a restaurant of New York Chef Daniel Boulud, has brought world-class French cuisine—housed in the former neoclassical American Embassy—to Beijing. See p. 85.
- **Best Asian** (non-Chinese): Stylish decor and stunning sushi make **Bei** the best Japanese option in Beijing. See p. 92.
- **Best Quintessential Beijing Setting: Dali Courtyard** has a beautiful courtyard setting and decent Yunnan (southwest Chinese) cuisine to match. See p. 88.
- **Best Decor:** If you're a fan of designer Philippe Starck, head over to **Lan** for a meal in the city's most splashy, nouveau riche Chinese atmosphere. See p. 93.
- **Best Brunch:** For a buffet extravaganza, visit the **Westin Beijing Chaoyang** for their Sunday champagne brunch, which is a great deal for its numerous stations offering everything from foie gras and sashimi to chocolate fondue and creative pastries. See p. 70.

2 RESTAURANTS BY CUISINE

American
Element Fresh (Xin Yuansu) ★ (Chaoyang, $$, p. 95)

Beijing
Beijing Da Dong Kaoya Dian ★★ (Chaoyang, $$, p. 94)
Made in China (Chang An Yi Hao) ★★ (City Center, $$$, p. 86)

Xian'r Lao Man ★ (Dong Cheng, $, p. 92)

Cantonese/Hong Kong
Le Galerie (Zhongguo Yiyuan) ★ (Chaoyang, $$, p. 95)
Lei Garden (Li Yuan) ★★ (Dong Cheng, $$, p. 89)

Key to Abbreviations: $$$$ = Very Expensive $$$ = Expensive $$ = Moderate $ = Inexpensive

Zen 1903 (Die 1903) ★ (City Center, $$$, p. 86)

Chinese
Duck de Chine (Quan Ya Ji) ★★ (Chaoyang, $$$, p. 93)

Continental/European
Blu Lobster (Lan Yun Xi Can Ting) ★★ (Haidian, $$$$, p. 102)
Capital M (Mishi Canting) ★★ (City Center, $$$, p. 85)
Vineyard (Putaoyuan'r) ★ (Dong Cheng, $$, p. 89)

Dumplings
Tianjin Bai Jiao Yuan (Beijing South, $, p. 101)
Xian'r Lao Man ★ (Dong Cheng, $, p. 92)

French
Maison Boulud (Bulu Gong Fa Canting) ★★★ (City Center, $$$$, p. 85)

Fusion
The CourtYard (Siheyuan) ★★ (City Center, $$$, p. 85)
Green T. House (Zi Yun Xuan) ★ (Chaoyang, $$$$, p. 92)
Lan ★ (Chaoyang, $$$, p. 93)
My Humble House (Dongfang Hanshe) ★★ (City Center, $$$, p. 86)

Guizhou
San Ge Guizhouren (Chaoyang, $, p. 98)

Hakka
Kejia Cai ★ (Back Lakes, $, p. 90)

Home-Style (Jiachang Cai)
Black Sesame Kitchen (Heizhima Chufang) ★ (Back Lakes, $$$, p. 87)
Huajia Yiyuan (Dong Cheng, $, p. 90)
Xiangyang Tun (Haidian, $, p. 103)
Xiao Wang Fu (Chaoyang, $$, p. 97)

Hot Pot
Ding Ding Xiang (Chaoyang, $, p. 98)
Huangcheng Lao Ma (Chaoyang, $$, p. 95)
Taipo Tianfu Shanzhen ★★ (Beijing South, $, p. 101)

Huaiyang
Kong Yiji Jiudian ★ (Back Lakes, $, p. 91)
Zhang Sheng Ji Jiudian, ★★ (Beijing West, $$, p. 103)

Indian
Taj Pavilion (Taiji Lou Yindu Canting) (Chaoyang, $$, p. 96)

Italian
Cepe (Yiwei Xuan) ★★ (Beijing West, $$$$, p. 102)

Japanese
Hatsune (Yin Quan) ★ (Chaoyang, $$, p. 95)
Yotsuba (Si Ye) ★★ (Chaoyang, $$$, p. 93)

Malaysian
Cafe Sambal ★ (Back Lakes, $$, p. 88)

Mediterranean
Sureño ★★ (Chaoyang, $$$, p. 93)

Muslim
Crescent Moon (Wan Wan Yue Liang) ★ (Dong Cheng, $, p. 90)

Northeastern
Dongbei Hu ★ (Yayun Cun, $, p. 103)
Xiangyang Tun (Haidian, $, p. 103)

Northern Asian
Bei ★ (Chaoyang, $$$$, p. 92)

Northwestern
Xibei Youmian Cun ★★ (Yayun Cun, $$, p. 102)

Persian
Rumi (Rumi) ★★ (Chaoyang, $$, p. 96)

Pizza
Hutong Pizza (Back Lakes, $$, p. 89)

Shanxi
Noodle Loft (Mian Ku Shanxi Shiyi) (Chaoyang, $, p. 98)
Xibei Youmian Cun ★★ (Yayun Cun, $$, p. 102)

Sichuan
Chuan Jing Ban Canting ★★ (Dong Cheng, $, p. 90)
Lan ★ (Chaoyang, $$$, p. 93)
Mala Youhuo ★★ (Beijing South, $, p. 100)
Source (Dujiangyuan) (Back Lakes, $$$, p. 88)
Yuxiang Renjia ★ (Chaoyang, $, p. 100)

Spanish
Agua ★★ (City Center, $$$$, p. 84)
Mare (Da Pa Shi) ★★ (Chaoyang, $$, p. 96)

Steakhouse
Aman Grill (Yihe Anman) ★★★ (Beijing West, $$$$, p. 101)

Taiwanese
Bellagio (Lu Gang Xiaozhen) (Chaoyang, $, p. 98)

Thai
Serve the People (Wei Renmin Fuwu) (Chaoyang, $$, p. 96)

Uighur
Pamer (Pami'er Shifu) ★ (Beijing South, $, p. 100)
Xiyu Shifu ★★ (Yayun Cun, $, p. 104)

Vegetarian
Baihe Sushi (Lily Vegetarian Restaurant) ★ (Beijing West, $, p. 103)
Pure Lotus (Jing Xin Lian) ★ (Chaoyang, $$, p. 96)

Vietnamese
Nuage (Qing Yun Lou) ★ (Back Lakes, $$, p. 89)

Yunnan
Dali Courtyard (Da Li) ★ (Back Lakes, $$, p. 88)
No Name Restaurant (Wu Ming Can Ting) (Back Lakes, $$, p. 89)
Yunnan Jin Kongque Dehong Daiwei Canguan (Haidian, $, p. 104)
Yunteng Binguan ★ (Beijing South, $, p. 101)

3 BEIJING CITY CENTER, AROUND WANGFUJING DAJIE

VERY EXPENSIVE

Agua ★★ SPANISH   Along with Maison Boulud, Agua is a highlight of Ch'ien Men 23, a former legation area that was recently converted into a hub of fine dining. Chef Jordi Valles often circulates around the dining room to greet his guests with an infectious energy, as he explains the processes behind making his delicious, beautiful Spanish tapas. The darkened, red-lit dining room decorated with tiles and arched ceilings makes a romantic spot for a meal, while a large patio overlooking the lawn of the legation area is the perfect place to spend a warm Beijing evening. Tapas are executed flawlessly—winners include the goose liver with red-pepper ice cream, suckling pig with apricot purée and baby onions, and a smooth pumpkin soup rumored to be a favorite of Jackie Chan's.

The wine list is reasonably priced, with a nice range of by-the-glass selections from Spain, France, Italy, and the New World.

Qianmen Dong Da Jie 23 前门东大街23号 Ch'ien Men 23, southeast corner of Tian'an Men Square; see map p. 106. ℂ 010/6559-6266. www.chienmen23.com. Reservations essential. Meal for 2 ¥1,000–¥1,200. AE, DC, MC, V. Daily 11:30am–2pm and 6–11pm. Metro: Qianmen.

Maison Boulud (Bulu Gong Fa Canting) 布鲁宫法餐厅 ★★★ FRENCH

Ever since New York celebrity chef Daniel Boulud opened his first Eastern outpost just before the 2008 Olympics, there's been little reason to go anywhere else in Beijing for French food. Housed in the former pre-1949 American embassy, Boulud's refined "soul" food gleams brilliantly amid a landscape of mediocre French restaurants in Beijing—everything at Boulud from the food to the wine list to the service to the atmosphere is top-notch. You'll find updated versions of classic dishes like coq au vin and French twists on contemporary American food like the signature "dB burger"—stuffed with foie gras and stewed short rib meat by executive chef Brian Reimer (Boulud visits Beijing several times a year to keep quality high). All of this comes at a hefty price, but you can expect to pay 25% less here than at Boulud's New York flagship, Daniel, which some would consider a bargain. If that's not enough to lure you, lunch and weekend brunch menus include set meals, which go for around ¥200.

Qianmen Dong Da Jie 23 前门东大街23号 Ch'ien Men 23; southeast corner of Tian'an Men Square; see map p. 106. ℂ 010/6559-9200. www.danielnyc.com/maisonboulud.html. Reservations essential. Meal for 2 ¥1,000–¥1,200. AE, DC, MC, V. Daily 11am–2:30pm and 6–10:30pm. Metro: Qianmen.

EXPENSIVE

Capital M (Mishi Canting) 米氏西餐厅 ★★ CONTINENTAL

Restaurateur Michelle Garnaut has used that adage about real estate—location, location, location—to her advantage, with incredible results: Capital M has a front-and-center view of Tian'an Men Square unique in all of Beijing. Though the restaurant is new to Beijing, Garnaut has already built up a loyal expat following among those who are familiar with her Hong Kong and Shanghai restaurants, M at the Fringe and M on the Bund. At the northern tip of the newly renovated Qianmen Pedestrian Street, Capital M serves up not only a gorgeous view, but a beautiful interior with terrazzo floors, steel columns, and a colorful mural by Richard Cartwright. Garnaut describes the cuisine as "comfort food" with an Australian and Middle Eastern flair; highlights include the crispy suckling pig and *fesen-jen*, an Iranian stew with braised duck leg. Weekend brunches, served with champagne and freshly baked bread, are a delicious treat. Leave room for dessert: the pavlova, an Australian meringue, is legendary.

Qianmen Pedestrian St. 2, 3/F 前门步行街2号3层 (just south of Tian'an Men Square); see map p. 106. ℂ 010/6702-2727. www.m-restaurantgroup.com. Meal for 2 ¥700–¥1,200. MC, V. Daily 11:30am–5pm and 6–10:30pm. Metro: Qianmen.

The CourtYard (Siheyuan) 四合苑 ★★ FUSION

If you read the food magazines, this may be the one Beijing restaurant you know. Owned by a Chinese-American lawyer with family roots in Beijing, the CourtYard serves admirable fare but wins the most accolades for its setting, in a restored courtyard-style house next to the Forbidden City. The house's gray brick exterior still blends with its old Beijing surroundings, but inside is a different world: modernist white and glass, with tall art-hung walls and a beckoning staircase that leads to a contemporary art gallery in the basement. The fare isn't genuine fusion; dishes are recognizably Occidental or Oriental with only a token mixing of styles, but they're delectable nonetheless. Foie gras brûlée, cashew-crusted lamb chop, and black cod with tomato marmalade are longtime favorites. The tender grilled chicken breast in lemon grass and coconut curry is superb, justifying rave reviews almost by itself. The wine list is more comprehensive and well thought out than anything this side of Hong Kong, with a surprisingly large number available by the glass. An intimate cigar lounge upstairs, furnished with leather couches, looks out across the Forbidden City's eastern moat.

Donghua Men Dajie 95 东华门大街95号 (10-min. walk, on north side of street); see map p. 106. ✆ 010/6526-8883. www.courtyardbeijing.com/home.html. Reservations essential. Meal for 2 ¥600–¥800. AE, DC, MC, V. Daily 6–10pm. Metro: Tian'an Men East; east side of Forbidden City.

Made in China (Chang An Yi Hao) 长安一号 ★★ BEIJING   This is a restaurant we regularly visit, for its fantastic Peking duck and its equally enthralling setting—a dining room placed in the middle of an open kitchen, illuminated by the occasional leaping flame from the stove. Made in China serves the capital's most palatable *dou zhi* (fermented bean purée), excellent *ma doufu* (mashed soybean), and the ubiquitous *zhajiang mian* (wheat noodles with black bean mince), a dish that has spawned its own chain of restaurants. The Peking duck is the highlight—the presentation and flavors are impeccable. There's the odd fusion twist such as foie gras with sesame pancake, and there are excellent plain dishes such as *tong hao* vegetable with rice vinegar and garlic sauce. Quite unexpected for a Chinese restaurant, Made in China does delicious desserts—the pear champagne and passion fruit sorbet packs a fruity punch. Right next door you'll find the sleek **Red Moon Bar,** perfect for an aperitif.

Dong Chang'an Jie 1 东长安街1号 (inside Grand Hyatt, p. 60); see map p. 106. ✆ 010/8518-1234, ext. 3608. Reservations essential. Meal for 2 ¥400–¥600. AE, DC, MC, V. Daily 11:30am–2:30pm and 5:30–10pm. Metro: Wangfujing.

My Humble House (Dongfang Hanshe) 东方寒舍 ★★ FUSION   There's nothing humble about this restaurant: The big players have come to town. Perched above Oriental Plaza, the dramatic light-filled atrium sports a slightly sickly bamboo forest on the north side, and a rippling pond to the south, in line with feng shui principles. The staff is relaxed and confident, there is a vast amount of space between tables, and the background music complements the experience without becoming a distraction. The superb fare is a mixture of genuine fusion and Hunan-influenced seafood dishes. The menu changes constantly, but the juicy tenderloin Angus beef with black pepper is not to be missed. If there are faults, it's the slim range of wine by the glass, and the inexperience of the bartenders, dumbfounded when asked for a dirty martini.

Dong Chang'an Jie 1 东长安街1号 (west side of Oriental Plaza, podium level); see map p. 106. ✆ 010/8518-8811. Meal for 2 ¥500–¥700. AE, DC, MC, V. Lunch 11:30am–2:30pm; afternoon tea 2:30–5:30pm; dinner 5:30–10:30pm. Metro: Wangfujing.

Zen 1903 (Die 1903) 蝶1903 ★ CANTONESE   Just around the corner from Tian'an Men Square, this Cantonese restaurant (the Chinese name is pronounced Dee-eh) makes a nice stopping point for a dim sum meal if you happen to be touring Beijing's central sites. Though it's part of the luxury complex of restaurants called Ch'ien Men 23, the prices are lower than those of its neighbors, which include Maison Boulud. Comfortable rounded banquettes in gray tones face floor-to-ceiling windows looking out at historical buildings lining Chang'an Jie—one of Beijing's main thoroughfares. Crispy pork cubes dipped in sugar and mustard make an excellent starter, while the shrimp dumplings—a dim sum fixture—are plump and covered with a delicate rice wrapper. There's

⟨Overrated⟩ Imperial Restaurants

Elaborately presented but seldom appetizing, dishes cooked in Beijing's much-hyped imperial style are one of the city's biggest scams. Famous imperial restaurants **Fang Shan Fanzhuang** in Bei Hai Park and **Li Jia Cai (Li Family Restaurant)** in the Back Lakes area are both set in picturesque surroundings but charge far too much for bad food and are therefore not included in this book. For a better dining experience in either location, pack a picnic. If you really want to drop a hundred bucks on camel paw and soup made from bird saliva, ask the concierge in your hotel to point the way. If you want to enjoy the cuisine of modern Mandarins, we recommend **Chuan Jing Ban** (p. 90) and the **Yunteng Binguan** (p. 101), the restaurants of the Sichuan and Yunnan provincial governments, respectively.

also an extensive menu of Cantonese steamed and braised dishes, including a delicious winter melon stewed with a mushroom and bamboo fungus sauce. The restaurant offers a weekend dim sum lunch buffet for a bargain price of ¥108.

Qianmen Dong Dajie 23 前门东大街23号 Ch'ien Men 23; southeast corner of Tian'an Men Square; see map p. 106. ☏ **010/6559-9608.** Reservations essential. Meal for 2 ¥400–¥1,000. AE, DC, MC, V. Daily 11am–10pm. Metro: Qianmen.

4 BACK LAKES & DONG CHENG

EXPENSIVE

Black Sesame Kitchen (Heizhima Chufang) 黑芝麻厨房 ★ HOME-STYLE   Full disclosure: Jen Lin-Liu, the co-author of this Frommer's edition, is the owner of this cooking school and private kitchen. After reviewing restaurants for years and learning how to cook in China, Jen figured out just the right formula for a restaurant of her own. Located in a residential courtyard just off of the popular alley Nan Luogu Xiang, the kitchen makes home-style Beijing and Sichuan cuisine, with an emphasis on fresh, quality ingredients (organic vegetables from a local farm are delivered weekly; the cooking oil is non-GM; the chefs use MSG only sparingly, with the permission of whoever's eating that night). The restaurant features a lofty eat-in kitchen where guests can watch all the cooking action, plus a separate lounge for a more relaxed experience. Signature dishes include pan-fried pork and pumpkin dumplings, fried shiitake mushrooms seasoned with bamboo shoots and coriander, and cashew kung pao chicken. Since Jen modeled the meals after dinner parties she held at home, wine—paired and matched with the food—is included with dinner. There's no menu, but diners can inform the kitchen ahead of time if they have any particular dietary preferences or restrictions. The kitchen runs hands-on cooking classes on Thursday and Saturday, and communal open dinners on Friday evenings seat up to 24 guests; otherwise, you may book classes or dinners daily by private appointment. Be sure to reserve early as the kitchen sometimes books several weeks in advance.

Heizhima Hutong 3 黑芝麻胡同3号旁南锣鼓乡 (just off of Nan Luogu Xiang); see map p. 106. ☏ **0/1369-147-4408.** www.blacksesamekitchen.com. Set meals ¥250–¥300 per person. No credit cards. Open for classes Thurs 11am–1:30pm and Sat 1–4pm and dinner Fri 7–10pm. Also available for private bookings. Reservations necessary. Metro: Gulou or Beixinqiao.

Cooking Schools in Beijing

A handful of cooking schools have popped up in Beijing in the past few years that put you right in front of a chopping board and stove. Aside from **Black Sesame Kitchen** (p. 87), you may want to try **Hutong Cuisine,** Dong Mianhua Hutong 15 (✆ **010/8401-4788;** www.hutongcuisine.com), or **The Hutong,** Jiudao Wan Zhong Xiang Hutong 1 (✆ **010/8915-3616;** http://thehutong.com/blog). Black Sesame Kitchen's classes are taught by professional Chinese chefs who speak to you through a translator, while Hutong Cuisine offers slightly cheaper classes taught by a home-trained chef. The Hutong offers a range of cuisines, often taught by foreign housewives. Restaurants offering cooking classes include **Bei** (p. 92), which offers sushi lessons, and **Salt,** Jiangtai Xi Lu 9, 1st Floor (✆ **010/6437-8457;** www.saltrestaurantbeijing.com), which offers creative continental cuisine classes.

Source (Dujiangyuan) 渡江源 SICHUAN   Frequented by expats, this restaurant in a Chinese courtyard is where you should go if you want to enjoy a quiet Sichuanese meal in style. The set menu, served in courses, can be hit-or-miss.

Kuanjie Nan Luogu Xiang Banchang Hutong 14 宽街南锣鼓巷板厂胡同14号 (next to Lusong Yuan hotel); see map p. 106. ✆ 010/6400-3736. Set meals ¥188–¥268 per person. AE, DC, MC, V. Daily 11am–2pm and 5–10pm. Metro: Zhangzizhong Lu.

MODERATE

Cafe Sambal ★ MALAYSIAN   Sambal embraces and surpasses all the clichés of a chic Beijing eatery. It's a cozy courtyard house decorated with antique and modern furnishings, relaxed service, and a well-balanced wine list. And then there's the food, prepared by a charming chef from Kuala Lumpur. You'll need to call a day in advance for the superb double-braised Australian lobster in *nyonya* sauce, or the incredibly fresh chili curry crab, served on a bed of curry leaves, dried shrimp, and chili paste. Try the fried four-sided bean with cashew-nut sauce, or the yogurt-based mutton curry. Don't miss the signature dish, Kapitan chicken, a mildly spicy dish with a nutty aftertaste, said to have been invented when Chinese migrants reached Penang during the Ming dynasty. The *kuih dadar,* shredded coconut fried with palm sugar and wrapped in a padang leaf roll, is delectable.

Doufu Chi Hutong 43 豆腐池胡同43号 (walk south along Jiu Gulou Dajie, it's near the corner of the 5th street on the left, marked by a red lantern); see map p. 106. ✆ 010/6400-4875. Reservations recommended for dinner. Meal for 2 ¥250–¥400. AE, DC, MC, V. Daily 11am–midnight. Metro: Gulou.

Dali Courtyard (Da Li) 大理 ★ YUNNAN   Romance, romance! Old jazz tunes play in this traditional Chinese courtyard decorated with coal furnaces and Art Deco furniture. There's no menu—the chef serves up a set meal in courses—so it's perfect for couples or small groups who want to try a range of southwestern Chinese dishes. Items include papaya salad, grilled fish, and stir-fried chicken—all fairly light and healthy. The restaurant is perfect for people who don't like the stress of ordering and would prefer to concentrate on the ambience. The food is perfectly fine, but nothing will knock you out of the courtyard.

Gulou Dong Dajie, Xiaojingchang Hutong 67 古楼东大街小经常胡同67号; see map p. 106. ✆ 010/8404-1430. www.dalicourtyard.com. Set meals ¥100–¥300 per person. AE, MC, V. Daily 11am–1:30pm and 5–10pm. Metro: Beixinqiao.

Hutong Pizza 胡同比萨 PIZZA   This hard-to-find pizzeria occupies the site of a former Buddhist nunnery and features untouched murals in the loft. There's no religious theme to the handmade thin-crust pizzas, but if you've arrived from the wilds of China, you may experience something akin to a spiritual experience. The only jarring touch is the presence of green pepper and black olives on an otherwise sublime three-cheese pizza.

Yinding Qiao Hutong 9 银锭桥胡同9号 (from Yinding Qiao walk west, taking the left fork, and then right at T-junction); see map p. 106. (C) 010/8322-8916. Meal for 2 ¥80–¥150. No credit cards. Daily 11am–11pm. Metro: Gulou.

Lei Garden (Li Yuan) 利苑 ★★ CANTONESE   Up until the recent opening of this Hong Kong chain restaurant, pickings were slim for authentic dim sum and Cantonese cuisine. But Lei Garden, regarded as one of Hong Kong's finest restaurants, has brought delicious egg tarts, pan-fried turnip cakes, and shrimp dumplings to the capital. The only drawback is that it's located in a sterile office building, but the restaurant makes up for it with stylish booths and attentive service. If you've got time for only one dim sum meal in Beijing, have it here. Book ahead, as it's often packed during the lunch rush.

Jinbao Rd. 89, Jinbao Tower 3/F 金宝街89号金宝大厦3层 (next to the Regent Hotel); see map p. 106. (C) 010/8522-1212. Meal for 2 ¥200–¥300. AE, DC, MC, V. Daily 11:30am–2pm and 5:30–9pm. Metro: Dengshikou.

No Name Restaurant (Wu Ming Can Ting) 无名餐厅 YUNNAN   The demolition of Bai Feng's much-loved No Name Bar is inevitable, but his charming new restaurant has some of its spirit. There are smart touches: Luminous inlaid stones, shimmering waterfalls, and maidenhair ferns create a soothing atmosphere. The minority-chic food is sublime; try the *nongjia shao jian ji* (spicy sautéed chicken fillet), which uses real bird's-eye chili, or the delectable grilled lemon grass fish *(daizu xiangmao cao kao yu)*, served wrapped in a lotus leaf. The finest dish is a juicy foil-wrapped beef marinated in mountain herbs *(se shao niurou)*. A range of fresh juices nicely complement the spicy fare, and the bar still makes a mean gin and tonic.

Da Jinsi Hutong 1 号大金丝胡同1号 (from Yinding Qiao head west and look for a narrow lane that soon forks right); see map p. 106. (C) 010/6618-6061. Meal for 2 ¥120–¥200. AE, MC, V. Daily 11am–midnight (kitchen closes at 11pm). Metro: Gulou.

Nuage (Qing Yun Lou) 庆云楼 ★ VIETNAMESE   Lake views from this restaurant's upstairs windows are matched only by its hallucinatory Hanoi-inspired interior. A long silver dragon snakes up the rear staircase to the main dining room, where the low light from red lanterns flickers on reed curtains and finely crafted wooden tables. The first floor has improbably stylish bathrooms, divided by an elaborate cut-glass pool, and the new rooftop section has breathtaking views of the Back Lakes. Food is not quite as impressive—portions are small and prices inflated—but there are some worthwhile gems. The grilled la lop leaf beef *(ye niurou juan)* is exquisite; and the *phô* (Vietnamese beef noodles in soup) has a smooth, flavorful broth, but at a price 10 times higher than in Vietnam. This is the closest thing Beijing has to a "hot" restaurant in the New York City sense, complete with a long-legged hostess who seems to take pleasure in turning people away. (Make reservations well in advance.) A dance club extends two floors underground.

Qian Hai Dong Yan 22 前海东沿 22号 (east of the Yinding Bridge, at the intersection of Qian Hai and Hou Hai); see map p. 106. (C) 010/6401-9581. Reservations required. Meal for 2 ¥300–¥400. Add 15% service charge for rooftop dining. AE, DC, MC, V. Daily 11:30am–2pm and 5:30–10pm. Metro: Gulou.

Vineyard (Putaoyuan'r) 葡萄院儿 ★ EUROPEAN   This is one of our favorite neighborhood haunts—the sunny outdoor patio is a great place to enjoy lunch or Sunday brunch. Their pizza is top-notch, and if you're looking for a healthy breakfast, try the granola and fresh yogurt. The cafe also has Wi-Fi access and a good wine selection. Service takes a sharp nose-dive when the restaurant gets busy, and you may find yourself repeatedly flagging down staff to get your food.

Wudaoying Hutong 31 五道营胡同31号 (just north of the Confucius temple); see map p. 106. ✆ 010/6402-7961. Meal for 2 ¥50–¥150. AE, DC, MC, V. Tues–Sun 11:30am–3pm and 6–10:30pm. Metro: Yonghegong.

INEXPENSIVE

Chuan Jing Ban Canting 川京办餐厅 ★★ ⓥ Value SICHUAN　Anyone who has dealt with Chinese officials knows that there is one topic they are all experts on: food. This constantly crowded restaurant occupies the former site of the Qing Imperial examination hall (no traces remain). It is now the headquarters of the Sichuan Provincial Government, and the masses can enjoy the fruits of their rulers' connoisseurship. The spicy *shui zhu yu* consists of sublime, tender fish floating on a bed of crisp bean sprouts, and kids will appreciate the sweet pork with rice crust (*guoba roupian*). Sichuan standards, such as *mapo doufu* (spicy tofu with chopped meat), are as authentic as the ingredients, which are flown in several times a week. The only evidence you're dining with cadres arrives later in the menu; two pages are dedicated to hard liquor and one to cigarettes.

Gongyuan Tou Tiao 5 贡院头条5号 (from metro, walk 1 block north along the Second Ring Rd., turn left into Dong Zongbu Hutong, Dong Cheng Qu); see map p. 106. ✆ 010/6512-2277. Meal for 2 ¥50–¥120. No credit cards. Daily 10:50am–2pm and 4:50–10pm. English menu. Metro: Jianguo Men.

Crescent Moon (Wan Wan Yue Liang) 弯弯月亮 ★ MUSLIM　Located down a narrow *hutong* alley, this restaurant, with a mosquelike facade, serves some of the best Xinjiang cuisine in central Beijing. Xinjiang cuisine, from northwestern China just on the border with Central Asia, specializes in lamb and mutton dishes, baked breads, and tomato-based dishes, and here the grilled lamb skewers offer huge hunks of meat and the *nang chao yangrou*, bits of lamb rendered in its own fat, is stir-fried with crisp bits of bread. Top off your meal with a pomegranate juice or fresh yogurt, or a toke on one of the hookahs for rent. The owner, a middle-aged Uighur man, can be a little pesky sometimes, but his all-female staff is gracious and accommodating.

Dongsi Liutiao 16 东四六条16号朝内北小街100米 (about 100m/328 ft. west of Chaoyang North Xiaojie); see map p. 106. ✆ 010/6400-5281. Meal for 2 ¥40–¥100. Daily 11am–11pm. Metro: Zhangzizhong.

Huajia Yiyuan 花家怡园 HOME-STYLE　The chef-owner behind this popular courtyard restaurant claims to have created a new Chinese supercuisine, assembled from the best of the country's regional cooking styles. Whether Huacai (his name for the cuisine) will ever spread beyond Beijing remains to be seen, but his long menu is one of the city's most impressive. The new restaurant is slightly less raucous than the recently demolished original, but locals still crowd around tables at night to devour heaped plates of spicy crawfish (*mala longxia*) and drink green "good for health" beer. Try the *larou douya juanbing,* a mix of spicy bacon and bean sprouts rolled in pancakes roast duck–style.

Dongzhi Men Nei Dajie 235东直门内大街235号; see map p. 106. ✆ 010/6403-0677. Meal for 2 ¥120–¥150. AE, DC, MC, V. Daily 10:30am–4:30am. Metro: Beixinqiao.

Kejia Cai 客家菜 ★ HAKKA　The Hakka, or "guest people" (*Kejiaren*), are Han who migrated southeast from central China generations ago, but never managed to integrate. Forced by discrimination to live in isolated communities in poor mountainous regions, they kept to their separate culture—and cooking traditions. A historically marginal cuisine,

6

(Moments) Dinner on the Lakes, by Candlelight

For roughly ¥400 plus the cost of food, Beijing's ancient roast-meat restaurant **Kaorou Ji** now arranges what may be the most charming dining experience in the city: a meal for up to eight people served aboard a narrow **canopied flat-bottom boat,** staffed by a lone oarsman who guides the craft in a gentle arc around the man-made serenity of Qian Hai and Hou Hai. The entire trip takes roughly 2 hours. A little extra money buys live traditional music and the opportunity to float candles in the lakes after dark falls—a cliché in the making, but who cares? The restaurant is located next to Nuage (p. 89) at Qian Hai Dong Yan 14, and a meal for two costs ¥120 to ¥160; open daily 9am to 2pm and 5 to 9pm. To make boat arrangements, call ✆ **010/6612-5717** or 010/6404-2554. *Note:* Boat-rental prices vary from season to season and will probably increase as time goes on.

Hakka food has over the past few years become the center of epicurean fashion in Beijing. The owner, a local artist, designed this space with a rustic motif: thick wood tables, stone floors, crinkled character-laden wallpaper next to patches of exposed brick, and waitresses in peasant garb. Enjoyable as the dining rooms are, it is the kitchen that keeps lines of customers winding through the door. The cooking style is hard to define vis-à-vis other cuisines available in the city, but ask regular patrons to explain the difference and most give a quick answer: It's good. The *yanju xia* (shrimp skewers served in rock salt) and *lancai sijidou* (diced green beans with ground pork) are both divine, as is the chicken with tea-mushroom soup *(chashugu bao laoji).* The one dish you'll find on every table is *mizhi zhibao luyu,* a "secret-recipe paper-wrapped fish"—tender and nearly boneless, in a sweet sauce you'll want to drink.

Southeast bank of Qian Hai 前海南沿 (50m/164 ft. north of Bei Hai Park north entrance); see map p. 106. ✆ **010/6404-2259.** Meal for 2 ¥120–¥140. No credit cards. Daily 11am–3:30pm and 5–10:30pm. Metro: Zhangzizhong Lu.

Kong Yiji Jiudian 孔乙己酒店 ★ HUAIYANG   This popular restaurant was named for the alcoholic scholar-bum protagonist of a short story by Lu Xun, the father of modern Chinese literature. It offers an enjoyable dining experience, although it is somewhat weighed down by its own popularity. Service is not what it once was. A small bamboo forest leads to a traditional space outfitted with calligraphy scrolls, traditional bookshelves, and other trappings of Chinese scholarship. The menu, written vertically in the old style, features several hair-raising dishes, including the infamous *zuixia* (drunken shrimp), served still squirming in a small glass bowl filled with wine. Less shocking, and highly recommended, are the *mizhi luyu,* a whole fish deep-fried and then broiled in tin foil with onions in a slightly sweet sauce; and the *youtiao niurou,* savory slices of beef mixed with pieces of fried dough. Nearly everyone orders a small pot of *Dongpo rou,* extremely tender braised fatty pork swimming in savory juice, and a plate of *huixiang dou,* anise-flavored beans. Fans of Lu's story will appreciate the wide selection of *huangjiu,* a sweet "yellow" rice wine aged for several years, served in silver pots, and sipped from a special ceramic warming cup. Less crowded branches have opened at Yayun Cun (✆ **010/8480-3966**) and Dong Si Bei Dajie 322 (✆ **010/6404-0507**).

Desheng Men Nei Dajie 德胜门内大街 (next to the octagonal Teahouse of Family Fu on the northwest bank of Hou Hai); see map p. 106. ✆ **010/6618-4917.** No reservations. Meal for 2 ¥140–¥160. AE, DC, MC, V. Daily 11:30am–2pm and 5–10:30pm. Metro: Jishuitan.

Xian'r Lao Man 馅老满 ★ BEIJING/DUMPLINGS   Sixty varieties of dumplings are available at this busy neighborhood hangout, decorated with black-and-white photos of Beijing and simple Chinese antiques reproductions. With dumpling skins made from high-quality flour and innovative fillings (including cabbage and peanut, or lotus root with pork), this inexpensive restaurant is popular with foreigners and locals alike. We've personally wrapped dumplings in the kitchen as part of a cooking internship, so we can vouch for the cleanliness of the operation!

Andingmen Nei Dajie 252 安定门内大街252 号; see map p. 106. ✆ 010/6404-6944. Meal for 2 ¥40–¥80. No credit cards. Daily 11am–10:30pm. Metro: Andingmen. Another branch at Ya Yuan 5, An Hui Bei Li, ✆ 010/6497-2097.

5 CHAOYANG

VERY EXPENSIVE

Bei 北 ★ NORTHERN ASIAN   Located in the Opposite House hotel in Sanlitun, this contemporary northern Asian restaurant has brought sophistication to the neighborhood. It's a good concept—blending the cuisines of Korea, Japan, and China, given the restaurant's location in the heart of China's capital, but the dishes are hit-or-miss. The basement space is decorated with whimsical flying light bulbs, minimalist white tables, and black wooden bucket seats. Some complain that the restaurant is an example of style over substance, but a visit is worthwhile if you like sushi, which is Tokyo-quality in freshness and cut. (The scallops are lightly sweet and reminded us of the texture of the first gumdrop you ever had.) Sake pairings and creative desserts like fried strawberry *mochi* (sticky rice balls) make this a unique dining experience.

Sanlitun Lu 11 三里屯路11号 (in the basement of the Opposite House, p. 68); see map p. 110. ✆ 010/6410-5230. www.beirestaurant.com. Meal for 2 ¥400–¥500. AE, DC, MC, V. Daily 5:30–10:30pm. Metro: Dongsi Shitiao.

Green T. House (Zi Yun Xuan) 紫云轩 ★ FUSION   It strikes us as a little too precious, but this restaurant was groundbreaking when it opened in the late 1990s for bringing unique design to Beijing's restaurant scene—the problem is nowadays, ultradesigned restaurants are a dime a dozen in Beijing, making this place seem a little outdated. Large oversized chairs, tree branches, and bird cages decorate the airy dining room. If it's too much for you, try Bellagio, right next door. The restaurant's name changes from purple to green in translation, and dining at Green T. is a similarly psychedelic experience. The imaginatively prepared food is light, with tea-infused flavors, but the cuisine is beside the point. The minimalist decor and attentive service attract a fashion-conscious crowd. A branch of the restaurant, called Green T. House Living, opened in the outskirts of Beijing, but isn't really worthwhile unless you think an extra dose of pretentiousness is worth the 45-minute drive.

Gongti Xi Lu 6 工体西路6号 (a subtly marked door, on the east side of Bellagio); see map p. 110. ✆ 010/6552-8310. www.green-t-house.com.cn. Reservations essential. Dinner for 2 ¥800–¥1,200. AE, DC, MC, V. Daily 11am–2:30pm and 6pm–midnight. Metro: Dongsi Shitiao. Other location, known as Green T. House Living 紫云轩茶事, far north of the city center at Cuigezhuang Xiang Hegezhuang Cun 318 崔各庄乡合各庄村318号, ✆ 010/6434-2519, daily 11:30am–11:30pm.

EXPENSIVE

Duck de Chine (Quan Ya Ji) 全鸭季 ★★ CHINESE   There's no mistaking what the main attraction is here—duck figurines decorate the lobby while ceramic duck chopstick holders sit on the tables. The juicy Peking duck, served with a traditional sweet flour paste and sesame sauce, comes with thin, chewy pancakes and steamed sesame buns. The restaurant also features a decent selection of northern and southern Chinese dishes, along with high-priced entries like abalone and shark's fin. As expected from a restaurant that caters to the overseas Chinese crowd and diners on an expense account, Duck de Chine also features an extensive wine list. Part of a Hong Kong dining complex called 1949, this restaurant is the standout attraction of the area, which is located in a renovated factory.

Gongti Bei Lu, Courtyard 4 in 1949 The Hidden City 朝阳区工体北路4号院 (behind Pacific Century Place); see map p. 110. ✆ **010/6501-8881.** Meal for 2 ¥600. AE, DC, MC, V. Daily 11:30am–2:30pm and 6–10:30pm. Metro: Tuanjiehu.

Lan 兰 ★ SICHUAN/FUSION   This has become *the* place to be seen in Beijing among the trendy set. European Renaissance-style paintings hang on the wall, and cabinets hold wacky items like stacks of canned tuna fish and Mao memorabilia. Designed by Phillip Starck, this flagship of a popular chain of Sichuan restaurants serves decent, if overpriced, dishes. Avoid the fusion fare at all costs, and stick to the basics like the kung pao chicken.

4/F, LG Twin Towers, Jianguomenwai Dajie Yi 12 建国门外大街乙12号LG双子楼4层; see map p. 110. ✆ **010/5109-6012.** www.lan-global.com. Meal for 2 ¥400–¥600. AE, DC, MC, V. Daily 11am–11pm. Metro: Yong'anli .

Sureño ★★ Mediterranean   The menu isn't particularly flashy—it's mainly pastas, pizzas, and grilled meats—yet the atmosphere and service make it almost a fine-dining experience (by Beijing standards, at least). Located in the Opposite House hotel, this sunken dining room featuring a small outdoor garden and an open kitchen gets all the basics right, and then some. A delicious citrus-butter spread accompanies complimentary warmed flat bread, and a range of tapas-like appetizers can be enjoyed at a leisurely pace before tackling a main entree like the simple yet well-executed rack of lamb and Wagyu tenderloin. The look is contemporary, with warm orange and brown leather seats, and simple unadorned banquettes. Frequented by business travelers on expense accounts and well-heeled expatriates, this is one of Beijing's more popular upscale restaurants to open in the past year.

Sanlitun Lu 11 三里屯路11号 (in the basement of the Opposite House, p. 68); see map p. 110. ✆ **010/6410-5240.** www.surenorestaurant.com. Meal for 2 ¥400–¥800. Daily 5:30–10:30pm. AE, DC, MC, V. Metro: Dongsi Shitiao.

Yotsuba (Si Ye) 四叶 ★★ JAPANESE   This tiny restaurant looks like it was plucked up in Tokyo and dropped in the middle of Beijing, what with its traditional Japanese booths and a bar where a Japanese chef (who speaks no Chinese or English) works his magic with bare hands and a slender sushi knife. Skip the booths and go directly to the bar, where you can sit and watch the action. This place is made for raw-fish aficionados—if you like your food cooked, you're out of luck. But for sushi fans, this is one of the best places to eat or try everything culled fresh out of the sea, including delicious cuts of *chu-toro* and *o-toro* (premium tuna) and more exotic items like ark shell, all imported from Dalian, a Chinese coastal city not far from Japan.

Xinyuanli Zhong Jie Building 2 新源里中街2号楼; see map p. 110. ✆ **010/6467-1837.** Meal for 2 ¥400–¥800. AE, DC, MC, V. Reservations recommended. Tues–Sun 11am–2pm and 3–11pm. Metro: Liangmaqiao.

ⓘ Tips **Where to Buy Picnic Supplies**

Picnicking is the most neglected tradition among travelers in Beijing, considering the city's wealth of picturesque parks and scenic areas. This was once due to a paucity of the necessary components, but the availability of nearly any food item from anywhere now means there is no excuse.

You can purchase basic **groceries** and Chinese-style **snacks** at local markets and the *xiaomaibu* (little-things-to-buy units) found nearly everywhere. Several fully stocked **supermarkets** and a handful of smaller grocers now carry imported wine and cheese, pesto sauce, American junk food, Newcastle Brown Ale, and just about anything else you could want, albeit at inflated prices. Supermarket Olé stocks a good selection of foreign items; find them in the China World Trade Center and the basement of the Ginza Mall at the Dongzhi Men metro stop. April Gourmet, opposite On/Off in Sanlitun, has sliced meats, rare Western vegetables, and a full selection of familiar breakfast cereals. Much the same can be found at Jenny Lou's (see chapter 9, p. 174).

Among **delis and bakeries,** the best is the Kempi Deli (on the first floor of the Lufthansa building; ⓒ **010/6465-3388,** ext. 5741). It offers satisfying crusty-bread sandwiches and a tremendous pastry and fresh baked bread selection that goes for half-price after 9pm. Mrs. Shanen's Bagels (ⓒ **010/8046-4301**) can whip up some mean bagel sandwiches, and if you can't make it to their inconvenient, far-northeast-suburbs location, they'll deliver.

Recommended picnic spots in the city proper include Bei Hai Park ★ (p. 136), Summer Palace (p. 127), and Ri Tan Park (p. 137), as well as Zizhu Yuan Gongyuan (Purple Bamboo Garden), west of Beijing Zoo. Outside Beijing, sections of the Great Wall provide a dramatic spot for an outdoor meal. Also try the Ming and Qing tombs and the Tanzhe and Jietai temples in the western suburbs.

MODERATE

Beijing Da Dong Kaoya Dian 北京大董烤鸭 ★★ BEIJING   No hundred years of history or obscure *hutong* location here, just a crispy-skinned and pleasing roast duck that many say is one of the best in town—it rivals that of our favorite place for duck, Made in China, and it's also cheaper. The restaurant claims to use a special method to reduce the amount of fat in its birds, although it seems unlikely that duck this flavorful could possibly be good for you. The birds come in either whole (¥198) or half (¥99) portions and are served in slices with a wide assortment of condiments (garlic, green onion, radish). Place the duck on a pancake with plum sauce and your choice of ingredients, and then roll and eat. An excellent plain broth soup, made from the rest of the duck, is included in the price. The English picture menu offers a wide range of other dishes, everything from mustard duck webs to duck tongue in aspic, plus a number of excellent *doufu* (tofu) dishes with thick, tangy sauces. Every meal comes with a free fruit plate and dessert. This is one of the few restaurants in Beijing with a nonsmoking room.

1-2/F Nanxincang International Plaza 南新仓国际大厦1-2层 (southwest corner of Dongsi Shitiao); see map p. 110. ⓒ **010/5169-0329.** Reservations essential. Meal for 2 (including half-duck) ¥300–¥500. AE,

DC, MC, V. Daily 11am–10pm. Metro: Dongsi Shitiao. An older location at Tuanjiehu Bei Kou 3团结湖北口3号 (on east side of E. Third Ring Rd., north of Tuanjiehu Park), see map p. 110, ✆ 010/6582-2892, metro: Tuanjiehu.

Element Fresh (Xin Yuansu) 新元素 ★ AMERICAN

If you're looking for healthy salads, smoothies, and light continental dishes, this Shanghai-based chain restaurant is the place to go. Located in the Sanlitun Village, this restaurant has a stylish interior with high ceilings and plenty of greenery and a nice outdoor patio for Beijing's warmer months. The restaurant is especially popular for Saturday and Sunday brunch, with American breakfast favorites like scrambled eggs with smoked salmon and pancakes. For lunch or dinner, try the laffa bread salad—which comes with a delicious miso yogurt dressing, crumbled feta cheese, and grilled chicken—and a tropical storm smoothie. The food is nothing extraordinary, but in a town with few salad options, it definitely is as close as one gets to healthy eating in Beijing.

Sanlitun Lu 19 in Sanlitun the Village S8-31 三里屯路19号三里屯 VILLAGE S8-31 (in the basement of the Opposite House); see map p. 110. ✆ 010/6417-1318. www.elementfresh.com. Meal for 2 ¥200–¥400. AE, DC, MC, V. Mon–Fri 10am–11pm; Sat–Sun 8am–11pm. Metro: Tuanjiehu.

Hatsune (Yin Quan) 隐泉 ★ JAPANESE

Hatsune is sushi sacrilege via Northern California, with a list of innovative rolls long and elaborate enough to drive serious raw-fish traditionalists to ritual suicide. The unconventional attitude is also reflected in the stylish space, high-ceilinged and sleek, with a long glass-and-metal entryway and a rock garden path leading to the bathrooms. Nearly every item on the menu is among the best of its kind in the city, but the rolls are what make this place truly special. With the single exception of the Beijing Roll, a roast-duck and "special sauce" gimmick, you simply can't go wrong. The 119 Roll, with bright red tuna inside and out, topped with a divine spicy-sweet sauce, absolutely should not be missed.

Guanghua Dong Lu, Heqiao Dasha C 光华东路和乔大厦C楼 (4 blocks east of Kerry Centre, opposite Petro China building); see map p. 110. ✆ 010/6581-3939. Meal for 2 ¥200–¥400; Mon–Fri prix-fixe lunch ¥75; weekend lunch buffet ¥158. AE, DC, MC, V. Daily 11:30am–2pm and 5:30–10pm. Metro: Dawang Lu.

Huangcheng Lao Ma 皇城老妈 HOT POT

Upmarket hot pot sounds like a contradiction in terms, but Huangcheng Lao Ma makes it work—and work well. Set inside a huge multistoried building with a hyperbolic, tile-eave facade and relatively pleasant decor, the restaurant is almost constantly packed. The reason is their special ingredient, "Lao Ma's beef," a magical meat that stays tender no matter how long you boil it. Also popular are the large prawns, thrown live into the pot. The traditional broth is eye-watering spicy; order the split *yuanyang* pot with mild *wuyutang* (water world essence) broth in a separate compartment, or risk overheating your tongue.

Dabeiyao Nan Qingfeng Zha Hou Jie 39 大北窑南庆丰闸后街39 (south of China World Trade Center; south along East Third Ring, take left after crossing river); see map p. 110. ✆ 010/6779-8801. Meal for 2 ¥200–¥300. AE, DC, MC, V. Daily 11am–11pm. English menu. Metro: Dawang Lu.

Le Galerie (Zhongguo Yiyuan) 中国怡园 ★ CANTONESE

Located on the south end of Ri Tan Park, this makes a nice stopping place for dim sum lunch if you happen to be near Silk Market or the Central Business District. It's as authentic as Lei Garden but slightly sloppier when it comes to service. Yet it makes up for it with delicious barbecue pork buns and other Cantonese treats, while a nice outdoor courtyard makes it a very pleasurable al fresco experience if the weather happens to be comfortable.

Ri Tan Park South Gate 日坛公园南门; see map p. 110. ✆ 010/8562 8698. Meal for 2 ¥200–¥400. Daily 10am–10:30pm. AE, DC, MC, V. Metro: Jianguo Men.

Mare (Da Pa Shi) 大怕世 ★★ SPANISH   The huge range of tapas, large wine list, and comfortable dining room make us regulars at this elegant restaurant, decorated to look like a lovely Spanish living room. We love the chicken croquettes, mushroom risotto, and deep-fried baby squid. The chocolate molten cake, flanked by small scoops of hazelnut and vanilla ice cream, is our favorite dessert in town.

Guanghua Lu 12, E-Tower光华路丙12号数码01大厦1层南侧; see map p. 110. ✆ 010/6595-4178. Meal for 2 ¥300–¥600. AE, MC, V. Daily 11:30am–11:30pm. Metro: Guomao.

Pure Lotus (Jing Xin Lian) 净心莲 ★ VEGETARIAN   The dimmed restaurant, decorated with prayer wheels and Buddhist statues, offers stylish vegetarian food that wows in taste and presentation. Highlights include the pumpkin soup and the vegetarian dumplings. A monk supposedly owns the restaurant, but we suspect that he's more of a businessman given the relatively high prices. The Holiday Inn Lido location is a bit of a trek from central Beijing, but offers a stylish, not-to-be-missed setting.

Nongzhanguan Nan Lu 10 朝阳区农展南里10号 (inside Zhongguo Wenlian); see map p. 110. ✆ 010/6592-3627. Meal for 2 ¥250–¥450. AE, DC, MC, V. Daily 11am–11pm. Metro: Gongti Bei Lu. Another branch at 3F, Holiday Inn Lido Hotel, Jiang Tai Lu 6, ✆ 010/6437-6288.

Rumi (Rumi) 入迷 ★★ PERSIAN   This is the only place dishing up Persian food in the city. Be forewarned, however: Alcohol is not served at Rumi, but they make up for it with an extensive offering of fruit juices, milkshakes, and teas. Plus, if you're looking for a buzz, the restaurant offers hookahs—long water pipes with fruit-flavored tobaccos. The portions are generous, grilled meats are seasoned with tasty spices, and the dips and sauces are divine. The bread, which can be on the dry and bland side, could use some sprucing up. Grab a seat on the outdoor terrace if the weather's nice, or otherwise dine in elegance among minimalist, off-white decor and vaulted ceilings.

Gongti Bei Lu Jia 1 工体北路甲1号 (across from Pacific Century Place); see map p. 110. ✆ 010/8454-3838. www.rumigrill.com. Dinner for 2 ¥200–¥300. MC, V. Daily 11am–1am. Metro: Gongti Bei Lu.

Serve The People (Wei Renmin Fuwu) 为人民服务 THAI   It's a sign of the times that Mao's best-known slogan can be used so frivolously by this chic Thai eatery. In the heart of the Sanlitun diplomatic quarter, you'll find Beijing's finest Thai food at very reasonable prices. The grilled beef salad and green chicken curry are highly recommended, and the *pad thai* (rice noodles with seafood in peanut sauce) is done to perfection. The small but interesting wine list has a limited by-the-glass selection. The temptation to use inappropriate local ingredients (such as cabbage!) plagues other Thai restaurants in the capital, but here the people are given their due.

Sanlitun Xi Wu Jie 1 三里屯西五街1号 (behind German embassy); see map p. 110. ✆ 010/8454-4580. Meal for 2 ¥200. AE, DC, MC, V. Daily 10:30am–10:30pm. Metro: Nong Zhan Guan; 1 long block west, right at the stoplights (Sanlitun), then first left.

Taj Pavilion (Taiji Lou Yindu Canting) 泰姬楼印度餐厅 INDIAN   One of Beijing's oldest Indian restaurants, the classy small dining room here holds only a few tables, nicely dressed in white linen, with subtle decor refreshingly free of camp. Food and service are both of consistently high quality. Recommended dishes include vegetable *kofta* curry (deep-fried vegetables in tomato-based curry sauce), *palak paneer* (spinach with chunks of soft cheese), *rogan josh* (mutton in spicy tomato curry), and chicken *tikka masala* (marinated chicken in rich tomato sauce)—all authentic, thick, and deceptively filling. A second branch recently opened at the Holiday Inn Lido.

(Value) Chinese on the Cheap

Affordable Chinese food is everywhere in Beijing, and not all of the places that provide it are an offense to Western hygiene standards. As with shopping in this city, high prices don't necessarily guarantee high quality in dining, and cheap restaurants often provide better food than expensive ones. Down-market dining also offers the best chance to connect with the average Beijing resident.

Most convenient is a stable of adequately clean **Chinese fast-food** restaurants, many of which deliberately try to ape their Western counterparts. Menus typically offer simple noodles, baked goods, and stir-fries. Top chains include Yonghe Dawang 永和大王 (with KFC-style sign) and Malan noodle outlets 马兰拉面 (marked with a Chicago Bulls–style graphic), both with locations throughout the city.

A better option is to visit one of the **point-to-choose food courts** on the top or bottom floor of almost every large shopping center. These typically feature a dozen or so stalls selling snacks, noodles, or simple precooked selections from different regions. Prices are reasonable, making it easy to sample a wide range. Just point to what looks good. The food court in the basement of the Oriental Plaza, requiring purchase of a card you use to pay for food at each stall, is the most extensive. Others can be found in the China World Mall, the Yaxiu Clothing Market, and Xi Dan Baihuo Shangchang north of the Xi Dan metro stop.

One of the most enjoyable local dining areas in Beijing, the legendary 24-hour food street on Dongzhi Men Nei Dajie known to most as **Ghost Street** (**Gui Jie** 簋街; the first Chinese character is a homonym for the Chinese word for ghost and actually refers to a vessel, but most Chinese and foreigners alike refer to it as "Ghost Street" or "鬼街"), took a hit from the wrecking ball but is still there in abbreviated form. From the Dong Si Bei Dajie intersection and running east, dozens of small eateries offer hot pot, *mala longxia* (spicy crayfish), and home-style fare through the lantern-lit night.

L1-28 West Wing of China World Trade Center, Jianguo Men Wai Dajie 1国贸中心; see map p. 110. ⓒ 010/6505-5866. www.thetajpavilion.com. Meal for 2 ¥200–¥400. Prix-fixe lunch ¥45–¥50, prix-fixe dinner ¥50–¥55. AE, DC, MC, V. Daily 11:30am–2:30pm and 6–10:30pm. Metro: Guomao.

Xiao Wang Fu 小王府 HOME-STYLE   Xiao Wang serves up tasty, traditional Chinese food in an atmospheric setting—and does a respectable Peking duck. While the food is not particularly imaginative, it does all the standards perfectly well—from kung pao chicken to the spicy Sichuan string beans. We prefer the Ri Tan Park location, which is slightly pricier, but has a nice alfresco patio and is set within one of Beijing's nicer parks.

North Gate of Ri Tan Park 日坛路日坛公园北门内; see map p. 110. ⓒ 010/8561-5985. Meal for 2 ¥250–¥350. AE, DC, MC, V. Daily 11am–2pm and 6–10pm. Metro: Chaoyangmen or Jianguo Men. Other locations at Building 2, Guanghua Lu Dongli 光华路东里2号楼, ⓒ 010/6591-3255; 15 Qianhai Beiyan 前海北沿15号, ⓒ 010/6617-5558.

Bellagio (Lu Gang Xiaozhen) 鹿港小镇 TAIWANESE   Taiwanese food, characterized by sweet flavors and subtle use of ginger, is one of the most appealing to Western palates. Bellagio's team of glam female waitstaff have an unjustified reputation for snooty service. The clientele of the Gongti branch, stumbling out from Babyface and Angel nightclubs, make for amusing people-watching. The decor is all sleek lines and shimmering beads. Don't miss the delicate *shacha niurou*, mustard greens combined perfectly with thinly sliced beef strips. *Taiwan dofu bao*, a tofu clay-pot seasoned with shallots, onion, chili, and black beans, is also remarkable, as is the signature dish, *sanbei ji* (chicken reduced in rice wine, sesame oil, and soy sauce). In summer, don't miss the enormous shaved-ice desserts: One serving is enough for four, but gobble it up before it comes tumbling down!

Xiaoyun Lu 35 霄云路35号 (opposite Renaissance Hotel); see map p. 110. (2) 010/8451-9988. Meal for 2 ¥120–¥200. AE, DC, MC, V. Daily 11am–4am. Metro: Dongsi Shitiao. Other branches at Gongti Xi Lu 6 工体西路6号 (south of Gongti 100 bowling center), see map p. 110, (2) 010/6551-3533, daily 11am–5am; Jian Guo Lu 87 Beijing Shin Kong Place 6F建国路87号新光天地6楼, (2) 010/6530-5658, daily 11am–10pm, metro: Da Wang Lu, exit C; An Hui Bei Li Block 2 Building #4安慧北里2区4号楼, (2) 010/6489-4300, daily 11am–midnight.

Ding Ding Xiang 鼎鼎香 (Finds) HOT POT   This Mongolian-style mutton hot pot restaurant is tremendously and justifiably popular for its signature dipping sauce *(jinpai tiaoliao)*, a flavorful sesame sauce so thick they have to dish it out with ice-cream scoops. Large plates of fresh sliced lamb *(yangrou)* are surprisingly cheap; other options include beef *(niurou)*, spinach *(bocai)*, and sliced winter melon *(donggua pian)*. Reservations strongly recommended.

Dongzhi Men Wai Dong Jie 14 东直门外东街14号 (opposite Donghuan Guangchang, in alley across from Guangdong Development Bank); see map p. 110. (2) 010/6417-2546. http://en.dingdingxiang.com.cn. Reservations highly recommended. Meal for 2 ¥100–¥200. DC, MC, V. Daily 11am–midnight. Metro: Dongzhi Men (214, exit C). Other branches (11am–10pm) at Building 31 Gan Jia Kou Xiaoqu 甘家口小区 31号楼, (2) 010/8837-1327; East Gate Plaza at Dong Zhong Jie 9东中街9号, (2) 010/6417-9289; Building 7 Guo Xing Jia Yuan, Shou ti Nan Lu 首体南路国兴家园7号楼, (2) 010/8835-7775; Jian Guo Lu 87 Beijing Shin Kong Place 6/F 建国路87号新光天地6层, (2) 010/6530-5997.

Noodle Loft (Mian Ku Shanxi Shiyi) 面酷山西食艺 SHANXI   Unheard of outside China and rarely found in such stylish surroundings, Shanxi cuisine is noted for its vinegary flavors, liberal use of tomatoes, and large variety of interesting noodles. The Noodle Loft's interior is ultramodern in orange and gray, with a large open kitchen featuring giant woks and steamers. An English menu makes ordering easy. Highlights include *yi ba zhua* (fried wheat cakes with chives), *qiao mian mao erduo* (cat's ear–shaped pasta stir-fried with chopped meat), and *suancai tudou* (vinegared potato slices).

Xi Dawang Lu 20 西大望路20号 (from bus stop, walk back 90m/285 ft.); see map p. 110. (2) 010/6774-9950. Meal for 2 ¥80–¥100. MC, V. Daily 11am–2:30pm and 5:30–10pm. From Dawang Lu metro stop, take bus 11 or 31 for 3 stops, getting off at Jiu Long Shan 九龙山. Other location at Heping Xijie 3 和平西街3号, (2) 010/5130-9655, metro: Hepingli Bei Jie.

San Ge Guizhouren 三个贵州人 GUIZHOU   Southern China's Guizhou Province is one of the country's poorest regions, which lends a certain irony to this restaurant's hip minimalist setting and rich artist clientele. The menu offers a stylish take on the province's Miao minority food with dishes that tend to be spicy, colorful, and slightly rough. Both tabletop hot pots—the Miao-style peppermint lamb and the cilantro-heavy dry

(Moments) Nightmarket Nosh

Late-night dining is a favorite Beijing pastime, and the most convenient way to experience it is to visit one of the several nightmarkets scattered about the city. This is street food, government regulated but not guaranteed to be clean, so the weak in stomach or courage may want to pass. Gastrointestinal gamble aside, the markets are a vivid and often delicious way to spend an evening.

The markets are typically made up of stalls, jammed side by side, selling all manner of snacks that cost anywhere from ¥.50 to ¥5. Most legendary are the little animals on sticks, a veritable zoo of skewers that includes baby birds and scorpions. Popular markets are on **Longfu Si Jie** 隆福寺街 (see chapter 8, p. 161) and **west of the Beijing Zoo** (at the Dongwuyuan Yeshi 动物园夜市), but the most celebrated is the **Donghua Men nightmarket** 东华门夜市, just off Wangfujing Dajie opposite the Xin Dong An Plaza.

With a history supposedly dating back to 1655, the Donghua Men was closed during the Cultural Revolution and reopened in 1984. Previously a charming mishmash of independent operators each in their own battered tin shacks, it was "reorganized" in 2000. The stalls are all now a uniform red and white, each with identical twin gas burners. Prices have risen into the ¥10 range and the food has fallen a bit in quality. The payoff is an increase in revenues from foreign tourists.

Below are the most common items you'll find for sale at the stalls.

- **Baozi** 包子: Steamed buns typically filled with mixtures of pork and vegetables, but occasionally available with just vegetables, for around ¥3 for a basket of five.
- **Jianbing** 煎饼: Large crepe with egg, folded around fried dough with cilantro and with plum and hot sauces, for ¥3.
- **Jiaozi** 饺子: Pork and vegetable filling with doughy wrapper, commonly boiled, ¥2 to ¥4 for 12.
- **Miantiao** 面条: Noodles, commonly stir-fried with vegetables or boiled in beef broth with cilantro, for ¥3 to ¥10.
- **Xianbing** 馅饼: Stuffed pancakes, usually filled with meat or vegetables, fried golden brown, around ¥2.
- **Yangrou chuan** 羊肉串: Lamb skewers with cumin and chili powder, either fried or roasted; also available in chicken (*jirou*), ¥1.

beef—are highly recommended, as is the flavorful but fatty *jueba chao larou* (bacon stir-fried with brake leaves). ***Note:*** Items listed on the menu as "vegetarian" are not.

Guanghua Xi Lu 3 光华西路3号 (walk north on Dong Da Qiao Lu from Yong'anli metro, turn down alley north of Mexican Wave, look for blue sign); see map p. 110. ℂ **010/6502-1733.** Meal for 2 ¥80–¥100. AE, DC, MC, V. Daily 10am–10pm. Metro: Yong'anli. Other branches at Building 7 Jianwai SOHO 建外SOHO 7 楼 (south of Guomao metro), ℂ **010/5869-0598,** daily 10am–10pm; 2/F of Ideal International Plaza on the Fourth Ring Rd. 北四环理想国际大厦2层, ℂ **010/8260-7670,** daily 11am–2pm and 5–10pm; Building 8 Gongti Xi Lu 工体西路8号, ℂ **010/6551-8517,** daily 24-hr.

Yuxiang Renjia 渝乡人家 ★ SICHUAN Franchise food in the Chinese capital doesn't carry the same connotations of blandness it does in the West. Yuxiang Renjia, a constantly crowded chain of restaurants with bright mock-village decor and a talent for producing authentic Sichuan fare, is a case in point. Dishes are slightly heavy on the oil but as flavorful as anything found outside Sichuan itself. The spicy familiar *gongbao jiding* (diced chicken with peanuts and hot peppers) is superb, putting American versions of "kung pao chicken" to shame. They also produce several worthwhile dishes you aren't likely to have tried before, including an interesting smoked duck (*zhangcha ya*) and the "stewed chicken with Grandma's sauce" (*laoganma shao ji*). Waitstaff sometimes gets overwhelmed, and the impressive decor isn't matched by the hygiene.

Chaoyang Men Wai Dajie 20 朝阳门外大街20号 (on 5th floor of Lianhe Dasha, behind Foreign Ministry Building 联合大厦); see map p. 110. ✆ 010/6588-3841. www.yuxiangrenjia.com (Chinese only). Meal for 2 ¥80–¥120. AE, DC, MC, V. Sun–Fri 11am–10:30pm; Sat 11am–10pm. Metro: Chaoyang Men.

6 BEIJING SOUTH

INEXPENSIVE

Mala Youhuo 麻辣诱惑 ★★ (Finds) SICHUAN Beijing's obsession with Sichuan cuisine seems to have no end, and this restaurant, where locals queue down the street on a Monday night, currently enjoys the most fanatical following. Service is surprisingly friendly for such a busy restaurant, and the mock-village decor is cheesy but fun. The signature dish, *shui zhu yu* (boiled fish with chili and numbing hot peppers) comes in three different varieties, grass carp (*caoyu*), catfish (*nianyu*), and blackfish (*heiyu*). We still prefer the traditional grass carp, but the slightly firmer and less slippery blackfish makes a nice change. For a walk on the culinary wild side, try *mala tianluo*, field snails stewed in chili and numbing hot pepper. Skewers are provided to extract the flesh from the sizable mollusks. Leave the innermost black part to the side, unless you want a serious tummy ache. A nice antidote to all the spice is a clear soup with seasonal leafy greens, *tutang shicai*. A second branch recently opened northeast of Da Zhong Si.

Guang'an Men Nei Dajie 81, Xuanwu Qu 广安门内大街81号 (just south of Baoguo Si); see map p. 114. ✆ 010/6304-0426. Meal for 2 ¥80–¥140. No credit cards. Daily 11:30am–2am. Metro: Changchun Jie (205, exit D1); walk south on Changchun Jie, then turn right (west) at 1st major road. Other branches at Da Zhong Si Taiyang Yuan 大钟寺太阳园, ✆ 010/8211-9966, daily 11am–10:30pm; Xi Dan Bei Dajie 176 Chung Yo Store 8/F 西单北大街176号中友百货8楼, ✆ 010/6603-7068, daily 11am–10pm; Xi Dan Bei Dajie 133 Juntai shopping mall 7F西单北大街133号君太百货7楼, ✆ 010/8265-6688, daily 11am–10pm; Sky Plaza 3F (300m/984 ft. east of Metro: Dongzhi Men, exit C) 天恒大厦三层 (东直门地铁C出口向东步行300米), ✆ 010/8460-8558, daily 11am–10:30pm; Chong Wen Men Wai Dajie 40 So Show Plaza 7/F 崇文门外大街40号搜秀商城7楼, ✆ 010/5167-1099, daily 11am–10pm.

Pamer (Pami'er Shifu) 帕米尔食府 ★ (Finds) UIGHUR Pamer isn't much to look at, but it is clean, and the food it serves is cheaper and better than anything at the more famous Afunti, which is now overrun by tour groups. Cumin-spiced lamb skewers (*yangrou chuan*) are immense and surprisingly low on fat. Also not to be missed are the *nang bao rou* (lamb and vegetable stew served on flat wheat bread) and *shouba fan* (rice with lamb and raisins).

Lianhua Chi Dong Lu 3 莲花池东路3号 (north side of Baiyun Qiao; large sign depicts dancing silhouettes); see map p. 114. ✆ 010/6326-3635. Meal for 2 ¥60–¥100. No credit cards. Mon–Fri 10am–2pm and 4:30–9:30pm; Sat–Sun 10am–9:30pm.

Taipo Tianfu Shanzhen 太婆天府山珍 ★★ HOT POT   To make the broth for their divine hot pot, this restaurant stews a whole black-skinned chicken with 32 different kinds of mushrooms and lets the mixture reduce for hours. The mushrooms are strained but the chicken stays, served with the by-now vibrant broth in a heavy clay pot kept boiling at your table. Already a fine meal on its own, it gets even better as you add ingredients—lamb *(yangrou)*, beef *(niurou)*, lotus root *(ou pian)*, spinach *(bocai)*, or, best of all, more mushrooms *(shanjun)*. Many of the mushrooms, shown in their uncooked form on a series of posters hung along the walls, are imported from the southern provinces. Good enough to make converts of fungus haters.

At south end of Er Qi Juchang Lu, behind east side of the Chang'an Shangchang 二七剧场路长安商场东侧 (east of metro stop); see map p. 114. ✆ **010/6801-9641.** Meal for 2 ¥100–¥120. MC, V. Daily 10am–11pm. Metro: Nanlishilu. Another branch at Anhui Li Er Qu Si Hao Bei Lou 2-3/F, Yayun Cun 亚运村安慧里二区4号北楼2-3层, ✆ **010/6496-9836.**

Tianjin Bai Jiao Yuan 天津百饺园 Dumplings   No restaurant has managed to fill the vacuum left by the inexplicable closing of Gold Cat, once Beijing's most charming outlet for *jiaozi* (ravioli-like dumplings), but Tianjin Bai Jiao Yuan comes closest. Staff are given to occasional catatonia, and the clichéd red-and-gold interior can't match Gold Cat's old courtyard setting, but the *jiaozi* are just as delicious. The *xiesanxian shuijiao* (dumplings with shrimp, crab, and mushroom filling) and *niurou wan shuijiao* (beef ball dumplings) are treasures, best accompanied by a steaming pot of *chenpi laoya shanzhen bao* (duck, mandarin peel, and mushroom potage). There's also a respectable range of Sichuan dishes, pictured on the menu.

Xin Wenhua Jie 12A 新文化街12号 (in alley opposite the Grand Mercure); see map p. 114. ✆ **010/6605-9371.** Meal for 2 ¥50–¥80. No credit cards. Daily 11am–2:30pm and 5–9:30pm.

Yunteng Binguan 云腾宾馆 ★ (Finds) YUNNAN   This is a low-key cadre restaurant with exceptionally fresh fare. Even though Yunnan is one of the poorest provinces in China, the Mandarins have their ingredients flown in several times each week. The decor exudes as much warmth as a hospital waiting room, but exceedingly friendly waitstaff more than compensate. The signature dish, *guoqiao mixian* (crossing-the-bridge rice noodles) is worth the trip in itself, a delicious blend of ham, chicken, chrysanthemum, chives, tofu skin, and a tiny egg, all blended at your table with rice noodles in chicken broth. *Zhusun qiguoji* (mushroom and mountain-herbs chicken soup) is ideal comfort food, and *zhutong paigu* (spicy stewed pork with mint), while not actually steamed in the bamboo tube it's served in, has hearty, complex flavors. Avoid choosing the enticing mushroom dishes on the picture menu without first checking the price; the Yunteng stocks some fancy fungi.

Dong Huashi Bei Li Dong Qu 7, Chongwen Qu 崇文区东花市北里东区 (follow Jianguo Men Nan Dajie south for 10 min.; on the south side of flyover); see map p. 114. ✆ **010/6713-6439.** Meal for 2 ¥100–¥160. MC, V. Daily 11:30am–10pm. Metro: Jianguo Men.

7 BEIJING WEST, HAIDIAN & YAYUN CUN

VERY EXPENSIVE

The Aman Grill (Yihe Anman) 颐和安曼餐厅 ★★★ STEAKHOUSE   Far from the center of town is this gorgeous steakhouse located at the new Aman Resort. If you happen to be at the Summer Palace or any of Beijing's northwestern tourist sites, this is well worth a visit, especially if you're in the mood for a luxurious, non-Chinese meal. The dining room with high, wooden-beamed ceilings, orchids, and lounge seats decorated with silk pillows feels elegant and subtly Chinese. Beyond the imported T-bone and rib-eye steaks that the restaurant specializes in, the kitchen also makes delicious starters and side dishes, from an enticing pork belly and scallop appetizer lightly seasoned with curry powder to a comforting scalloped bacon-and-cheese potatoes. A Bible-sized wine list with descriptions of all selections from the resident "cellar master"—a graduate of New York's Culinary Institute of America—completes the fine package.

Gongmenqian St. 15, Aman Beijing at the Summer Palace (p. 56) 北京颐和园宫门前街15号颐和安缦酒店; see map p. 116. ✆ 010/5987 9999. Meal for 2 ¥600–¥1,500. AE, DC, MC, V. Daily 7–10:30am, 12–2:30pm, and 6–10:30pm.

Blu Lobster (Lan Yun Xi Can Ting) 蓝韵西餐厅 ★★ CONTINENTAL   It's worth the trip to this out-of-the-way restaurant if you're looking for a gourmet Spanish-tinged seafood meal. Led by talented 30-something Spaniard Jordi Villegas Serra, the menu features expensive imported ingredients like lobster alongside local items like delicious hami melon. He's got a penchant for citrus, which flavors many dishes, from his king crab, mushroom, and avocado salad to his beet-root and parsley cream roll. The menu is nicely presented with a number of set menu choices from which you can mix and match dishes, starting at ¥388 for three courses. For decadent eaters who aren't concerned about their cholesterol, the ¥888 "Lobster Addict" set menu features eight courses made with the crustacean, from lobster thermidor to Wagyu beef in a lobster reduction.

Zizhuyuan Lu 29 (first floor of Shangri-La Hotel, p. 76); see map p. 116. ✆ 010/6841-2211. Meal for 2 ¥800–¥2,000. AE, DC, MC, V. Tues–Sun 5:30–10pm.

Cepe (Yiwei Xuan) 意味轩 ★★ ITALIAN   This restaurant serves the best upscale Italian fare in the city. The waitstaff wear sleek pinstripe suits and are incredibly attentive, zipping over to your table at the merest hint of a frown or inquiring look. This is a place to indulge in a leisurely meal. You must order a pasta dish, as the noodles are perfectly al dente and freshly made each morning. The decor is contemporary, with an open kitchen housed behind a giant silk screen of a portobello mushroom. There are romantic, semi-private nooks with curtains and leather chaise lounges alongside the back wall. Jazz music and, every now and then, an upbeat Laura Pausini song play in the background.

Jinchengfang Dong Jie 1 金成坊冻街1号 (inside Ritz-Carlton, Financial Street, p. 75); see map p. 116. ✆ 010/6601-6666. Dinner for 2 ¥600–¥1,500. AE, MC, V. Daily 11:30am–3pm and 6–11pm. Metro: Fuxing Men.

MODERATE

Xibei Youmian Cun 西贝莜面村 ★★ (Kids) NORTHWESTERN/SHANXI   This place is worth the trip out to Yayun Cun in itself. Friendly staff and bright, faux-rural decor make this the best "family restaurant" in Beijing, and the cuisine (a hybrid of Mongolian and Shanxi fare) will have you looking through the picture menu to plan your next visit. The signature dish is *youmian wowo* (steamed oatmeal noodles) served with mushroom *(sushijun retang)* or lamb *(yangrou retang)* broth, with coriander and chili on the side. Familiar *yangrou chuan'r* (mutton skewers with cumin) and yogurt *(suannai)* with honey make excellent side dishes, while the house salad *(Xibei da bancai)* is a meal in itself, crammed with unusual ingredients such as wild greens, radish, and purple cabbage, and topped with a delicious sesame dressing. The one dish you must try is *zhijicao* *kao niupai* (lotus leaf–wrapped roast beef with mountain herbs). Roast beef will never be **103** the same.

Yayun Cun Anyuan 8 Lou 亚运村安慧北里与慧忠路街角 (corner of Anhui Bei Li and Huizhong Bei Lu). ℂ **010/6498-4455.** Meal for 2 ¥140–¥240. AE, DC, MC, V. Daily 11am–2pm and 5–9pm.

Zhang Sheng Ji Jiudian 张生记酒店 ★★ HUAIYANG   It may lack the ambience of Kong Yiji Jiulou, but this branch of Hangzhou's most successful restaurant delivers more consistent Huaiyang fare. Service is no-fuss, and there's a pleasing amount of space between tables and a high ceiling. For starters, try the flavorful *jiuxiang yugan* (dried fish in wine sauce). The recently added *mati niuliu* (stir-fried beef with broccoli, water chestnuts, and tofu rolls) is excellent, and nearly every table carries the signature *sungan laoya bao* (stewed duck with dried bamboo shoots and ham), which has complex, hearty flavors. You can explore the English picture menu without trepidation; Huaiyang cuisine is delicately spiced, and largely eschews endangered species.

Bei San Huan, Zhejiang Dasha 北三环浙江大厦 (west of Anzhen Qiao on N. Third Ring Rd.); see map p. 116. ℂ **010/6442-0006.** Meal for 2 ¥200–¥300. AE, DC, MC, V. Daily 11am–2pm and 5–9pm. Metro: Hepingxiqiao.

INEXPENSIVE

Baihe Sushi (Lily Vegetarian Restaurant) 百合素食 ★ VEGETARIAN   Chinese vegetarian restaurants often get bogged down torturing meaty flavors out of gluten, but here you'll find delectable dishes with high-quality ingredients. Start with the hearty *shanyao geng* (yam broth with mushrooms) and the slightly fruity *liangban zi lusun* (purple asparagus salad), followed by *ruyi haitai juan* (vegetarian sushi rolls) and the excellent *huangdi sun shao wanzi* (Imperial bamboo shoots and vegetarian meatballs). When in season, their vegetables are sourced from an organic farm west of Beijing, so ask if they have any organic vegetables *(youji shucai)*. Monks dine free, so you're likely to meet a few from Guangji Si in the evening. Watch your head in the bathroom.

Yi He Yuan Kun Ming Hu Lu 50, 100m (328 ft.) south to the Xin Jian Gong Men (main gate of Yi He Yuan) 颐和园昆明湖路50号; see map p. 116. ℂ **010/6202-5284.** Meal for 2 ¥80–¥140. Daily 9am–9pm. Metro: Bagou. Another branch at Dongzhi Men Nei Bei Xiao Jie, Cao Yuan Hutong 23东直门内北小街草园胡同 23号, ℂ **010/6405-2082.**

Dongbei Hu 东北虎 ★ NORTHEASTERN   Natives of Dongbei (the Northeast) are famously direct, and few hesitate for more than a picosecond before nominating this raucous establishment as the source of Beijing's best Dongbei cuisine. Welcoming staff dressed in florals usher you upstairs past an open kitchen with whole cuts and huge jars of wine on show. Start with the refreshing cold rice noodle dish, *da lapi,* served in a sesame and vinegar sauce. Your table will groan under the weight of the signature dish, *shouzhua yang pai* (lamb chops roasted with cumin and chili). Filling snacks, such as *tiebingzi* (corn pancakes cooked on a griddle) and *sanxian laohe* (seafood and garlic chive buns), are delicious, as is the sweet-and-sour-battered eggplant *(cuipi qiezi)*. So cheap, you won't begrudge the taxi fare out to Yayun Cun.

Anhui Li Er Qu Yi Lou, Yayun Cun 安慧里二区一楼 (300m/984 ft. east of intersection with Anli Lu). ℂ **010/6498-5015.** Meal for 2 ¥50–¥80. No credit cards. Daily 11am–10pm.

Xiangyang Tun 向阳屯 HOME-STYLE/NORTHEASTERN   Set in a new courtyard-style complex in northwestern Beijing, this nostalgia restaurant is one of the only venues in the city for *errenzhuan,* a raunchily entertaining style of opera rarely performed outside the frigid northeast. The opera stage sits at one end of the cavernous main hall, decorated in an exaggerated Cultural Revolution–era countryside theme with bright red tables and propaganda-heavy newspapers from the 1960s plastered on the walls. Dishes are large and simple in the northeastern tradition. Good choices are the *Dongbei fengwei dapai* (Northeast-style braised ribs) and the *nongjia xiaochao,* an authentic combination of soybeans, green onion, Chinese chives, and bell peppers in a clay pot. Combine a stop here with an afternoon visit to the Summer Palace.

Wanquan He Lu 26 海淀区万泉河路26号 (in Haidian, across from the Zhongyi Yiyuan [Chinese Traditional Medicine Hospital]); see map p. 116. ✆ 010/6264-5522 or 010/6264-2907. Meal for 2 ¥60. No credit cards. Daily 9:30am–2pm and 5–9pm. Metro: Suzhou Jie.

Xiyu Shifu 西域食府 ★★ UIGHUR

Directly opposite Olympic Park you'll find the best Uighur food this side of Turfan. The decor (typical of Yayun Cun) is a nouveau riche fantasy of arches, Romanesque gold light fittings, and pictures of desert scenes hanging from marble walls, but it's spotless and welcoming, with an imaginatively translated menu. You'll find intriguing dishes, along with authentic Xinjiang favorites. The *da pan ji* (diced chicken, pepper, potatoes, and thick noodles in tomato sauce) is spicy, so when they ask if you like it hot, be honest. The piping-hot *nan* (flat bread) is perfect for sopping up the delicious sauce, and the *shou zhua fan* (rice with lamb and carrot), which often appears as a limp version of fried rice with raisins this far east, is as tasty as anything you'll find in Kashgar. Although spicy mutton skewers with cumin and chili *(yangrou chuan)* ranks as Beijing's most popular dish, too often the spices are heavy, usually to disguise less than fresh meat. Not here.

Corner of Beichen Dong Lu and Datun Lu, Yayun Cun 亚运村北辰东路与大屯路街角. ✆ 010/6486-2555. Meal for 2 ¥80–¥100. AE, MC, V. Daily 11am–2:30pm and 5–10pm. Metro: Olympic Park.

Yunnan Jin Kongque Dehong Daiwei Canguan 云南金孔雀德宏傣味餐馆

Ⓥ Value YUNNAN The street north of the Minorities University (Minzu Daxue) was once a claustrophobic *hutong* packed with Uighur, Korean, and Dai restaurants. Chaps who addressed you as "Hashish" are gone, along with most of the restaurants. But this holy grail of Dai cuisine remains, offering a superb synthesis of Thai and Chinese fare. Mirrors, tiled floors, and predictable bamboo furnishings lend it a sterile feel, but the gracious waitstaff more than compensates. Must-devour dishes include crispy *tudou qiu* (deep-fried potato balls with chili sauce), delectable *boluo fan* (pineapple rice), *zhutong zhurou* (steamed pork with coriander), *zhutong ji* (chicken soup), and *zha xiangjiao* (deep-fried banana) for dessert. Wash it all down with sweet rice wine *(mi jiu),* served in a bamboo cup.

Minzu Daxue Bei Lu 1 民族大学北路1号 (cross footbridge, head right, take the 1st street on your left); see map p. 116. ✆ 010/6893-2030. Meal for 2 ¥80–¥100. No credit cards. Daily 11am–10pm. Bus: no. 205 or 106 to Weigong Cun from Xi Zhi Men metro.

Exploring Beijing

by Jen Lin-Liu

Sightseeing in Beijing can be an overwhelming prospect. No other city in China, and few other cities in the world, offers so many must-see attractions. It is technically possible to see the big names—the **Forbidden City, Temple of Heaven, Summer Palace,** and **Great Wall**—in as little as 3 days, but you'll want at least a week to get any sort of feel for the city. People spend years here and still fail to see everything they should. ***Note:*** Most major sights now charge different prices for admission in summer and winter. The summer high season officially runs from April 1 to October 31 and the winter low season from November 1 to March 31.

HOW TO SEE BEIJING

Beijing's traffic is appalling. Do *not* plan to see too many sights that are far apart, unless you want your memories of the capital to consist of staring helplessly out of a taxicab window. Regardless of whether you choose to get around by taxi, metro, bus, bike, or foot, plan each day to see sights that are close together.

The best option for reaching sights within Beijing is to take the metro to the stop nearest the attraction you plan on seeing, and duck into one of the many waiting taxis. As an example, the **Summer Palace** is a short ¥20 cab ride from the new light rail station at Wudaokou. Buses are slow but plentiful and relatively safe, especially if you choose the air-conditioned 800-series buses. Maximum freedom (and usually speed) is realized by hiring a bike for the day. More convenient still is to hire a normal taxi for the day (see section 3, "Getting Around," in chapter 3).

The standard of organized tours in Beijing leaves much to be desired. But if this is your preference, most hotels have offices of China International Travel Service (CITS) or Dragon Tours, which offer overpriced tours to the major attractions (see section 11, "Organized Tours," in this chapter). The advantage is that transport and language barriers are removed, but the freedom to visit smaller attractions and meet locals is sacrificed. The fast pace of these tours can leave you giddy.

The last and least recommended option is to hire a car through your hotel. You will be charged up to five times what you should pay. Aside from convenience, the only conceivable plus is that if you are staying at a foreign-run, luxury hotel, they have a reputation for good service to protect. Organizations such as CITS do not.

1 TIAN'AN MEN SQUARE (TIAN'AN MEN GUANGCHANG)

This is the world's largest public square, the size of 90 American football fields (40 hectares/99 acres), with standing room for 300,000 people. It is surrounded by the Forbidden City in the north, the Great Hall of the People in the west, and the museums of

🚌 Bus Station
¥ Bank
ⓘ Information
✉ Post Office
🏢 Rail Station
PSB Public-Security Visas

Metro & Station
MUXIDI
112

文慧园路
Wenhuiyuan Lu

北京北站
Beijing North
Railway Station

西直门北大街
Xi Zhi Men Bei Dajie

新街口外大街
Xinjiekouwai Dajie

Desheng
Men

德胜门外大街
Desheng Men Wai Dajie

Desheng Men 德胜门
鼓楼 Gulou

Gaoling Qiao Xiejie
高梁桥斜街

XI ZHI MEN
201

Xi Zhi
Men

西直门内大街
Xi Zhi Men Nei Dajie

JISHUITAN
218

Xi Hai 西海

Hou Hai 后海

Beijing Zoo
北京动物园

Xi Zhi Men Wai Dajie
西直门外大街

XI ZHI MEN
西直门

西直门南大街
Xizhimennan Dajie

Nan Dajie

新街口北大街
Xinjiekou Bei Dajie

新街口南大街
Xinjiekou Nan Dajie

德胜门内大街
Desheng Men Nei Dajie

Hou Hai 后海

Luyin 绿荫

Chegongzhuang Dajie 车公庄大街

Ping'anli
Xi Dajie

平安大道 Ping 'an
Dadao

地安门西大街
Di'an Men Xi Dajie

西什库大街
Xishiku Dajie

展览路 Lu

展览路
Zhanlanguan
Lu

CHEGONGZHUANG
202

赵登禹路
Zhaodengyu Lu

西四北大街
Xisi Bei Dajie

XI SI
西四

San Li He Lu 三里河路

Fucheng Men Wai Dajie
阜成门外大街

Fucheng
Men

Fucheng Men Nei Dajie
阜成门内大街

西安门大街
Xi'an Men Dajie

Fuyou Jie 府右街

FUCHENG MEN
203

西四南北大街
Xidan Bei Dajie

金融街
Jin rong jie

太平桥大街
Tai Ping Qiao
Dajie

西城
XI CHENG

XI DAN
西单

San Li He 三里河

Yuetan Nan Jie 月坛南街

Picai Hutong 辟才胡同

Fuxing Men Wai Dajie
复兴门外大街

Fuxing
Men

复兴门内大街
Fuxing Men Nei
Dajie

XI DAN
115

Xi Chang'an Jie
西长安街

北新华街
Bei Xinhua Jie

MUXIDI
112

NAN LISHI LU
113

FUXING MEN
114/204

闹市口大街
Naoshikou
Dajie

宣武门内大街
Xuanwu Men
Nei Dajie

白云路 Bayun Lu

White Cloud
Temple

CHANGCHUN JIE
205

XUANWU MEN
宣武门

宣武门东大街
Xuanwu Men
Dong Dajie

HEPING
MEN
207

Changchun Jie

宣武门西
Men Xi门西
Dajie 大街

宣武门外
Xuanwu Wai
大街

0   1/2 mi
0   0.5 km

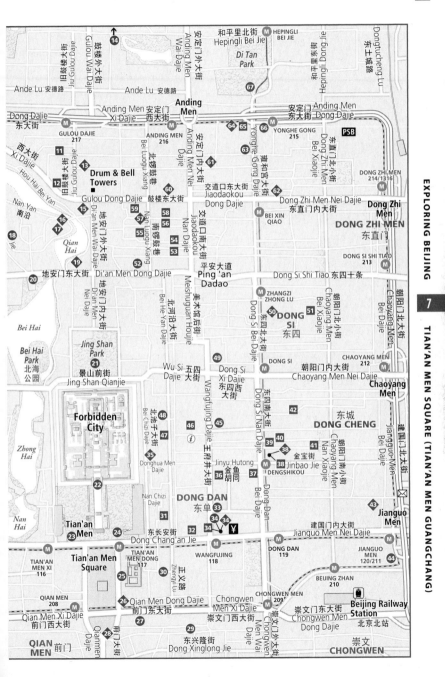

EXPLORING BEIJING

7

TIAN'AN MEN SQUARE (TIAN'AN MEN GUANGCHANG)

ACCOMMODATIONS ■

Beijing Downtown Backpackers
 Accommodation **55**
(Dōng Táng Qīngnián Lǚshè)
东堂青年旅社

Bamboo Garden Hotel **11**
(Zhu Yuan Binguan)
竹园宾馆

Confucius International Youth Hostel **65**
(Běijīng Yōng Shèng Xuān
 Qīngnián Jiǔdiàn)
北京拥圣轩酒店

Courtyard 7 (Qīhào Yuàn) **59**
七号院

Crowne Plaza Hotel **46**
(Guoji Yiyuan Huangguan Fandian)
国际艺苑皇冠饭店

Days Inn Forbidden City **31**
(Běijīng Xiāngjiāng Dàisī Jiǔdiàn)
北京香江戴斯酒店

The Emperor (Huángjiā Yìzhàn) **47**
 皇家驿栈

Du Ge Hotel **56**
(Dùgé Sìhéyuàn Yìshù Jīngpǐn Jiǔdiàn)
杜革四合院艺术精品酒店

Grand Hyatt Beijing **34**
(Beijing Dongfang Junyue Dajiudian)
北京东方君悦大酒店

Gu Xiang 20 (Gu Xiang Er Shi) **58**
古巷20 58

Han's Royal Garden Hotel **53**
(Hánzhēn Yuán Guójì Jiǔdiàn)
涵珍园国际酒店

Haoyuan Binguan **39**
好园宾馆

Hotel Côté Cour S.L. **42**

Hilton Beijing Wangfujing **36**
(Běijīng Wángfǔjǐng
 Xīěrdùn Jiǔdiàn)
北京王府井希尔顿酒店

Park Plaza Beijing **38**
(Beijing Li Ting Jiu Dian)
北京丽亭酒店

The Peninsula Beijing **37**
(Wangfu Bandao Fandian)
王府半岛饭店

Qomolangma Hotel **12**
(Zhumulangma Binguan)
珠穆朗玛宾馆

Raffles Beijing **32**
(Beijing Fandian Laifoshi)
北京饭店莱佛士

Red Capital Residence **51**
(Xin Hong Zi Julebu)
新红资俱乐部

The Regent Beijing **38**
(Beijing Li Jing Jiu Dian)
北京丽晶酒店

Saga Youth Hostel **41**
(Shijia Guoji Qingnian Lushe)
实佳国际青年旅社

Shi Jia House **40**
(Shǐ Jiā Hùi Guǎn)
史家会馆

DINING ◆
Agua **26**

Black Sesame Kitchen **57**
(Hēizhīma Chúfáng)
黑芝麻厨房

Cafe Sambal **13**

Capital M (Mishi Canting) **28**

Chuan Jing Ban Canting **43**
川京办餐厅

The CourtYard (Siheyuan) **35**
四合苑

Crescent Moon **50**
(Wān Wān Yuè Liàng)
弯弯月亮

Dali Courtyard (Da Li) **60**
大理

Huajia Yiyuan **62**
花家怡园

Hutong Pizza **17**
胡同比萨

Kong Yiji Jiudian **8**
孔乙己酒店

Kejia Cai **19**
客家菜

Lei Garden (Lì Yuán) **38**
利苑

Made in China (Chang An Yi Hao) **34**
长安一号

Maison Boulud **26**
(Bùlǔ Gōng Fǎ Cāntīng)
布鲁宫法餐厅

My Humble House 34
(Dongfang Hanshe)
东方寒舍

No Name Restaurant 16
(Wú Míng Cān Tīng)
无名餐厅

Nuage (Qing Yun Lou) 15
庆云楼

Source (Dujiangyuan) 54
渡江源

Vineyard (Putaoyuan'r) 64
葡萄院儿

Xian'r Lao Man 61
馅老满

Zen 1903 (Dié 1903) 26
蝶1903

ATTRACTIONS ●
Ancient Observatory 44
(Gǔ Guānxiàng Tái)
古观象台

Bai Ta Si 3
(White Dagoba Temple)
白塔寺

Beihai Park 20
(Běihǎi Gōngyuán)
北海公园

Beijing Planning and
  Exhibition Hall 27
(Běijīng Guīhuà Bówùguǎn)
北京规划博物馆

Běijīng Hǎiyángguǎn 1
(Beijing Aquarium)
北京海洋馆

Dàxīn Fǎngzhī Gōngsī 7
大新纺织公司

Dì Tán Gōngyuán 67
(Temple of Earth)
地坛公园

Dìxià Chéng 29
(Underground City)
地下城

Dōng Táng 45
(East Church or
  St. Joseph's Cathedral)
东堂

Forbidden City 22
(Gù Gōng)
故宫

Gōng'ānbù Dìyī Yánjiūsuǒ 30
公安部第一研究所

Gǔdài Qiánbì Zhǎnlǎnguǎn 9
(Ancient Coin Exhibition Hall)
古代钱币展览馆

Guo Zi Jian and Kong Miao 63
(Directorate of Education and Confucian Temple)
国子监／孔庙

Jewelry Street (Zhubao Yi Tiao Jie) 5
珠宝一条街

Jing Shan Gongyuan (Jing Shan Park) 21
景山公园

Lǎo Shě Jìniànguǎn 48
(Former Residence of Lao She)
老舍纪念馆

Lìdài Dìwáng Miào (Temple of Past Emperors) 4
历代帝王庙

Nanluoguxiang (Nán Luógǔ Xiàng) 52
南锣鼓巷

National Museum of China (Guójiā Bówùguǎn) 25
国家博物馆

Olympic Park (Aolinpike Gongyuan) 14
奥林匹克公园

Oriental Plaza (Dōngfāng Xīn Tiāndì) 34
东方新天地

Prince Gong's Mansion (Gōng Wáng Fǔ) 18
恭王府

Sanlian Taofen Tushu Zhongxin 49
三联韬奋图书中心

Sòng Qìnglíng Gùjū 10
(Former Residence of Soong Ching Ling)
宋庆龄故居

Sun Dong An Plaza (Xīn Dōng'ān Shìchǎng) 33
新东安市场

Tai Miao 24
太庙

Yán Chéng Yǔ (Over Workshop) 6
闫澄宇

Yōnghé Gōng 66
(Lama Temple)
雍和宫

Zhōngguó Gōngyì Měishùguǎn 2
(National Arts & Crafts Museum)
中国工艺美术馆

Zhōngshān Gōngyuá 23
中山公园

Chinese History and Chinese Revolution in the east. In the center of the square stands the Monument to the People's Heroes (Renmin Yingxiong Jinian Bei), a 37m (121-ft.) granite obelisk erected in 1958, engraved with scenes from famous uprisings and bearing a central inscription (in Mao's handwriting): THE PEOPLE'S HEROES ARE IMMORTAL. The twin-tiered dais is said to be an intentional contrast to the imperial preference for three-tiered platforms; the *yin* of the people's martyrs contrasted with the *yang* of the emperors (see the "Lucky Numbers" box on p. 124).

The area on which the square stands was originally occupied by the **Imperial Way**—a central road that stretched from inside the Forbidden City, through Tian'an Men, and south to Da Qing Men (known as Zhonghua Men during the Nationalist era), which was demolished to make way for Mao's corpse in 1976 (see the review for Chairman Mao's Mausoleum, below). This road, lined on either side with imperial government ministries, was the site of the pivotal May Fourth movement (1919), in which thousands of university students gathered to protest the weakness and corruption of China's then-Republican government. Mao ordered destruction of the old ministries. The vast but largely empty **Great Hall of the People** rose from the rubble to the west, and equally vast but unimpressive **museums** were erected to the east, as part of a spate of construction to celebrate 10 years of Communist rule. But the site has remained a magnet for politically charged assemblies; the most famous was the gathering of **student protesters** in late spring of 1989. That movement, and the government's violent suppression of it, still defines Tian'an Men Square in most minds. You'll search in vain for bullet holes and bloodstains. The killing took place elsewhere. Brutal scenes were witnessed near Fuxing Men and Xi Dan (west of the square), as workers and students were shot in the back as the regime showed its true colors, bringing a halt to a decade of intermittent political reform. Today, stiff-backed soldiers, video cameras, and plainclothes police still keep a close watch on the square.

Other than flying a kite and playing "spot the plainclothes policeman," there isn't much to do in the square, but early risers can line up in front of Tian'an Men at dawn to watch the **flag-raising ceremony,** a unique suffocation-in-the-throng experience on National Day (Oct 1), when what seems like the entire Chinese population arrives to jostle for the best view.

Chairman Mao's Mausoleum (Mao Zhuxi Jinian Guan)

This is one of the eeri-est experiences in Beijing. The decision to preserve Mao's body was made hours after his death in 1976. Panicked and inexperienced, his doctors reportedly pumped him so full of formaldehyde his face and body swelled almost beyond recognition. They drained the corpse and managed to get it back into acceptable shape, but they also created a wax model of the Great Helmsman just in case. There's no telling which version—the real or the waxen—is on display at any given time. The mausoleum itself was built in 1977, near the center of Tian'an Men Square. However much Mao may be mocked outside his tomb (earnest arguments about whether he was 70% right or 60% right are perhaps the biggest joke), he still commands a terrifying sort of respect inside it. It's not quite the kitsch experience some expect. The tour is free and fast, with no stopping, photos, drinks, or bags allowed inside. *Note:* The lineup to get into the mausoleum gets *very* long as early as 9am, so get there early to secure your spot.

South end of Tian'an Men Square; see map p. 119. ℂ **010/6513-2277.** Free admission. Tues–Sun 8–noon. Bag storage in a small building across the street, directly west: ¥4/bag, ¥5/camera. Metro: Qian Men.

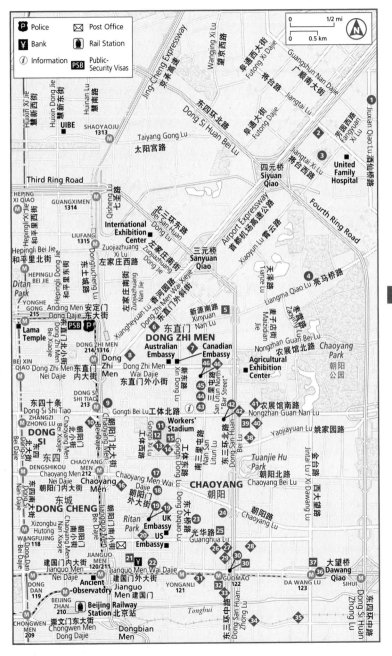

ACCOMMODATIONS ■
A.hotel **15**

China World Hotel **30**
(Zhōngguó Dàfàndiàn)
中国大饭店

Hotel G **12**

Kerry Centre Hotel **25**
(Beijing Jiali Zhongxin Fandian)
北京嘉里中心饭店

Opposite House **46**
(Yú Shè)
瑜舍

Park Hyatt **32**
(Běijīng Bǎiyuè Jiǔdiàn)
北京柏悦酒店

Ritz-Carlton Beijing **37**
(Běijīng Lìsī
    Kǎěrdùn Jiǔdiàn)
北京丽思卡尔顿酒店

St. Regis Beijing **21**
(Beijing Guoji Julebu Fandian)
北京国际俱乐部饭店

Traders Hotel Beijing **30**
(Guomao Fandian)
国贸饭店

Westin Beijing Chaoyang **5**
(Jīn Mào Běijīng
    Wēisītīng Dà Fàndiàn)
金茂北京威斯汀大饭店

Zhaolong Qingnian Lǚguan **39**
兆龙青年旅馆

DINING ◆
Běi **46**
北

Beijing Da Dong Kaoya Dian **10, 38**
北京大董烤鸭店

Bellagio (Lu Gang Xiaozhen) **13**
鹿港小镇

Ding Ding Xiang **8**
鼎鼎香

Duck de Chine (Quán Yā Jì) **42**
全鸭季

Element Fresh (Xīn Yuánsù) **46**
新元素

Green T. House (Zi Yun Xuan) **13**
紫云轩

Hatsune (Yin Quan) **28**
隐泉

Huángchéng Lǎo Mā **34**
皇城老妈

Lan **31**
兰

Le Galerie (Zhōngguó Yíyuán) **20**
中国怡园

Mare (Da Pa Shi) **27**
大怕世

Noodle Loft **35**
(Miàn Kù Shānxī Shíyì)
面酷山西食艺

Pure Lotus **2, 40**
净心莲

Rumi (Rumi) **41**
入迷

San Ge Guizhouren **14, 33**
三个贵州人

Serve The People (Wei Renmin Fuwu) **7**
为人民服务

Sureño **46**

Taj Pavilion (Taiji Lou Yindu Canting) **2, 29**
泰姬楼印度餐厅

Xiǎo Wáng Fǔ **19, 26**
小王府

Yotsuba (Si Ye) **6**
四叶

Yuxiang Renjia **16**
渝乡人家

ATTRACTIONS AND SHOPPING ●
Bai Nao Hui **18**
百恼汇

China World Trade Center Shopping Center **30**
(Zhongguo Guoji Maoyi Zhongxin)
中国国际贸易中心

Chinese Culture Club (Kente Zhongxin) **4**
肯特中心

Da Guo Shou **9**
大国手

Dong Yue Miao **17**
东岳庙

Factory 798 **1**
七九八工场 "大山子"

Friendship Store (Youyi Shangdian) **22**
友谊商店

Nali Patio (Nàlǐ Huāyuán) **45**
那里花园

Pacific Century Place **42**
太平洋百货

The Place **23**
世贸天阶

Ri Tan Park (Ri Tan Gongyuan) **19**
日坛公园

Shin Kong Place (Xinguang Tiandi) **36**
新光天地

Spin (Xuán) **3**
旋

The Village at Sanlitun (Sānlǐtún Tàigǔ Guǎngchǎng) **44**
三里屯太古广场 "The Village at 三里屯"

Worker's Stadium (Gongren Tiyuchang) **11**
工人体育场

Yashow Market (Yaxiu Fuzhuang Shichang) **43**
牙秀服装市场

3501 PLA Surplus Store **24**
三五零一工场

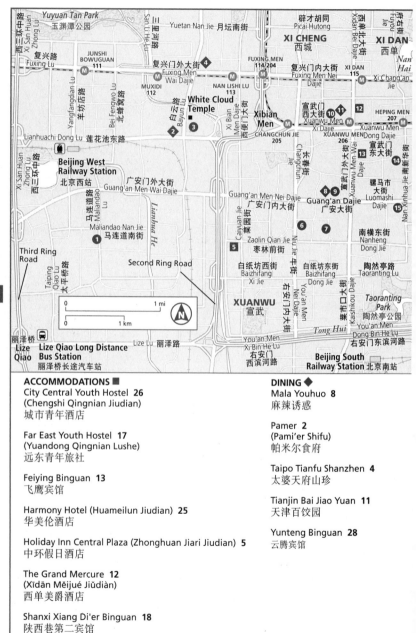

ACCOMMODATIONS ■

City Central Youth Hostel **26**
(Chengshi Qingnian Jiudian)
城市青年酒店

Far East Youth Hostel **17**
(Yuandong Qingnian Lushe)
远东青年旅社

Feiying Binguan **13**
飞鹰宾馆

Harmony Hotel (Huameilun Jiudian) **25**
华美伦酒店

Holiday Inn Central Plaza (Zhonghuan Jiari Jiudian) **5**
中环假日酒店

The Grand Mercure **12**
(Xīdān Měijué Jiǔdiàn)
西单美爵酒店

Shanxi Xiang Di'er Binguan **18**
陕西巷第二宾馆

DINING ◆

Mala Youhuo **8**
麻辣诱惑

Pamer **2**
(Pami'er Shifu)
帕米尔食府

Taipo Tianfu Shanzhen **4**
太婆天府山珍

Tianjin Bai Jiao Yuan **11**
天津百饺园

Yunteng Binguan **28**
云腾宾馆

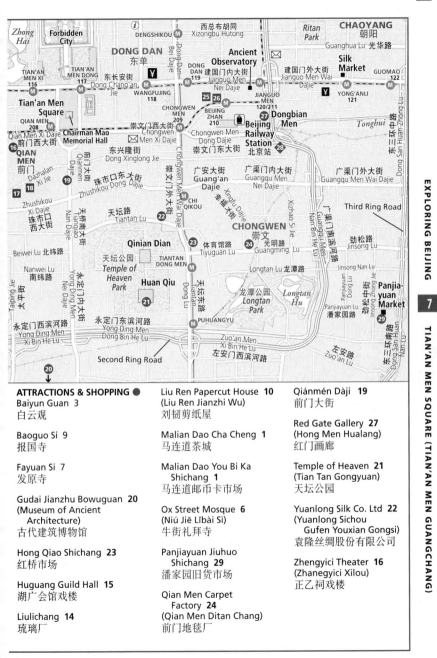

ATTRACTIONS & SHOPPING ●

Baiyun Guan **3**
白云观

Baoguo Si **9**
报国寺

Fayuan Si **7**
发原寺

Gudai Jianzhu Bowuguan **20**
(Museum of Ancient
   Architecture)
古代建筑博物馆

Hong Qiao Shichang **23**
红桥市场

Huguang Guild Hall **15**
湖广会馆戏楼

Liulichang **14**
琉璃厂

Liu Ren Papercut House **10**
(Liu Ren Jianzhi Wu)
刘韧剪纸屋

Malian Dao Cha Cheng **1**
马连道茶城

Malian Dao You Bi Ka
   Shichang **1**
马连道邮币卡市场

Ox Street Mosque **6**
(Niú Jiē Lǐbài Sì)
牛街礼拜寺

Panjiayuan Jiuhuo
   Shichang **29**
潘家园旧货市场

Qian Men Carpet
   Factory **24**
(Qian Men Ditan Chang)
前门地毯厂

Qiánmén Dàji **19**
前门大街

Red Gate Gallery **27**
(Hong Men Hualang)
红门画廊

Temple of Heaven **21**
(Tian Tan Gongyuan)
天坛公园

Yuanlong Silk Co. Ltd **22**
(Yuanlong Sichou
   Gufen Youxian Gongsi)
袁隆丝绸股份有限公司

Zhengyici Theater **16**
(Zhanegyici Xilou)
正乙祠戏楼

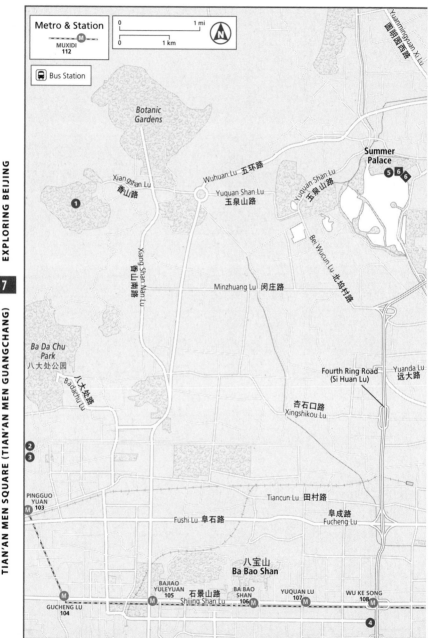

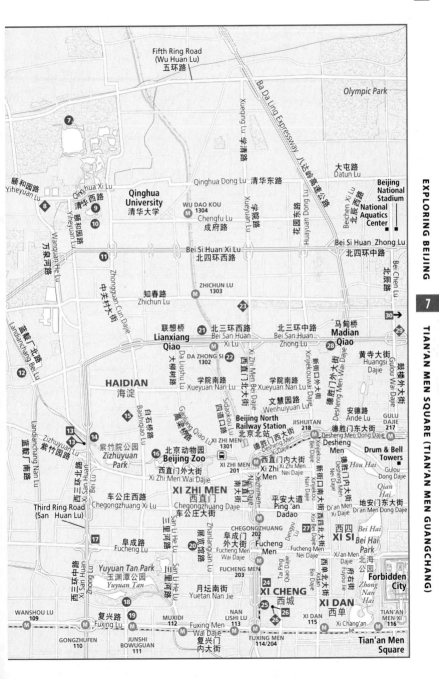

ACCOMMODATIONS ■

Aman Beijing **6**
(Běijīng Ānmàn Wénhuà Jiǔdiàn)
北京安曼文化酒店

Beijing Marriott West **17**
(Beijing Jinyu Wanhao Jiudian)
北京金域万豪酒店

Crowne Plaza Park View Wuzhou **30**
(Wuzhou Huangguan Jiari Jiudian)
五洲皇冠假日酒店

Red Lantern House **27**
(Hóng Dēnglóng Kèzhàn)
红灯笼客栈西院

Ritz Carlton, Financial Street **26**
(Jinrong Jie Lijia Jiudian)
金融街丽嘉酒店

Shangri-La Beijing **13**
(Xianggelila Fandian)
香格里拉饭店

The Westin Beijing,
   Financial Street **24**
(Wei Si Ting Da Jiu Dian)
威斯汀大酒店

DINING ◆

The Aman Grill (Yíhé Ānmàn) **6**
颐和安曼餐厅

Bǎihé Sùshí **23**
(Lily Vegetarian Restaurant)
百合素食

Blu Lobster **13**
(Lan Yun Xi Can Ting)
蓝韵西餐厅

Cepe (Yiwei Xuan) **26**
意味轩

Xiangyang Tun **8**
向阳屯

Yunnan Jin Kongque
   Dehong Daiwei Canguan **15**
云南金孔雀德宏傣味餐馆

Zhang Sheng Ji Jiudian **29**
张生记酒店

ATTRACTIONS AND SHOPPING ●

Altar to the Century **18**
(Zhonghua Shiji Tan)
中华世纪坛

Baoguo Si Wenhua Gongyipin Shichang **10**
报国寺文化工艺品市场

Beijing Sheying Qicai Cheng **4**
北京摄影器材城

Fahai Si **2**
法海寺

Five Pagoda Temple (Wu Ta Si) **16**
五塔寺

Fragrant Hills Park **1**
(Xiang Shan Gongyuan)
香山公园

Great Bell Temple (Da Zhong Si) **21**
大钟寺

Jin Wuxing Baihuo Pifa Cheng **22**
金五星百货批发城

Lane Crawford **25**
连卡佛

Lima Guandi Miao **12**
立马关帝庙

Military Museum of the Chinese People's
   Revolution (Jūnshì Bówùguǎn) **19**
军事博物馆

Old Summer Palace (Yuan Ming Yuan) **7**
圆明园

Peking University (Beijing Daxue) **9**
北京大学

Sanfo Outdoors (Sanfu Huwai Yongpin) **28**
三夫户外用品

Summer Palace (Yihe Yuan) **5**
颐和园

Tian Yi Mu **3**
田义墓

Tianyi Xiaoshangpin Pifa Shichang **20**
天意小商品批发市场

Wanshou Si **14**
万寿寺

Zhongguan Cun **11**
中关村

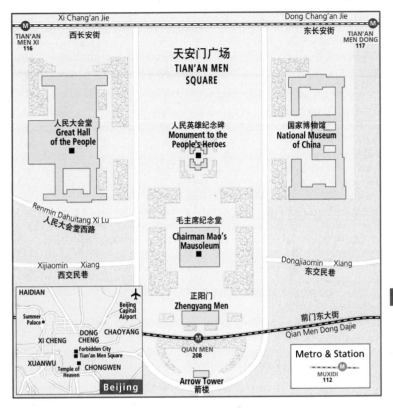

Qian Men (Front Gate) The phrase *Qian Men* is actually a reference to two separate towers on the south side of the square which together formed the main entrance to the Tartar (or Inner) City. The southernmost Arrow Tower (Jian Lou) is no longer open to the public. You can, however, still climb up inside the rear building, called the Zheng-yang Men, where an enjoyable photo exhibition depicts life in Beijing's pre-1949 markets, temples, and *hutong*.

South end of Tian'an Men Square; see map above. ℂ **010/6511-8101.** Admission ¥20. 8:30am–4pm. Metro: Qian Men.

---

2 FORBIDDEN CITY (GU GONG)

The universally accepted symbol for the length and grandeur of Chinese civilization is undoubtedly the Great Wall, but the Forbidden City is more immediately impressive. A 720,000-sq.-m (7,750,016-sq.-ft.) complex of red-walled buildings and pavilions topped by a sea of glazed vermilion tile, it dwarfs nearby Tian'an Men Square and is by far the largest and most intricate imperial palace in China. The palace receives more visitors than any other attraction in the country (over seven million a year, the government says), and has been praised in Western travel literature ever since the first Europeans laid eyes on it in the late 1500s. Yet despite the flood of superlatives and exaggerated statistics that inevitably go into its description, it is impervious to an excess of hype, and it is large and compelling enough to draw repeat visits from even the most jaded travelers. Make more time for it than you think you'll need.

The palace, most commonly referred to in Chinese as Gu Gong (Former Palace), is on the north side of Tian'an Men Square across Chang'an Dajie (© **010/6513-2255**; www.dpm.org.cn). It is best approached on foot or via metro (Tian'an Men Dong), as taxis are not allowed to stop in front. The palace is open daily from 8:30am to 5pm during summer and from 8:30am to 4:30pm in winter; last tickets are sold an hour before the doors close. Regular admission *(men piao)* in summer costs ¥60, dropping to ¥40 in winter. Various exhibition halls and gardens inside the palace charge additional fees, usually ¥10. All-inclusive tickets *(lian piao)* had been discontinued at press time, perhaps in an effort to increase revenues (see the box "The Big Makeover," below), but it's always possible these will be reinstated. *Tip:* If you have a little more time, it is highly recommended that you approach the entrance at **Wu Men (Meridian Gate)** via Tai Miao (p. 122) to the east, and avoid the gauntlet of tiresome touts and tacky souvenir stalls.

Ticket counters are marked on either side as you approach. **Audio tours** in several languages (¥40 plus ¥100 deposit) are available at the gate itself, through the door to the right. Those looking to spend more money can hire **"English"-speaking tour guides** on the other side of the gate (¥200 for a 1-hr. tour, ¥300 for 1½ hr., ¥400 for 2½ hr.). The tour-guide booth also provides **wheelchairs** and **strollers** free of charge, with a ¥500 deposit. *Note:* Only the central route through the palace is wheelchair-accessible, and steeply so.

BACKGROUND & LAYOUT

Sourcing of materials for the original buildings began in 1406, during the reign of the Yongle emperor, and construction was completed in 1420. Much of it was designed by a eunuch from Annam (now Vietnam), Nguyen An, but without improvements to the Grand Canal, construction would have been impossible—timber came from as far away as Sichuan, and logs took up to 4 years to reach the capital. The Yuan palace was demolished to make way for the Forbidden City, but the lakes created during the Jin (1122–1215) were retained and expanded. Between 1420 and 1923, the palace was home to 24 emperors of the Ming and Qing dynasties. The last of these was Aisin-Gioro Puyi, who was forced to abdicate in 1912 but remained in the palace until 1924.

The Forbidden City is arranged along a north-south meridian, aligned on the Pole Star. The Qing court was unimpressed when the barbarians designated Greenwich Royal Observatory as the source of the prime meridian in 1885; they believed the Imperial Way marked the center of the temporal world. Major halls open to the south. Farthest south and in the center is the symmetrical **outer court,** dominated by immense ceremonial halls where the emperor conducted official business. Beyond the outer court and surrounding it on both sides is the **inner court,** a series of smaller buildings and gardens that served as living quarters. During the Ming, only eunuchs were allowed to pass between the two courts, enhancing their power.

> ### Map of the Forbidden City
>
> For a map of the palace, see the inside back cover of this book.

The Big Makeover

An immense **$75-million renovation of the Forbidden City,** the largest in 90 years, will be completed in two phases (the first by 2008, the second by 2020). Work began on halls and gardens in the closed western sections of the palace in 2002. Effort was concentrated on opening the **Wuying Dian (Hall of Valiance and Heroism)** in the southwest corner of the palace; the **Jianfu Gong Huayuan (Garden of the Palace of Building Happiness)** in the northwest; and then the **Cining Huayuan (Garden of Love and Tranquillity)** next to the Taihe Dian. **Wuying Dian,** formerly the site of the Imperial printing press, should be open when you arrive, displaying a collection of Buddhist sutras, palace records, and calligraphy. Also slated to reopen is **Jianfu Gong Huayuan,** which has undergone an ambitious restoration as the entire section was devastated by fire in 1923. **Cining Gong** (the Palace of Compassion and Tranquillity) should be open by early 2010 and will display a collection of Buddhist sculptures. **Shoukang Gong** (the Palace of Longevity and Good Health) will be under restoration for all of 2010. At press time, officials were still uncertain about when Shoukang Gong would reopen to the public.

On the other side of the palace, within the northern section of the Ningshou Gong Huayuan, a remarkable building is undergoing restoration with assistance from the World Cultural Heritage Foundation. Qianlong commissioned the European Jesuit painters in his employ to create large-scale *trompe l'oeil* paintings, which were used both in the Forbidden City and in the Yuan Ming Yuan (p. 138). **Juanqin Zhai,** an elaborately constructed private opera house, houses the best remaining examples of these paintings, including a stunning image of a wisteria trellis, almost certainly painted by Italian master Castiglione.

The palace has been ransacked and parts destroyed by fire several times over the centuries, so most of the existing buildings date from the Qing rather than the Ming. The original complex was said to contain 9,999 rooms, testament to the Chinese love of the number nine (see the box "Lucky Numbers," p. 124), and also to an unusual counting method. The square space between columns is counted as a room *(jian),* so the largest building, **Taihe Dian,** counts as 55 rooms. Using the Western method of counting, there are now 980 rooms. Only half of the complex is open to visitors (expected to increase to 70% after repairs are completed in 2020; see the box "The Big Makeover," above), but this still leaves plenty to see.

THE ENTRANCE GATES

Tian'an Men (Gate of Heavenly Peace) ★★   This gate is the largest in what was once known as the Imperial City and the most emblematic of Chinese government grandeur. Above the central door, once reserved for the emperor, now hangs the famous **portrait of Mao,** flanked by inscriptions that read: LONG LIVE THE PEOPLE'S REPUBLIC OF CHINA (left) and LONG LIVE THE GREAT UNITY OF THE PEOPLES OF THE WORLD (right). Mao declared the founding of the People's Republic from atop the gate on October 1,

1949. There is no charge to walk through, but tickets are required if you want to ascend to the **upper platform** for worthwhile views of Tian'an Men Square. You might imagine yourself as the Great Helmsman addressing a sea of Red Guards, all struggling to understand your thick Hunan accent while waving your little red book. Note the pair of *huabiao* (ornamental columns) topped with lions, wreathed in dragons and clouds, and facing the square. In their original form, *huabiao* were wooden posts in the shapes of a battle-axes, upon which subjects would attach petitions or scrawl their grievances to the king. Over time, their function was reversed. Turned to stone and wreathed in the ultimate symbol of the emperor's mandate—the dragon—they became a warning to the ruled to keep out. *Tip:* If you're traveling in a group of two or more, split up and have one person line up to buy tickets and the other queue to check bags; you'll save yourselves both time and frustration.

North of Tian'an Men Square; ticket office to left as you enter. Admission ¥15. Daily 8am–5pm, last ticket sold at 4:30pm. Mandatory bag storage (¥2–¥6) behind and to left of ticket booth; cameras allowed.

Taihe Men (Gate of Great Harmony)   Immediately inside the Meridian Gate entrance is a wide courtyard with five marble bridges spanning the Jin He (Golden River), followed by Taihe Men. Ming emperors came here to consult with their ministers; this function moved farther inside under the Qing.

Wu Men (Meridian Gate)   Built in 1420 and last restored in 1801, Wu Men is the actual entrance to the Forbidden City. The emperor would sit atop the gate to receive prisoners of war, flanked by a battalion of imperial guards clad in full battle armor. The prisoners, clad in chains and red cloth, knelt in the courtyard while charges were read before the emperor confirmed they would be taken to the marketplace for execution. The order would be repeated first by two, then four, then eight officers, until the entire battalion was thundering the edict in unison. The watchtowers extending out either side of the gate *(que)* are an expression of imperial power. This style was prevalent during the Han dynasty (206 B.C.–A.D. 220); this is the only example from the Ming and Qing. The trees leading up to this gate are recent additions. Originally no trees were planted along the Imperial Way, stretching over 2km (1¼ miles) from **Da Qing Men** (now demolished) to **Qianqing Men (Gate of Heavenly Purity)** in the Inner Court, as according to the "five processes" *(wu xing)*, wood (green) subdues earth (yellow), the element associated with the emperor (hence the yellow glazed tiles).

THE OUTER COURT (QIAN CHAO)

Baohe Dian (Hall of Preserving Harmony)   This last hall, supported by only a few columns, is where the highest level of imperial examinations was held until the exams were suspended in 1901 and abolished in 1905. To the southwest, you can spy **Wenyuan Ge** (the former Imperial Archive), easily recognized by its black-tiled roof with green trim. (Black is associated with water, which, it was hoped, would protect the building from fire.) At the rear is an impressive carved marble slab weighing about 180 tons; during the reign of the Wanli emperor (1573–1620), 20,000 men spent 28 days dragging it to this position from Fangshan, roughly 50km (31 miles) to the southwest.

Taihe Dian (Hall of Great Harmony) ★★   Located beyond Taihe Men, and across an even grander stone courtyard, is an imposing double-roofed structure mounted atop a three-tiered marble terrace with elaborately carved balustrades. This is the largest wooden hall in China, and the most elaborate and prestigious of the palaces' throne halls; it was therefore rarely used. Emperors came here to mark the New Year and winter solstice. Note the row of ceramic figurines on the roof, led by a man on a chicken (a despotic prince) fleeing a terrible dragon that heads a group of nine animal figures. The number of figures reflects the importance of the building.

Zhonghe Dian (Hall of Middle Harmony)   The second great hall of the outer court houses a smaller imperial throne. The emperor would prepare for annual rites, such as sowing the fields at the Altar of Agriculture (Xian Nong Tan; see Gudai Jianzhu Bowuguan, p. 139) in spring, by examining the appropriate manuals here.

THE INNER COURT (NEI TING)

During the Ming, only the emperor, his family, his concubines, and the palace eunuchs (who numbered 1,500 at the end of the Qing dynasty) were allowed in this section. It begins with the **Qianqing Men (Gate of Heavenly Purity),** directly north of the Baohe Dian, fronted by a magnificent pair of **bronze lions** ★ and flanked by a **Ba Zi Yingbi** (a screen wall in the shape of the character for "eight"), both warning nonroyals not to stray inside. Beyond are three palaces designed to mirror the three halls of the Outer Court.

The first of these is the **Qianqing Gong (Palace of Heavenly Purity),** where the emperors lived until Yongzheng decided to move to the western side of the palace in the 1720s. Beyond is **Jiaotai Dian (Hall of Union),** containing the throne of the empress and 25 boxes that once contained the Qing imperial seals. A considerable expansion on eight seals used during the Qin dynasty, the number 25 was chosen because it is the sum of all single-digit odd numbers (see the box "Lucky Numbers," p. 124). Next is the more interesting **Kunning Gong (Palace of Earthly Tranquillity),** a Manchu-style bedchamber where a nervous Puyi was expected to spend his wedding night before he fled to more comfortable rooms elsewhere.

At the rear of the inner court is the elaborate **Yu Huayuan (Imperial Garden)** ★, a marvelous scattering of ancient conifers, rockeries, and pavilions, largely unchanged since it was built in the Ming dynasty. The crags allowed court ladies, who spent their lives inside the Inner Court, a glimpse of the world outside. Puyi's British tutor, Reginald Fleming Johnston, lived in the **Yangxin Zhai,** the first building on the west side of the garden (now a tea shop).

From behind the mountain, you can exit the palace through the **Shenwu Men (Gate of Martial Spirit)** and continue on to Jing Shan and/or Bei Hai Park. Those with time to spare, however, should take the opportunity to explore less-visited sections on either side of the central path.

WESTERN AXIS

Most of this area is in a state of heavy disrepair, but a few restored buildings are open to visitors. Most notable among these is the **Yangxin Dian (Hall of Mental Cultivation),** southwest of the Imperial Garden. The reviled Empress Dowager Cixi, who ruled China for much of the late Qing period, made decisions on behalf of her infant nephew, the Guangxu emperor, from behind a screen in the east room. This is also where emperors lived after Yongzheng moved out of the Qianqing Gong.

EASTERN AXIS

This side tends to be peaceful and quiet even when other sections are crowded. Entrance costs ¥10 and requires purchase of useless overshoe slippers, which quickly disintegrate

(Fun Facts) Lucky Numbers

The layout of imperial Beijing is based on an ancient system of numerology that still resonates today. Odd numbers are seen as *yang* (male, positive, light) and are more auspicious than even numbers, which are viewed as *yin* (female, negative, dark). **Three** is a positive number, as seen in the three-tiered platforms that are reserved for Beijing's most sacred structures—Taihe Dian in the Forbidden City; Tai Miao, the Hall of Prayer for Good Harvests at Tian Tan; and Chang Ling at the Ming Tombs. It's also the number chosen for China's latest political theory, the Three Represents, which explains how a Communist party can be staffed by capitalists. **Four** *(si)*, as a *yin* number, signifies submission. When the emperor carried out sacrifices at the Temple of Heaven, he would face north and bow four times. It is also pronounced the same as death *(si)*, and is the most inauspicious number. Many Chinese apartment buildings lack a fourth floor. **Five** is revered as the center of the Luo Diagram (which allows single-digit numbers arranged in noughts-and-crosses formation to add up to 15). It also signifies the "five processes" *(wu xing)*—metal, wood, water, fire, and earth, which also correspond to the five points of the Chinese compass and to the five colors. Significant imperial buildings are five rooms *(jian)* deep; five openings welcome you into Tian'an Men; and until Zhonghua Men was razed to make way for Mao's corpse, the Imperial Way had five gates. Though an even number, **eight** has gained popularity because it is homophonous with "get rich" in Cantonese: The Olympic Games opened on August 8, 2008. **Nine**, situated at the top of the Luo Diagram and the largest single-digit odd number, was reserved for the imperial house, with grand buildings measuring nine rooms across.

(¥2). The most convenient ticket booth is 5 minutes' walk southwest of the Qianqing Men, opposite **Jiulong Bi (Nine Dragon Screen),** a 3.5m-high (11-ft.) wall covered in striking glazed-tile dragons depicted frolicking above a frothing sea, built to protect the Qianlong emperor from prying eyes and malevolent spirits (that are able to move only in straight lines). The Qianlong emperor (reign 1736–95) abdicated at the age of 85, and this section was built for his retirement, although he never really moved in, continuing to "mentor" his son while living in the Yangxin Dian, a practice later adopted by Empress Dowager Cixi, who also partially took up residence here in 1894.

Zhenbao Guan (Hall of Jewelry) ★, just north of the ticket booth, has all 25 of the Qing imperial seals, ornate swords, and bejeweled minipagodas—evidence that the Qing emperors were devoted to Tibetan Buddhism. One of the highlights is the secluded **Ningshou Gong Huayuan** ★★★, where the Qianlong emperor was meant to spend his retirement. Water was directed along a snakelike trough carved in the floor of the main pavilion. A cup of wine would be floated down the miniature stream, and the person nearest wherever it stopped would have to compose a poem, or drink the wine. The

Qianlong emperor, whose personal compendium of verse ran to a modest 50,000 poems, was seldom short of words.

East of the garden is the **Changyin Ge,** sometimes called Cixi's Theater, an elaborate green-tiled three-tiered structure with trapdoors and hidden passageways to allow movement between stages. Farther north is sumptuous **Leshou Tang ★★**, built entirely from sandalwood, where the Qianlong emperor would read, surrounded by poems and paintings composed by loyal ministers set into the walls and framed by blue cloisonné tablets. Cixi slept in the room to the west. The following hall, **Yihe Xuan,** is not a good place to bring friends from Mongolia or Xinjiang. The west wall has an essay justifying the Qianlong emperor's decision to colonize the latter, while the east wall has a poem celebrating the invasion of Mongolia. In the far northeastern corner is **Zhen Fei Jing (Well of the Pearl Concubine),** a surprisingly narrow hole covered by a large circle of stone. The Pearl Concubine, one of the Guangxu emperor's favorites, was 25 when Cixi had her stuffed down the well by a eunuch as they were fleeing in the aftermath of the Boxer Rebellion. According to most accounts, Cixi was miffed at the girl's insistence that Guangxu stay and take responsibility for the imperial family's support of the Boxers.

Also worth seeing is the **Hall of Clocks (Zhongbiao Guan),** a collection of timepieces, many of them gifts to the emperors from European envoys. Entrance to the exhibit costs ¥10.

3 TEMPLE OF HEAVEN (TIAN TAN GONGYUAN)

At the same time that the Yongle emperor built the Forbidden City, he also oversaw construction of this enormous park and altar to Heaven directly to the south. Each winter solstice, the Ming and Qing emperors would lead a procession here to perform rites and make sacrifices designed to promote the next year's crops and curry favor with Heaven for the general health of the empire. It was last used for this purpose by the president of the Republic, Yuan Shikai, on the winter solstice of December 23, 1914, updated with photographers, electric lights (the height of modernity at the time), and a bulletproof car for the entrance of the increasingly unpopular president. This effectively announced his intent to promote himself as the new emperor, but few onlookers shared his enthusiasm. Formerly known as the Temple of Heaven and Earth, the park is square (symbolizing Earth) in the south and rounded (symbolizing Heaven) in the north.

ESSENTIALS

Temple of Heaven Park (Tian Tan Gongyuan; ✆ 010/6702-8866) is south of Tian'an Men Square, on the east side of Qian Men Dajie. It's open daily from 6am to 8pm (may close earlier in winter, depending on weather and staff decisions), but the ticket offices and major sights are open only from 8am to 6pm, last ticket sold at 5pm. All-inclusive tickets *(lian piao)* cost ¥35 (¥30 in winter); simple park admission costs ¥15. The east gate *(dong men)* is easily accessed by public transport; take the no. 39, 106, or 110 bus just north of the Chongwen Men metro stop (exit B) to Fahua Si. However, the best approach is from the south gate *(nan men),* the natural starting point for a walk that culminates in the magnificent Hall of Prayer for Good Harvests.

During the Cultural Revolution, Tian Tan lost its perfect symmetry as large bites were taken out of the southwest and southeast corners. There's no sign that the land will be returned, with massive apartment blocks ready to sprout on both corners, but it's still a vast park that takes at least 2 hours to see in any depth. The west gate is convenient to the Altar of Agriculture (see Gudai Jianzhu Bowuguan, p. 139) and Wansheng Juchang (see section 1, "Performing Arts," in chapter 10). At the northeast corner lie the shopping delights of Yuanlong Silk Co. Ltd. (p. 180) and Hong Qiao Shichang (see section 2, "Markets & Bazaars," in chapter 9).

Circular Altar (Yuan Qiu)   This three-tiered marble terrace is the first major structure you'll see if you enter from the south gate *(nan men)*. It was built in 1530 and enlarged in 1749, with all of its stones and balustrades organized in multiples of nine (see the box "Lucky Numbers," p. 124). Here, a slaughtered bull would be set ablaze, the culmination of an elaborate ceremonial entreaty to the gods.

Hall of Abstinence (Zhai Gong)   Yuan Shikai fasted for 3 days in his own residence rather than here, as tradition dictated. Perhaps this was his undoing (he died 1½ years later). Real emperors would fast and pray for 5 days, spending their final night in the **Living Hall (Qin Dian)** at the rear of this compound. Note the rare swastika emblems, a symbol of longevity in China, on the door piers. This green-tiled double-moated compound faces east, the best side at which to enter. The grounds are agreeably dilapidated, and are on a more human scale than the rest of the compound.

Hall of Prayer for Good Harvests (Qinian Dian) ★★   Undoubtedly the most stunning building in Beijing, this circular wooden hall, with its triple-eaved cylindrical blue-tiled roof, is perhaps the most recognizable emblem of Chinese imperial architecture outside of the Forbidden City. Completed in 1420, the original hall was struck by lightning and burned to the ground in 1889 (not a good omen for the dynasty), but a near-perfect replica was built the following year. Measuring 38m (125 ft.) high and 30m (98 ft.) in diameter, it was constructed without a single nail. The 28 massive pillars inside, made of fir imported from Oregon (China lacked timber of sufficient length), are arranged to symbolize divisions of time: The central 4 represent the seasons, the next 12 represent the months of the year, and the outer 12 represent traditional divisions of a single day. The hall's most striking feature is its ceiling, a kaleidoscope of painted brackets and gilded panels as intricate as anything in the country. Don't skip the **Imperial Hall of Heaven (Huangqian Dian),** a smaller building to the north where the emperor would pray before the wooden tablets of his ancestors. Although Red Guards destroyed the tablets, the balustrades surrounding this prayer hall are elegantly carved.

Imperial Vault of Heaven (Huang Qiong Yu)   Directly north of the Circular Altar, this smaller version of the Hall of Prayer (see above) was built to store ceremonial stone tablets. The vault is surrounded by the circular **Echo Wall (Huiyin Bi).** In years past, when crowds were smaller and before the railing was installed, it was possible for two people on opposite sides of the enclosure to send whispered messages to each other along the wall with remarkable clarity. You can still experience this magical acoustic effect at the Western Qing Tombs (see section 4 in chapter 11), but there's little hope of enjoying it here.

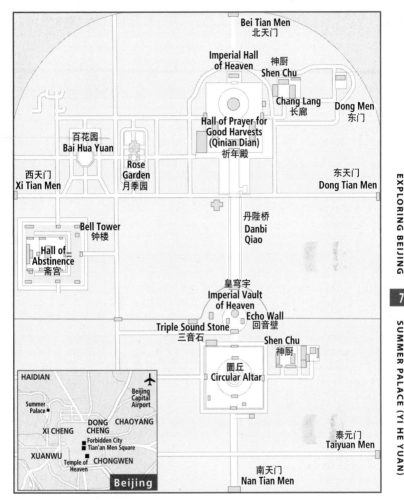

Bei Tian Men
北天门

Imperial Hall
of Heaven
神厨
Shen Chu

Chang Lang
长廊

Dong Men
东门

Hall of Prayer for
Good Harvests
(Qinian Dian)
祈年殿

百花园
Bai Hua Yuan

Rose
Garden
月季园

西天门
Xi Tian Men

东天门
Dong Tian Men

丹陛桥
Danbi
Qiao

Bell Tower
钟楼

Hall of
Abstinence
斋宫

皇穹宇
Imperial Vault
of Heaven

Echo Wall
回音壁

Triple Sound Stone
三音石

Shen Chu
神厨

圜丘
Circular Altar

HAIDIAN

Summer
Palace

Beijing
Capital
Airport

DONG
CHENG

CHAOYANG

XI CHENG

Forbidden City
Tian'an Men Square

XUANWU

Temple of
Heaven

CHONGWEN

Beijing

泰元门
Taiyuan Men

南天门
Nan Tian Men

4 SUMMER PALACE (YI HE YUAN)

This expanse of elaborate Qing-style pavilions, bridges, walkways, and gardens, scattered along the shores of immense Kunming Lake, is the grandest imperial playground in China, constructed from 1749 to 1764. Between 1860 and 1903, it was twice leveled by foreign armies and rebuilt; hence it is often called the New Summer Palace, even though it predates the ruined Old Summer Palace (Yuan Ming Yuan, p. 138). The palace is most often associated with the Empress Dowager Cixi, who resided here for much of the year and even set up a photographic studio. The grounds were declared a public park in 1924 and spruced up in 1949.

ESSENTIALS

The **Summer Palace** (✆ **010/6288-1144**) is located 12km (7½ miles) northwest of the city center in Haidian. Take **bus no. 726** from just west of Wudaokou light rail station; or take a 30- to 40-minute **taxi** ride for ¥60 from the center of town. A more pleasant option is to travel there by **boat** along the renovated canal system; slightly rusty "imperial yachts" leave from the Beizhan Houhu Matou (✆ **010/8836-3576**), behind the Beijing Exhibition Center just south of the Beijing Aquarium (from 10am to 4pm every hour, or every 30 min. during student summer holidays [early July to late Aug]; 50-min. trip; ¥40 one-way; ¥70 round-trip; ¥100 including entrance ticket), docking at Nan Ruyi Men in the south of the park. The gates open daily at 6am; no tickets are sold after 5:30pm in summer and 5pm in winter. Admission is ¥30 for entry to the grounds or ¥60 for the all-inclusive *lian piao,* reduced to ¥20 and ¥50, respectively, in winter (Nov–Mar). The most convenient entrance is Dong Gong Men (East Gate). Go early and allow at least 4 hours for touring the major sites on your own. Overpriced **imperial-style food** in a pleasant setting is available at the Tingli Guan Restaurant, at the western end of the Long Corridor. The area around the lake is perfect for a picnic, and Kunming Lake is ideal for skating in the depths of winter.

EXPLORING THE SUMMER PALACE

This park covers roughly 290 hectares (717 acres), with **Kunming Lake** in the south and **Longevity Hill (Wanshou Shan)** in the north. The lake's northern shore includes most of the buildings and other attractions and is the most popular area for strolls, although walking around the smaller lakes (Hou Hu) behind Longevity Hill is more pleasant. The hill itself has a number of temples as well as **Baoyun Ge (Precious Clouds Pavilion),** one of the few structures in the palace to escape destruction by foreign forces. There are literally dozens of pavilions and a number of bridges on all sides of the lake, enough to make for a full day of exploration. Rather slow electric-powered boats may be rented; they are an appealing option on muggy summer days.

Long Corridor (Chang Lang) ★   Among the more memorable attractions in Beijing, this covered wooden promenade stretches 700m (nearly half a mile) along the northern shore of Kunming Lake. Each crossbeam, ceiling, and pillar is painted with a different scene (roughly 10,000 in all) taken from Chinese history, literature, myth, or geography. Politely rebuff the "students" who offer to show you their "original art" at this spot.

Marble Boat (Shi Fang)   Docked at the end of the Long Corridor is an odd structure which is "neither marble nor a boat," as one novelist observed. Locals, keen to blame the Empress Dowager for China's decline during the Qing dynasty, wring their hands and cite it as the symbol of China's demise. Cixi funded a general restoration of the palace using money intended for the Chinese navy, and the (completely frivolous) boat is said to be Cixi's backhanded reference to the source of the funds. Shortly after the restoration was completed in 1888, China's paltry fleet was destroyed in a skirmish with Japan, the most glaring evidence yet of China's weakness in the modern era.

Renshou Dian (Hall of Benevolence and Longevity)   Located directly across the courtyard from the east gate entrance, Renshou Dian is the palace's main hall. This

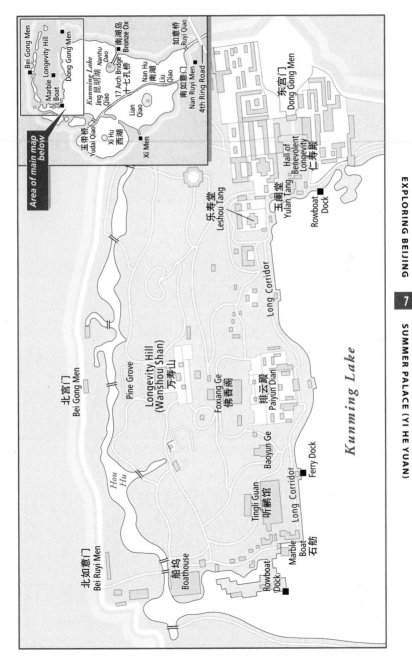

Area of main map below

北宫门 Bei Gong Men

北如意门 Bei Ruyi Men

船坞 Boathouse

听鹂馆 Tingli Guan

石舫 Marble Boat

Long Corridor

Rowboat Dock

Ferry Dock

Baoyun Ge

排云殿 Paiyun Dian

佛香阁 Foxiang Ge

万寿山 Longevity Hill (Wanshou Shan)

Pine Grove

乐寿堂 Leshou Tang

Long Corridor

玉澜堂 Yulan Tang

仁寿殿 Hall of Benevolent Longevity

东宫门 Dong Gong Men

Rowboat Dock

Kunming Lake

Hou Hu

Bei Gong Men

Marble Boat

Longevity Hill

Dong Gong Men

昆明湖 Kunming Lake Jing

玉带桥 Yudai Qiao

西湖 Xi Hu

西门 Xi Men

Lian Qiao

Liu Qiao

南湖岛 Nanhu Dao

南湖 Nan Hu

十七孔桥 17 Arch Bridge

南如意门 Nan Ruyi Men

4th Ring Road

南湖岛 Bronze Ox

如意桥 Ruyi Qiao

Impressions

"Most people hate the Old Buddha (Cixi) for diverting the naval funds. How unjust! Any navy we built in those days would have been destroyed in the first battle. Which of our enemies would have helped us build a fleet capable of destroying a single ship of theirs? They would have sent our fleet to the bottom of the sea and then charged us with the costs of the action, as they always did! As it is, the Old Buddha's palace still stands—they say there is nothing equal to it in the world! Could anyone, Chinese or foreign, of our generation duplicate it?"
—*Professor Ch'eng, quoted in John Blofeld,* City of Lingering Splendour, *1961*

is where the Empress Dowager received members of the court, first from behind a screen and later, all pretenses dropped, from the Dragon Throne itself. North of the hall is Cixi's private theater, now a museum that contains an old Mercedes-Benz—the first car imported into China.

Seventeen-Arch Bridge (Shiqi Kong Qiao) ★   This marble bridge, 150m (492 ft.) long, connects South Lake Island (Nan Hu Dao) to the east shore of Kunming Lake. There is a rather striking life-size bronze ox near the eastern foot of the bridge.

5 TEMPLES, MOSQUES & CHURCHES

While signs around Beijing whip up indignation at the destruction of Chinese temples by foreign forces in 1860 and 1900, most destruction was carried out by the Chinese themselves, particularly after 1949. Medium-size houses of worship—Buddhist, Christian, Confucian, Daoist, and Muslim alike—fared badly; many were torn down straightaway, while others were converted to factories, hospitals, schools, or police stations. With the realization by the Chinese authorities that tourists are willing to pay money to inspect them, some have been converted back to a semblance of their original form, if not function.

Bai Ta Si (White Dagoba Temple)   Seemingly continuously under renovation, this Liao dynasty temple features the largest Tibetan pagoda (also called *chorten, dagoba,* or stupa) in China, towering over the neighborhood at 51m (167 ft.) tall. A Nepali architect built it over 700 years ago (completed 1279) by order of Kublai Khan, one of the first Mongols to convert to Tibetan Buddhism. Originally known as Miao Ying Si, the temple has undergone numerous reconstructions, usually as a result of fire. The Dajue Dian (Hall of the Great Enlightened Ones), the first building, contains thousands of little Buddhas in glass cases, set into the columns. An earthquake in 1976 turned up numerous artifacts, some of which are now on display in the museum. You'll find Buddhist statuary demonstrating ritualistic hand positions *(mudra)* and vivid *thangka* (silk hangings depicting Buddhist images).

Fucheng Men Nei Dajie 171, Xi Cheng Qu (a 10-min. walk east from the metro stop); see map p. 106. *✆* 010/6616-0211. Admission ¥20. 9am–4:30pm. Metro: Fucheng Men.

Baiyun Guan ★★   If the incense here somehow smells more authentic, it's because this sprawling complex, said to have been built in 739, is the most active of Beijing's Daoist temples. Chinese visitors seem intent on actual worship rather than smug tourism, and the blue-frocked monks wear their hair in the rarely seen traditional manner—long and tied in a bun at the top of the head. The temple acts as headquarters for the Chinese Daoist Association. Although the texts of Daoism (China's only native religion) decry the pursuit of wealth and honors as empty, the gods of wealth attract the most devotees. One notable structure is the Laolu Tang, a large cushion-filled hall in the third courtyard originally built in 1228, now used for teaching and ceremonies.

On Baiyun Guan Lu, east of the intersection with Baiyun Lu, Haidian Qu (1st right north of Baiyun Qiao, directly across from Baiyun Guan bus stop); see map p. 114. ✆ 010/6346-3531. Admission ¥10. 8:30am–4:30pm. Bus: no. 727 from Muxidi metro to Baiyun Guan.

Dong Tang (East Church or St. Joseph's Cathedral) This gray Gothic structure has endured a torrid history. Built on ground donated by the Shunzhi emperor in 1655, this Jesuit church was toppled by an earthquake in 1720, then gutted by fire in 1812, after which it was leveled by an increasingly antiforeign regime. It was rebuilt after foreigners forced their way into Beijing in 1860, and was razed again during the Boxer Rebellion of 1900. Chinese Christians were the first targets of the xenophobic Boxers, who disparagingly referred to them as "lesser hairy ones." Local converts were slaughtered in the hundreds before the Boxers (who also murdered women with unbound feet) worked up the courage to kill a real foreigner. Yet they are usually portrayed as a "patriotic" movement in China's history books. After a major renovation in 2000, Dong Tang is notable for its wide, tree-lined forecourt, a favorite spot for Beijing's skateboarders. Its counterpart in the south of town, **Nan Tang (South Church)** is just northeast of the Xuanwu Men metro stop, and has services in English. Call ✆ 010/6603-7139 to check times. *Note:* Catholic churches in Beijing are not recognized by the Roman Catholic Church.

Wangfujing Dajie 74, Dong Cheng Qu (walk north for 10 min.); see map p. 106. ✆ 010/6524-0634. Sat services in Latin at 6:30 and Chinese at 7am. Metro: Wangfujing.

Dong Yue Miao ★ Reopened to the public in 1999, one of Beijing's most captivating Daoist temples stands largely disregarded. Founded in 1322 by the devotees of the Zhengyi sect, the temple is dedicated to the god Dong Yue, who resides in the sacred mountain of Tai Shan. Aside from coping with the hordes of tourists who now visit his abode, Dong Yue is charged with supervising the 18 layers of Hell and the 76 departments.

The garishly represented emissaries of these departments may be found in the 72 halls that ring the main courtyard of the temple. Worshipers present themselves at the relevant hall, with offerings of money, incense, and red tokens inscribed with their names *(fupai)*. With 76 departments (some are forced to share a cubicle), there are emissaries for every conceivable wish, and if viewed as a straw poll of China's preoccupations, the results are not encouraging. The Department for Accumulating Wealth ("justifiable" is added in the translation) is busy, while the Department of Pity and Sympathy, depicting beggars, awaits its first petition, and there are an alarming number of donations for the Department for Implementing 15 Kinds of Violent Death. This may or may not be related to the ongoing popularity of the Department of Official Morality, which rails against corrupt government.

A glassed-in stele at the northeast corner of the courtyard is written in the fine hand of Zhao Mengfu, recording the building of the temple and the life of its founder, Zhang Liusun, who died soon after purchasing the land. At the north of the complex stands the two-story **Minsu Bowuguan** (Folk Museum). This hosts exhibitions to remind Beijingers of their marvelous but largely forgotten traditions.

Chaoyang Men Wai Dajie 141, Chaoyang Qu (10-min. walk east on the north side); see map p. 111. ✆ 010/6551-0151. Admission ¥10; free during festivals. Tues–Sun 8:30am–4:30pm. Metro: Chaoyang Men.

Fahai Si   Located in the far west of Beijing, this early Ming temple, a must for those with an interest in Buddhist art, is easily combined with a visit to the cemetery for eunuchs, Tian Yi Mu (p. 143). The decoration of this temple in 1443 was funded by Li Tong, a wealthy eunuch who attracted artists from the Imperial court to produce stunning murals and statuary. The statues didn't survive the Cultural Revolution, but Red Guards failed to notice the exquisite **Buddhist murals** ★★ in the gloom of the main hall. These murals, miraculously preserved intact, were modeled on the art of the Tang, but show influences of Song dynasty landscape painting, and later Ming innovations in the use of perspective and depth in portraiture. The brushwork, particularly in the depiction of robes, clouds, and flowers, is extraordinarily fine.

Moshi Kou Dajie, Shijing Shan Qu (from bus stop, continue up the rise and take a right after 5 min.; pass Tian Yi Mu, take a left turn, continue uphill to a T-junction, and take a right turn; the temple is a further 5 min. up the hill); see map p. 116. ℂ 010/8871-5776. Admission ¥20. 8:30am–4:30pm. Bus: no. 959 or 746 from left of Pingguo Yuan metro stop to Shougang Xiaoqu. *Note:* This temple was being renovated at time of writing. New prices had not yet been decided. It should be open by the time you read this.

Fayuan Si (Source of Dharma Temple) (Finds)   Despite guides droning on about a long and glorious history, most of Beijing's sights are relatively new, dating from within the past 600 years. This temple, constructed in 645 in what was then the southeast corner of town, retains both an air of antiquity and the feel of a genuine Buddhist monastery. Orange-robed monks, housed in the adjacent Buddhist college, go about their business in earnest, and the visitors are asked to "respect religious ceremonies: Do not interfere with religious activities." The ancient *hutong* immediately surrounding the temple are "protected" and worth a wander. Lanman Hutong, just to the east, was formerly a moat that marked the boundary of the old town during the Tang dynasty.

Fayuan Si Qian Jie 7, Xuanwu Qu; see map p. 114. Admission ¥5. Thurs–Tues 8:30–11am and 1:30–4pm. Metro: Xuanwu Men.

Guo Zi Jian and Kong Miao ★   Buried down a tree-shaded street west of the Lama Temple (see below), **Kong Miao,** China's second-largest Confucian temple, is on the right, and **Guo Zi Jian (Directorate of Education)** is on the left; both were originally built in 1306. Two stelae at the front *(xia ma bei)* instruct you to park your horse in six different languages. The front courtyard of the temple contains 198 stelae inscribed with the names of successful candidates in the *jinshi* (highest level) imperial examinations during the Yuan, Ming, and Qing dynasties. Staff admit they see few local visitors, except during the weekend before the university entrance examinations, when students and their parents descend in droves to ask for the Great Sage's assistance. The main hall, **Dacheng Dian,** is the focus for students, who must throw their incense on the shrine rather than burn it, because of fire regulations. Ancient musical instruments, which Confucius saw as essential to self-cultivation, are the main point of interest. Behind the hall and to the left are 189 stelae, which contain the 630,000 characters that make up the Thirteen Confucian Classics—incredibly, copied by one man over a 12-year period. The attendant enhances the mood of antiquity by earnestly reciting old texts.

Success in the imperial examination was the key to social advancement, so **Guo Zi Jian** wielded immense power. It was originally joined to Kong Miao by Chijing Men, to the right as you enter. They will be reunited when the Ministry of Culture (housed in Guo Zi Jian) and the Ministry of Cultural Relics (housed in Kong Miao) can sort out their differences. A striking yellow glazed-tile *pailou* (gate) with elaborately carved stone arches leads to **Bi Yong Dadian** ★, a square wooden hall encircled by a moat. The emperor would deliver a lecture on the classics here at the start of his reign, although the irrepressible Qianlong visited three times—after assuming the throne, after renovations were completed to mark the 50th anniversary of his reign, and when handing the throne over to his son, the Jiaqing emperor. He even wrote poems to decorate the sandalwood screen behind the throne. Ministers and the royal family were permitted inside, while three criers (to the west, south, and east) would repeat the emperor's words to students and minor officials kneeling outside.

Kong Miao at Guo Zi Jian Jie 13, Dong Cheng Qu (walk south from station along west side of Lama Temple, turn right onto street marked with arch); see map p. 106. © 010/8401-1977. Admission ¥20 to both. Kong Miao 8:30am–5:30pm; Guo Zi Jian 9am–5pm. Metro: Yong He Gong/Lama Temple.

Lidai Diwang Miao (Temple of Past Emperors) ★ (Finds)

Lidai Diwang Miao is where Ming and Qing emperors made sacrifices to the emperors of previous dynasties. Built on the grounds of a former Buddhist temple (Bao'an Si), there's nary a Buddha in sight. Rulers didn't always come in person, but their representatives diligently carried out sacrifices in spring and autumn. The Yongzheng emperor, who killed his brother to usurp the throne, had more reason to pray than most, and made five appearances during his short reign. The layout is akin to Tai Miao in miniature, with an imposing spirit wall opposite the entrance, and two horse-dismounting tablets on either side of the entrance. There were originally three marble bridges and a spectacular wooden memorial arch (*pailou*) outside the entrance; these feudal elements were demolished in 1953 and 1954. Curatorial standards are improving: Patches of the original ceiling have been left in their original state, touch-screen displays in the exhibition halls roughly translate the captions, and there is even an admission of past vandalism. The original wooden tablets, once housed in the impressive twin-eaved main hall, were smashed during the Cultural Revolution. Their replacements look inauthentic, but the original order has been preserved. Central position goes to the legendary ruler Fuxi, and his successors are arranged outward in order of venerability, one to the left, one to the right (*yi zuo yi you*), a seating arrangement still followed by China's rulers. The most striking feature is the intricately carved stelae (nearly 8m/26 ft. tall) set to the east and west of the main hall.

Fucheng Men Dajie 131 (a 5-min. walk east from metro); see map p. 106. © 010/6612-0186. Admission ¥20. 8:30am–4:30pm. Metro: Fucheng Men.

Niu Jie Libai Si (Ox Street Mosque)

This is Beijing's largest mosque and the spiritual center for the city's estimated 200,000 Muslims. Built in 996, the complex looks more Eastern than Middle Eastern, with sloping tile roofs similar to those found in Buddhist temples. Halls are noticeably free of idols, however. A small courtyard on the south side contains the tombs and original gravestones of two Arab imams who lived here in the late 13th century. The main prayer hall is ghostly quiet except on Friday, the traditional day of worship.

Niu Jie 88, Xuanwu Qu (on east side of street); see map p. 114. © 010/6353-2564. Admission ¥10 for non-Muslims. 4am–9:30pm. Bus: no. 10 or 66 to Libai Si from Changchun Jie metro stop.

Tai Miao ★★ (Finds)

Sometimes the biggest surprises are under your nose. Just east of Tian'an Men stands the only example of an imperial ancestral hall (*zu miao*) remaining in China; here are grand imperial edifices in a sleepy, atmospheric setting. Laid out in accordance with the ancient principle from the Rites of Zhou, "ancestors to the left, land to the right" (*zuo zu you she*), the wooden tablets (*paiwei*) that represented the ancestors of the imperial house were housed to the left of the Forbidden City (the land was offered its due at the Altar of Land and Grain, housed in Zhongshan Gongyuan to the west). Beyond the Halberd Gate (Ji Men), untouched since it was constructed in 1420, the three main buildings are lined up on a central axis. Sacrifices to the ancestors took place in the southernmost building (Xiang Dian). This is one of only four buildings in Beijing to stand on a three-tiered platform, a hint that it was the most sacred site in imperial Beijing. Mao renamed it the Workers' Cultural Palace (Laodong Renmin Wenhua Gong), and the wooden tablets were pilfered during the Cultural Revolution. The workers have moved on, and the complex is largely deserted. Once you reach the moat at the northern end of the complex, turn left. Immediately opposite is **Zhongshan Gongyuan;** to the right stands **Wu Men** and the Forbidden City. Infinitely preferable to running the souvenir vendor gauntlet north from Tian'an Men, entering the Forbidden City from Tai Miao may be the best ¥2 you'll ever spend.

East of Tian'an Men, Dong Cheng Qu; see map p. 106. © 010/6525-2189. June–Sept 6:30am–8:30pm; Oct–May 7am–8:30pm. Admission ¥2; admission to bell exhibit ¥10. Metro: Tian'an Men Dong.

Wanshou Si ★ The Longevity Temple, now home to the **Beijing Art Museum (Beijing Yishu Bowuguan),** was funded by a eunuch and was originally constructed in 1577. It later became a stopping point for the Qianlong emperor and his successors (particularly the Empress Dowager Cixi) on their way to the Summer Palace by boat, a route now followed by tour boats departing from just north of the zoo. The long sequence of heavily restored but low-key halls now houses an odd set of exhibitions, featuring everything from early ceramics, iron, and copperware, to late and very intricate lacquerware and carved ivory. Puzzlingly, the museum's most interesting exhibit, highly decorated and ancient seals *(zhuanzhang)* wrought from a variety of precious and semiprecious materials, are now kept in storage. At the rear of the complex is a rock garden from whose top Cixi is supposed to have admired the surrounding countryside, now long built over. Also visible are the original east and west wings of the complex, now occupied by squatters and staff, although there are plans to renovate the west wing.

Xi San Huan Bei Lu 18, Haidian Qu (on north side of Chang He, east side of the W. Third Ring Rd.); see map p. 116. © 010/6841-3380. Admission ¥20; ¥60, including cup of tea. 9am–4:30pm (last ticket sold at 4pm). Bus: no. 811 from Gongzhu Fen metro stop to Wanshou Si.

Wu Ta Si (Five Pagoda Temple) More correctly known as Zhenjue Si (Temple of True Awakening), the one ancient building remaining on this site is a massive stone block with magnificently preserved Indian Buddhist motifs carved out of the bare rock. Peacocks, elephants, and dharma wheels adorn the base, which is also decorated with sutras copied out in Sanskrit (the large script) and Tibetan (the small script). The central pagoda has an image of two feet, harking back to an age when artisans could only hint at the presence of Buddha through symbols. The circular pavilion was added by the Qianlong emperor to honor his mother, an act of architectural vandalism which ruined the original simplicity and symmetry of the pagoda. The surrounding courtyard is gradually filling up with stone tombstones, spirit-way figures, and stelae commemorating the construction or renovation of temples; most are refugees from construction and road-widening projects around the capital. The wonderfully curated **Shike Yishu Bowuguan (Stone Carving Museum)** ★★ is at the rear of the complex. Beijing Aquarium is a 15-minute walk to the northeast.

Wu Ta Si Cun 24, Haidian Qu (from Beijing Tushuguan walk south and turn left at the Nanchang Canal; the walk takes 10 min.); see map p. 116. © 010/6217-3836. Admission ¥20. 9am–4:30pm. Bus: no. 808 from just east of Xi Zhi Men metro stop to Beijing Tushuguan.

Yonghe Gong (Lama Temple) ★★★ If you visit only one temple after the Temple of Heaven, this should be it. A complex of progressively larger buildings topped with ornate yellow-tiled roofs, Yonghe Gong was built in 1694 and originally belonged to the Qing prince who would become the Yongzheng emperor. As was the custom, the complex was converted to a temple after Yongzheng's move to the Forbidden City in 1744. The temple is home to several rather beautiful **incense burners,** including a particularly ornate one in the second courtyard that dates back to 1746. The Falun Dian (Hall of the Wheel of Law), second to last of the major buildings, contains a 6m (20-ft.) bronze statue of Tsongkapa (1357–1419), the founder of the reformist Yellow Hat (Geluk) sect of Tibetan Buddhism, which is now the dominant school of Tibetan Buddhism. He's easily recognized by his pointed cap with long earflaps. The last of the five central halls, the Wanfu Ge (Tower of Ten Thousand Happinesses), houses the temple's prize possession—an ominous Tibetan-style **statue of Maitreya** (the future Buddha), 18m (59 ft.) tall, carved from a single piece of white sandalwood. Once something of a circus, Yonghe Gong is slowly starting to feel like a place of worship, as there are now many Chinese devotees of Tibetan Buddhism.

Yong He Gong Dajie 12, south of the N. Second Ring Rd. (entrance on the south end of the complex); see map p. 106. ✆ 010/6404-3769. Summer 9am–4:30pm; winter 9am–4pm. Admission ¥25; audio tours in English additional ¥25 plus ¥200 deposit. Metro: Yong He Gong/Lama Temple.

6 PARKS & GARDENS

Olympic Park (Aolinpike Gongyuan) ★ Everything in Beijing is big. Tian'an Men Square is roughly the size of 90 football fields, wandering through the Forbidden City feels like a minimarathon, and of course the Great Wall is . . . very long. It is fitting then that hosting the Olympics in Beijing meant building awe-inspiring, people-dwarfing structures. And all at a sizable price tag of $40 billion.

Beijing's **Olympic Green** is the main attraction. Wear comfortable shoes, because the green covers an area roughly six times the size of Athens' Olympic Green and three times the size of New York's Central Park. Electric trolleys with tours in Chinese only will take you around the green for ¥20, round-trip. The biggest draw here is the **Beijing National Stadium,** dubbed "the Bird's Nest" because its oblong shape and interlocking steel grids closely resemble the twigs and branches of, well, a bird's nest. The original design featured an innovative retractable roof, but that was scrapped a year before the XXIX Olympiad due to cost and time pressures. But even without a fancy convertible-like ceiling, the Bird's Nest is an impressive architectural feat. It was designed by architecture darlings Jacques Herzog and Pierre de Meuron, cost roughly $400 million, and can hold 91,000 spectators. It hosted the opening and closing ceremonies, as well as athletics events and football. The ¥50 entrance fee (ticket booths are at the north end of the nest) gets you into the stadium, where you can walk right onto the field and have your picture taken with the Olympic torch for ¥15. A post office on-site sells commemorative stamps and a few other stores sell Olympic kitsch inside. A healthy stone's throw away from the Bird's Nest is the **National Aquatics Center,** also known as "the Water Cube" (it's actually a rectangle, but "Water Rectangle" didn't have the same ring). From the outside, it looks like a giant cube made up of hundreds of bubbles. Swimming, diving, synchronized swimming, and water polo events were held here. If you've been to a high-school swim meet, save yourself the ¥30 entrance fee, because the indoor view of the Water Cube is pretty much the same. You can swim at the Water Cube, but only in the warm-up pool. Head to the ticket booths on the western side of the aquatics center. The ¥50 entrance ticket buys you 2 hours of swimming in crowded, often chaotic lanes. A mandatory swim test (100m in the stroke of your choice) is required and you must wear a swim cap. North of the Water Cube is the **National Indoor Stadium,** which hosted gymnastics and handball events. Its design plays on the theme of a traditional Chinese folding fan. Unlike its neighbors, it doesn't have a cutesy nickname.

Behind the Olympic Green is the **Olympic Forest Park.** During the Olympics, the park hosted tennis, archery, and hockey events. This spacious bit of greenery includes **Main Mountain,** a man-made pile of 3.98 million cubic meters (141 million cubic ft.) of earth, and **Main Lake,** a 110-hectare (272-acre, roughly 205 football fields) body of water shaped like the Olympic torch. While this is Beijing's largest city park at 640 hectares (1,581 acres), there's nothing terribly special here. It's over 1km (less than a mile) north of the Water Cube and Bird's Nest, so if your feet are already aching, you can skip this attraction.

Beichen Dong Lu; see map p. 106. ⓒ **010/8437-3017.** Free admission to the Olympic Green. 24-hr. Admission to National Stadium ¥50, free for children under 1.2m (4 ft.) and seniors; National Aquatics Center ¥30, ¥15 children under 1.5m (5 ft.) and seniors 65–69. 9am–5:30pm. Opening times for both stadiums will vary in the case of sporting or entertainment events. Swimming at National Aquatics Center ¥50. 2–9pm. Free admission to Olympic Forest Park. Mar 15–Nov 15 6am–8pm; Nov 16–Mar 14 8am–6pm. Metro: Olympic Sports Centre.

Bei Hai Gongyuan (Beihai Park) ★ An imperial playground dating back to the Tartar Jin dynasty (1115–1234), Bei Hai lies to the north of Zhong Hai and Nan Hai, which were also opened to the public in 1925. In the best tradition of *Animal Farm,* the Communist leaders created a new Forbidden City and named it Zhong Nan Hai. Bei Hai was left to the masses. Although it's a convenient way to combine a morning visit to the Forbidden City with a more relaxing afternoon in the Back Lakes area, most visitors have a quick peek at the southern half and then disappear. Unfortunately, they miss the north side of the park, which is more interesting.

Entering from the south, you come to **Tuan Cheng (Round City),** a small citadel on a raised platform whose most notable structure, **Chengguang Dian,** houses a 1.5m-tall (5-ft.) statue of a feminine-looking Buddha, crafted from Burmese white jade. Crossing the Yong'an Bridge to **Qiong Dao (Qiong Islet),** you soon reach **Yong'an Si,** where the founder of the prominent Geluk sect, Tsongkapa, was the focus of devotion. He is now portrayed as a Chinese reformer of corrupt Tibetan Buddhism, on the grounds that he was born in Qinghai rather than "autonomous" Tibet. From here, boats run to the north side of the park for ¥5, or you can walk around the east side, passing calligraphers wielding enormous sponge-tipped brushes to compose rapidly evaporating poems on the flagstones.

Boats pull in to the east of **Wu Long Ting (Five Dragon Pavilion),** where aspiring singers treat the public to revolutionary airs popular in the 1950s. Off to the left is an impressive green-tiled *pailou* (memorial arch; the green tiles signify a religious purpose, in contrast to the yellow imperial tiles of the Forbidden City and Guo Zi Jian). Continue on to the square-shaped **Jile Shijie Dian** ★, encircled by a dry moat. Built by the Qianlong emperor to honor his mother, the sandalwood structure is exquisite, topped with a priceless gold dome (apparently too high for either foreign troops or local warlords to reach). The gaudy fiberglass statuary inside brings you back to the present. To the west stands an impressive **Nine Dragon Screen,** which guarded the entrance to a now-vanished temple. Farther east is **Daci Zhenru Bao Dian** ★★, an atmospheric Buddhist hall built during the late Ming from unpainted cedar; topped with a black roof (to protect the precious wood from fire), it has a cool slate floor. Continue east to the northern exit onto Ping'an Dadao, which marks the southern end of the Shicha Hai (Back Lakes) area.

Wenjin Jie 1, Xi Cheng Qu (south entrance is just west of the north gate of the Forbidden City; east entrance is opposite the west entrance of Jing Shan Park); see map p. 106. ℂ 010/6404-0610. Admission summer ¥10; winter ¥5; ¥10 extra for Yong'an Si; ¥1 extra for Tuan Cheng. 6am–10pm. Bus: no. 812 or 814 from Dong Dan metro stop to Bei Hai.

Jing Shan Gongyuan (Jing Shan Park)

If you want a clear aerial view of the Forbidden City, you'll find it here. The park's central hill was created using earth left over from the digging of the imperial moat and was the highest point in the city during the Ming dynasty. It was designed to enhance the feng shui of the Forbidden City, by blocking the harsh northern wind and by burying a Mongol Yuan dynasty pavilion, the Yanchun Ge. In something of a riposte to the Chinese Ming dynasty, the Manchu Qianlong emperor built a tower by the same name (albeit in a very different style) in the Jianfu Gong Huayuan, within the Forbidden City. A tree on the east side of the hill marks the spot where the last Ming emperor, Chongzhen, supposedly hanged himself in 1644, just before Manchu and rebel armies overran the city. The original tree, derided as the "guilty sophora" during the Qing, was hacked down by Red Guards who failed to recognize a fellow anti-imperialist.

Jing Shan Qian Jie 1, Dong Cheng Qu (opposite Forbidden City north gate); see map p. 106. ℂ 010/6404-4071. Admission ¥5. Jan–Mar and Nov–Dec 6:30am–8pm; Apr–May and Sep–Oct 6am–9pm; June–Aug 6am–10pm. Bus: no. 812 from Dong Dan metro stop (exit A) to Gu Gong.

Ming Chengqiang Gongyuan (Ming City Wall Park) ★

The section of wall presented here, running a mile east-to-west from Dongbian Men to Chongwen Men, was originally built in the Yuan dynasty (1279–1368) and reconstructed in the mid-1500s by the Ming. Modern restoration work on the section began in 2002 and is still in progress, using bricks from the original Ming reconstruction collected from nearby residents (some of whom employed them to build toilets after the wall was demolished in the 1950s). A pleasant park runs east along the length of the wall to the dramatic Dongnan Jiaolou (Southeast Corner Tower; daily 9am–5pm; ¥10), with its dozens of arrow slots; a contemporary art gallery and interesting exhibition on the history of Chongwen can be found inside.

East of metro stop. ℂ 010/6527-0574. 24-hr. Metro: Chongwen Men.

Ri Tan Gongyuan (Ri Tan Park)

The Temple of the Sun (Ri Tan) served as an altar where the emperor conducted annual rites. Built in 1530, Ri Tan is a pleasant park with a delightful outdoor **teahouse** ★ and a **rock-climbing wall.** Fishponds, a pedal-powered monorail, kites, and a bonsai market also keep the locals amused.

The other imperial altars are located in similar city parks, roughly marking the five points of the Chinese compass. To the north is **Di Tan Gongyuan (Temple of Earth),** just north of the Lama Temple; to the west is **Yue Tan Gongyuan (Temple of the Moon);** and the much grander **Tian Tan Gongyuan (Temple of Heaven)** marks the southern point. **She Ji Tan (Altar of Land and Grain)** in Zhongshan Gongyuan, southwest of the Forbidden City, predates them all by several centuries, and marks that peculiarly Chinese compass point, the center.

Ri Tan Lu 6, Chaoyang Qu; see map p. 111. ℂ 010/8561-1389. Free admission. 6am–9:30pm (6:30am–9pm in winter). Metro: Yong'an Li.

Yuan Ming Yuan ★ **Kids**   An amalgamation of three separate imperial gardens, these ruins create a ghostly and oddly enjoyable scene, beloved for years as a picnic spot. Established by the Kangxi emperor in 1707, Yuan Ming Yuan is a more recent construction than the New Summer Palace to the west, but it is misleadingly called the Old Summer Palace because it was never rebuilt after French and British troops looted and burned it down during the Second Opium War of 1860. Ironically, some of the buildings were Western-style and filled with European furnishings and art. Two Jesuit priests, Italian painter Castiglione and French scientist Benoist, were commissioned by Qianlong to design the 30-hectare (75-acre) **Xi Yang Lou (Western Mansions)** in the northeast section of the park. Perhaps the most remarkable structure was a zodiac water clock which spouted from 12 bronze heads, 3 of which (an ox, a monkey, and a tiger) are now housed in the otherwise unremarkable **Poly Art Museum,** immediately above Dong Si Shi Tiao metro stop. Inaccurate models suggest that the structures were entirely European in style, but they were curious hybrids, featuring Imperial-style vermilion walls and yellow-tiled roofs. A few restorations have begun, starting with the **Wanhua Zhen (10,000 Flowers Maze),** a nicely reconstructed labyrinth in the **Changchun Yuan (Garden of Eternal Spring).** Recently, the park has been the center of environmental controversy. Park management and the district government decided to line the lakes (an integral part of Beijing's water ecology and a magnet for bird life) with plastic sheeting to save on water bills and raise the water levels to allow for a duck-boat business.

Qinghua Xi Lu 28, Haidian Qu (north of Peking University); see map p. 116. © **010/6262-8501.** 7am–7pm (to 5:30pm in winter). Admission ¥10; ¥15 to enter Xi Yang Lou. Bus: no. 743 or 375 from east of Wudaokou metro stop to Yuan Ming Yuan.

7 MUSEUMS

In keeping with the Communist (and Confucian) passion for naming and quantification, Beijing has a museum for everything—police, bees, even the humble watermelon. If you share this passion and plan on spending a week or more in the capital, invest in a *bowuguan tong piao* (¥80), which grants you free (or half-price) admission to 98 sites in and around Beijing. You can buy the museum pass at full-service post offices around town.

Beijing Guihua Bowuguan (Beijing Planning and Exhibition Hall) ★ **Kids**
This high-tech museum gives you of a glimpse of tomorrow's Beijing. Several of the exhibitions are interactive, including the scale model of Beijing that you can actually walk on. We highly recommend the short movies, offered at half-hour intervals and in English on request. The 3-D movie, complete with the funny glasses, tells the history of Beijing's development. The 4-D movie—more like a ride at an amusement park—whisks you on a tour of Beijing's future subway lines, which will supposedly connect any two points in Beijing in less than an hour. Even if it is propaganda, it's still good fun.

20 Qianmen Dong Lu. © **010/6702-4559.** www.bjghzl.com.cn. Admission ¥30; ¥10 additional for each movie. Tues–Sun 9am–5pm, last ticket sold at 4pm. Metro: Qianmen.

Capital Museum (Shou Du Bowuguan) ★ **Kids**   This surprisingly well-curated museum of Beijing history and culture includes plenty of English subtitles that are often too scarce at other Beijing museums. Exhibitions on Chinese courtyard architecture and Buddhist sculpture are some of the highlights. Especially fun for the kids is the fifth floor's folk exhibition, which includes displays on Chinese traditional dress and live demonstrations of Peking Opera on Saturdays.

Da Zhong Si (Great Bell Temple)

Da Zhong Si (Great Bell Temple)   An attraction to bring out the hunchback in any-one, this Qing temple now houses the **Ancient Bell Museum (Gu Zhong Bowuguan),** best visited on the way to the Summer Palace or in conjunction with **Wanshou Si** (p. 134), which lies to the southwest along the Third Ring Road. The temple was known as Juesheng Si (Awakened Life Temple). But the 47-ton bell transported here on ice sleds in 1743 clearly took center stage, hence the temple's current moniker. The third hall on the right houses clangers garnered from around Beijing. Some were donated by eunuchs wishing the rele-vant emperor long life, with hundreds of donors' names scrawled on their sides. But frus-tratingly, none of this is fleshed out. The main attraction is housed in the rear hall, carved inside and out with 230,000 Chinese and Sanskrit characters. The big bell tolls but once a year, on New Year's Eve. Visitors rub the handles of Qianlong's old wash basin, and scramble up narrow steps to make a wish while throwing coins through a hole in the top of the monster. But it is no longer the "King of Bells"—that honor now goes to the 50-ton bell housed in the **Altar to the Century (Zhonghua Shiji Tan),** constructed in 1999 to prove that China could waste money on the millennium, too.

Bei San Huan Xi Lu 31A, Haidian Qu (west of metro stop, north of Lianxiang Qiao on the northwest side of the Third Ring Rd.); see map p. 116. ℰ **010/6255-0819.** Admission ¥10; ¥2 extra to climb the Bell Tower. Tues–Sun 8:30am–4:30pm. Free admission for the first 200 visitors on Wed. Metro: Da Zhong Si.

Gudai Jianzhu Bowuguan (Museum of Ancient Architecture) ★★

Gudai Jianzhu Bowuguan (Museum of Ancient Architecture) ★★   This exhibition, a mixture of models of China's most famous architecture and fragments of buildings long disappeared, is housed in halls as dramatic as those on the central axis of the Forbidden City. These were once part of the **Xian Nong Tan,** or Altar of Agriculture, now as obscure as neighboring Tian Tan, the Temple (properly Altar) of Heaven, is famous. From about 1410, emperors came to this once-extensive site to perform rituals in which they started the agricultural cycle by playing farmer and plowing the first fur-rows. The site where they once toiled is now a basketball court.

The exhibition in the surviving halls is striking in its extensive English explanations of everything from the construction of the complicated bracket sets, which support temple roofs, to the role of geomancy in Chinese architectural thinking, and curiosities from now-razed sites such as Longfu Si. Models of significant buildings around Beijing can help you select what to see in the capital during the remainder of your trip.

The rearmost **Taisui Dian (Hall of Jupiter)** of 1532, with its vast, sweeping roof, is exceeded in magnificence only by the Forbidden City's Hall of Supreme Harmony.

Dong Jing Lu 21, Xuanwu Qu (from bus stop, take 1st right into Nan Wei Lu and walk 5 min.; look for an archway down a street on the left); see map p. 114. ℰ **010/6301-7620.** Admission ¥15. 9am–4pm. Bus: no. 803 from just south of Wangfujing or Qian Men metro stops to Tian Qiao Shangchang.

Military Museum of the Chinese People's Revolution (Junshi Bowuguan) ★

Military Museum of the Chinese People's Revolution (Junshi Bowuguan) ★
Fighter planes, missiles, and tanks—oh my! Walk past the giant marble Mao Zedong statue in the foyer and head straight to this museum's awesome Hall of Weapons. Here you'll find mid-20th-century F-series fighter planes modeled after Russia's MIG-17, tanks, rocket mine-layers (whose accompanying English explanation has a typo identify-ing them as "pocket mine-layers") and other big and scary items surrounding the biggest, scariest item of all: a giant DF-1 ballistic missile. The weapons hall's second floor show-cases gobs of 1950s and 1960s American guns and rifles captured from the Kuomintang during the Revolutionary War, as well as a busy store selling toy weapons (mini AK-47

EXPLORING BEIJING

7

MUSEUMS

for the li'l one, perhaps?). The fourth-floor ancient war exhibition is also worth a peek for its Ming dynasty canons, and replicas of long-range weapons and ancient Chinese warships. Unfortunately, a lot of the cool exhibits in this section—terra-cotta warriors, ancient bronze horsemen, and stone reliefs—are only copies of originals housed in other museum collections, a common practice in Chinese museums.

Fuxingmenwai Dajie A9; see map p. 116. ℂ **010/6686-6244.** Free admission. English audio tours ¥10, deposit ¥100. 8:30am–5pm. Metro: Military Museum.

National Museum of China (Guojia Bowuguan) ★

The Museum of the Chinese Revolution and the Museum of History have been united in a single building, but renovations won't be completed until 2010. Until then, a series of exhibits emphasizing the greatness of the Chinese civilization will be shown. Some effort has been made to spruce things up, and English captions have been added to a number of the displays, although they are conspicuously lacking from the hilarious wax figure hall. In the past, interest centered on who was omitted from Chinese history; now it focuses on who is included. Former unpersons such as Liu Shaoqi and Lin Biao, Mao's ill-fated heirs apparent, are displayed alongside their tormentors. The Party line is scrupulously followed: The passive and obsequious Lin, whose death went unreported for nearly a year, is still said to have plotted to seize power from Mao.

East side of Tian'an Men Square, Dong Cheng Qu; see map p. 106. ℂ **010/8468-9019.** www.nmch.gov. cn. Admission ¥30 for *tong piao* (all-inclusive), or ¥10–¥20 for each exhibit; English audio tours ¥30. 9am–3:30pm. Metro: Tian'an Men East.

Zhongguo Dianying Bowuguan (China National Film Museum)

If you're a Chinese movie buff, you'll love this place. The black and white building is loosely designed to look like a giant screen and a movie clipboard. Inside, you'll find a huge IMAX theater on your right; to your left is a four-story circular ramp leading to exhibits stuffed with black-and-white photos, old camera equipment and movie memorabilia, and even a mini-set of Old China. Wall-mounted plasma TVs show clips from various films. In the special effects hall on the fifth floor, fork over ¥10 to buy yourself a ride on a motorcycle or carpet and choose from seven different blue screen backgrounds—escaping the snapping jaws of a T-rex, or floating peacefully over the Temple of Heaven. You'll get a CD of your ride afterward, and yes, it will look very cheesy. There are English translations for introductions to exhibits, but otherwise information is in Chinese only. The biggest drawback of this museum is its location—it's halfway to the airport. Combine a visit here with a trip to nearby art district 798 (p. 141).

20 Nanying Lu. ℂ **010/6431-9548.** www.cnfm.org.cn. Free admission. Tues–Sun 9am–4:30pm, last entrance at 3:30pm.

Zhongguo Gongyi Meishuguan (National Arts & Crafts Museum)

At this museum, located on the fifth floor of Parkson Department Store (Baisheng Gouwu Zhongxin), you'll find no ancient, dusty treasures. This is a museum to prove that contemporary Chinese craftsmanship is every bit as good as it was during the Tang dynasty. Many items suggest otherwise, particularly large chunks of jade painstakingly carved into monuments to bad taste, and ceramic statues of arhats picking wax from their ears. But it's a good introduction to traditional crafts in their places of origin. Striking exhibits include clay figurines from Jiangsu, cloisonné from Beijing, lacquerware from Fujian, and ceramics from Jingde Zhen which steal the show.

Fuxing Men Nei Dajie 101, Xi Cheng Qu; see map p. 106. ℂ **010/6605-3476.** Admission ¥8. Tues–Sun 9:30am–4pm. Metro: Fuxing Men.

8 FORMER RESIDENCES & OTHER CURIOSITIES

Constructing memorial halls to the heroes of past and present dynasties has a long history, and the Communists have adopted this tradition with élan. As before, historical accuracy matters little; cultivating patriotic subjects is the goal.

Ancient Observatory (Gu Guanxiang Tai)   Most of the observatory's large bronze astronomical instruments—mystifying combinations of hoops, slides, and rulers stylishly embellished with dragons and clouds—were built by the Jesuits in the 17th and 18th centuries. You can play with reproductions of the Chinese-designed instruments they superseded (the originals were moved to Nanjing in 1933 and, for unexplained reasons, haven't been returned) in the grassy courtyard below. At the back of the garden, a "we-invented-it-first" display outlines the achievements of Song dynasty astronomer Guo Shoujing, who also has his own memorial hall on the northern tip of Xi Hai. To the right of the entrance is a more useful exhibition, which houses a photo of a bone from 1300 B.C. on which China's first astronomers etched a record of solar eclipses, details of which are still used in present-day astronomy.

Jianguo Men Dong Biaobei 2, Dong Cheng Qu (southwest side of Jianguo Men intersection, just south of metro); see map p. 106. ℂ 010/6512-8923. Admission ¥10. Tues–Sun 9am–4pm. Metro: Jianguo Men.

Dixia Cheng (Underground City) ★ (Kids)   A sign near the entrance proclaims this seldom-visited attraction a HUMAN FAIRYLAND AND UNDERGROUND PARADISE. Far from it. Aside from odd recent additions, such as a silk factory, these tunnels are dark, damp, and genuinely eerie. A portrait of Mao stands amid murals of ordinary folk "volunteering" to dig tunnels, and fading but catchy slogans (DIG THE TUNNELS DEEP, ACCUMULATE GRAIN, OPPOSE HEGEMONY, and FOR THE PEOPLE: PREPARE FOR WAR, PREPARE FOR FAMINE). Unintentional humor is provided by propaganda posters from the era, which advise citizens to cover their mouths in the event of nuclear, chemical, or biological attack. Built during the 1960s, with border skirmishes with the USSR as the pretext, the tunnels could accommodate all of Beijing's six million inhabitants upon completion—or so it was boasted. Army engineers were said to have built a secret network of tunnels connecting the residences of Party leaders at Zhong Nan Hai to the Great Hall of the People and the numerous military bases near Ba Da Chu to the west of town. Suspicions were confirmed in 1976 and 1989 when large numbers of troops emerged from the Great Hall of the People to keep the people in check. The construction boom means that this is the only remaining entrance to the nonsecret tunnels; it may disappear soon.

Xi Damochang Jie 64, Chongwen Qu (from metro stop walk west; take the 1st left into Qinian Dajie, then the 2nd right; entrance is on south side, just past Qian Men Xiaoxue); see map p. 106. ℂ 010/6702-2657. Admission ¥20. 8:30am–5:30pm. Metro: Chongwen Men.

Factory 798 (Qijiuba Gongchang) ★★   Optimistically billed as a rival to New York's Soho district, this Soviet-designed former weapons factory is a center for local modern art and fashion. Factory 798's long-term survival is uncertain, with Beijing's mayor musing that they would "look, regulate, and discuss" the use of the space, which the owners and the Chaoyang municipal government hope will become a technology park. Purchase a map for ¥2 on arrival. From entrance no. 4 (Jiuxian Qiao Lu 4), you'll soon arrive at the impressive **UCCA** (admission ¥15; closed Mon), a nonprofit, spacious gallery that often hosts intriguing and buzz-worthy exhibitions that merge the international and

Chinese modern art worlds. Keeping west, hang a right and on your left is the remarkable Bauhaus-inspired **798 Space,** still daubed with slogans offering praise to Mao. The most consistently interesting exhibitions are held by **798 Photo,** immediately opposite. Turn right and right again as you emerge from the building to find the first gallery to open in Factory 798, **Beijing Tokyo Art Projects** (www.tokyo-gallery.com), which has a formidable stable of local and international artists. Turn left and duck down a narrow lane, to emerge at the Gao Brothers' cuddly **Beijing New Art Projects** (℡ 010/8456-6660). If a visit to 798 whets your appetite for more avant-garde Chinese art, many of 798's artists, faced with spiraling rents and an increasingly commercial atmosphere, have moved to **Song Zhuang,** a village to the east of town (www.artistvillagegallery.com).

Jiuxian Qiao Lu 4, Chaoyang Qu (north of Dashanzi Huandao); see map p. 111. www.798space.com. 10:30am–7:30pm (some galleries closed Mon). Bus: no. 813 east from Chaoyang Men metro to Wangye Fen.

Lao She Jinianguan (Former Residence of Lao She)

The courtyard home of one of Beijing's best-loved writers, Lao She (1899–1966), is the most charming of many converted homes scattered around Beijing's *hutong.* Despite being granted this home by Zhou Enlai in 1950, the writer refused to become a cheerleader for the regime, and his post-revolution years were remarkably quiet for such a prolific writer. He recently came in at no. 5 in an online survey of "China's leading cultural icons," ahead of pop diva Wang Faye but well behind the no. 1 choice, the iconoclastic writer Lu Xun (who has a memorial hall in the west of town; see chapter 8, p. 162). Lao She is renowned for the novel *Rickshaw (Luotuo Xiangzi),* a darkly humorous tale of a hardworking rickshaw puller, Happy Boy.

Start in Hall 3, to the right, which records his early years in London, the United States, and Shandong Province. Hall 2 is an attempt to re-create the mood of his original study and sitting room, with his personal library untouched and his desk calendar left open at the day of his disappearance—August 24, 1966. While the date of his death is certain, the details are murky. The official line has him committing a poetic suicide in nearby Taiping Hu (pictured in Hall 1) after enduring a "struggle session" at Kong Miao. It's possible that he was simply murdered by Red Guards.

Fengfu Hutong 19, Dong Cheng Qu (from Wangfujing Dajie, turn left at the Crowne Plaza along Deng-shikou Xi Jie to the 2nd *hutong* on your right); see map p. 106. ℡ 010/6514-2612. Free admission. 9am–4pm. Metro: Wangfujing.

Prince Gong's Mansion (Gong Wang Fu)

This splendid imperial residence belonged to several people, including the sixth son of the Guangxu emperor (Prince Gong) who, at the age of 27, was left to sign the Convention of Peking in 1860, after the Qing royal family took an early summer holiday when British and French forces advanced on the capital. The convention (which ratified the ill-enforced Treaty of Tianjin) is reproduced in an exhibition hall. But other than one picture, there's little information concerning the original owner, Heshen (1750–99), the infamously corrupt Manchu official. Thought to have been the Qianlong emperor's lover, he ruled China for his own gain when Qianlong abdicated in 1796, embezzling funds earmarked for suppressing the White Lotus rebellion. After Qianlong's death, his demise was swift. While he was mourning in the Forbidden City, officials were dispatched to this mansion. Though the extent of his graft was widely known, officials were shocked by the piles of gold and silver ingots uncovered. His remaining friends at court managed to persuade the Qianlong emperor's son to spare him from "death by a thousand cuts," but he was soon hanged. The labyrinthine combination of rockeries and pavilions here offers plenty to see, but you're seeing only half of the mansion and it's often overrun by tour groups. Short but sweet performances of opera and acrobatics are served up in the three-story "Grand Opera House."

Liuyin Jie 17 (signposted in English at top of Qian Hai Xi Dajie running north off Ping'an Dadao opposite north gate of Bei Hai Park; turn left at sign and follow alley past large parking lot; entrance is marked with huge red lanterns); see map p. 106. ✆ 010/8328-0385. Admission ¥40; ¥70 including guide and opera performance. 7:30am–4:30pm. Metro: Jishui Tan.

Song Qingling Guju (Former Residence of Soong Ching Ling)

Song Qingling is as close as you'll get to a modern Chinese Communist saint—wealthy, obsessed with children, and a friend of Mao to boot. She married Sun Yat-sen, 30 years her senior, a diminutive man acknowledged as the "father of modern China" (even though he was in Denver during the 1911 Revolution). Qingling showed some sympathy to the Communist cause only after her husband's death in 1925. Her younger sister married Chiang Kai-shek (leader of the Nationalist Party and China's public enemy no. 1 until his death in 1975), while Qingling nearly died during the "white terror" of 1927 when the Nationalist Party was purged of Communist sympathizers. Mao rewarded Qingling for her loyalty by granting her this mansion in 1963, and she lived here until her death in 1981, devoting much time to education. The grounds are well kept, making them the most popular spot in Beijing for soon-to-be-weds to be photographed. The exhibition on her life seems to contain nearly every article of clothing she wore and every letter she wrote. It's all a little too perfect.

Hou Hai Bei Yan 46, Xi Cheng Qu (northeast shore of Hou Hai); see map p. 106. ✆ 010/6404-4205. Admission ¥20. 9am–5pm (to 4:30pm in winter). Metro: Jishui Tan.

Tian Yi Mu ★ (Finds)

The first Ming emperor had a dim view of eunuchs, noting "not one or two of these people out of thousands are good . . . These people can only be given sprinkling and sweeping jobs," but upon the accession of the Wanli emperor (reign 1573–1620), the Imperial City housed nearly 20,000 eunuchs (*huanguan,* later *taijian*), from powerful bureaucrats enjoying their own mansions, down to junior eunuchs scraping by through petty graft. This cemetery was built in 1605 for Wanli's favorite eunuch, Tian Yi, who served three emperors and acted as Wanli's mentor and confidant. It has a spirit way, an underground tomb complex, and memorial stelae wreathed in dragons, an unprecedented honor for a eunuch. It's away from the city center, best combined with a visit to Tanzhe Si or Cuan Di Xia (see chapter 11 for both) and Fahai Si (p. 132), a 10-minute walk to the northeast. The cemetery has survived almost intact, and provides insight into their fraught spirituality. Buddhist and Taoist motifs are carved onto their graves, along with images depicting morality tales.

A small exhibition hall is set to the left of the entrance, but all captions are in Chinese. China's last eunuch, Sun Yaoting (1902–96) is pictured making a visit to the Forbidden City in 1993, his first since Puyi was driven out in 1924. He is said to have taken issue with the accuracy of the captions there. On the right a naive letter describes his years in service. Castrated at the age of 8, he was devastated when the emperor abdicated months later, although he continued to serve Puyi. He earned enough money to adopt a son, but lost his "treasure" during the Cultural Revolution (see the box "Eunuchs: The Unkindest Cut," below).

Cixi is photographed with a large entourage of eunuchs at the Summer Palace, and the temples pictured were sponsored by eunuchs. Buddhism, with its emphasis on celibacy and renunciation, had more appeal for eunuchs than Confucianism. Wealthier eunuchs

Eunuchs: The Unkindest Cut

The practice that created eunuchs is said to date back 4,000 years, when it was an alternative to the death penalty, often used in the case of political crimes. By the Ming dynasty, most eunuchs submitted to this operation voluntarily, usually as a way out of poverty. The eunuch's abdomen and upper thighs were bound tightly with coarse rope or bandages; his penis was anesthetized with hot pepper water. He was then seated in a semireclining chair, with waist and legs held down by three assistants. At this point, he was asked if he would have any regrets. Consent given, the small curved blade flashed and "fountains of red, white, and yellow liquid spouted from the wound" as both the testes and the penis were removed. A goose quill would then quickly be inserted into the urethra to prevent it from closing, and the wound was plugged with cloth previously dipped in wax, sesame oil, and pepper. The surplus organs (or "treasure") were plopped in a jar and jealously guarded, as they were necessary to establish a eunuch's credentials for promotions, and to pass into the next life as complete men. After the patient (often unconscious by this point) had endured 3 days without food or drink, the plug was removed. If urine gushed out, the operation was a success, and a lifetime in service waited. If not, there would be a horrible, lingering death. A less violent alternative involved slitting the scrotum and removing the testicles. Both operations were preferable to criminal castration, where the testicles were beaten off with a club.

would adopt sons, but most relied on Buddhist monks to tend their graves. A second eunuch museum will be opening soon inside a late Qing temple, **Lima Guandi Miao.** Built for one of Cixi's most trusted eunuchs, Liu Chengyin, the keeper of the imperial seals, it stands south of the Summer Palace in an area akin to a eunuch retirement village.

Moshi Kou Dajie 80, Shijing Shan Qu (from bus stop, continue up the rise; take a right after 5 min.; cemetery is on the left); see map p. 116. ✆ **010/8872-4148.** Admission ¥8. 9am–4pm. Bus: no. 959 or 746 from left of Pingguo Yuan metro stop to Shougang Xiaoqu.

9 HUTONG & SIHEYUAN (LANES & COURTYARD COMPOUNDS)

As distinct as Beijing's palaces, temples, and parks may be, it is the *hutong* that ultimately set the city apart. Prior to the 20th century, when cars and the Communist love of grandeur made them impracticable, these narrow and often winding lanes were the city's dominant passageways. Old maps of Beijing show the city to be an immense and intricate maze composed almost entirely of *hutong,* most no wider than 10m (33 ft.) and some as narrow as 50cm (20 in.).

Beijing's other famous feature is the *siheyuan* (**courtyard houses**)—traditional dwellings typically composed of four single-story rectangular buildings arranged around a central courtyard with a door at one corner (ideally facing south). Originally designed to house a single family, they now house up to five or six families. Mao brought the countryside to the city during the Cultural Revolution, and most of these squatters never left. Foreign visitors charmed by the quaintness of the old houses often assume migration into modern apartment buildings is forced, and it often is. But many move willingly, eager for central heating, indoor plumbing, and, most important, security of ownership. Many locals will try to convince you that *hutong* are inherently run-down, but why would you renovate a house that could be torn down next week?

The *hutong* are being leveled so rapidly the term **"fast-disappearing"** is now a permanent part of their description. With the 2008 Olympics, destruction carried the imprimatur of modernization. Never mind that visitors prefer quiet lanes to endless blocks of identical flats. But the main driving force behind the destruction is banal: taxes. Municipal governments are desperately short of revenue (following reforms implemented by the oft-lauded Zhu Rongji), and land is the one thing they can sell. Property developers, who now rely on evictees for one-third of their sales, are happy to oblige. Drunk from these runoff influxes of capital, municipal governments expand further. New departments are created, and new jobs are found for friends and relatives. So the next time around, the hit has to be bigger. The Dong Cheng government in particular has a reputation for ordering forceful evictions and arranging unfavorable resettlement schemes.

The most dynamic of these *hutong* can be found around the alley of Nan Luogu Xiang, a gentrifying neighborhood filled with Chinese hipsters, grungy French and Americans, and old Beijingers. Nan Luogu Xiang is the name of the north-south alley filled with a growing number of cafes, bars, restaurants, and hotels listed throughout our pages. Bar highlights include MAO Livehouse (p. 187) and Pass-By Bar (p. 192), one of

Our Favorite Hutong Names

The names of *hutong* are a link to the history and humor of the capital. **San Bu Lao Hutong,** a couple of blocks west of Prince Gong's Mansion, is named for its famous former resident, Admiral Zheng He, whose nickname was San Bao (three treasures, possibly a reference to his eunuch status). As described in *1421: The Year China Discovered America,* this Hui Muslim led a vast armada of ships to Southeast Asia, India, Ceylon, the Persian Gulf (where he was able to visit Mecca), and West Africa over seven voyages between 1405 and 1433. Detachments of his fleet probably reached Australia, but the central contention of the book is dubious. Other names hint at long-forgotten markets. **Yandai Xie Jie (Tobacco Pipe Lane),** east of Yinding Qiao, now harbors the capital's hippest cafes, but it once provided smoking paraphernalia for the capital's numerous opium dens. The meaning of **Xian Yu Kou Jie (Fresh Fish Corner Street)** seems straightforward, but locals swear it's a corruption of *xianyu* (salty fish), a reference to a man who burned down half the street while preparing his favorite meal. **Shoushui Hutong (Gathering Water Lane),** where you'll find the Liu Ren Papercut House (see below), was originally known by the less-salable name of **Choushui Hutong (Smelly Water Lane),** as it was a ditch which ran along the north side of the old city wall.

the first establishments to open on the street in the early 2000s. Hotels in the area include Du Ge, Han's Royal Garden, Courtyard 7, Gu Xiang 20, Beijing Downtown Backpackers Accommodation, and Confucius International Youth Hostel.

Intriguing swathes of *hutong* still stand south of **Heping Men** and **Qian Men** (though parts of them are quickly being demolished), as well as northwest of **Xi Si,** surrounding **Bai Ta Si.** Here you may hear strange humming sounds, produced by pigeons wheeling overhead with small whistles attached to their feathers. For now, the destitution of these areas makes them unattractive to property developers, but their long-term survival is improbable. See them now. The *hutong* most likely to survive because of their popularity with tourists are in the **Back Lakes (Shicha Hai)** area and in nearby **Di'an Men.** Pedicab tour companies offer to bike you around this area and take you inside a couple of courtyards, but they all charge absurd rates. It's much cheaper, and far more enjoyable, to explore on your own by foot or bicycle (see chapter 8 for suggested routes). If you must, the **Beijing Hutong Tourist Agency** (© 010/6615-9097) offers tours in English for ¥70 for the whole trip. It takes about 2½ hours. You can also book ahead for a ¥240 trip, which takes the same route and includes a meal at local resident's home. *Tip:* However you travel, *never* enter a *siheyuan* uninvited.

10 ESPECIALLY FOR KIDS

Competition for the disposable income of Beijing's one-child families is intense—advertising ruthlessly targets children. Alas, few of Beijing's just-for-kids attractions are of a standard that will appeal to Western children, and those few tend to be overcrowded. Some exceptions are noted below.

Beijing Haiyangguan (Beijing Aquarium) ★ "The world's largest inland aquarium" attracted plenty of opposition from local environmental groups when it opened in 1999, and the logic of keeping countless marine animals so far from the sea is questionable. Efforts to compensate are obvious—an environmental message is laid on thickly in the Chinese captions. Introducing Chinese children to the concept that shrimp can exist somewhere other than in a sea of garlic sauce has to be commended, although descriptions of "horrible" sharks show there's a ways to go in its efforts. **Dolphin shows** at 11am and 3pm pack in the one-child families. **Beijing Zoo (Beijing Dongwuyuan)** lies to the south, and despite improvements to some areas—notably the **Panda House**—the zoo is more likely to traumatize your child than provide entertainment. It is possible to take a boat from the canal south of the aquarium to the Summer Palace (50-min. trip; ¥40 one-way, ¥70 round-trip).

Gaoliang Qiao Xie Jie 18B, Haidian Qu (from Beifang Jiao Da cross road and walk west; north gate of the Beijing Zoo); see map p. 106. © **010/6217-6655.** Admission ¥120 includes admission to Beijing Zoo; children ¥60; 2 children (under 1.2m/4 ft.) free with 1 paid adult ticket. 9am–5pm (to 9pm during summer holidays). Bus: no. 16 *(zhi xian)* from Xi Zhi Men metro stop to Beifang Jiao Da.

Beijing Huanle Gu (Happy Valley Amusement Park) ★ Beijing's answer to Disneyland, this theme park features stomach-turning roller coasters, and themed sections called Shangri-La Land, Mayan Aztec Village, and Greek Town. Lines for rides can be 3 hours long, so arrive early and avoid the weekends. Opened by overseas Chinese investors and designed with the help of Westerners, the roller coasters are supposedly state-of-the-art.

Xiao Wu Ji Bei Lu, Dong Si Huan (E. Fourth Ring Rd.). ℂ **010/6738-9898**. Admission ¥160 adults, ¥80 kids **147** 1.2–1.4m (4–4¹/₂ ft.), free for kids under 1.2m (4 ft.). Apr 1–Nov 14 daily 9am–7:30pm (last ticket at 5:30pm), Nov 15–Mar 31 10am–5pm.

Gudai Qianbi Zhanlanguan (Ancient Coin Exhibition Hall)　If your child is at the collecting phase, this may or may not be a wise place to visit, although the vast range of shells, coins, and notes is as likely to bewilder as to fascinate. While the tour guides' chant of "5,000 years of history" rings hollow, "5,000 years of retail" rings true. Confucius and Mao both railed in vain against the mercantile spirit. The exhibition should also impress upon you how simple it is to mint coins; the stalls of the **Ancient Coin Market (Gudai Qianbi Jiaoyi Shichang)** outside are testament to how easy they are to duplicate—*don't* make large purchases. **Desheng Men Jianlou (Desheng Men Arrow Tower),** which houses the exhibition, is akin to an imposing castle, with many dark crannies to explore.

Desheng Men Jianlou, Bei Er Huan Zhong Lu, Xi Cheng Qu (north side of N. Second Ring Rd., just east of metro stop); see map p. 106. ℂ **010/6201-8073**. Admission ¥10. Tues–Sun 9am–4pm. Metro: Jishui Tan.

Liu Ren Papercut House (Liu Ren Jianzhi Wu)　The art of paper cutting might not sound exciting, but self-taught artist Liu Ren, who works out of a charming courtyard house, works up such a good spiel you may be converted. Paper cuttings *(jianzhi)* were gifts in rural China, to be stuck on windows, doors, or lanterns. There's nothing subtle about the traditional paper cuttings—a baby with a large member marks the birth of a boy, and a baby surrounded by protective wolves is appropriate for a girl. Liu Ren knows her craft, and is happy to provide instruction (¥200 per hour; ¥60 if taught by her students). Call ahead to book.

Shou Shui He Hutong 16, Xi Cheng Qu (walk south on Xuanwu Men Wai Dajie, take the 2nd *hutong* on the right, turn left down the 1st lane, then take the 1st right); see map p. 114. ℂ **010/6601-1946**. Admission Sat–Sun ¥50, Thurs–Fri ¥100. Metro: Xi Dan.

Milu Yuan (Milu Park) ★★ ⓕ**inds**　Located on the site of the Southern Marshes (Nan Haizi), where Yuan, Ming, and Qing emperors would hunt deer, rabbit, and pheasant, and practice military exercises, this ecological research center is the most humane place to view animals in Beijing. The main attraction is Père David's deer *(milu)*, a strange deerlike creature that became extinct in China toward the end of the Qing dynasty. The *milu* you see today are the descendants of 18 animals that were collected in 1898 by the far-sighted Lord Bedford from zoos around Europe. In 1985, a group of 20 *milu* was reintroduced to China; they now number about 200, and over 400 animals have returned to the wild. The expansive marshlands attract migratory birds, and also house other endangered animals, a maze, plots of land where members can grow vegetables without pesticides, and the chillingly effective World Extinct Wildlife Cemetery, which illustrates the plight of endangered species.

Nan Haizi Milu Yuan, Daxing Qu. ℂ **010/8796-2105**. www.milupark.org.cn. Free admission. Tues–Sun 9am–4pm. Bus: no. 729 from Qian Men metro stop to Jiu Gong. Change for minibus no. 4, which will drop you at the signposted turnoff.

Sony ExploraScience (Suoni Tan Meng) ⓚ**ids**　This museum has live science shows (in Chinese) and plenty of interactive exhibits. We love the swipe cards, which act as keys that unlock the secrets of each science station (English text provided). This is an excellent place to spend a few hours if it's raining or too hot and humid outside.

Inside Chaoyang Gongyuan (Chaoyang Park), Chaoyang Qu. © 010/6501-8800. www.sony.com.cn/ses/index.html. Admission ¥30 adults, ¥20 students, free for kids under 1.2m (4 ft.). Buy your tickets at the park's south or east gates and you won't have to buy park entry tickets. Mon–Fri 9:30am–5:30pm; Sat–Sun until 6:30pm.

11 ORGANIZED TOURS

During a visit to Bei Hai, writer John Blofeld chanced upon an elderly eunuch, and inquired as to how he was making a living. He touchily replied, "I manage well. I am a guide—not one of those so-called guides who live by inventing history for foreigners and by making commissions on things they purchase. I have not fallen that far yet . . ." Little has changed. In a country where children are taught that South Korea and their American allies started the Korean War when they invaded innocent North Korea, many modern historical accounts are inventions. Many visitors assume locals have a unique insight into their own culture. In China, and Beijing in particular, all-pervasive censorship and a general lack of curiosity ensures this is rarely the case. You *do not* need the services of a local guide.

Several companies offer guided group tours of Beijing for English speakers, but these are almost always overpriced, often incomplete, and best thought of as an emergency measure when time is short. The most popular operator is **BTG Travel** (© 010/9609-6798; www.btgtravel.com), which has offices scattered through the four- and five-star hotels. City highlight tours by air-conditioned bus typically cost around ¥300 per person for a half-day and around ¥500 for a full day with a mediocre lunch. **China International Travel Service (CITS)** (© 010/6522-2991; www.cits.net), offers tours that are more customizable, but at a much higher fee. The options listed below are infinitely preferable.

The **China Culture Center** (© 010/8462-2081; www.chinaculturecenter.org) organizes outings, lectures, and film screenings for expatriates with an interest in Chinese culture. There's usually a weekend half-day or full-day tour. Events are often led by prominent lecturers, and discussions go well beyond the palaver you're subjected to at CITS. They are constantly on the lookout for new attractions, and multiday tours to sites far afield are now offered. A smaller operation with a similar philosophy is **Cycle China** (© 010/6402-5653; www.cyclechina.com). Many sights around Beijing, such as the Ming tombs, are more appealing on two wheels than on two feet. *Hutong* cycle tours are a specialty.

Surrounded by mountains on three sides, the environs of Beijing provide tremendous scope for 1- or 2-day walks taking in scenery, ancient villages, and, of course, the Great Wall. **Beijing Hikers** (contact Huijie at © 0/1391-002-5516 or Vicky at © 0/1381-016-5056; www.beijinghikers.com) organize day hikes for ¥200 for adults, ¥150 for children 11 and under departing from the Lido Hotel. Though popular with North American expatriates, groups are often too large. A cheaper and more interesting alternative is to join a hike organized by **Sanfo Outdoors** (© 010/6201-5550; www.sanfo.com.cn). Originally a small club at Peking University, they now have at least four hikes every weekend advertised (in Chinese) on their website. Visit one of their shops (p. 178) to obtain information on the weekend's activities, but take the grading system seriously—difficult hikes are really tough, while outings with all luxuries provided are humorously referred to as "corrupt" *(fubai).*

12 STAYING ACTIVE

Foreign-run five-star hotels offer the cleanest and best-equipped fitness centers and swimming pools for those desperate to work out. Most locals can't afford this, and head for the parks—which were off-limits to the common folk in Imperial times—early in the morning to practice *taijiquan* or ballroom dancing, or walk the bird (walking the dog is prohibited during daylight hours). At night, Beijing's undersize canines emerge, along with seniors dancing (waddling, really) and beating drums to the rhythm of rice-planting songs *(yang ge)*.

ACTIVITIES A TO Z

BOWLING (BAOLINGQIU)   With bottles of Johnnie Walker Red Label and French perfume readily traced, and visits to "karaoke" clubs easily photographed, the favorite way to curry favor with a Chinese official is . . . bowling. During the 1990s, more than 15,000 alleys were built, many in Beijing. The biggest and most fun place to bowl is 24-hour **Gongti Yibai** at Gongti Xi Lu 6 (just south of the west gate of the Worker's Stadium), with 100 lanes, thumping music, and flashing video games to bring in the kids (✆ **010/6552-2688;** ¥30 per game).

GOLF (GAO'ERFUQIU)   If playing golf in a region desperately short of land and water doesn't bother you, then try negotiating the water hazards of **Beijing International Golf Club (Beijing Guoji Gao'erfu Julebu;** ✆ **010/6076-2288)**, northwest of town near the Ming Tombs. Eighteen holes including caddie fees cost ¥800 during the week, rising to ¥1,400 on weekends.

ICE-SKATING (LIUBING)   Beijing has superb outdoor ice-skating in the winter at **Bei Hai Gongyuan, Qian Hai,** and the **Summer Palace.** Skate-rental outfits charge about ¥20, but you might not find boots that fit. Even more popular in winter are "ice cars" *(bing che),* box sleds propelled by ski poles. Warnings about the thickness of ice sheets apply—global warming makes for a shorter skating season each year. Beijing's largest skate rink is **Le Cool,** Guomao Liubing Chang (✆ **010/6505-5776**), in the underground shopping center that connects Traders Hotel to China World Hotel. Open Monday through Friday from 10am to 9pm, Saturday from 10am to 10pm, and Sunday from 10am to 7:30pm. The rink charges ¥30 for 90 minutes from 10am to 9pm, ¥40 from 6 to 10pm, and ¥50 on Saturday and Sunday.

KITE-FLYING (FANG FENGZHENG)   Flying kites in China began at least 2,000 years before they were seen in Europe. The humble kite has been used in the sport of kite fighting, and even as a device to frighten enemy troops. But most locals fly kites peacefully, particularly at **Tian'an Men Square** (where you can rent kites) or in parks such as **Ri Tan Gongyuan.** You can purchase kites at several markets; good selections are available at Guanyuan Shichang and on the fourth floor of Yaxiu Fuzhuang Shichang (see section 2, "Markets & Bazaars," in chapter 9).

TABLE TENNIS (PING PONG QIU)   Every community center in Beijing has a ping-pong table with willing opponents. It's an excellent way to meet locals, but humiliating when your conqueror is a generation or two older than you. There's a Ping Pong Club (mostly Chinese-speaking, but who needs to talk during ping-pong?) at Peking University (✆ **010/6261-1188**).

Winding Down

While Beijing is fascinating, it is *not* relaxing. A slew of hotel spas have opened recently, including the **Ritz-Carlton, Financial Street** spa (℄ **010/6601-6666**). The signature Treasure Island treatment (¥1,127) is 90 minutes of bliss. The **Chi Spa** at the Shangri-La Beijing (℄ **010/6841-2211**) offers Tibetan-style treatments in a dimmed, meditative environment. Another choice for unwinding is the **St. Regis Spa** (℄ **010/6460-6688,** ext. 2745). One of the best values in town and a favorite with expats is **Bodhi** (℄ **010/6417-9595;** www.bodhi. com.cn) at Gongti Bei Lu 17 (opposite the north gate of the Workers' Stadium). A full-body massage before 5pm costs as little as ¥78 per hour from Monday to Thursday and includes complimentary food and beverages. Open 11am to midnight. Traditionally, massage was a profession reserved for the blind. Experience *mangren anmo* (blind massage) at the friendly **Lesheng Mangren Baojian Anmo Zhongxin,** Dengshikou Xi Jie 32 (℄ **010/6525-7532,** ext. 3201; daily 11am–midnight), on the second floor of Donghua Fandian, a long block west of the Crowne Plaza in Wangfujing. A 1-hour massage costs ¥88.

TAIJIQUAN   Tai chi practitioners can visit any park at daybreak, and enjoy the thrill of practicing with hundreds of others. The **Chinese Culture Center** (see above) has a regular course in English.

YOGA (YUJIA)   The **Yoga Yard,** Gongti Lu 17 (6/F, above Bodhi; ℄ **010/6413-0774;** www.yogayard.com), offers hatha yoga classes for all levels.

SPECTATOR SPORTS

Gongren Tiyuchang (Workers' Stadium) is the home of the capital's football (soccer) team, formerly known as Beijing Guo An, now called **Beijing Xiandai** (named for the Hyundai car company). A fanatical green-and-white army of fans follows the team, which perennially wallows in mid-table mediocrity. Referees are usually corrupt, and fans shower them with invective you won't find in any language textbook. Tickets can be purchased at the Workers' Stadium north gate, **Lisheng Tiyu Shangsha,** Wangfujing Dajie 201 (℄ **010/6525-0581;** Sun–Thurs 9am–9pm; Fri–Sat 9am–10pm). The season runs April through November.

Beijing Strolls

by Jen Lin-Liu

Taking a stroll in Beijing can be hard work. The main boulevard, Chang'an Dajie, is a soulless and windswept thoroughfare, and the rest of town seems to be a huge construction site choking on dust and car fumes. These strolls will show you a gentler Beijing, where older Beijingers push cane shopping carts through even more ancient tree-lined *hutong,* where young lovers clasp hands nervously as they gaze across the Back Lakes, and where potbellied cab drivers quaff beer while enjoying boisterous games of poker or chess in the middle of the sidewalk.

You'll need to keep your wits about you. No one in Beijing seems capable of walking in a straight line. Pedestrian crossings are decorative, and newly installed crossings with traffic lights are often ignored by motorists. The car, particularly the four-wheel drive, dominates both the road and the sidewalk. Cars are the main source of the air pollution that blankets the capital. Beijing already has the highest rate of car ownership in China, and more than a thousand new cars hit the road every day—a suicidal path, akin to turning New York into Los Angeles.

Renting or purchasing a bike moves you one rung up the traffic food chain and is a less tiring way to get around. Youth hostels rent out bikes for around ¥30 per day, while bike parking stations next to metro stops are cheaper yet at ¥10 per day, but you'll need a native speaker to assist you. You can purchase a secondhand bike from a streetside repair stall for less than ¥100; new bikes start from ¥140. Bike traffic is orderly, and unlike Guangzhou and Shanghai, the capital has yet to block off large numbers of streets to cyclists. Whether you walk or ride a bike, avoid sudden changes of direction, and go with the substantial flow around you.

WALKING TOUR 1	LIULICHANG & DA ZHALAN

START:	Zhengyi Ci Xilou, just south of the metro on Qian Men Xi Heyan Jie (metro: Heping Men).
FINISH:	Qian Men, south end of Tian'an Men Guangchang (metro: Qian Men).
TIME:	3 hours.
BEST TIMES:	Any weekday starting at about 9am or 2pm.
WORST TIMES:	Weekends are crowded. Most shops close about 8:30pm.

This pleasant stroll takes in many of Beijing's most famous shops. Even if you're not interested in buying anything, it makes an agreeable break from the fumes of the capital's constantly gridlocked streets. **Liulichang,** named for a factory that once turned out the glazed roof tiles that clearly delineated the rank of Beijing's buildings, was renovated in the 1980s to capture the look and atmosphere of the late Qing dynasty. Scholars and art connoisseurs once frequented Liulichang, and it is still home to the most famous art-supplies store in China, **Rongbao Zhai.** A cluster (at times it feels like a gauntlet) of shops sells art books, scrolls, rubbings, handmade paper, paintbrushes, ink sticks, "jade," and antiques (which are nearly all fakes). Liulichang runs about 6 blocks east-west. Southeast of it is **Da Zhalan,** an ancient, but more plebeian, shopping street that has been converted into a cobblestoned pedestrian-only mall. There are many ancient shops on Da Zhalan, including tailors, shoe stores, and apothecaries selling traditional medicines. North of Da Zhalan, the market streets of **Langfang Er Tiao** and **Langfang Tou Tiao** wind their ways toward **Qian Men (Front Gate)** overlooking **Tian'an Men Square.**

Walk south from the Heping Men metro station down Nan Xinhua Jie, and take the first left onto Qian Men Xi Heyan Jie, where you'll find on the right:

❶ Zhengyi Ci Xilou

The original theater, which was demolished to make way for a new theater in the same place, dated back more than 340 years, and began as a Buddhist temple during the Ming dynasty. The new theater holds occasional evening performances.

Backtrack to the main road and go south for a few minutes. On the left, extending to the corner of Liulichang Dong Jie, you will see:

❷ Zhongguo Shudian (No. 115)

Although it's sprawling and state-run, the largest branch of China Books offers a wide range of new and used books on Chinese art, architecture, and literature without the markups that plague arty bookstores.

Cross the main road to Liulichang Xi Jie. On the left-hand side of the road is:

❸ Cathay Bookshop (No. 18)

One of several branches of China Books, this bookshop (south side of street; ✆ **010/ 6301-7678**) has an interesting paper-cutting exhibit upstairs and a great range of art materials—paper, ink stones, chops, brushes, and frames—at reasonable prices.

Across the street is:

❹ Rongbao Zhai (No. 19)

The most renowned art shop in China (north side of street) greets you with what may be the world's largest ink stone. Rongbao Zhai sells wood-block prints, copies of famous calligraphy, historic paintings (reproductions), and art supplies. The handful of workers who are more interested in doing their jobs than in

reading the paper are gold mines of information on Beijing's art scene.

Farther west, the street has more shops and traditional-style facades for another 100m (328 ft.), until you get to the wall explaining the history of glazed tile. When you are finished, backtrack to Nan Xinhua Jie and cross over to Liulichang Dong Jie. Continue east to browse:

❺ Curio Shops

Liulichang Dong Jie eventually peters out into a series of touristy shops that sell Buddhist statues, ceramics, and reproductions of Tang Dynasty horses and emperors. No. 71 sells good chrysanthemum and green tea. Most of the street contains shops that sell the same knickknacks, but no. 58 carries some quality antiques and reproductions like grandfather clocks and jewelry. Just before no. 65, turn right down an alley marked with a gate bafflingly labeled PRADIPRION SCULPTURE, and follow the signs that say ANTIQUE CARPETS to 54 Dong Bei Yun Hutong. A couple sells Mongolian and Tibetan carpets in their small courtyard living room. No. 28 Liulichang Dong Lu sells elegant grey-green celadon teapots and vases.

Liulichang Dong Jie ends at Yanshou Jie. Turn right, then left on Yangmei Zhu Xie Jie. When you reach the large T-intersection, turn right, then left on:

❻ Da Zhalan (Dashilanr in Beijing Dialect)

Known as Langfang Si Tiao during the Ming dynasty, its name was changed to Da Zhalan after a large stockade was built, presumably to give peace of mind to the wealthy retailers who set up shop here. Now the proletarian answer to Wangfujing, it's a bustling pedestrian-only street with some of Beijing's oldest retailers.

BEIJING STROLLS

8

LIULICHANG & DA ZHALAN

1 Zhèngyǐ Cí Xìlóu
正乙祠戏楼

2 Zhōngguó Shūdiàn (No. 115)
中国书店

3 Cathay Bookshop (No. 18)
来薰阁

4 Róngbǎo Zhāi (No. 19)
荣宝斋

5 Curio Shops

6 Dà Zhàlán
大栅栏

7 Nèi Lián Shēng Xiédiàn (No. 34)
内联升鞋店

8 Tóngréntáng (No. 24)
同仁堂

9 Ruìfúxiáng Chóubù Diàn (No. 5)
瑞蚨祥绸布店

10 Bā Dà Hútòng (Eight Great Lanes)
八大胡同

11 Lángfáng Èr Tiáo
廊房二条

12 Qián Mén (Front Gate)
前门

On the right side, you'll find:

❼ Nei Lian Sheng Xiedian (No. 34)

Established in 1853, this famous shoe store ((© 010/6301-4863) still crafts cloth "happy shoes" (*qianceng buxie*) and delicately embroidered women's shoes by hand. Using a little bit of charm, you may get a peek at the workshop out back.

Continue east, and on the right is a well-known restaurant selling traditional steamed buns as well as other Chinese dishes:

TAKE A BREAK
Locals certainly love the steamed buns sold by the steamer basket at **Goubuli Baozi Dian** (Da Shilan 29; © 010/6353-3338), a recently renovated and attractive restaurant. We prefer the ¥22 buns stuffed with wild vegetables and pork (ask for the *yeshu bao*) to the original pork flavored buns. On the west side of Meishi Jie are a number of cafes if you prefer coffee and Western food.

❽ Tongren Tang (No. 24)

Beijing's most celebrated Chinese-medicine pharmacy was established in 1669. In the western wing, you can make an appointment to see a Chinese-medicine doctor while in the main hall people of all ages—from youthful 20-somethings to senior citizens pushing ancient-looking wooden carts—browse the medicine counters. On the second floor, a precious ginseng root that was harvested 80 years ago in Manchuria sells for a staggering ¥680,000.

You're nearly at the east end of Da Zhalan. Don't miss its most famous store, on the left (north) side:

❾ Ruifuxiang Choubu Dian (No. 5)

Established in 1893 on the north side of Da Zhalan is the steel baroque facade of a fabric store that once supplied silk to the Qing Dynasty royalty. The company brochure claims that one of the first Chinese flags raised by Chairman Mao was also made from Ruifuxiang fabric.

When you reach the end of the street you should be at the newly renovated Qianmen Dajie. Turn right and explore the quiet lanes of the area once known as:

❿ Ba Da Hutong (Eight Great Lanes)

A 1906 survey found that the capital was home to 308 brothels (more than the number of hotels or restaurants), most of them in this district. While there are assuredly now many multiples of that number in Beijing, the government is embarrassed by this area, and forbids local tour agents from visiting or even mentioning Ba Da Hutong. Lanes were once graded into three levels, from "lower area" (*xia chu*) streets such as Wangpi Hutong, where prostitutes satisfied the needs of the masses, up to lanes such as Baishun Hutong, where "flower girls" versed in classical poetry and music awaited. Money was no guarantee of success; there were various manuals on the etiquette of wooing courtesans. The Tongzhi emperor (reign 1862–74) was notorious for creeping out at night to sample the delights of "clouds and rain." He died of syphilis. These days, hair salons in nearby alleys are unlikely to house courtesans skilled in the arts of conversation and playing the lute, but the basic requirements of the masses are provided for.

North of the east end of Da Zhalan, the *hutong* becomes Zhubaoshi Jie, a jumble of stands, shops, and carts peddling cheap clothing and bric-a-brac. Take the first left into:

⓫ Langfang Er Tiao

During the Qing dynasty, this *hutong* was renowned for its jade and antiques vendors, but by the time you get here, it may all be bulldozed. Two- and three-story houses with beautifully carved wooden balconies hint at past wealth. To the south is Langfang San Tiao, the heart of the former banking district.

Head right (north) along Meishi Jie up to Langfang Tou Tiao, known as Lantern Street (Deng Jie) during the Qing dynasty. Turn right (east), then left (north) when the street ends. Ahead looms:

⓬ Qian Men (Front Gate)

North of Zhubaoshi Jie is the south end of Tian'an Men Square. To the northeast

1 Wángfǔjǐng Palaeolithic Museum
王府井古人类文化遗址博物馆

2 Oriental Plaza
    (Dōngfāng Xīn Tiāndì)
东方新天地

3 Gōngměi Dàshà (No. 200)
工美大厦

4 Shèngxīfú (No. 196)
盛锡福

5 Wuyutai Tea Shop (no. 186)
吴裕泰茶庄

6 Foreign Language
    Bookstore (No. 235)
外文书店

7 Dōng Táng (East Church)
东堂

8 Lǎo Shě
    Jìniànguǎn (No. 19)
老舍纪念馆

9 Fùqiáng Hútòng
富强胡同

10 Zhōngguó Měishùguǎn
    (National Art Museum of China)
中国美术馆

11 Lóngfú Sì Jiē
隆福寺街

12 Dōng Sì Qīngzhēn Sì
东四清真寺

American and European brand-name stores, and hit the more unusual Chinese shops. The mall also includes a good basement-level cinema and food court. Shop AA10 **Shanghaixu** has a large selection of *qipao*, traditional tight-fitting, high-collared Chinese dresses. If they don't have anything you like, you can get one made to order. Next door, **Emperor** has a nice assortment of embroidered napkins and housewares. A few shops down at AA20, **Art of Shirts** has a nice collection of button-down and casual shirts for men and women. **The Herborist** at EE05 carries a line of traditional Chinese medicine toiletries.

Emerging from the west side of the mall, stick to the right (east) side and head north up Wangfujing Dajie, passing the huge but chaotic Wangfujing Bookstore. Cross the road to:

❸ Gongmei Dasha (No. 200)

You're guaranteed to get the real thing at this large jade store, rather than the colored glass you might find elsewhere. Bargain down to a third of the marked price (☏ 010/6528-8866; daily 9am–9:30pm).

Continue along the right-hand side of Wangfujing Dajie to:

❹ Shengxifu (No. 196)

Established in 1912, this famed hat shop is the place to get your proletarian Mao cap or a furry hat with earflaps decorated with Communist red stars. Return to Wangfujing Dajie, and continue north along the left (west) side to the next attraction.

Return to the main street, and continue north. On the right (east) side is:

❺ Wuyutai Tea Shop (No. 186)

The second floor of this quality tea shop has an interesting exhibition of tea culture, including a collection of teapots, and a lively teahouse.

Return to the main street and head north for a few steps. On the left (west) side is a place to:

> **TAKE A BREAK**
> Our favorite stalls in town for street food are at **Wangfujing Xiaochi Jie (Small Eats Street)**. Don't be afraid to try the lamb skewers or the squid on a stick— though they may look suspect, we assure you, they are clean and scrumptious!

Return to the main street and continue north to:

❻ Foreign Language Bookstore (No. 235)

The Waiwen Shudian (☏ **010/6512-6911;** daily 9:30am–9:30pm) houses Beijing's largest selection of English-language materials on the first and third floors. The second floor has a surprisingly wide range of CDs featuring local alternative bands, as well as Beijing opera and soothing instrumental music.

Continue north. It's hard to miss:

❼ Dong Tang (East Church)

Also known as St. Joseph's Cathedral, this gray Gothic structure has endured a torrid history. Built on ground donated by the Shunzhi emperor in 1655, this Jesuit church was toppled by an earthquake in 1720, gutted by a fire in 1807, and completely razed during the Boxer Rebellion of 1900. After a major renovation from 1999 to 2000, the church became notable for its wide, tree-lined forecourt, the favorite spot of Beijing's skaters. Sunday services are held at 6:15, 7, and 8am.

Across the street are two narrow lanes. Take the lane on the left to reach this memorial hall:

❽ Lao She Jinianguan

Lao She was one of China's most famous writers. When Lao She returned to a newly Communist China in 1950, then-premier Zhou Enlai gave him this court-yard residence with the hopes that he would write propaganda novels for the new government. But he never turned out another famous novel, and he drowned himself during the Cultural Revolution.

Retrace your steps back to the street, and take the right alley into:

❾ Fuqiang Hutong

This alley is immodestly named "Rich and Powerful Alley." Note the finely carved roof lintels with Buddhist swastikas and the lotus-emblazoned door piers at no. 18. While the rectangular door pier indicates that the residents weren't officials (whose houses were marked by circular door piers), they must have been well-off to be able to afford skilled stonemasons. Party General Secretary Zhao Ziyang, who was ousted during the Tian'an Men Massacre, lived at no. 3 under house arrest until his death in January 2005.

Loving Life Massage Center

Chinese believe that the blind make superior masseuses because, with the loss of one sense, they are supposed to have a heightened sense of touch. The **Lesheng Mangren Baojian Anmo Zhongxin (Loving Life Massage Center),** 32 Dengshikou Xi Jie (© **010/6525-7531,** ext. 3201) offers 1-hour full-body and foot massages for ¥88 each. You can also try cupping, in which hot glass jars are used to suck out bad energy from your back, leaving funny-looking red welts. The massage center is on the second floor of the Donghua Hotel. Hours are daily 11am to midnight.

Following the *hutong* to the end, turn right to get back on Wangfujing. Then turn left, heading north until you reach the intersection with Wusi Dajie. Across the street on the left is:

⑩ **Zhongguo Meishuguan (National Art Museum of China).** This museum has a good permanent collection of Chinese oil paintings and hosts international exhibitions curated by the likes of New York's Guggenheim.

Turn left out of the museum, and make a left at the next intersection. On the right side of the street is:

⑪ **Longfu Si Jie** 'n this small alley you'll find bargain clothes, music, and street food that make

an interesting contrast to the bustle and commercial flair of Wangfujing.

At the archway at the end of the alley, turn right and head south to Dongsi Nan Dajie. On the right side of the street is:

⑫ **Si Qingzhen Si (Dong Si Mosque)** One of Beijing's oldest mosques, Dong Si Qingzhen Si has been around since the 14th century. The second courtyard is especially serene—a nice place to unwind and rest your feet.

WALKING TOUR 4   LIDAI DIWANG MIAO & HUGUO SI

START:	Lu Xun Bowuguan (metro: Fucheng Men).
FINISH:	Desheng Men Jianlou (metro: Jishui Tan).
TIME:	4 to 5 hours.
BEST TIMES:	Any time between 9am and noon.
WORST TIMES:	Mondays, when some of the museums and sites are closed.

With the Shicha Hai area increasingly overrun with bar touts, "To the Hutong" tours, and Beijing's nouveau riche blocking the way with their Audis, this walking tour will let you rub shoulders with real *Beijingren.* You'll ramble along tree-lined quiescent lanes too narrow for automobiles, uncovering recently reopened and long-forgotten temples; you'll explore the tranquil former residences of two of China's most influential artists and a lively local wet market; you'll meet bonsai and Peking opera aficionados and drink tea in a former concubine's residence. *Tip:* **Take this tour soon.** Much of the area is threatening to disappear by way of the wrecking ball . . .

Taking exit B from the metro, turn left (east) along Fucheng Men Nei Dajie, taking the first left (north) into Fucheng Men Nei Bei Jie. Ahead is:

❶ Lu Xun Bowuguan

An online poll saw Lu Xun (1881–1936), an acerbic essayist, outpoll pop divas and basketball stars as the most popular figure in China. Young visitors display something approaching reverence when they photograph the desk where the young Lu carved the character for early *(zao)* to remind him not to be late for school. Seek out a gruesome photo of a Japanese soldier beheading a Chinese national during the Russo-Japanese war of 1905. His Chinese compatriots look on with blank countenances. Lu, then a medical student in Japan, saw this as symptomatic of a national sickness, and credited the picture with changing the direction of his life toward literature. His charming residence (one of three in Beijing) is set to the west side (¥5; Tues–Sun 9am–3:30pm).

Walk back down Fucheng Men Nei Dajie, turn left at the next alley, then right at the T-intersection, then left on the main street and continue until you see on the left:

❷ Bai Ta Si

Having undergone a makeover just before the Olympic Games, this white stupa (p. 130) commissioned by Mongolian ruler Kublai Khan and built by a Nepalese architect glitters with shiny paint though it is more than 700 years old. The surrounding temple is still worth a gander, with one hall showing thousands of carved Buddhas behind glass encasements. A new exhibit in the western hall shows a chilling vision for "modernizing" the surrounding area. Open daily from 9am to 4pm; admission ¥20.

Turn left as you exit. On the right are the new towering skyscrapers of the financial district. Continue until you see on the left:

❸ Lidai Diwang Miao

This icon-free temple (p. 133), whose grounds were occupied by a school until recently, is where Ming and Qing emperors would come to pay tribute to their predecessors. It has impressive stone carvings and signs of improvement in local curatorial standards—some of the original roof murals have been left untouched; there are touch-screen displays; and there's even admission of past vandalism. Open daily 8:30am to 4:30pm; admission ¥20.

Turn left, and continue down the main street until you find:

❹ Guangji Si

This is the closest thing Beijing has to a real Buddhist temple. The 1st and 15th day of the lunar calendar are especially busy here. Built in the Jin Dynasty, the temple also contains Buddhist statues made of yellow sandalwood and copper-cast statues of arhats dating back to the Ming Dynasty. If you'd like to meet the monks, visit **Lily Vegetarian Restaurant** (p. 103), where they often dine.

Backtrack west in the direction of Lidai Diwang Miao, taking the third right turn into Yao Jia Hutong; follow the alley, which jumps slightly left after one intersection and winds to the right until you reach the T, which brings you to:

❺ Xisi Bei San Tiao

Formerly known as Bozi Hutong, this is where bamboo screens for writing were produced. From this lane northward, the original Yuan street grid remains intact, with east-west *hutong* spaced exactly 79m (259 ft.) apart. Many of the original entrances and door piers *(men dun'r)* are in excellent condition, and this lane may be spared from development.

Turn right, and walk down to no. 3, which reveals a striking monastery gate, embellished with faded murals, which formerly marked the entrance to:

❻ Shengzuo Longchang Si

A Buddhist temple dating from the Ming, this was the site of scripture reproduction, transcribed on the bamboo strips the street was famed for. It is possible to (discreetly) wander among the former halls; the original outlay of the temple is readily discerned. There are no plans for restoring these ancient halls.

1 Lǔ Xùn Bówùguǎn
鲁迅博物馆

2 Bái Tǎ Sì
白塔寺

3 Lìdài Dìwáng Miào
历代帝王庙

4 Guǎngjǐ Sì
广济寺

5 Xīsì Běi Sān Tiáo
西四北三条

6 Shèngzuò Lóngcháng Sì
圣祚隆长寺

7 Rénmín Jùchǎng
人民剧场

8 Tiānmíng Pénjǐng Qíshíguǎn
天明盆景奇石馆

9 Rùndéli Zōnghé Shìchǎng
润得立综合市场

10 Xú Bēihóng Jìniànguǎn
徐悲鸿纪念馆

Continue east to the busy Xi Si Bei Dajie, turn left, and continue north past electronics shops until you reach a Bank of China. At this point, carefully cross the road and duck into the alley labeled Zhong Mao Jia Wan. The south side of this street was the residence of Mao's ill-fated deputy, Marshal Lin Biao. Appropriately, the residence is now occupied by the army. After 60m (197 ft.) turn left and continue up this winding *hutong*. At the main road, turn left to continue north, crossing Di'an Men Xi Dajie into Hucang Hutong. This area was formerly a prince's mansion, Zhuang Qin Wang Fu. Turn left at a busy Huguo Si Jie and look for no. 74, which is:

➐ Renmin Juchang

Built in honor of Mei Lanfang (see the "Back Lakes Ramble" walking tour, p. 155) during the 1950s, this impressive wooden structure has been deemed too much of a fire hazard to host performances.

Immediately opposite is:

> **TAKE A BREAK**
> From the late Yuan onward, **Huguo Si Xiaochi** (daily 5:30am–9pm) was the site of a huge temple fair (second only to Longfu Si; see the "Wangfujing" walking tour, p. 161), held on the seventh and eighth days of Chinese New Year. Beijing's most renowned snack shop claims to be faithful to temple fairs of the past, and at lunchtime, it's as chaotic as one. Tasty dishes include *xingren doufu* (chilled almond pudding), *shaobing jia rou* (miniburgers inside sesame buns), *wandou huang* (green pea pudding), and *saqima* (candied rice fritter).

Turn left to head north along Huguo Si Xi Jie, right next to the snack shop. You'll pass a neighborhood notice board on the right, and shortly on the left, at no. 33, you'll find:

➑ Tianming Penjing Qishiguan

While bonsai is normally associated with Japan, quite a number of elderly *Beijingren* are passionate about its antecedent, *penjing*. The owner of this exhibit is a quietly fanatical collector and creator of stunted trees and bizarrely shaped rocks.

Continue up the alley, which bears right, and make your way back to Mianhua Hutong (which is just Hucang Hutong under a different name) and continue north, passing old men playing chess and selling grasshoppers. Shortly, you'll arrive at a more densely forested section, and you'll notice people emerging from a lane to your right with bags of fruit and vegetables. Follow them to the source to find:

➒ Rundeli Zonghe Shichang

Still widely known as Si Huan Shichang, this is one of the few large open food markets (known as a wet market) still located within the city. There are vast stalls hawking clothing and fabric, animals (not intended as pets), and colorful spices.

Duck back out to Luo'r Hutong (again, just Hucang Hutong under another name) and continue north until you reach a major intersection, just before a hospital gate. Turn left into bustling Xinjiekou Dong Jie. This soon runs into still livelier Xinjiekou Bei Dajie, crammed with clothing and music shops. Continue north. On the left (west) side you'll soon find:

➓ Xu Beihong Jinianguan

The work on display in this memorial hall at Xinjiekou Bei Dajie 53 (¥5; Tues–Sun 9am–4pm) is instantly familiar—copies of the watercolors of Xu Beihong are on display at most tourist sites. Xu did much to revive a moribund art, combining traditional Chinese brushwork with Western techniques he assimilated while studying and traveling in Europe and Japan.

Head north along this bustling thoroughfare and turn right (east) onto Ban Qiao Tou Tiao, which leads to Xi Hu (West Lake), a peaceful area where locals fish. At this point, you can join up with the "Walking Tour 2: Back Lakes Ramble," or when you spy the waters of Hou Hai, keep to the right side and you'll reach:

> **WINDING DOWN**
> The **Kong Yiji Jiudian** (p. 91), named for the drunken hero of one of Lu Xun's best-known short stories, serves delicate Huaiyang cuisine in a scholarly setting. Slightly farther south is the tranquil **Teahouse of Family Fu** (p. 156).

Shopping

by Sherisse Pham

Writer Wang Shuo once observed that there were still devout Communists to be found in China, all of them safely under lock and key in a mental asylum. Consumerism is the official ideology of China, and shopping is the national sport. Spend, spend, and spend some more is the message drummed into China's willing citizens at every turn.

Dusty, empty, and useless state-run department stores are thankfully a thing of the past, though the **Friendship Store** still stands as an amusing reminder of the old days. Megamalls, shopping streets, and the few remaining open-air markets fight for a share of the spoils. Avoid shopping forays on weekends and evenings, when it can feel as if all of Beijing's 15 million residents line up at the cash registers to do their bit for the economic miracle.

Note: Unless otherwise noted, shops are open daily from between 9 and 10am to 9 or 10pm.

1 THE SHOPPING SCENE

Western-style shopping malls are flexing their muscles in Beijing, replacing the traditional storefronts, Chinese department stores, and alley markets. Even the new, privately run stores on major shopping streets tend to be versions of the boutiques and specialty outlets familiar to shoppers in the West. But there are still plenty of open-air markets and streetside vendors offering more traditional arts and crafts, collectibles, and clothing, usually at prices far below those in the big plazas and modern stores.

BEIJING'S BEST BUYS
Stores and markets in Beijing sell everything from cashmere and silk to knockoff designer-label clothing and athletic wear, antiques, traditional art, cloisonné, lacquerware, Ming furniture, Mao memorabilia, and enough miscellaneous Chinesey doodads to stuff Christmas stockings from now until eternity. Prices are reasonable (certainly lower than in the Asian goods boutiques back home), though increasingly less so. Cheap one-time-use luggage is widely available for hauling your booty if you get carried away.

Before you rush to the ATM, it is important to remember that not all that is green and gleams in Beijing is jade. Indeed, the majority of it is colored glass. The same principle holds for pearls, famous-brand clothing, antiques, and just about everything else. If you plan to make big purchases, you should educate yourself about quality and price well beforehand.

BEIJING'S TOP SHOPPING AREAS
The grandest shopping area in Beijing is **Wangfujing Dajie,** east of the Forbidden City. The street was overhauled in 1999, and the south section was turned into a pedestrian-only commercial avenue lined with clothing outlets, souvenir shops, fast-food restaurants, and two very popular malls—the Sun (Xin) Dong An Plaza and Oriental Plaza

---

Warning! "Hello, I'm an Art Student"

Be leery of any English-speaking youngsters who claim to be **art students** and offer to take you to a special exhibit of their work. This is a **scam.** The art, which you will be compelled to buy, almost always consists of assembly-line reproductions of famous (or not so famous) paintings offered at prices several dozen times higher than their actual value. You are almost sure to encounter this nonsense in the **Wangfujing** and **Liulichang** areas.

(Dongfang Guangchang). **Dong Dan Bei Dajie,** a long block east, is a strip of clothing boutiques and CD shops popular among fashionable Beijing youth. On the western side of town is the mirror image of Dong Dan, bustling **Xi Dan,** and farther north, **Xinjiekou Dajie.**

The extremely popular **The Village at Sanlitun** is a new shopping and entertainment complex in the heart of Beijing's famous bar district. On any given evening you will run into a fascinating cross section of Beijing all commingling in the Village's courtyard: migrant workers walking through after a hard day's work, Beijing yuppies shopping for new threads, and local expats sipping on iced lattes.

South of Tian'an Men is the newly constructed **Qianmen Dajie.** Originally built in 1436, it is one of the city's oldest commercial streets. All the buildings here are new, but modeled after traditional Chinese architecture.

Other major Westernized shopping areas include the section of **Jianguo Men Wai Dajie** between the Friendship Store and the China World Trade Center, and the neighborhood outside the **Northeast Third Ring Road North,** southeast of San Yuan Qiao around the new embassy district.

Beijing's liveliest shopping zone, beloved for its atmosphere and Chinese-style goods, is the centuries-old commercial district southwest of Qian Men. **Liulichang** is an almost too-quaint collection of art, book, tea, and antiques shops. The stores are lined up side by side in a polished-for-tourists Old Beijing–style *hutong,* running east-west 2 blocks south of the Heping Men metro stop. The street is good for window-shopping strolls and small purchases—like the unavoidable **chop** (*tuzhang;* stone or jade stamp), carved with your name. But beware of large purchases: Almost everything here is fake and overpriced. In a similar setting but more raucous, *Da Zhalan* ("Dashilanr" in the Beijing dialect) is the prole alternative. Located in a pedestrian-only *hutong* 2 blocks south of Qian Men, it is jammed on either side with cheap clothing outlets, restaurants, and luggage shops (see "Walking Tour 1: Liulichang & Da Zhalan," in chapter 8).

2 MARKETS & BAZAARS

Although malls and shopping centers are becoming more popular, the majority of Beijing residents still shop in markets. Whether indoors or out, these markets are inexpensive, chaotic, and, for the visitor, tremendously interesting. Payment is in cash, bargaining is essential, and pickpockets are plentiful. Perhaps the most common item you'll find in the markets these days is not silk, souvenirs, or crafts, but designer-label clothing, much of it knockoffs with the upscale labels sewn in, although some items are factory seconds or

overruns (sometimes smuggled out of legitimate brand-name factories). Before you stock
up on too many fake items, however, check the customs website of your home country
(p. 29) to see what you are allowed to bring home. Many countries, including the U.S.,
ban knockoff goods.

The most popular market is Yaxiu **Fuzhuang Shichang,** the best for jewelry is **Hong
Qiao Shichang,** and the most interesting is **Panjiayuan Jiuhuo Shichang;** but there are
others worth browsing.

HONG QIAO SHICHANG ★   Also called the **Pearl Market,** Hong Qiao Shichang is
located at Tian Tan Lu 9 (© **010/6713-3354;** see map p. 115), just northeast of Tian
Tan Gongyuan (Temple of Heaven Park) and north of Tiyuguan Lu. Hong Qiao began
life as a fascinating curio market outside Tian Tan Gongyuan, but like most outdoor
markets it was forced indoors and now sits above a malodorous wet market. Popular
purchases include reproductions of 1920s Shanghai advertisements for "cow soap." Also
popular is Cultural Revolution kitsch: Look out for flamethrower-like cigarette lighters
that play "The East is Red" *("Dongfang Hong")* when you light up. Elsewhere in the store,
you'll need to bargain hard for brand-name clothing, footwear, luggage, watches, and
pearls (see below), which attract swarms of bottle-blonde Russian women. The **toy
market** *(wanju shichang),* housed in a separate building at the back, is overlooked by
visitors, so starting prices are more reasonable; there are candles, incense, and stationery.
A post office is on the fourth floor. From Chongwen Men metro, take bus no. 807 to
Hong Qiao, and cross the footbridge. Open daily from 8:30am to 7pm.

PANJIAYUAN JIUHUO SHICHANG ★★★   Eureka! This is the Chinese shopping
experience of dreams: row upon crowded row of calligraphy, jewelry, ceramics, teapots,
ethnic clothing, Buddha statues, paper lanterns, Cultural Revolution memorabilia, PLA
belts, little wooden boxes, Ming- and Qing-style furniture, old pipes, opium scales, and
painted human skulls. The market is also known as the Dirt or Ghost Market. There are
some real antiques scattered among the junk, but you'd have to be an expert to pick them
out. Locals arrive Saturday and Sunday mornings at dawn or shortly after (hence the
"ghost" label) to find the best stuff; vendors start to leave around 4pm. Initial prices given
to foreigners are always absurdly high—Mao clocks, for instance, should cost less than
¥40 rather than the ¥400 you'll likely be asked to pay. Handily located just south of

---

(Tips) Buying Pearls

Most of the pearls on sale at **Hong Qiao Shichang** are genuine, although of too
low quality to be sold in Western jewelry shops. However, some fakes are floating
around. To test if the pearls you want to buy are real, try any one of the following:

- Nick the surface with a sharp blade (the color should be uniform within and
  without)
- Rub the pearl across your teeth (this should make a grating sound)
- Scrape the pearl on a piece of glass (real pearls leave a mark)
- Pass it through a flame (fake pearls turn black, real ones don't)

Oddly, vendors are generally willing to let you carry out these tests, and may
even help, albeit with bemused faces. If you'd rather not bother (most don't),
assume the worst, shop for fun, and spend modestly.

Panjiayuan on the west side of Huawei Qiao, **Curio City** (**Guwan Cheng;** © 010/6774-7711) has four floors of jewelry (including diamonds and jade), old clocks, cloisonné, furniture, and porcelain, as well as curios and the odd genuine antique. International shipping is provided. Curio City is open daily from 10am to 6:30pm. Panjiayuan market is located on the south side of Panjiayuan Lu, just inside the southeast corner of the Third Ring Road. It's open Saturday and Sunday from noon to about 4pm. See map p. 115.

SILK ALLEY (XIUSHUI JIE)   Herded indoors in 2005, Beijing's most famous market among foreign visitors is a crowded maze of stalls with a large selection of shoes and clothing (and very little silk). Vendors formerly enjoyed so much trade they could afford to be rude, but the knockoff boot is now firmly on the shopper's foot, as Silk Alley now sees only a fraction of the business of Yaxiu (see below). Most of the original vendors are gone, unwilling (or unable) to pay the new steep rental fees. Good riddance. Under no circumstances should you pay more than ¥150 for a North Face (or "North Fake," as the expats call it) jacket, ¥50 for a business shirt, or ¥100 for a pair of jeans. Stores which sport a red flag are purported to "subscribe to higher ethics." Spot the ethical pirates. Corner of Jianguo Men Wai Dajie and Xiushui Dong Jie, above the Yong'anli metro stop.

YAXIU FUZHUANG SHICHANG ★   Whatever you may think of their business practices, Beijing's clothing vendors are nimble: Here you'll find refugees from two now-extinct outdoor markets, Yabao Lu and Sanlitun. Opened in 2002, the market occupies the old Kylin Plaza building (Qilin Dasha) and retains at least one feature of the old Kylin: excellent tailors can be found on the third floor. The fourth floor is a fine hunting ground for souvenirs and gifts—there are kites from Weifang in Shandong, calligraphy materials, army surplus gear, tea sets, and farmers' paintings from Xi'an (laughably claiming to be originals by Pan Xiaoling, the most frequently copied artist). You can even treat yourself to a ¥20 manicure. The basement and the first two floors house a predictable but comprehensive collection of imitation and pilfered brand-name clothing, shoes, and luggage. The market has been "discovered" by fashion-conscious locals, and starting prices are often ridiculous. *Note:* Be especially aware of pickpockets in this market; we know of friends who have had their cellphones stolen while shopping. The market is just west of Sanlitun Jiuba Jie, at Gongti Bei Lu 58 (© **010/6415-1726**). Metro: Tuanjiehu.

SHOPPING WITH THE LOCALS

These markets are unknown to visitors and most expatriates. Asking prices are more reasonable than at the markets listed above, and the quality of goods is often superior. **Tianyi Xiaoshangpin Pifa Shichang** is the ultimate "Made in China" shopping experience. You'll find it 4 blocks west of the Fucheng Men metro stop at Fucheng Men Wai Dajie 259 (© **010/6832-7529;** see map p. 116), on the north side of the road. Everything is here, crammed into hundreds of stalls in a spanking-new five-story building tucked behind the old market. The range of toys, sporting equipment, electronic appliances, and luggage is eye-popping. Open daily from 7:30am to 5:30pm.

   Jin Wuxing Baihuo Pifa Cheng (© **010/6222-6827;** see map p. 116), a single-story wholesale market just south of Da Zhong Si metro, is even more comprehensive and more chaotic. They have every item imaginable, including the kitchen sink! Open 8:30am to 7pm. **Baoguo Si Wenhua Gongyipin Shichang** (Guanganmennei Dajie; © **010/6303-0976;** see map p. 116), Panjiayuan in miniature, is more relaxing. This delightful market has been a site of commerce since the Qing dynasty, and is set in the leafy grounds of a Liao dynasty (930–1122) temple. It offers mostly bric-a-brac, but vendors aren't pushy, and asking prices are reasonable. Coins, antiquarian books, and Cultural Revolution memorabilia abound. The market is liveliest on Thursday and Saturday mornings. From Changchun Jie metro, walk south along Changchun Jie and take the third right onto a tree-lined avenue that ends at the east gate of Xuanwu Yiyuan. Turn left and follow your nose southwest through the *hutong* to Baoguo Si. It's open daily from 9am to 4pm.

3 SHOPPING A TO Z

ANTIQUES & CURIOS

The **Panjiayuan Jiuhuo Shichang** market (see above) was once *the* place to look for antiques, and it still is for bric-a-brac and oddities. If you're not in town on the weekend, visit *Baoguo Si Wenhua Gongyipin Shichang* market (see above), which has similar curiosities in a more pleasant setting. Any cracked and dusty treasure you find is almost certainly fake, but you won't have trouble taking it home. Genuine antiques are not allowed out of the country without bearing an official **red wax seal,** and pieces made prior to 1795 cannot be exported at all. "Certified" antiques are available at astronomical prices in the **Friendship Store** (p. 111), at a few hotel gift shops, and in some of the nicer malls. But determined antiques lovers should look elsewhere.

Guang Han Tang ★   Set in a delightful courtyard house constructed from the ruins of a derelict factory, all of Guang Han Tang's pieces could be described as partially restored, as they maintain a feeling of antiquity. Furniture made from fir *(shanmu)* and elm *(yumu)* is disparagingly referred to as "firewood" *(chaimu)* by the locals, though the sturdiness of the latter wood is recognized in the expression for a die-hard traditionalist, *yumu naodai,* literally "elm brain." Furniture made from rosewood (*zitan* or *hongmu*) commands a higher price. Prices are serious, but so is the owner, Mr. Liang. No fakes here. Open daily 9am to 6pm. Caochangdi. ✆ 010/8456-7943. Bus: no. 418 from Dong Zhi Men metro stop to Caochangdi. Take the Da Shanzi exit off the airport expressway., follow Jichang Fu Lu northeast, and take the 2nd right onto Nan Gao Lu. After passing under the railway line, take the left fork in the road and follow the signs.

Lu Ban Gudian Jiaju Cheng (Finds)   Just east of town is **Gaobeidian**—one of the largest antique furniture markets in China. Lu Ban was the first shop to open at the location in 1991, but it's remarkable that over a decade later so few locals know of its existence. This outlet is the most reliable of the many furniture stores in Gaobeidian. But if you know what you're looking for, the real bargains can be found in small workshops opened by enterprising peasants from Shandong, Shanxi, and Anhui. At least half of the merchandise is bogus, and any furniture marked with a tag that says TIBETAN should be regarded as counterfeit until proven otherwise. Open daily 8am to 7pm. Gaobeidian 4 Dui (from Gaobeidian bus stop continue south for around 90m/295 ft.; turn left just before the railway tracks). ✆ 010/8575-6516. Bus: no. 363 from Sihui Dong metro stop to Gaobeidian.

ART SUPPLIES

Liulichang (see "Walking Tour 1: Liulichang & Da Zhalan," in chapter 8) has many small shops and stalls selling calligraphy brushes, brush racks, chops, fans, ink stones, paper, and other art supplies. The best bargains are found in the stalls toward the far-west

SHOPPING A TO Z

end. The most famous outlet is **Rongbao Zhai,** Liulichang Xi Jie 19 (𝄪 **010/6303-6090;** metro: Hepingmen), although its prices are pushed ever higher by tour groups. Even if you can't afford the prices, take a peek at the gallery on the second floor. It's open daily 8am to 6pm. Many art-supply shops cluster around the **National Gallery,** just opposite the north end of Wangfujing shopping street. **Baihua Meishu Yongpin,** located diagonally across from the gallery at Wusi Dajie 10–12 (𝄪 **010/6525-9701**), stocks a wide range of modern art supplies and also has a reliable framing service. It's open daily 9am to 6:30pm. The largest art store in Beijing is **Gongmei Dasha** at Wangfujing Dajie 200 (𝄪 **010/6528-8866**), although its prices are high. Metro: Wangfujing.

BIKES

Qian Men Zixingche Shangdian   One of Beijing's largest bike stores is dominated by new brands, such as Giant and Strong. However, you can still find some old-style Forever *(Yongjiu)* bicycles. Sadly, there's not a Flying Pigeon in sight. Open daily 9am to 6:30pm. Luo Ma Shi Da Jie 31, Xuanwu Qu. 𝄪 **010/6313-2092.**

BOARD GAMES

Xing Qiyi Yuan Shangmao Zhongxin   Better known in the West by the Japanese name of *go,* the complex game of strategy, *weiqi,* is undergoing a welcome resurgence in its native land, if the number of TV programs dedicated to its exposition are any guide (although it doesn't make for great television). This friendly shop outside the south gate of the National Sports Training Center, where many of China's *weiqi* masters work, sells boards and the 361 black and white pieces that fill in the spaces. These start at ¥40 for metal pieces in a wicker basket, and rise to ¥3,600 for agate stones in a jade bowl. "Traditional" Chinese chess, or *xiangqi,* is more commonly seen on the street. Elaborate *xiangqi* sets are also sold. Open weekdays 9am to 5pm; weekends 9am to 4pm. Tian Tan Dong Lu 80. 𝄪 **010/6711-4691.** Metro: Chongwen Men, then bus no. 807 to Dong Ce Lu; cross bridge and head south, then turn left onto Chang Qing Lu.

BOOKSTORES

Maps of any place in China can be found on the first floor of **Wangfujing Bookstore,** Wangfujing Dajie 218 (𝄪 **010/6527-7787**). The finest library of English-language books and magazines can be found at the **Bookworm** (p. 193).

Foreign Language Bookstore (Waiwen Shudian) ★   A few years ago, China's strict censorship laws restricted the stock in this bookstore to boring Western classics. Nowadays, we're happy to find the latest bestsellers, novels by Haruki Murakami, and good biographies alongside classics by the likes of Jane Austen. Wangfujing Dajie 235, Dongcheng Qu. 𝄪 **010/6512-6903.** Metro: Wangfujing.

Sanlian Taofen Tushu Zhongxin   Come here for the most interesting selection of Chinese-language books in Beijing, although **Wansheng Shudian,** south of Qinghua University in Haidian, runs a close second. A quiet cafe is on the second floor, but most patrons prefer the stairwell. Meishuguan Dong Jie 22, Dongcheng Qu. 𝄪 **010/6400-1122.** Bus: no. 803 from north of Wangfujing metro stop to Meishuguan. See map p. 106.

Sanwei Shuwu   Public outrage spared Beijing's original "dissident bookstore" from being converted into a patch of lawn in 2002. Downstairs is a small bookstore with a few English-language titles. Upstairs is a tranquil, traditional teahouse, ideal for a quiet read during the day. Fuxing Men Nei Dajie 60, Xicheng Qu (west of the metro stop, opposite Minzu Wenhua Gong, on the corner of Tonglinge Lu). 𝄪 **010/6601-3204.** Metro: Xidan.

has the best selection of art books in town. The decor is converted factory chic, with bookshelves nestled against exposed brick-and-cement walls. They are located in **Factory 798** (p. 111), so if you're a little rusty on your contemporary Chinese art, pop in here to refresh your memory before hitting the nearby galleries. Open Sunday to Thursday 10am to 9pm, and Friday and Saturday 10am to 11pm. Jiuxianqiao Lu 4, Chaoyang Qu. ✆ **010/ 8459-9332.**

CAMERAS & FILM

Color film and processing are readily arranged, but you're probably better off waiting until you return home or pass through Hong Kong. For black-and-white processing (the only choice for depicting Beijing in winter), try **Aitumei Caise Kuoyin Zhongxin,** Xinjiekou Nan Dajie 87 (✆ **010/6616-0718**). Beijing is not the place to buy new cameras and accessories, but those looking for secondhand parts for their old SLR camera, or wanting to experiment with ancient Russian swing lens cameras, have the two excellent markets listed in this section.

Beijing Sheying Qicai Cheng (Finds) Beijing's largest camera market has a bewildering array of equipment—one shop sells only lens filters! If you're looking for the old, obscure parts they just don't make any more, you'll find them here. Competition between vendors is fierce. Open daily 9am to 6pm. Xi Si Huan Lu 40, Xicheng Qu (a mile south of the metro stop on the west side). ✆ **010/8811-9797.** Bus: no. 748 from south of Wukesong metro stop to Zhengchang Zhuang. See map p. 116.

Malian Dao Sheying Qicai Cheng Located on the top floor of Malian Dao Tea City is a cluster of secondhand camera shops. **Hongsheng Sheying Fuwu Zhongxin,** on the north side, has the widest range of gear and the best repair service. Open daily 9am to 7pm. Malian Dao 11 (cross road and walk south for 5 min.). ✆ **010/6339-5250.** Bus: no. 719 from Fucheng Men metro stop to Wanzi.

CARPETS

Qian Men Carpet Factory Most modern Chinese carpets are testaments to what azo compounds are capable of if they fall into the wrong hands. Fortunately, the carpets in this dusty basement emporium (which was once a bomb shelter) are largely antiques. Rugs from Gansu and Ningxia in northwest China feature swastikas, dragons, phoenixes, and other auspicious symbols, and are free of alarming pinks and oranges. Antiques include Tibetan prayer rugs, Xinjiang yurt rugs, and Mongolian saddle rugs, all handmade using natural dyes. The factory also makes antique "reproductions" and Henan silk carpets. Cleaning and repair services are available. The factory is located at the back of the Chongwen Worker's Cultural Palace; follow the ANTIQUE CARPETS signs. Open daily 9:30am to 5pm. Xingfu Dajie 59, Chongwen Qu (opposite the east side of Tian Tan Fandian). ✆ **010/6715-1687.** Bus: no. 807 from Chongwen Men metro stop to Beijing Tiyuguan. See map p. 114.

Torana Gallery (Tu Lan NaYouyi Shangdian) Run by Englishman Chris Buckley, a guidebook writer turned entrepreneur, Torana sources its exquisite Tibetan and Chinese wool rugs from Gangchen Carpets and Michaelian and Kohlberg. Chris has a passion for Tibet, and often hosts photographic exhibitions. No bargains, but if you're looking for a genuine hand-woven rug, and lack the time or expertise to hunt one down, Torana should be your first choice. Open daily 10:30am to 6:30pm. Shun Huang Lu 60, Shunyi District. ✆ **010/8459-0785.**

Coin collectors and philatelists rub shoulders in Beijing. The largest market is **Malian Dao You Bi Ka Shichang** at Malian Dao 15 (daily 8:30am–5pm; see map p. 114), tucked away behind the tea shops, just south of yet another Carrefour supermarket. Housed in a half-empty building that resembles an aircraft hangar, you'll find stamps and envelopes commemorating great moments in Chinese diplomacy (more than you'd expect), coins and notes of all imaginable vintages, phone cards (popular with locals—there's even a Phone Card Museum), and a large range of Cultural Revolution memorabilia. To get here, take bus no. 719 from the Fucheng Men metro stop to Wanzi, cross the road, and walk south for 5 minutes. Larger post offices also have special sections offering limited-issue stamps. Coin collectors should make the trip to the **Ancient Coin Market (Gudai Qianbi Jiaoyi Shichang;** 🕾 **010/6201-8073;** daily 9am–4pm) at Desheng Men (p. 147).

COMPUTERS

In a recent local soap opera, **Zhongguan Cun** (touted as China's Silicon Valley), to the northwest of Beijing, was depicted as innovative, dynamic, and even sexy. Alas, with an education system that stifles creativity and a legal system incapable of enforcing intellectual property laws, copying software remains China's forte. (And software engineers are seldom sexy.) Don't rely on pirated software, but computer games usually work and computer whizzes have been known to build a computer from scratch here. Take bus no. 808 from Xi Zhi Men.

Bai Nao Hui   Less dodgy and easier to reach than Zhongguan Cun, this four-story amalgam of stores sells computers, digital cameras, and accessories. Software is not sold inside, but a gaggle of gentlemen from Anhui loitering outside greet you with a chorus of "Hello. CD-ROM!" Open daily 9am to 8pm. Chaowai Dajie 10 (10-min. walk east, on the south side of the street). 🕾 **010/5876-1166.** Metro: Chaoyang Men. See map p. 111.

DEPARTMENT STORES

Friendship Store (Youyi Shangdian)   Friendship Stores were once the only places where locals and foreigners alike could purchase imported goodies. You even needed "foreign exchange currency" to obtain the viciously overpriced merchandise. This is the largest store, and it was recently spared demolition when plans for a high-rise complex caused a stir among nearby embassies, but its days are numbered. You can bargain for their overpriced wares, but it's really not worth your while. The first-floor bookshop stocks a decent range of English-language magazines. Open daily 9:30am to 8:30pm. Jianguo Men Wai Dajie 17, Chaoyang Qu. 🕾 **010/6500-3311.** Metro: Jianguo Men. See map p. 111.

Pacific Century Place   This department store is packed with familiar brand names like Nine West, Hush Puppies, Esprit, and Columbia. Expat and local mommies swear by the toy selection on the sixth floor. It is located a short block east of Yashow, and is a great place to shop for authentic labels in a sterile, hassle-free environment. Gongti Bei Lu A2. 🕾 **010/6539-3888.** Metro: Tuanjiehu. See map p. 111.

DRUGSTORES

International SOS   Sure they charge high prices, but they are probably the safest place in town to purchase medicine. They have a good selection of familiar Western names. Open Monday through Friday from 8am to 8pm and Saturday and Sunday from 8:30am to 6pm. The pharmacy actually provides 24-hour service, although there is a

surcharge for after-hours purchases (¥50 for SOS members, and ¥60 for nonmembers).
Sanlitun Xi Wu Jie 5. ☏ 010/6462-9112. Metro: Liangmaqiao.

Wangfujing Drugstore   This emporium has a small selection of Western cosmetics and health aids, along with a large selection of traditional Chinese medicines. Open daily 8:30am to 10pm. Wangfujing Dajie 267, Dongcheng Qu. ☏ 010/6524-0199. Metro: Wangfujing.

Watson's   Another pawn in the Li Ka-Shing empire, Watson's has been quick to expand in the nation's capital. At the time of writing, there were 36 stores occupying prime Beijing real estate. This should be your first choice for Western cosmetics and toiletries, though the range of over-the-counter medicines is limited. Open daily 10:30am to 9:30pm (Holiday Inn Lido branch 9:30am–9:30pm; Oriental Plaza branch 10am–10pm). Branches at Holiday Inn Lido, ☏ 010/6436-3813, metro: Chaoyang Men; and at Oriental Plaza (see below), ☏ 010/8518-6426.

FASHION

Fashion is a baby industry in Beijing. For the most part, the city is not known for being fashion-forward. However, there are interesting independent ateliers emerging at Factory 798 (p. 111), and you can find funky stores with original designs.

Botao Haute Couture (Botao Gaojishi Zhuang Zhan) ★   Head to Botao if you want to order high-quality, original Chinese designs. The store employs a team of young Chinese designers, several of whom studied abroad in fashion hot spots like Paris, and most clothing is made-to-order. You get to choose from the store's fantastic fabric collection. Allow yourself several weeks for fittings. Dongzhimenwai Dajie 18, Chaoyang Qu. ☏ 010/6417-2472. Metro: Agricultural Exhibition Center (Nongzhan Guan).

Exception de Mixmind   Exceptional indeed. This Guangzhou-based store offers an original selection of women's clothing using high-quality knitwear, funky linens, and soft cottons. The designs all play off basic, conventional designs. A floor-length loose-knit sweater is topped with a gigantic hood, or simple tank tops come with a skewed neckline. Definitely a place to check out if you're looking to support innovative Chinese design. Store BB104 China World Shopping Center, Jianguo Men Wai Dajie 1, Chaoyang Qu. ☏ 010/6505-2268. Metro: Guomao.

Lane Crawford ★   The mother ship has landed. This upscale department store is doing everything in its power to transform Beijing into a fashion capital. The Hong Kong–based behemoth stocks the usual suspects (LV, Gucci, and so on) alongside a healthy selection of fashion-insider labels like Marni, Vanessa Bruno, and 3.1 Phillip Lim. And unlike at snooty flagship stores, staff at Lane Crawford are ultrafriendly and helpful. Store L130 Seasons Place Shopping Mall, Jinchengfang Jie 2 (next to the Ritz-Carlton Financial Street), Xicheng Qu. ☏ 010/6622-0808. See map p. 116.

Nali Patio (Nali Huayuan) ★   A couple of gems are housed in this multistory Mediterranean-style building. The hallways on the south side have a number of small shops carrying a mixture of fake and real clothes, often just one copy of whatever is on the racks. Bargain hard. The north side showrooms feature independent local designers. We love the elegant, feminine designs that mix Parisian chic with Oriental lines at Elysée Yang's eponymous showroom on the first floor (Shop D109; ☏ 010/5208-6070). Another favorite is Lu 12.28 (Shop D305; ☏ 010/5208-6105), which stocks young, edgy designs from Parsons-educated Liu Lu. Relegated to the south side, but full of a fine selection of original cashmere accessories and separates by freelance designer Ellede Zhang, is **Non**

Season (Shop 517; ☎ 010/8668-9255). Sanlitun Bei Lu 81, just north of The Village at Sanlitun, Chaoyang Qu. Metro: Tuanjiehu.

Nanluoguxiang ★★ This popular tourist-friendly *hutong* is lined with eclectic boutiques. The street is constantly changing, with cafes being torn down one week and new shops being put up the next. But on any given day you'll find stores stuffed with hip young clothes and independent boutiques offering creative, original designs such as **NLGX** at no. 33, or **Plastered T-Shirts** at no. 61 (see below). Most stores open until 10pm. Nan Luogu Xiang, between Gulou Dong Dajie and Di'anmen Dong Dajie, Dongcheng Qu. Metro: Bei Xin Qiao. See map p. 106.

Plastered T-Shirts ★ Simply the best place to get a quirky, original souvenir T-shirt. A British-Canadian couple opened the store over 3 years ago, and it is going strong. Shirts bear cute designs like *I "heart" BJ* (pun intended, we think), as well as some nods to Beijing life like the blown-up label of *Erguotou*, a 56-proof rice wine that sells for less than ¥20. Their newest collection features designs inspired by the artistry of Cultural Revolution posters. Open daily 10am till 11pm. Nan Luogu Xiang 61, Dongcheng Qu. ☎ 139/1020-5721. Metro: Bei Xin Qiao.

Ri Tan Shangwu Lou ★★ Not as cheap as Yaxiu, but a far more pleasant experience. If you lack the patience to wade through cheap copies of designer clothing in search of the genuine (or near-genuine) item at the markets listed above, or simply wouldn't be seen dead wearing such clothes, then swan on down to Ritan Office Building. From outside, it looks like an uninspiring office building, but inside is shopping nirvana: more than 70 shops stocking high-quality women's clothing, footwear, and accessories. There is a smattering of shops for chaps too. Open daily 10am till 8pm. Guanghua Lu 15A, Chaoyang Qu (just east of the south gate of Ri Tan Park, next to Schindlers). ☎ 010/8561-9556. Metro: Yong'anli metro stop.

Su Ren ★★ This place carries fantastic leather goods. It is our favorite place to buy quality bags and shoes that aren't knockoffs or cheap fakes. Styles are original and quirky, like leather gladiator-style sandals embellished with horsehair, or slender wallets tied with silk string looped through a jade stone. Jinyu Hutong 3, Chaoyang Qu. ☎ 010/6513-5580. Metro: Wangfujing. Other stores at Yaxiu Market, store 18 right beside the main entrance, on the east side, 10am–9:15pm, ☎ 010/8700-0099; and Huaqing Jia Yuan 2, Chengfu Lu, 10am–10pm, ☎ 010/8286-5563.

FOOD

Carrefours dot the city, but the most convenient supermarkets for travelers to stock up on snacks are found in the malls above the metro stops, including **Olé** (at China World Shopping Mall) at Guomao metro, Oriental Plaza at Wangfujing metro, and Oriental Kenzo at Dong Zhi Men metro), **Parksons** (Fuxing Men metro), and **Sogo** (Xuanwu Men metro).

April Gourmet This place carries excellent fresh fruits and vegetables, with decent cheese, bread, and wine selections. They will deliver within 2.5km (1½ miles) for purchases over ¥50. Their best-stocked branch is on Xingfu Ercun. Open daily 8am to midnight. Xingfu Ercun, Jiezuo Dasha, Chaoyang Qu. ☎ 010/6417-7970. Another convenient location is at Sanlitun Bei Xiao Jie 1. Daily 8am–9pm. ☎ 010/8455-1245. Metro: Nong Zhan Guan.

Jenny Lou's (Tianshun Chaoshi) Similar to April Gourmet, though with a less impressive cheese and bread selection, Jenny's empire continues to expand, with six outlets in total. The best branches are at Sanlitun Bei Xiao Jie and Chaoyang Park. Open daily 7am to 10pm. Sanlitun Bei Xiao Jie 6. ✆ 010/6461-6928. Metro: Nong Zhan Guan. Other location at Chaoyang Park West Gate. Daily 8am–midnight. ✆ 010/6507-5207.

JEWELRY

The **Hong Qiao Shichang** (see section 2 of this chapter), also known as the Pearl Market, has dozens of jewelry stalls (mostly pearls and jade) on its third and fourth floors. Unless you're an expert, this is not a place to make large purchases.

Beijing Gongmei Dasha   The third-floor stalls stock all varieties of jade, from green Khotanese nephrite to Burmese jadeite. They're terribly popular with Hong Kong visitors. Count on paying no more than a third of the marked price. Open daily 9:30am to 9:30pm. Wangfujing Dajie 200, Dongcheng Qu. ✆ 010/6528-8866. Metro: Wangfujing.

Shard Box Store (Shendege Gongyipin)   The wall of JCB, Amex, and Visa credit card stickers on the front door are fair warning—you aren't the first to discover this charming jewelry shop. The shard boxes—supposedly made from fragments of porcelain vessels smashed during the Cultural Revolution—are gorgeous. The rather more ordinary jewelry is a mixture of colorful curiosities gathered from Mongolian and Tibetan regions, and pieces crafted in nearby workshops. Jewelry can also be made to order. Open daily 9am to 7pm. Ritan Bei Lu 1, Chaoyang Qu (continue east from northeast corner of Ri Tan Gongyuan). ✆ 010/8561-3712. Metro: Yong'anli.

Things of the Jing   Local designer Gabrielle Harris creates original jewelry that merges Eastern designs with Western functionality. Find abacus earrings (with tiny beads that actually move), gorgeous streamlined silverware, and beautiful rings and pendants with inlaid turquoise, amber, and jade. The main store at Shunyi is a bit of a hike, so head to the more centrally located Bookworm (p. 193) to view a small sample. Since this store is out in the suburbs, the best way to get there is by cab. Open daily 10:30am to 6pm. Houshayu, Xi Baixinzhuang, Kaifa Jie. ✆ 0136/9151-3985.

Xincang Zhubao   Jewelry Street (Zhubao Yi Tiao Jie) is another traditional market cleaned up and forced indoors. This is the largest of more than 20 shops. The first floor stocks a full range of gemstones, wedding rings, and necklaces. Have a peek at the second floor's Western antiques—Swiss gramophones, American Bibles, old telephones, and a suit of plate armor. There's even some fine French chinoiserie, which has come full circle. Open daily 9am to 7pm. Yangrou Hutong 2, Xicheng Qu (cross over and continue north; Jewelry St. is marked by an archway). ✆ 010/6618-2888. Bus: no. 808 from north of Xidan metro stop to Xisi. See map p. 106.

MALLS & SHOPPING PLAZAS

China's new generation of leaders would love nothing better than to wake up and find a more populous version of Singapore outside the gates of Zhong Nan Hai. With the increasingly growing middle class and the arrival of swanky malls like **the Place** (p. 111) and **Shin Kong Place** (p. 111), this may be a reality sooner than any of us had ever imagined.

China World Trade Center Shopping Center (Zhongguo Guoji Maoyi Zhongxin)   Usually simply called "Guomao," this three-level mall caters to foreign business travelers and expatriate families. The ground level of China World contains airline offices, American Express, a food court, and Beijing's first (but now far from only) Starbucks. There are stores such as Louis Vuitton and Jack and Jones, as well as an Olé

Supermarket and a specialty wine shop. Jianguo Men Wai Dajie 1, Chaoyang Qu. ℰ **010/6505-2288.** Metro: Guomao.

Oriental Plaza (Dongfang Xin Tiandi)   Beijing's second-largest shopping complex stretches from Wangfujing to Dong Dan (the largest is Golden Resources Mall, an empty shopping complex in the west of town). Supplanting the world's biggest McDonald's, the project was backed by Hong Kong billionaire Li Ka-Shing. The two-story arcade houses hip clothing stores such as Art of Shirts (shop AA20) and multibrand retailer i.t (BB60-62); the Wangfujing Paleolithic Museum; and another Olé supermarket. The Grand Hyatt (p. 60) stands above all the consumption. In summer, it is open daily 10am to 10:30pm; winter daily 9:30am to 10pm. Dong Chang'an Dajie 1, Dongcheng Qu. ℰ **010/8518-6363.** www.orientalplaza.com. Metro: Wangfujing. See map p. 106.

The Place (Shimao Tianjie)   This behemoth, marked by a huge outdoor screen playing clips of random fashion shows, sees plenty of fashionista traffic. Spanish retailer Zara chose to open its first Beijing shop here; their arrival in Beijing was highly anticipated by locals and expats alike. Makeup guru MAC also chose The Place for its Beijing flagship store. Other retailers like French Connection, Mango, and adidas ensure that this place is virtually bargain hunter–free. Guanghua Lu Jia 9. ℰ **010/8595-1755.** Metro: Yong'anli metro stop. See map p. 111.

Qianmen Dajie   This renovated commercial street is tourist-oriented and a bit Disney-esque: Multistory shops modeled after traditional Chinese architecture line the street and an old-fashioned trolley runs down the center. That said, the city's first H&M is here, and a second Apple Experience Store should be open by the time you read this. Combine a trip here with a trip to Tian'an Men Square. Qianmen Dajie, Dongcheng Qu. Metro: Qian Men. See map p. 114.

Shin Kong Place (Xin Guang Tiandi)   Shin Kong Place sets the gold standard in Beijing luxury shopping. The indoor mall has all the labels that break the bank: Coach, Gucci, Salvatore Ferragamo, and Marc Jacobs, as well as high-end but more affordable retailers like Juicy Couture, Diesel, and Club Monaco. Jianguo Lu 87, Chaoyang Qu. ℰ **010/6530-5888.** Metro: Dawang Lu. See map p. 111.

Sun Dong An Plaza (Xin Dong'an Shichang)   This huge mall is filled with designer clothing shops. Aside from the usual Western food chains—Baskin-Robbins, Pizza Hut, McDonald's, KFC, Starbucks, and Délifrance—an excellent hot pot restaurant, Dong Lai Shun, is on the fifth floor. Chinese medicine outlets, tea shops, and tacky "Old Beijing Street" await in the basement. Wangfujing Dajie 138, Dongcheng Qu. ℰ **010/5817-6688.** Metro: Wangfujing. See map p. 106.

The Village at Sanlitun ★★   This is *the* place to see and be seen. A team of well-known and international names from the architect world is responsible for the look of this modern shopping complex, which is composed of several free-standing, multistory buildings connected by covered walkways. Shoppers congregate in the central outdoor courtyard to people-watch or refuel with a Frappuccino. Anchor stores include the first Apple Experience Store in Asia and the world's largest adidas flagship. Aside from shopping, popular restaurants are on the second and third floors, a movie theater is in the basement, and cafes are on the main level. For now, only the south "phase" is open, composed of midrange labels like Mango and United Colors of Benetton. The swankier north phase beside the Opposite House hotel will host luxury brands; it should be open by the time you read this. Sanlitun Bei Lu 19, Chaoyang Qu. www.thevillage.com.cn. Metro: Tuanjiehu. See map p. 111.

Many branches of traditional Chinese art have been on the wane since the Tang dynasty (A.D. 618–907). So rather than encourage the 5,000-year-old tradition of regurgitation, look for something different. It's a much better investment.

798 (**Dashanzi** or simply 798 in Chinese, **Qi Jiu Ba**)   This art district (www.798space. com) has become a bit less arty and more youth-culture driven these days, but it's still a worthwhile place to visit, if just to soak up the local vibes of Beijing's "bo-co" (bohemian-commercial) culture. A few worthwhile galleries in this former factory district turned art hub include Ullens Centre for Contemporary Art (ⓒ **010/8459-9269**), Long March Space (ⓒ **010/5978-9768**), Farschou (ⓒ **010/5978-9316**), and 798 Photo (ⓒ **010/ 6438-1784**). Get a map of the area at Timezone 8 Bookstore and Café (ⓒ **010/8456/ 0336**), 500m (1,640 ft.) east of 798's south entrance (no. 4 gate).

Caochangdi   This blossoming art district has become a destination for serious art collectors. Even if you don't have millions of yuan to blow, it's worthwhile to check it out to see pieces by China's new up-and-coming artists. Rent a car and driver for half a day to make it convenient to get in between the galleries. Visit Three Shadows Photography Art Centre (ⓒ **010/6432-2663**), Chambers Fine Arts (ⓒ **010/5127-3298**), Pekin Fine Arts (ⓒ **010/5127-3220**), ShanghART(ⓒ **010/6432-3202**), and White Space (ⓒ **010/ 8456-2054**).

East Gallery (Yisen Hualang)   Although quality varies, the East Gallery is the best of the locally run modern art galleries. The backdrop is magnificent, as you clamber up the narrow stairwells of the Desheng Men arrow tower (p. 147). You can visit the Ancient Coin Exhibition Hall downstairs. Open daily 9am to 5:30pm. Bei Er Huan Lu, Desheng Men Jianlou, Xicheng Qu (just east of the metro stop). ⓒ **010/8201-4962**. Metro: Jishuitan.

Red Gate Gallery (Hong Men Hualang) ★   Opened by the delightfully camp Brian Wallace in the early 1990s, Red Gate has regular exhibitions featuring the work of its dozen or so artists. The Dongbian Men watchtower (¥5) provides an airy and atmospheric viewing space. Open daily 10am to 5pm. Chongwen Men Dong Dajie, Dongbian Men Jiaolou, Dongcheng Qu (10-min. walk south). ⓒ **010/6525-1005**. www.redgategallery.com. Metro: Jianguo Men. See map p. 114.

MUSIC

Despite numerous well-publicized and photogenic police crackdowns, pirated *(daoban)* CDs and DVDs are readily available in Beijing, and with the proliferation of illegal music download sites, even the pirates are having it rough. If you want to support local music, go to a concert and buy the music directly from the band. The second floor of the **Foreign Language Bookstore** (p. 170) has a wide range of Chinese music. There's maddening cross-talk *(xiangsheng)*, bland mandopop, and even a small alternative *(fei zhuliu)* music section featuring local bands such as Thin Man and Second Hand Rose. The alternative philosophy doesn't extend to the Western music section, which relies on Richard Clayderman, Kenny G, and Avril Lavigne.

Beijing Yangguang Yunzhi Shudian   An essential stop for those looking to develop an appreciation (or at least an understanding) of Peking Opera. Located next to the People's Theater, this tiny shop is crammed with DVDs and CDs featuring Peking opera's leading man, Mei Lanfang. Traditionally, only three instruments were essential—the ubiquitous two-stringed erhu; its smaller cousin, the *jinghuu;* and the banjolike *yueqiin.* Elegant handmade versions of all three are found here. Lessons can be arranged.

Open daily 8am to 6:30pm. Huguo Si 4 Dajie 74, Xicheng Qu 1 (next to Renmin Juchang). C **010/6617-2931.** Metro: Jishuitan.

Beijing Yinyue Shudian   At this store, located just to the east of the north end of the Wangfujing pedestrian mall, the top floor has a large range of sheet music at prices far cheaper than in the West. Composers' names are in Chinese, of course, but names are transliterated (Beethoven becomes Beiduofen, Liszt is rendered as Lisite), so you may be able to make yourself understood. If not, names are often written in English above the scores. 1/F open daily 9:30am to 10:30pm, 2/F–4/F open to 9:30pm only. Dong'an Men Dajie 16. C **010/6525-4458.** Metro: Wangfujing.

ODDITIES

Gong'anbu Diyi Yanjiusuo (Finds)   More *Get Smart* than James Bond, the commercial outlet of the "No. 1 Police Research Unit" is a bizarre example of socialist marketization. Aside from authentic Chinese police gear—bulletproof vests, sturdy boots—there's a full range of dated surveillance equipment, including nifty spy pens. Suspicious (often with good reason) wives are said to be their main clients. Open daily 9am to 5:30pm. Zhengyi 4 Lu, Dongcheng Qu (walk east to 1st intersection and turn right, walk for a few minutes; opposite Beijing City Government He   uarters). C **010/6842-0099.** www.fri.com.cn. Metro: Tian'an Men Dong.

Pyongyang Art Studio   More disturbing tha.. `1, this tiny shop, opened by a Brit who has been traveling to the DPRK since 1993, is crammed with North Korean goods and socialist realist art. Cultural Revolution kitsch, while in questionable taste, has some distance to it. This is more confronting: There are anti-U.S. tracts, and paeans to the Dear Leader, Kim Jong-Il , the only man to card a perfect 18 in a round of golf. His love of cinema is described in "Great Man and Cinema," while "A Great Mind" celebrates his father, Kim Il-Sung. There are propaganda posters (many hand-painted), magazines, flags, T-shirts, cigarettes, and even North Korean hooch. Compelling. Open Monday to Friday 10am to 6pm. Chunxiu Lu 10, Chaoyang Qu (inside the Red House). C **010/6416-7810.** www.pyongyangartstudio.com.

3501 PLA Surplus Store (3501 Gongchang) ★   The official disposal store of the world's largest army is a delightful mix of fur-lined boots, army greatcoats, and kitsch Communist memorabilia. Where else will you find Lei Feng hats, sturdy compasses and binoculars, and waist watches commemorating the 50th anniversary of liberation? Open daily 9am to 5pm. Dong San Huan 23, Dongcheng Qu (just south of Jing Guang Zhongxin). C **010/6585-9312.** Metro: Guomao. See map p. 111.

OUTDOOR EQUIPMENT

Decathlon (Value)   A place to get the real stuff—we think. This is basically an outlet of the sporty French retailer. It has everything for the outdoors, from tents to hiking boots, at significantly lower prices than what you would find back home. And for the ladies, this is the only place in Beijing where we have found nonpadded sports bras. Open Sunday through Thursday from 9am to 9pm, and Friday through Saturday until 10pm. Dongsihuan Zhong Lu 195 (corner of Nanmofang Lu and E. Fourth Ring Rd.). C **010/8777-8788.**

Sanfu Huwai Yongpin (Sanfo Outdoors) (Value)   This shop began life as an outdoor club at Peking University, and has a dedicated following among students and young professionals. Unlike the knockoffs for sale at Hong Qiao and elsewhere, Sanfo stocks

only the genuine article, and most products come with a warranty. They have their own
line of sleeping bags, and still organize weekend trips to the wilderness around Beijing.
There are branches in Jin Zhi Qiao Dasha west of Guomao, and northwest of Peking
University. Open daily 10am to 8:30pm. Madian Nan Cun 4 Lou 5. ℂ 010/8202-1113, ext. 12.
www.sanfo.com.cn. Metro: Jishuitan, then bus no. 919 to Beijiao Shichang. See map p. 116.

PORCELAIN

Spin ★★   This innovative boutique has a loyal local and international following.
Everything in here is creatively masterminded by a trio of Shanghai-based artists. The
store's interior looks like a lovingly stocked gallery, with beautifully crafted dishware,
vases, and quirky tea sets lining the shelves and central display area. You'll find timeless
streamlined designs here as well as unconventional pieces, such as square plates with a
small wrinkle worked into the porcelain, or slender coffee cups that tilt to one side. Wares
are made from thin porcelain with green-white glaze, china-blue, underglaze red, or
jingdezhen (a fine white porcelain). Prices are incredibly reasonable to boot. It's a short
cab ride away from the art district, so combine a trip here with your 798 visit. Open daily
11am to 9pm. Fangyuan Xi Lu 6, Chaoyang Qu. ℂ 010/6437-8649. See map p. 111.

SHOES

Lao Fan Jie Fuzhuang Shichang (Alien's Street)   It's hard to imagine anything
more chaotic than the original Yabao Lu Market, but this brushed-down version comes
close. It is impossible not to get lost. The first floor houses shoes, shoes, and more shoes,
which mercifully come in sizes suitable for Western feet. Cheap, expansive, and often
nasty, this market is popular with Russian traders. Open daily 9:30am to 6:15pm. Yabao
Lu, Chaoyang Qu (head east from the metro stop and take the 2nd right; continue south, and
the market is on the left side). ℂ 010/8561-4647. Metro: Chaoyang Men.

Nei Lian Sheng Xiedian   Cloth-soled "thousand layer happy shoes" *(qianceng
buxie)*, loved by martial arts stars and aging Communist leaders alike, are hard to find.
Cheaper plastic-soled shoes are taking their place. A workshop behind this shop, founded
in 1853, still turns them out; these shoes are well stitched and very comfortable. There
are also some gorgeous women's shoes, modeled on Qing fashions. Fortunately, they are
now available in larger sizes. Bargaining is fruitless. Dazhalan Jie 34. ℂ 010/6301-4863. Metro:
Qian Men.

SILK, FABRIC & TAILORS

The third floor of **Yashow Market** (**Yaxiu Fuzhuang Shichang;** see map p. 111) is a fine
place to look for a tailor.

Beijing Sichou Dian (Beijing Silk Store)   Tucked away in a narrow *hutong* just
west of and running parallel with Qian Men Dajie, this bustling store is said to date from
1840. Prices for tailoring and raw materials are affordable. Open daily 9am to 8:30pm.
Zhubao Shi 5, Chongwen Qu (just south of metro stop). ℂ 010/6301-6658. Metro: Qian Men.

Daxin Fangzhi Gongsi (Value)   It might not be as prestigious as other tailors, but
with hand-tailored *qipao* (body-hugging one-piece dress) typically costing less than ¥200,
it's impossible to argue with the price. Open daily 8:30am to 8pm. Chao Nei Dajie 253
(northeast corner of Dongsi Shitiao, take metro line 5 get off at Dongsi). ℂ 010/6403-2378.

Ruifuxiang Choubu Dian ★   You'll find piles of gorgeous silk brocade at this store, in the trade for 110 years. They specialize in *qipao* for ¥500 and up. It takes 1 week to tailor, with a couple of fittings. If you're pushed for time, they can complete it in 2 days for an additional charge. They also have an outlet at Wangfujing Dajie 190 (✆ **010/ 6525-0764**), just north of Gongmei Dasha. Aim to bargain 30% to 50% off the marked prices. Open daily 9:30am to 8:30pm. Dazhalan Jie 5, west off Qian Men Dajie, Chongwen Qu. ✆ **010/6303-5313.** Metro: Qian Men.

Yuanlong Sichou Gufen Youxian Gongsi (Yuanlong Silk Co. Ltd.)   A huge range of silk fabric occupies the third floor; prices are clearly marked and surprisingly competitive. A *qipao* or suit can be made in a couple of days, but it's best to allow at least a week. Exquisite (and expensive!) silk carpets from Henan are sold on the first floor. Try not to visit at midday, when the third floor is overrun by tour groups. Open daily 10am to 6:30pm. Tian Tan Lu 55, Chongwen Qu (northeast side of Tian Tan Gongyuan). ✆ **010/6702-2288** or 6701-2854. Bus: no. 807 from Chongwen Men metro stop to Hong Qiao. See map p. 114.

SKATE WEAR

Yan Cheng Yu (Over Workshop) ⟨**Kids**⟩   With acres of empty concrete, the capital is a skateboarder's paradise. The skating park in Tian'an Men Square is a distant memory, but the owners of this shop can steer you in the right direction. Decks and wheels are imported, but local skate fashions feature striking designs. Danny Way, who skated over the Juyong Guan section of the Great Wall in 2005, figures prominently. Some designs can be viewed online at www.skatechina.com and www.shehuisk8.com. Open daily 10am to 6pm. Xinjiekou Xi Li Yi Qu 1 6-002, Xicheng Qu (cross road, take 1st right after Xu 2 Beihong Memorial Hall, inside a block of yellow apartments on left side). ✆ **010/8201-1266.** Metro: Jishuitan. See map p. 106.

TEA

Geng Xiang   With a survey finding that more than half of Beijing's teas have traces of pesticides or heavy metals, organic teas are a sensible choice. The largest retailer of organic tea in Beijing, Geng Xiang, survived the scandal with its reputation enhanced. Their green tea *(lu cha)* is among the best in China. Open daily 9am to 8pm. Di'an Men Wai Dajie 116, Xicheng Qu (south of Drum Tower on east side of street). ✆ **010/6404-0846.** Metro: Gu Lou Dajie.

Malian Dao ★★   This might not be all the tea in China, but with over a mile of shops hawking tea leaves and tea paraphernalia, it feels like it. Shops are run by the families of tea growers from Fujian and Zhejiang, and many rate this friendly street as the highlight of their visit. The four-story Tea City *(Cha Cheng),* halfway down the street, is a pleasant spot to start. Black tea *(hong cha)* and Pu'er tea (sold in round briquettes, a tea that improves with age) are usually sold by the same vendors. The Beijing outlet of **Menghai Chachang** (ext. 8165), at the south end of the first floor, stocks exquisite black tea. Oolong tea *(wulong cha)* is usually encountered in the West in substandard form: Here is the genuine article. There is such a wide range of flavors—from flowery *gaoshan* to caffeine-laden *tie guanyin,* from milky *jinxuan* to the sweet aftertaste of *renshen* (ginseng)—that most shoppers find a brew to suit. Try **Taiwan Tianbaoyang Mingcha** (ext. 8177), on the west side of Tea City's first floor. Ceramic and cloisonné tea sets are the other big draw. **Ziyu Taofang** (✆ **010/6327-5268;** daily 8am–7pm), on the east side of the second floor, sells fine pots and cups molded from Yixing clay. Bargain hunters should visit **Jingmin Chacheng,** an older wholesale market, farther south on the same side of the street. Open daily 8:30am to 7pm. Malian Dao Cha Cheng, Fengtai Qu. ℂ 010/ 6328-1177.

Tian Fu Jituan (Ten Fu Tea)   While not quite the McDonald's of tea, at last count there were 70 branches in Beijing. This store is the largest. Their jasmine tea *(hua cha)* is excellent. Open daily 10am to 11pm. Wangfujing Dajie 176, Dongcheng Qu. ℂ 010/6524- 0958. Metro: Wangfujing.

TOYS

Mass-produced toys can be found at the **toy market** *(wanju shichang)* behind Hong Qiao Shichang, or at **Alien's Street Market.** Check carefully before you purchase: There are no warranties or safety guarantees. We infinitely prefer:

Bannerman Tang's Toys and Crafts (Shengtang Xuan) ★   A world away from the baubles produced in the sweatshops of Shenzhen, this tiny shop offers delightful handcrafted toys. It's run by fifth-generation toymaker Tang Yujie and stocked with a delightful collection of figurines, paper lanterns, and other childish delights made from wood, clay, paper, and cloth. Toys depict scenes from old Beijing—the street barber, the fortuneteller, and old men playing chess. Beijing opera figurines betray influences from Japanese *manga.* Open daily 9am to 7pm. Guo Zi Jian Jie, Dongcheng Qu (just west of Kong Miao, on the south side of the street). ℂ 010/8404-7179. Metro: Yonghe Gong/Lama Temple.

Beijing After Dark

by Sherisse Pham

If you measure a city's nightlife by the number of chances for debauchery it offers, then Beijing has never held (and probably will never hold) a candle to such neon-lit Babylons as Shanghai and Hong Kong. If, instead, you measure nightlife by its diversity, the Chinese capital rivals any major city in Asia.

Such was not always the case. As recently as a decade ago, Beijing's populace routinely tucked itself into bed under a blanket of Mao-inspired Puritanism shortly after nightfall, leaving visitors with one of two tourist-approved options: Attend Beijing opera and acrobatic performances in a sterile theater, or wander listlessly around the hotel in search of a drink to make sleep come faster.

Since then, the government has realized there is money to be made on both sides of the Earth's rotation. The resulting relaxation in nocturnal regulations, set against the backdrop of Beijing residents' historical affinity for cultural diversions, has helped remake the city's nightlife. Opera and acrobatics are still available, but now

in more interesting venues, and to them have been added an impressive range of other worthwhile cultural events: teahouse theater, puppet shows, intimate traditional music concerts, live jazz, even the occasional subtitled film.

This diversity continues with Beijing's drinking and dance establishments, of which there are scores. Some are even beginning to rival Shanghai's for style and, unfortunately, price. With the opening of a few modern dance clubs, the city's cheesy old discos are thankfully no longer the only dance option, although the latter can still be tremendously entertaining for kitsch value. The same goes for karaoke, a favorite in China as it is in Japan. Foreign–Chinese interaction in bars hasn't progressed much beyond the sexual exploitation rampant in the 1920s and 1930s, but this is by no means a necessary dynamic. The traveler not afraid to bumble through language barriers can often connect with local people over a bottle or two of beer.

1 PERFORMING ARTS

BEIJING OPERA

Beijing opera *(jingju)* is described by some as the apogee of traditional Chinese culture and, at least according to one modest Chinese connoisseur, is "perhaps the most refined form of opera in the world." Many who have actually seen a performance might beg to differ with these claims, but few other Chinese artistic traditions can match it for sophistication and pure stylized spectacle.

The Beijing tradition is young as Chinese opera styles go. Its origins are most commonly traced to 1790, when four opera troupes from Anhui Province arrived in Beijing to perform for the Qing court and decided to stay, eventually absorbing elements of a popular opera tradition from Hubei Province. Initially performed exclusively for the royal family, the new blended style eventually trickled out to the public and was well received as a more accessible alternative to the elegant but stuffy operas dominant at the time.

How it could have ever been considered accessible is mystifying to most foreign audiences. The typical performance is loud and long, with archaic dialogue sung on a screeching pentatonic scale, accompanied by a cacophony of gongs, cymbals, drums, clappers, and strings. This leaves most first-timers exhausted, but the exquisite costumes and martial arts–inspired movements ultimately make it worthwhile. Probably the opera's most distinctive feature is its elaborate system of face paints, with each color representing a character's disposition: red for loyalty, blue for bravery, black for honesty, and white for cruelty.

Communist authorities outlawed the "feudalistic" classics after 1949 and replaced them with the Eight Model Plays—a series of propaganda-style operas based on 20th-century events that focus heavily on class struggle. Many of these are still performed and are worth viewing if only to watch reactions from audience members, some of whom have seen these plays dozens of times and loudly express their disgust when a mistake is made. But the older stories, allowed again after Mao's death, are more visually stunning. Among the most popular are *Farewell My Concubine,* made famous through Chen Kaige's film of the same name, and *Havoc in Heaven,* which follows the mischievous Monkey King character from the Chinese literary classic *Journey to the West.*

Several theaters now offer shortened programs more amenable to the foreign attention span, usually with English subtitles or plot summaries. Most people on tours are taken to the cinema-style **Liyuan Theater (Liyuan Juchang)** inside the Qian Men Hotel (nightly performances at 7:30pm; ✆ **010/6301-6688;** ¥200–¥580) or to one of several other modern venues. These are affordable but supremely boring. Your time and money are much better spent at one of the traditional theaters below.

Huguang Guild Hall (Huguang Huiguan Xilou)   This combination museum-theater, housed in a complex of traditional buildings with gray tile roofs and bright red gables, has a connection with Beijing Opera dating back to 1830. To the right of the main entrance is a small museum filled with old opera robes and photos of famous performers (including the legendary Mei Lanfang), probably interesting only to aficionados. On the left is the expertly restored theater, a riot of color with a beautifully adorned traditional stage, paper lanterns hung from the high ceilings, and gallery seating on all three sides. Subtitles are in Chinese only, but brochures contain brief plot explanations in English. Performances take place nightly at 7:30pm. Hufang Lu 3 (at intersection with Luomashi Dajie; plaza out front contains colorful opera mask sculpture). ✆ **010/6352-9134.** Tickets ¥150–¥580. Metro: Heping Men; walk south 10 min.

Mei Lanfang Grand Theatre (Mei Lanfang Da Ju Yuan)   This brand-new, multistory theater was built specifically for Peking Opera. The performance quality and times vary so be sure to check the schedule ahead of time. If you don't want to chance sitting through a bad Peking opera show, the ultramodern glass theater and the giant bust of Mei Lanfang in the foyer are worth viewing on their own. Ping'anli Xi Dajie 32. ✆ **010/5833-1288.** Tickets ¥20–¥150.

Teahouse of Prince Gong's Mansion (Gong Wang Fu Chaguan)   Not a traditional opera venue, Prince Gong's teahouse is nevertheless picturesque, with a rare bamboo motif on the exterior beams and columns and an intimate interior outfitted with

Rainbow Sexuality Under the Red Flag

Same-sex relationships between men have a history of acceptance in China dating as far back as the Zhou period (1100–256 B.C.). In official records of the Han dynasty (206 B.C.–A.D. 220), 10 emperors are described as openly bisexual and are listed with the names of their lovers. In the centuries following the Han, homosexuality was generally accepted among men, so long as it didn't interfere with their Confucian duty to marry and perpetuate the family name. Partly due to the influence of Western missionaries, homosexuality was outlawed by official decree in 1740, but Judeo-Christian notions of shame never fully took root in China and the practice persisted. Under the Communists, however, homosexuality came to be seen as disruptive of the social order, and persecution of gays was sanctioned during the Cultural Revolution.

The situation has improved markedly over the past decade. In 2002, the government rescinded its 1989 edict describing homosexuality as a psychological disorder, but laws still prohibit expat magazines from talking about gay bars (described instead as bars "for the alternative set"). *Time Out,* a popular expat periodical, runs a monthly column that gets around the censors with a subtle header: G&L. The general populace tends to ignore the existence of gay relationships, made easier by the fact that it's considered normal for men to be physically affectionate regardless of sexual orientation. As in ancient times, many gay men still marry and have children to satisfy their parents.

The best gay club in Beijing is **Destination (Mudidi;** p. 189; ⓒ **010/6551-5138)** at Gongti Xi Lu 7, south of the Worker's Stadium west gate, where the crowd revels and the beats are right. Things have turned a tad seedy in recent times, but the crowds still flock to this venue, which now includes a bar, a restaurant, and even an Internet cafe.

For lesbians, the scene is slightly grimmer. Women perceived as homosexual are often subject to harassment. In the context of Chinese patriarchy, lesbianism has never received much attention. Outside a brief appearance in the Chinese classic *Dream of the Red Mansion,* it is invisible in literature, and the pressures of China's skewed gender ratio—an excess of boys brought on by age-old prejudices in response to the one-child policy—has made many single Chinese men resentful of any reduction in the pool of potential wives.

Aside from Thursday nights at Destination, try the Feng Bar, just east of the south gate of the Worker's Stadium, on Saturday nights. As the scene is still developing, try connecting online, through Beijing's Other Attractions (www.boaevents.com), or more general websites for lesbians in Asia, such as www.fridae.com or www.utopia-asia.com.

polished wood tables and pleasing tea paraphernalia. This is opera for tourists, kept short and sweet, with a guided tour of the surrounding gardens included in the price (see Prince Gong's Mansion, p. 142). There are several performances daily until 4:30pm. Liuyin Jie 17. (Signposted in English at top of Qian Hai Xi Dajie [running north off Ping'an

ACROBATICS

China's acrobats are justifiably famous, and probably just a little bit insane. This was the only traditional Chinese art form to receive Mao's explicit approval (back flips, apparently, don't count as counterrevolution). While not culturally stimulating, the combination of plate spinning, hoop jumping, bodily contortion, and seemingly suicidal balancing acts make for slack-jawed entertainment of the highest order. Shanghai is the traditional home of acrobatics and has its best troupes, but the capital has done a fair job of transplanting the tradition.

The city's best acrobatics *(zaji)* venue is the **Wansheng Juchang** on the north side of Bei Wei Lu just off Qian Men Dajie (west side of the Temple of Heaven); performances are by the famous Beijing Acrobatics Troupe (*©* **010/6303-7449;** nightly shows at 5:30 and 7:15pm; ¥180). The acrobats at the **Chaoyang Theatre** (**Chaoyang Juchang;** Dong San Huan Bei Lu 36, south of Tuanjie Hu Park; *©* **010/6507-2421;** nightly shows at 7:15pm; ¥180–¥680) are clumsier but the theater is more conveniently located, a short taxi ride from the main bar district. Metro: Hujialou.

PUPPETS

Puppet shows *(mu'ou xi)* have been performed in China since the Han dynasty (206 B.C.–A.D. 220). The art form has diversified somewhat over the past 2 millenniums, coming to include everything from the traditional hand puppets to string and shadow varieties. Plotlines are simple, but the manipulations are deft and the craftsmanship is exquisite. Most performances, including weekend matinees, are held at the **China Puppet Art Theater (Zhongguo Mu'ou Juyuan),** in Anhua Xi Li near the North Third Ring Road (*©* **010/6424-3698**); tickets cost ¥90 to ¥380.

OTHER VENUES

Beijing hosts a growing number of international music and theater events every year, and its own increasingly respectable outfits—including the Beijing Symphony Orchestra—give frequent performances. Among the most popular venues for this sort of thing is the **National Centre for Performing Arts** (also known as "The Egg"), the modern egg-shaped glass structure next the Great Hall of the People (Xi Chang'an Jie 2; *©* **010/6655-0000**), the **Forbidden City Concert Hall** inside Zhongshan Park (*©* **010/6559-8285**), and the **Beijing Concert Hall** (**Beijing Yinyue Ting;** *©* **010/6605-5812**), at Bei Xinhua Jie in Liubukou (Xuanwu). The **Poly Theater** (**Baoli Dasha Guoji Juyuan;** *©* **010/6506-5343**), in the Poly Plaza complex on the East Third Ring Road (northeast exit of Dong Si Shi Tiao metro station), also hosts many large-scale performances, including the occasional revolutionary ballet. For information on additional venues and the shows they're hosting, check one of the expatriate magazines or ticket sellers Piao (Dongzhong Jie 32, 7/F; *©* **010/6417-0018;** www.piao.com) or Ticketmaster (North Gate of Worker's Stadium; *©* **400/707-9999;** www.ticketmaster.cn).

2 TEAHOUSE THEATER

Traditional teahouse entertainment disappeared from Beijing after 1949, but some semblance survives in a number of modern teahouses that have grown up with the tourism industry. Snippets of Beijing opera, cross-talk (stand-up) comedy, acrobatics, traditional music, singing, and dancing flow across the stage as you sip tea and nibble on snacks. If you don't have time to see these kinds of performances individually, the teahouse is an adequate solution. If you're looking for a quiet place to enjoy a cup of jasmine and maybe do some reading, look to one of the real teahouses listed later in this chapter.

De Yun She   The Tianqiao puts on essentially the same show as Lao She's Teahouse, but in a gallery seating framed in dark lacquered wood and a less eye-straining color scheme. The quality of the performances has declined markedly, however: Many performers are well past their prime. Bei Wei Lu (just west of intersection with Qian Men Dajie, west side of Temple of Heaven). ℂ **010/6304-0617.** Tickets ¥20–¥60.

Lao She's Teahouse (Lao She Chaguan)   This somewhat garishly decorated teahouse is named for one of the most famous plays by celebrated Chinese writer Lao She (see Lao She Jinianguan [Former Residence of Lao She], p. 142). Performances change nightly but always include opera and acrobatics. It pays to buy the more expensive tickets, as views from the rear seats are frequently obscured. Nightly shows at 7:50pm. Qianmen Xi Dajie 3 (west of Qian Men on south side of the street). ℂ **010/6303-6830.** www.laosheteahouse.com. Tickets ¥180–¥380.

3 CINEMAS

State limitations on freedom of expression, the profusion of black market DVDs, and ready access to illegal download sites have taken their toll on China's film industry, but the "movie theater experience" has taken off in recent years and Beijing now has enough film fanatics to support a healthy number of theaters. **Cherry Lane Movies** (ℂ **010/6530-5508** or 0/1390-113-4745; www.cherrylanemovies.com.cn; ¥20–¥40), run by a long-tenured and long-winded American expatriate, shows older and some new Chinese films with English subtitles on the weekends; films are listed at www.cherrylanemovies.com.cn and are screened at Yugong Yishan Zhangzizhong Lu 3 (ℂ **010/6404-2711;** metro: Zhangzizhong Lu). **Box Cafe (Hezi Kafeiguan;** Xi Wang Zhuang Xiaoqu 5; ℂ **010/6279-1280),** a smallish cafe near the east gate of Tsinghua University (Qinghua Daxue), offers free screenings on Sunday (screenings usually start at 3pm; ¥20) of Chinese independent and experimental films and a few foreign films of the same nature. Be sure to call ahead as screening days may change from month to month. Several full-scale theaters show undubbed Hollywood blockbusters (the ones that make it through the censors, anyway). Tickets are generally ¥30 to ¥120. The new **MegaBox** (basement of The Village at Sanlitun, Sanlitun Bei Lu 19; ℂ **010/6417-6118;** www.imegabox.com; metro: Tuanjie Hu) offers roughly 50% discounts off ticket prices when you sign up for a free membership card *(huiyuan ka).* Other options include **Star City (Xinshi Ji Ying Cheng;** inside Oriental Plaza on the east side of the mall; ℂ **010/8518-6778;** metro: Wangfujing), **UME International Cineplex (Huaxing Guoji Yingcheng;** Shuangyushu Xueyuan Nan Lu 44; ℂ **010/8211-5566)** just north of the Third Ring Road and southeast of Renmin University, and **Wanda International Cinema (Wanda Guoji Dianying Cheng;** 3/F, Building B, Wanda Plaza Jianguo Lu 93; ℂ **010/5960-3399;** metro: Da Wang Lu). Have your hotel concierge double-check that the movie you want to see has English subtitles.

When international film festival directors go looking for new, edgy films, they visit **Hart Center of Arts** (**Hate Shalong;** © 010/6435-3570; www.hart.com.cn) in the Factory 798 complex (see chapter 7, p. 141), which hosts festivals with themes no one else is game to touch, and regularly screens movies at 8pm on Saturday (call to check). Most of the work shown here has not passed the censors.

4 LIVE MUSIC

Most of the bars on Sanlitun North Bar Street offer nightly live "music" performances by cover bands, usually of scant talent and almost invariably Filipino in origin. But several small venues, most of them in Chaoyang, host an increasingly varied lineup of musical acts. Performers range from traditional folk instrumentalists to jazz ensembles and rock outfits, and are usually interesting, if not always good. (See chapter 2 for more on the city's better bands.) Most venues are bars open nightly from around 5pm to 1 or 2am, although few offer live acts every night. There is usually a small cover charge of about ¥5 to ¥50 on performance nights, depending on the number of acts and their prestige. *Time Out* and *The Beijinger* maintain somewhat accurate listings of what is playing where and when.

CD Jazz Cafe (Sendi Jueshi)   After much upheaval, this amalgamation of CD Cafe and the short-lived Treelounge is the best place to see local jazz and blues acts in Beijing. If it's a special act, get there early. Dong San Huan, south of the Agricultural Exhibition Center (Nongzhanguan) main gate (down small path behind trees that line sidewalk). © **010/6506-8288.** No cover. Metro: Nongzhanguan.

D-22 ★   It's a long way from the center of town, but this tight two-floor venue is the best place for experimental music acts. On certain weekdays, the club hosts art house movie nights. Chengfu Lu 13. © **010/6265-3177.** www.d-22.cn. Cover ¥30–¥40. Metro: Wudaokou.

MAO Livehouse   This live music venue is backed by Japanese label Bad News, home of local punk band Brain Failure. Plenty of aspiring punk rocksters have already become loyal fans, to both the band and the bar. The exterior looks like a rusty, unfinished steel warehouse. Inside, the decor is an eclectic mix of chairs and tables sandwiched between black walls. Performances generally start at 8:30pm. Guloudajie 111. © **010/6402-5080.** Cover ¥40–¥60. Metro: Bei Xin Qiao.

Salud   This cozy bar often hosts local live music acts, usually upbeat South American music or jazz. They've got fabulous loft seating, and an understated decor of blond wood with a couple of artsy paintings on the wall. Glass jars filled with the bar's homemade rum line one wall. Service is horrible when things get busy, but the French owners proudly shrug it all off: "We're not 'ere to make money!" A refreshing sentiment. Nan Luogu Xiang 66. © **010/6402-5086.** Metro: Bei Xin Qiao.

The Star Live   The cool music acts (Ziggy Marley, The Roots, Sonic Youth) are finally coming to Beijing, and they seem to like playing at Star Live. This place is nothing like its thumping, downstairs neighbor Tango; it is small and intimate and has excellent acoustics. Ticket prices depend on the artist, but expect to pay between ¥50 and ¥300. 3/F, Tango, Heping Xijie 70 (50m/164 ft. north of metro station). © **010/6425-5677.** www.thestar live.com. Metro: Yonghegong.

188 Yugong Yishan This wonderful performance space is the best live music venue in Beijing, period. The owners have a knack for turning up the best local acts. Run by the owners of the now-defunct Loup Chante, the diverse lineup—from punk to Mongolian mouth music, and everything in between—means you can visit night after night. Having enjoyed a successful 2-year run in the parking lot across from the Worker's Stadium, the bar moved to their new space near Lotus Lane in Hou Hai in 2007. Daily 2pm to 2am. Zhangzizhong Lu 3, east of Lotus Lane. ℂ 010/6404-2711. www.yugongyishan.com. Cover varies for performances. Metro: Zhangzizhong Lu.

---

5 CLUBS & DISCOS

The average Chinese will lump all dancing establishments into a single category—*tiaowudian* (dancing place), or, if they try it in English, "dee-si-ko." But while the distinction between a Beijing disco and a Beijing dance club is lost on most locals, it is readily apparent to any foreigner. Discos are typically old and cavernous, with exaggerated decor, horrible music, and a wholly Chinese clientele whose attempts to imitate Western modes of style and dance will send shivers down your spine. Clubs, by contrast, are newer, smaller, and more stylish, with a DJ-dominated atmosphere closer in feel to what you'd find in the United States or Europe. The club clientele is wealthier, more diverse (with both Chinese and foreigners), and not quite as clueless.

Both discos and dance clubs charge high covers, at anywhere from ¥50 to ¥150. Both tend to get crowded on weekends around 10pm and empty around 3am, although a few clubs will host special parties that last until dawn. There is some activity on Thursday nights, but the rest of the week is slow. Discos predate the days of the drinking district and hence are scattered randomly around the city. Clubs tend to be situated next to bars, in foreigner-heavy areas like Sanlitun and Chaoyang Park.

Alfa ★ This Southeast Asian bar recently transformed their patio into a covered, harem dream world. It's as spacious as ever, with two glowing floor pools and cozy bed nooks covered in drapes and pillows. Inside, private booths on the second floor are where crowds gather to people-watch while shooting back green tea and whiskey. The small, claustrophobic dance floor is fun on Fridays, when the DJ spins '80s music. Xingfu Yicun 5 (in the alley opposite the Workers' Stadium west gate). ℂ 010/6413-0086. No cover.

Babyface Definitely not a place to come for a quiet chat, Babyface serves it up for the wealthy young elite of the capital. Dance floors are small and much of the clientele has an air of studied boredom, but it's near impossible to fault the music (often supplied by Ministry of Sound DJs) and the stylish metal-and-glass decor. Try not to scratch the paint on anyone's Mercedes when you stumble back outside, disoriented by the thumping bass and the potent shooters. Gongti Xi Lu 6 (just south of the Workers' Stadium west gate). ℂ 010/6551-9081. When there's a cover charge (depends on the night and the DJ), it's usually ¥50; ladies usually get free entry.

Banana Banana is one of Beijing's oldest and most popular discos. This new, larger location is a classic bit of 1990s Miami Beach postmodernism with fake palm trees and white Doric columns. The crowd is mostly black-clad men and skinny women who wear sunglasses at night. The sound system produces enough bass to loosen tooth fillings. Jianguo Men Wai Dajie 22 (in front of Scitech Hotel). ℂ 010/6528-3636. Cover ¥40, includes 1 drink.

> **(Moments)** **Karaoke: Down That Drink, It's Time to Sing**
>
> No one knows why Asian cultures have embraced karaoke (pronounced "*kala okay*" in Mandarin) with such red-faced gusto, or why so many foreigners become just as enthusiastic once they're on Eastern soil. Maybe the food lacks some amino acid crucial to the brain's shame function. Or maybe it's just fun to get soused and pretend you have talent, thousands of miles away from home. Spend enough time in Beijing and sooner or later you'll find yourself standing before a TV screen, beer and microphone in hand, with a crowd of drunkards insisting you sing to the Muzak version of a Beatles hit. Refuse and your Chinese host loses face; comply and you receive applause. Resistance is futile. Most karaoke venues in Beijing are seedy and given over to less-than-legal side entertainment, so if you have any choice in the matter, head to **Party World**, also known as the Cash Box (Qian Gui; ✆ **010/6588-3333;** 24 hr.), the city's classiest and best-equipped do-it-yourself concert venue. It's located southeast of the Full Link Plaza, at the corner of Chaowai Shichang Jie and Chaowai Nan Jie, and there's another location at Teng Da Da Sha, Xi Zhi Men Wai Dajie (✆ **010/8857-6566** is the reservation service line for both branches). Cash Box has a hotel-like lobby, pleasantly decorated private rooms, and a wide selection of Western songs, with some even released in the past decade. Prices range from ¥60 to ¥360 per hour, depending on the size of the room and night of the week. There's usually a line, so you'll have to give them your name early. You wouldn't want to embarrass yourself anywhere else.

Bling ★   Despite the fact that it is housed in a mall that looks like it was airlifted out of San Diego, Bling draws a steady crowd with its hip-hop, rap, and R & B. The dance floor is long and narrow and booty shakers cluster around the front end of a Rolls-Royce Phantom DJ booth. The car is roped off and serious-faced security guards stand by to ensure no one touches the shiny chrome surface. Scantily clad bar dancers are around on weekends. The mixed drinks are just okay—given the prices, you're better off ordering beer. Inside Solana Mall, #5-1 Solana (northwest corner of the mall), Chaoyang Gongyuan Lu 6. ✆ **010/5905-6999.** Cover ¥50 depending on the night and the DJ.

Destination (Mudidi)   Jokingly renamed "Desperation" by locals, Beijing's most successful (almost openly) gay club is indeed a fine spot to meet locals of the same sex, without the rent boy seediness that now afflicts On/Off. Bare grey concrete walls, dark lounges, and odd subtitled video footage that never quite seems to match the tunes doesn't sound like a successful formula, but somehow it works. Beautiful hunky men crowd the sweaty nightclub featuring a bouncing dance floor. The music isn't so loud that you can't duck into a corner for a chat, and is slightly camp without being cliché. Insanely crowded on weekends. Gongti Xi Lu 7 (south of the west gate of the Workers' Stadium, opposite Bellagio). ✆ **010/6551-5138.** Cover ¥30, includes 1 drink.

Mix (Mi Ke Si)   If you want thumping hip hop beats, young gyrating bodies, and a sweaty dance floor, then Mix is the place for you. They've also got some of the tallest, beefiest bouncers in town—no small feat considering we're in China! The relaxation zone, featuring trance music, is a great place to unwind from the main dance floor. Otherwise, music is hip-hop and R & B. Gongti Bei Men Xi Ce (inside Workers' Stadium north gate, on the west side). ☎ 010/6530-2889. Cover ¥30, free entrance for ladies on Mon, Tues, Thurs, and Sun.

Propaganda   The place to see (and hope that you're not seen), Propaganda is the bass-pumping club of the student district. Its dance floor has witnessed many a hot and heavy make-out session. Huaqing Jiayuan Don Men Wang Bei (100m/328 ft. north of the east gate of Huaqing Jiayuan). ☎ 010/8286-3679. Metro: Wudaokou. Cover ¥20.

Vic's (Wei Ke Si)   Vic's is located directly opposite Mix (see above) and patrons who come here are often flipping a coin, deciding between Vic's 'n' Mix. They recently renovated, adding flashier lights and a multicolored psychedelic decor. Girls in heels: Watch out for the unexpected steps on the long, floor-lit catwalk entrance. Music formula follows that of Mix (see above). Gongti Bei Men Dong Ce (inside Worker's stadium north gate, on the east side). ☎ 010/5293-0333. No cover Sun–Thurs, ¥50 after 10pm Fri–Sat.

White Rabbit   It's a wonder you don't have to give a cryptic password to get into this white light–lit, two-story underground dance club, accessed by a small door at street level. Come here for thumping dance tunes of the electronica or house varieties. If you've got glow sticks, this is the place to crack 'em open. Haoyun Jie C2 (Lucky St.), Zaoying Lu 29, Maizidian. ☎ 133/2112-3678.

6 BARS

Although most average Chinese still prefer to get drunk at dinner, the Western pub tradition has gained ground among younger locals, and the city has a large, ever-growing population of establishments devoted exclusively to alcohol.

Drinking in Beijing occurs in one of several districts, each with its own atmosphere and social connotations. The city's oldest and still most popular drinking district is **Sanlitun,** located between the East Second and Third ring roads around the Workers' Stadium (Gongren Tiyuchang). The area's name comes from Sanlitun Lu, a north-south strip of drinking establishments a long block east of the Workers' Stadium that at one time contained practically all of the city's bars. Now known as Sanlitun Bar Street (Sanlitun Jiuba Jie), it has been overshadowed by other clusters of bars in the Xingfu Cun area north of the stadium and scattered around the stadium itself. Bars here are rowdy and raunchy, and packed to overflowing on weekends. Similar watering holes surround the south and west gates of **Chaoyang Gongyuan** (park) to the east, an area the government has tried to promote as the new drinking district because it has fewer residential buildings. The development of **Lucky Street,** north of the Kempinski Hotel, followed a similar logic. Bars and clubs in **Haidian,** the city's university district to the northwest, are clustered around the gates of several universities and cater to a crowd of local English majors and foreign students.

The fastest-growing spot for late-night drinking is the **Back Lakes** (**Shicha Hai** or **Hou Hai**), a previously serene spot with a few discreetly fashionable bars north of Bei Hai Park. It has exploded into a riot of neon, capped by Lotus Lane. **Nan Luogu Xiang,** to the east of the Back Lakes area, was previously home to only one cafe; now the bars are wall-to-wall. Perhaps the most notable trend is the resurgence of hotel bars. These are

the most appealing and stylish spots in Beijing, most notably **Xiu** and **China Bar** (Park
Hyatt), and **Mesh** (The Opposite House).

Beijing bars generally open around 5 or 6pm and stay open until the last patrons leave or the staff decides it wants to go home, usually by 2am on Friday and Saturday nights. Several of the Back Lakes bars double as cafes and open as early as 11am.

Bed Bar (Chuang Ba) ★★   The risqué decor of this courtyard bar is the work of a New York designer. All bare concrete, gauze, four-poster beds, and antique furnishings, Bed pushes the boundaries of what constitutes an acceptable leisure space for wholesome Socialist citizens. The olive tapenade is ideal finger food; the sangria and mojito are suitably refreshing. Bed is a block north of its sister establishment, Cafe Sambal, and attracts a similar crowd of design professionals. The rear courtyard is sublime on a warm summer evening. Mixed drinks are well done and reasonably priced. Zhangwang Hutong 17 (from Gulou Dajie metro station, head south along Jiu Gulou Dajie and take the 4th lane on your left). ℂ 010/8400-1554.

China Bar ★   This bar has fantastic panorama views of Beijing's lively city sprawl. It is perched on the 65th floor of the new Park Hyatt and you have to take two elevators to get here. If you want to snag one of the booths and catch a gorgeous sunset over the mountains (provided you are visiting on one of Beijing's rare blue-sky days), come early—outrageous minimum table charges start after 8pm. The menu has a solid selection of scotch, whisky, and other hard liquors, and the mixed drinks are worth the steep price tags (expect to pay ¥80 per cocktail). About 59 floors down is **Xiu,** the Park Hyatt's other bar. Xiu has a sleek indoor space as well as a huge outdoor rooftop courtyard that is an excellent choice on warm summer days. 65th floor of the Park Hyatt, Jianguomenwai Dajie 2. ℂ 010/8567-1234. Metro: Guomao.

Club Suzie Wong (Suxi Huang Julebu)   Named for the fictional Hong Kong hooker who falls for a much older William Holden (ironic given the current dynamic of the bar), this is the see-and-be-seen venue for nouveau riche Chinese and newly arrived expatriates. DJs so cool it hurts play music for head-bobbers in the main room, and there's a Ming-style canopy bed next to the bar where the exhibitionists sit. Get there early to stake out one of the row of semiprivate alcoves to the side, luridly lit and luxuriously outfitted with plush couches covered in brocaded pillows. The rooftop seating makes for a cool getaway during summer months. West gate of Chaoyang Park. ℂ 010/6500-3377. www.suziewong.com.cn.

Face Bar (Fei Si) ★   Penny-pinching Beijing expats complain about the exorbitant prices for drinks here, but it's still an upscale bar that's far cheaper than Hong Kong or New York. Plus, you get a classy, Southeast Asian–inspired decor that incorporates Buddhist statues. The first bar has an annoying pool table smack in the center of everything, but just bypass that room and head for the outdoor terrace or one of the cozy opium beds. Dongcaoyuan 25, Gongti Nanlu (just south of Workers' Stadium south gate). ℂ 010/6551-6738.

Fez ★   A superb rooftop terrace keeps the crowds coming, despite Fez's awkward location far, far away from the rest of Beijing's nightlife. Mixed drinks are well made, but come with hefty price tags. The views of the Forbidden City and surrounding Qianmen area are fantastic. Inside the Ch'ien Men 23 complex, Qianmen Dong Dajie 23. ℂ 010/8567-1234.

La Baie des Anges ★★   This intimate wine bar is one our favorite places in Hou Hai. The wine list is long and affordable options abound. The tiny space is a mix of regular tables, cozy booths, and a few tall tables with bar stools. It is an excellent place for a first date. DJs and live jazz music occasionally play on weekends, but it is always a relaxed and chill environment. Nanguanfang Hutong 5. ℂ 010/6657-1605.

Lush Students on a budget love the affordable drinks at this bar, located in Wu Dao Kou, the heart of the student district. By day, the young ones come and pretend to study while they check out who else is there. By night, they come for drinks, dancing, and debauchery. Sunday open-mic nights are a big hit. Open 24 hours. 2/F, Building 1, Huaqing Jia Yuan. ℂ 010/8286-3566. Metro: Wudaokou.

Pass-By Bar (Guoke Jiuba) Relocated in a restored courtyard house down a *hutong* east of Qian Hai in 2002, Tibetan-themed Pass-By is more gathering place than nightspot, with an extensive English-language library, a useful message board, and rotating photo exhibits on the walls. There's great Italian food, free Wi-Fi, and a separate non-smoking section—almost unheard-of in a Beijing bar. The courtyard is idyllic in the summertime. Nan Luogu Xiang 108 (Back Lakes; alley is to left/west of a Muslim restaurant on the north side of Ping'an Dadao; walk north 150m/492 ft.). ℂ 010/8403-8004.

Mesh ★★ This chic new lounge is the place to see and be seen in Beijing. A big bonus is location—inside the Opposite House hotel in the heart of Sanlitun Bar Street. Mesh is dimly lit, is sparsely decorated, and has large overstuffed, backless couches—the kind of seating that forces you to sit up and suck it in or lean forward to chat it up with one of the hottie patrons. Cocktails here are excellent, and Thursday nights 2-for-1 drinks are a bargain. **Punk** is the hotel's other bar. The drinks and environs are similar to those of Mesh, with the addition of a small dance floor and live DJ. Inside the Opposite House hotel, Sanlitun Bei Lu. ℂ 010/6417-6688. Metro: Tuan Jie Hu.

Q Bar ★★ Don't be put off by the drab interior of the hotel that houses Q Bar. The bar, located on the top floor, is an oasis of style, with dim lighting, lounge music, and a long bar nestled against a window with panoramic views. Here you will find the best martinis in town. Unfortunately, the love and devotion owners George and Echo pour into those drinks often translate into slow service. The expansive rooftop seating is fantastic and DJs spin lounge and house music on weekends. Nan Sanlitun Lu (on top floor of Eastern Inn Hotel). ℂ 010/6595-9239. Metro: Nong Zhan Guan.

The Saddle Cantina ★ A huge outdoor balcony, a pool table, Top-40 hits, and giant servings of slushy margaritas—no wonder Beijing's expatriates love this place. The Mexican-themed bar has a sunny interior, with sombreros on the walls and solid-wood furniture throughout. Nan Sanlitun Lu (on top floor of Eastern Inn Hotel). ℂ 010/6595-9239. Metro: Nong Zhan Guan.

Stone Boat Bar ★★ This is our favorite place for a Sunday-afternoon coffee and a game of Scrabble . . . but also our favorite evening spot for live music, ranging from local drumming groups to experimental ambient music. This little gem by the lake in Ri Tan Park also features a tiny upstairs alcove great for romantic dates. Open 10am to 11pm. Southwest corner of Ri Tan Park (south end of the lake). ℂ 010/6501-9986.

The Tree (Yinbi de Shu) Uprooted from South Bar street, the former Hidden Tree sports a new tree but is slightly more tranquil than its former incarnation. It still offers an unmatched selection of Belgian beer: Trappist and abbey ales, lighter wild-fermented lambics, and several wheat (white) beers. The stock changes, but there's always bottled Chimay and draft Hoegaarden. Passable single malts, cigars, thin-crust pizzas, and a pleasant but unpretentious brick-and-wood interior complete the picture. Open 10am to 2am. West of Sanlitun Bei Lu (behind Poachers Inn). ℂ 010/6415-1954. Metro: Gongti Bei Lu.

Yin Bar (Yin Ba) ★   This rooftop bar has the best views of the Forbidden City's serried rooftops, as well as the temple at nearby Jingshan Park. The best time to come is at sunset, when you can cast your eye west and take in the low cityscape (ignore skyscrapers in the distance) at its best. The service is appallingly slow, so if you want your drink quickly, stick to bottled beers. The food menu is passable. Qihelou Dajie 6/F. ℂ **010/6526-5566.**

7 CAFES & OTHER DRINK SPOTS

Just like the Manchurian hordes did 3½ centuries earlier, **Starbucks** swept into Beijing in the 1990s and quickly conquered it. Branches are everywhere, including the China World complex, the Oriental Plaza, and the Pacific Century Plaza near Sanlitun. They were, however, recently driven out of the inner court of the Forbidden City. By far the city's most popular coffee chain, it is particularly beloved of young local women in search of eligible expatriates. But there are other options (see below), many of which offer a better brew.

Despite the coffee invasion, Beijing is still ultimately tea territory, and the most pleasant sipping experiences can be found in small teahouses scattered about the city.

The Bookworm (Lao Shu Chong)   Come here for a quiet read—better yet, there's no need to bring your own book. This Sanlitun fixture has a library of 6,000 English-language titles, including most of the works recommended in chapter 2. The spacious venue is divided into three large rooms. Floor-to-ceiling bookshelves housing the impressive library are found in each room. The backroom is where you'll find the bookstore and a small kids' corner. Open 9am to 2am. Nan Sanlitun Lu Si Lou (behind Pacific Century shopping center, near The Loft). ℂ **010/6586-9507.** Metro: Gongti Bei Lu.

Café Zarah ★★   This is our favorite cafe in Beijing. It plays good music at the right volume, the exposed wooden beams and comfy chairs make for welcoming environs, the Wi-Fi is strong and reliable, and the iced lattes are the best in town. It's a popular place for breakfast on the weekends. Open 10am to midnight. 42 Gulou Dong Dajie. ℂ **010/8403-9807.** www.cafezarah.com. Metro: Beixinqiao.

Comptoirs de France (Fa Pai)   The best place to stock up on chocolate and calories. Apart from perfect chocolate truffles, this cafe also makes the best opera slices and strawberry tarts in town. And they serve excellent coffee to boot! The location at China Central Place is more charming than the Dongzhi Men cafe, but go to whichever one is closest to you—you won't be disappointed. Open 7am to 9pm. China Central Place 102, Jianguo Lu 89 (on the left side of the main walkway heading into the apartment complex). ℂ **010/6530-5480.** Other convenient location at East Lake Club, Dongzhi Men Wai Dajie 35. ℂ **010/6461-1525.** Metro: Dongzhi Men.

Gustamenta   This is the best place in town to get gelato. They're on the northern end of Sanlitun Bar Street, perfectly placed to satisfy those midnight sweet tooth cravings. They also serve a mean espresso. Open daily 8am to midnight. Sanlitun Lu 24. ℂ **010/6417-8890.** Other location at 1301 SOHO New Town. Daily 7am–midnight. ℂ **010/8580-5111.** Metro: Nongzhanguan.

Mima Café (Zuo You Jian)   The coffee and cuisine are just passable, but if you need a touch of serenity, visit Mima on a weekday afternoon or a summer evening. Located just north of the east gate of Yuan Ming Yuan (p. 138), outdoor courtyard seating is covered over by rice paper domes, set around clusters of bamboo. The washroom is the most stunning we have ever encountered, and worth the trek in itself. Open daily from 10am to midnight. Yuan Ming Yuan Dong Men Nei Bei Liu Jian Yuan. ✆ **010/8268-8003.**

Sculpting in Time (Diaoke Shiguang)   This was once Beijing's most famous film cafe, but it's since lost that title to Box Cafe (see section 3 of this chapter) when it moved from its location in a charming (now demolished) *hutong* east of Peking University. Now at the Beijing Institute of Technology, it seldom shows films but is still popular with students, foreign and Chinese both. A second branch, south of the main entrance to Fragrant Hills Park (✆ **010/8259-0040**), has a pleasant remoteness and a large outdoor deck with views of the park, while the largest branch, just west of Wudaokou metro stop (✆ **010/8286-7025**), has less charm but is handy to the university district. This coffee shop is on the rise, and they have a total of seven branches throughout the city. All serve adequate coffee and Western snacks, and have Wi-Fi. Open daily from 9am to midnight. Weigongcun Xi Kou 7 (Ligong Da Nan Men), just to left of the university's south gate. ✆ **010/6894-6825.**

The Teahouse of Family Fu (Cha Jia Fu)   Located in a unique octagonal building on the south bank of Hou Hai, the Fu family's teahouse is among the city's most charming, furnished throughout with a pleasantly haphazard assortment of Ming reproduction furniture. Owned by a former mechanics professor and run with help from his friendly English-speaking mother, it sometimes plays host to poetry readings, lectures, and classical Chinese music performances. Teas are reasonably priced at ¥50 to ¥152 for a pot with unlimited refills, presented on a fan. There are also free snacks. Semiprivate rooms branch off to all sides. Open from 10:30am to midnight. Hou Hai Xibei An (northwest side of Hou Hai, next to Kong Yiji). ✆ **010/6657-1588.**

The Great Wall & Other Side Trips

by Sherisse Pham

The ancient hills around Beijing are dotted with fascinating sights, the foremost, of course, being the **Great Wall.** Many of the sights listed in this chapter can be seen in a single excursion, which can include other sights just on the outskirts of the city. Nearly all organized tours include a stop at the **Ming Tombs** on the way to the Great Wall at **Ba Da Ling** and **Juyong Guan. Tanzhe Si** and **Jietai Si** are readily combined as an agreeable day trip, and the intriguing **Tian Yi Mu** is on the road to the quiet courtyard houses of **Cuan Di Xia.**

Surprisingly, the most enjoyable way to reach many of these sights is by public transportation. Although slower than an organized tour, public bus or train travel is flexible, doesn't drag you to dubious attractions, and costs a fraction of the overpriced tours offered by hotels. If you're short on time, an option is to hire a taxi for the day (see "Getting Around," in chapter 3). An entertaining (if slightly rushed) choice is to join a Chinese bus tour. Air-conditioned buses for these tours leave when full, early in the morning from various metro stations, and make stops at two or three sites. Your last resort should be hiring a car through your hotel or a tour agency for a ludicrous fee.

When heading out of town, avoid weekend mornings, when traffic can be gridlocked. Attempting to return on Sunday afternoon is also frustrating. Even on weekdays, allow at least half a day, and usually a full day, to explore the sights listed in this chapter. Have a picnic and take your time.

1 THE GREAT WALL (WANLI CHANGCHENG; 长城) ★★★

Even after you dispense with the myths that it is a single continuous structure and that it can be seen from space (it can't, any more than a fishing line can be seen from the other side of a river), China's best-known attraction is still mind-boggling. The world's largest historical site is referred to in Mandarin as **Wanli Changcheng** ("10,000-Li Long Wall" or simply "Very Long Wall"). The Great Wall begins at Shanhaiguan on the Bo Hai Sea and snakes west to a fort at Jiayu Guan in the Gobi Desert. Its origins date back to the Warring States Period (453–221 B.C.), when rival kingdoms began building defensive walls to thwart each other's armies. The king of Qin, who eventually conquered the other states to become the first emperor of a unified China, engaged in large-scale wall building toward the end of his reign, although tales of 300,000 conscripted laborers are embellishments of subsequent dynasties. During the Han dynasty (206 B.C.–A.D. 220), the Wall was extended west, and additions were made in completely different locations, according to the military needs of the day.

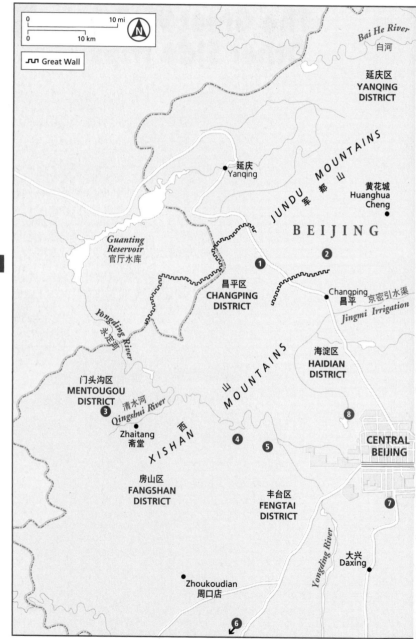

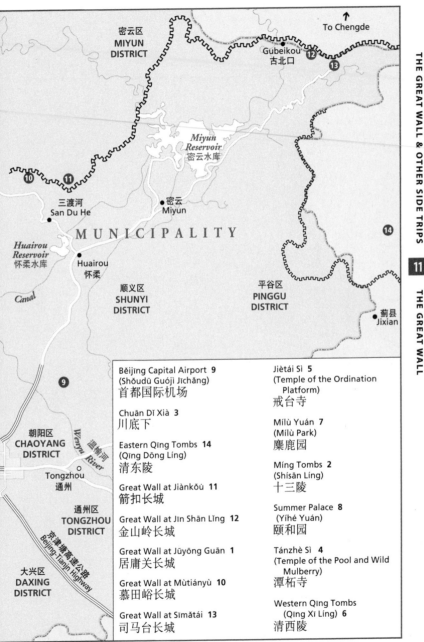

密云区
MIYUN DISTRICT

To Chengde

Gubeikou
古北口 **12**

13

Miyun Reservoir
密云水库

10

11

三渡河
San Du He

密云
Miyun

MUNICIPALITY

14

Huairou Reservoir
怀柔水库

Huairou
怀柔

Canal

顺义区
SHUNYI DISTRICT

平谷区
PINGGU DISTRICT

蓟县
Jixian

9

朝阳区
CHAOYANG DISTRICT

Wenyu River
温榆河

Tongzhou
通州

通州区
TONGZHOU DISTRICT

京津塘高速公路
Beijing-Tianjin Highway

大兴区
DAXING DISTRICT

Běijīng Capital Airport **9**
(Shǒudū Guójì Jīchǎng)
首都国际机场

Chuān Dǐ Xià **3**
川底下

Eastern Qīng Tombs **14**
(Qīng Dōng Líng)
清东陵

Great Wall at Jiànkǒu **11**
箭扣长城

Great Wall at Jīn Shān Lǐng **12**
金山岭长城

Great Wall at Jūyōng Guān **1**
居庸关长城

Great Wall at Mùtiányù **10**
慕田峪长城

Great Wall at Sīmǎtái **13**
司马台长城

Jiètái Sì **5**
(Temple of the Ordination Platform)
戒台寺

Mílù Yuán **7**
(Mílù Park)
麋鹿园

Míng Tombs **2**
(Shísān Líng)
十三陵

Summer Palace **8**
(Yíhé Yuán)
颐和园

Tánzhè Sì **4**
(Temple of the Pool and Wild Mulberry)
潭柘寺

Western Qīng Tombs **6**
(Qīng Xī Líng)
清西陵

Impressions

I think that you would have to conclude that this is a great wall, and it had to be built by a great people.
— President Richard Nixon during his trip to China; much to the president's dismay, most American newspapers left out the second part of his quote!

Although many tour guides will try to persuade you otherwise, the Ming Wall you see today is unrelated to the Qin Wall, which lies far to the north. The Ming even went to the trouble of calling their wall Bian Qiang (Frontier Wall) to avoid comparisons with the tyrannical first emperor of China, Qin Shi Huangdi. The original Wall was built almost entirely from tamped earth, and often crumbled away within decades of being constructed. Talk of satellite-mapping the current Wall is fanciful—for most of its length, the structure is barely visible from the ground. This, and the fact that there is no single "Great Wall," makes it impossible to pin down the Wall's precise length.

Those with an interest in exaggerating Chinese xenophobia portray Wall building as an essential part of the national psyche, but after the Han, few dynasties bothered with Wall construction, and relied mostly on trade, diplomacy, and the odd punitive expedition to keep the peace. Even during the inward-looking Ming dynasty, the Wall was viewed by many at court as an ancient version of the Star Wars missile-defense idea—ineffective, absurdly expensive, and successful only in antagonizing China's neighbors. With the Ming wracked by internal rebellion, the Qing armies simply bribed the demoralized sentries. The Qing left the Wall as a monument to folly, and while early Western visitors were awed, it became a source of national pride only recently. Dr. Sun Yat-sen was among the first to view it as a symbol of national strength, an idea the Communists adopted, including it in the National Anthem.

The Wall's most easily visited sections are **Ba Da Ling** and **Juyong Guan,** while **Mutianyu, Jin Shan Ling,** and the vertiginous **Simatai** require a full day's outing. Appealing options for overnight stays are **The Red Capital Ranch** at Mutianyu and the more basic **Simatai YHA.**

THE GREAT WALL AT JUYONG GUAN (居庸关)
59km (37 miles) NW of Beijing

Just before you get to the madness of Ba Da Ling, the most touristed and tacky section (we don't recommend it), lies this relatively peaceful stretch of the Wall. The most conveniently accessed section of the Wall is also the most historically significant. Guarding one of the two crucial passes to Beijing (the other is to the northeast, at Gu Bei Kou) and the vast North China Plain, **Juyong Guan (Dwelling in Harmony Pass)** was the site of pitched battles, involving Jurchen, Mongol, and, more recently, Japanese invaders. There may have been fortifications here as early as the 6th century, before Beijing existed. Climbing the steep section to the left offers marvelous views of Ba Da Ling, snaking up the mountains to the north, and south toward Beijing (in the event of a clear day). Restorations from 1993 to 1997 created over 4km (2½ miles) of wall, but railings mar the effect; there's little feeling of antiquity. All the construction must have eaten into the advertising budget, as crowds are thinner here than at Ba Da Ling.

It's worth stopping at Juyong Guan to view the ancient and remarkable **Yun Tai (Cloud Platform)** ★★★, which once stood astride the old road running northwest into Mongol territories. Dating from 1342, it was the base for three Tibetan-style stupas, which were toppled by an earthquake and replaced during the Ming dynasty by a Chinese-style Buddhist temple, also destroyed (by fire) during the early Qing. The central tunnel is carved with elephants, Buddha figures demonstrating different *mudra* (hand positions), the four heavenly kings, and six different scripts. Facing north, the languages on the right-hand wall are Chinese, Xi Xia (the script of a vanished Tibetan race, decimated by Genghis Khan's armies during the 14th c.), Uighur, and Mongolian. The top script is Sanskrit, with Tibetan below.

Essentials

VISITOR INFORMATION The ticket office at Juyong Guan (© 010/6977-1665) is open daily from 7:30am to 5pm. Admission is ¥45, ¥25 for students.

GETTING THERE A round-trip **taxi** should cost less than ¥400, driver's fee for waiting included.

WHERE TO STAY Giving the Red Capital Ranch (see below) a run for its money is **The Commune** (© 010/8118-1888; www.commune.com.cn). This hotel's stunning architecture and location near the Great Wall make it a perfect place to retreat from the city. The 12 original villas designed by international architects are often rented for lavish parties while copies of the homes have been subdivided into more affordable hotel rooms. Some guests have complained about service, but overall, it's still a pleasant experience. A large kids' club offers free babysitting and an outdoor wading pool. Doubles run for ¥1,700 to ¥2,500 plus a 15% service charge and include breakfast. Exit at Shuiguan, Ba Da Ling Highway.

ⓘ Tips   On the Wild Wall

Travelers with time and the inclination to explore beyond the typical tourist haunts are strongly encouraged to join a trip to the crumbling **"unofficial" sections of the Wall** that snake through more remote areas north of Beijing. Great Wall researcher and conservationist William Lindesay, a Briton who has been walking along and writing about the Great Wall since the mid-1980s, organizes excursions for the company **Wild Wall.** Joining one of his tours is the best way to learn about the Wall's construction and destruction, by both human and natural forces, from a knowledgeable source.

Wild Wall is based out of two modernized farmhouses, the first and more fully outfitted just north of Beijing, and the second somewhat more primitive (but still comfortable) in Hebei. Wild Wall's most common weekend trips run 3 days (Fri–Sun) and cost $450 (prices are quoted in U.S. dollars), including guided hikes, 2 nights' accommodations in a farmhouse, six meals, drinks and snacks, research and conservation contribution, and book. Although pricey, these weekend trips are highly recommended and typically take place two or three times a month. Day hikes and strenuous "Extreme Treks" are also available. For details see **www.wildwall.com**.

> **(Tips) Travelers with Disabilities**
>
> Exploring the Great Wall is tough enough for people in good shape. For those with disabilities, the Wall is a nightmare. At Mutianyu a cable car provides access, but there are still steps to negotiate up to the cable car, and steep steps up to the Wall. There are no elevators or wheelchair assists at any of the sections.

THE GREAT WALL AT MUTIANYU (幕田峪) ★

90km (56 miles) NE of Beijing

The Great Wall at Ba Da Ling proved so popular that authorities restored a second section of the Wall to the east in 1986. **Mutianyu** is slightly less crowded than Ba Da Ling, but it does have its own traffic jams in summer. Located in a heavily forested area, it's especially photogenic in rainy, misty weather. You can hop over a fence to see more tempting, unrestored sections, but those planning to survey the entire length of restored wall will find themselves with little energy remaining. There is a cable car to help those who need it.

Essentials

VISITOR INFORMATION The ticket office (℗ **010/6162-6505**) is open from 7:30am to 5:30pm. Admission is ¥40; the cable car costs ¥50 round-trip.

GETTING THERE Most hotels can arrange **guided group tours** for around ¥250. The **tourist (*you*) bus no. 6** combines a trip to Mutianyu with visits to a temple and a lake; it leaves from the northeast side of the Xuanwu Men metro stop (Sat–Sun 6:30–8am, every 30 min.; ¥50). The bus stops at Mutianyu for about 3 hours. A **taxi** will cost around ¥500, driver's fee for waiting included.

WHERE TO STAY In a quiet river valley close to Mutianyu and similar to the Red Capital Residence (p. 66), is the **Red Capital Ranch ★★** (℗ **010/8401-8886; ¥1,415–¥1,500** including breakfast, plus 15% service charge; Apr–Nov). All 10 rooms are thoughtfully decorated with antique furnishings. The oddly shaped Yan'an room has considerable charm and a *very* firm bed. The Ranch sits next to a dramatic section of the wall that is good for a challenge; there's a steep drop toward the end to the last tower that should be attempted only by advanced hikers. (*Tip:* You may also choose to hike this section of the wall without staying at the Ranch—arrange your own driver [see Jiankou, below] and grab a post-hike tea in the Ranch's lodge.) Fishing, biking, and even a Tibetan essential oil massage are offered. A twice-daily shuttle bus connects with the Red Capital Residence.

THE GREAT WALL AT JIN SHAN LING (金山岭)

130km (81 miles) NE of Beijing, 90km (56 miles) SW of Chengde

Located in Hebei Province, this is the least visited and least spoiled of the Wall sections listed in this chapter. **Jin Shan Ling** is 10km (6¼ miles) east of Gu Bei Kou (Old Northern Pass), through which Qing royalty passed on the way to their summer retreat at Chengde (Jehol). The Wall here is in good condition, as it was a recent (after 1570) rebuild of an existing Ming wall, and construction was overseen by the outstanding general, Qi Jiguang. The defensible pass, whose heart lies to the west at Gu Bei Kou, was 27km (17 miles), stretching all the way to Simatai in the east. Bricks are smaller, reflecting advances in wall-building technique. The Wall features unusual circular towers and elaborate defensive walls leading up to towers. Management dreams of tourist hordes—a cable car has been built, along with gradually rusting amusements—but the remoteness of the site makes large-scale tourism unlikely. The walk to **Simatai** (see below) is reason enough to visit.

Essentials

VISITOR INFORMATION   The ticket office (© **010/8402-4628**) is open from 8am to 5pm. Admission is ¥50.

GETTING THERE   The easiest way to get to Jin Shan Ling is to hire a taxi for the day, which will cost ¥600, driver's fee for wait time included. A cheaper alternative is to take the 980 express bus from Dong Zhi Men to Miyun for ¥15 (buses run 6am–8pm), and then transfer to a local taxi for the remaining trip, which should cost ¥100 each way. Jin Shan Ling can also be reached by **train** from the Beijing Bei Zhan (North Railway Station), just north of the Xi Zhi Men metro stop. A special tourist train for Gu Bei Kou, the L671, departs daily from mid-April to October at 7:25am (2½-hr. trip). The rest of the year, the slower L815, departing at 8am, will take you there (4-hr. trip; ¥10). Returning trains depart at 3:05 and 4:15pm, respectively. Walking down from the station, you can either find lodgings in Gu Bei Kou Hexi Cun village, or take a minivan directly to the Wall (25-min. trip, ¥20). From Xi Zhi Men bus station, some **buses** to Chengde (daily 6am–5:30pm, about every 20 min.; 2½-hr. trip; ¥46 for an Iveco or similar) also pass the turnoff, where you face either a 6km (3¾-mile) hike or haggling for a minivan (¥10).

WHERE TO STAY   Standard rooms start at ¥140 in the dull but clean **Jin Shan Ling Binguan,** to the right just inside the entrance of the wall. Staying at one of the simple courtyard houses in **Gu Bei Kou Hexi Cun,** just below the railway station, is a cheaper and more appealing option; accommodations are usually ¥10 per person, and home-cooked meals are similarly priced.

THE GREAT WALL AT SIMATAI (司马台) ★★

124km (77 miles) NE of Beijing

Somewhat tamed after a series of deaths led to the closing of its most dangerous stretch, Simatai nevertheless remains one of the best options for those who want more of a challenge from the Great Wall. The most harrowing portion, steep and unrestored, is on the east (right) side of the Miyun Reservoir. Several gravel-strewn spots require all four limbs to navigate. The endpoint is the **Wangjing Ta,** the 12th watchtower. Beyond this is the appropriately named **Tian Qiao (Heavenly Bridge),** a thin, tilted ridge where the Wall narrows to only a few feet—the section that is now off-limits. Despite the danger, Simatai can get rather crowded on weekends, especially since a cable car was installed, and souvenir vendors can be a nuisance. Those who speak Chinese would do well to pretend otherwise, or risk listening to hard-luck stories ("I've walked all the way from Mongolia"). The round-trip hike to Tian Qiao takes 3 hours at a moderate pace. The section of Simatai west of the reservoir is initially better restored and connects to Jin Shan Ling (see above), in Hebei Province.

VISITOR INFORMATION   The ticket office (℡ 010/6903-1051), a 10-minute walk away in a village south of the reservoir, is open 8am to 5pm. Admission is ¥40. The cable car runs from 8am to 4:30pm, April to November; a round-trip ride to the no. 8 Tower costs ¥50, or ¥30 one-way. Those walking west to Jin Shan Ling will be charged ¥5 to cross a bridge.

GETTING THERE   The best no-hassle option is to visit with one of the **Youth Hostelling International tours** (℡ 010/6551-5362), from the Beijing City Central Youth Hostel at Beijing railway station. The van leaves once a day and costs ¥220 from May to October and ¥200 from November to April. The **tourist *(you)* bus no. 12** travels to Simatai from northeast of the Xuanwu Men metro stop (Apr to mid-Oct Sat–Sun 6:30–8:30am, every 30 min; ¥70); you get about 3 hours at the site. A round-trip **taxi** ride should cost ¥600, driver's fee for wait time included.

WHERE TO STAY   Responding to the popularity of the Jin Shan Ling to Simatai hike, **Simatai YHA** (℡ 010/8188-9323; dorm bed ¥70; standard room ¥320) opened in 2004. Courtyard-style rooms are basic, but the coffee is world-class, and the view of the Wall from the patio is wonderful.

THE GREAT WALL AT JIANKOU (箭口) ★★★
70km (43 miles) NE of Beijing

This is our favorite part of the Wall. Few tourist buses make the journey here, and there is no cable car shuttling out-of-shape tourists to the top. Even more amazing, there are no touts selling knickknacks. We've spent plenty of time near here, since we rent a house in the nearby countryside. This section is for serious hikers only. Start at Xin Zhai Zi Cun where the road dead-ends into a parking lot, following the trail up to the Wall. Turn left once you reach the wall, and prepare yourself for an intense 5-hour hike. The tallest watchtower in the distance is Jiankou, and just before you reach it, there is a turnoff point that is marked by a flat, paved section of the Wall that leads you back down to the road. From the road, it's a 20-minute walk back to the parking lot.

Essentials

VISITOR INFORMATION   Admission is ¥20. Villagers charge ¥5 for parking. Open 24 hours. Bring your own lunch. Bottled water is usually available at the parking lot— bring plenty of water for the hike.

GETTING THERE   Since it's a remote location, you'll have to arrange a private car. Have your hotel concierge arrange a driver, or have them call one of two drivers: Mr. Liu (℡ 0/13661162308) or Mr. Zhang (℡ 0/13501189730) (neither speaks English, so you may need your concierge to help ring them up). The return trip takes 4 hours (plus figure in 5 hr. of wait time for your hike) and will cost ¥500, more if arranged by your hotel.

WHERE TO STAY   Many small peasant homes at the base of the mountain (near the parking lot) offer accommodations, but we don't recommend any in particular as the area is rather rustic. If you'd like to overnight, your best bet is to head to **Mountain Bar Lodge** (Hong Zun Yu Yi Tiao Gou; ℡ 010/6162-7396; www.ourshanba.com), 30 minutes away from Jiankou, on the return trip to Beijing. The Chinese resort offers small chalets perched on a hill and excellent fare at its massive, meandering restaurant that serves up to 1,000 people per night. Try the excellent barbecued pork ribs *(kao zhupai)* and the mixed eggplant, potato, and green peppers *(disanxian)*.

2 MING TOMBS (SHI SAN LING; 十三陵)

48km (30 miles) NW of Beijing

Of the 16 emperors who ruled China during the Ming dynasty (1368–1644), 13 are buried in a box canyon at the southern foot of Tianshou Shan (hence the Chinese name Shisan Ling, the 13 Tombs). The first emperor of the Ming, Hongwu, is entombed in Xiao Ling, near Nanjing. The location of the second emperor's tomb is uncertain, while the unfilial seventh emperor, who usurped the throne after his brother was taken by the Mongols, was buried near the Summer Palace among the graves of concubines. Despite these omissions, this is the most extensive burial complex of any Chinese dynasty. A red gate sealed off the valley, guards were posted, and no one, not even the emperor, could ride a horse on these grounds. The site was chosen by the Yongle emperor, who also oversaw the construction of the Forbidden City. Protected from the bitter northern winds by a mountain range, the tombs are constructed in conventional fashion, with memorial halls at the front and burial chambers to the rear.

The entrance to the **Ming Tombs,** a long and celebrated *shen dao* **(spirit way)** is lined with statues of guardian animals and officials. Only three of the Ming Tombs—**Ding Ling, Chang Ling,** and **Zhao Ling**—have been restored, and only one (Ding Ling) has been fully excavated. Many of the buildings mirror Ming palaces found in the city. Because of this, the sight can be boring to people who've had their fill of imperial architecture. The Ming Tombs are at their most charming along the *shen dao* and on the grounds of **unrestored tombs** (free admission). In contrast, the restored tombs are dank, overcrowded, and uninspiring. The Ming Tombs are so unpopular with foreign tourists that they are often excluded from tour-group itineraries.

ESSENTIALS

GETTING THERE   The valley is just off the freeway that goes to Ba Da Ling. Many **Chinese bus tours** to Ba Da Ling also come here, visiting the spirit way and one of the tombs at blinding speed, but if you want time to explore some unrestored tombs (highly recommended), you'll have to make a separate trip. The most comfortable means of public transport is to take the air-conditioned **bus no. 345** from the Jishuitan metro stop to Changping and then cross the street and take **bus no. 314** to the Nan Xin Cun stop, which is adjacent to the entrance to the spirit way. From there, you can continue north to either Ding Ling Daokou to visit Ding Ling, a further 2km (1¼-mile) walk to the west, or on to the terminus at Chang Ling. A **taxi** hired in Beijing should cost ¥500, driver's fee for wait time included.

EXPLORING THE AREA

The **spirit way** *(shen dao)* ★ (Apr–Nov ¥30, Dec–Mar ¥20; daily 8:30am–6pm) should not be missed. The main entrance to the valley is the **Da Hong Men (Great Red Gate),** beyond which is a pavilion housing China's largest memorial stele, and beyond that the spirit way. The path, slightly curved to fool malevolent spirits, is lined on either side with willows and remarkable **carved stone animals** and human figures, considered among the best in China. The statuary includes pairs of camels, lions, elephants, and mythical beasts, such as the *qilin,* a creature of immense virtue referred to as the "Chinese unicorn" even though it has two horns.

The largest and best preserved of the 13 tombs is 4km (2½ miles) ahead: **Chang Ling** (¥45 summer, ¥30 winter; daily 8:30am–5:30pm), the tomb of the Yongle emperor (reign 1403–24). The layout is identical to that of the tomb of the first Ming emperor in Nanjing. It feels like the Forbidden City in miniature, and is perhaps disappointing if you've seen the palace already. Most striking is **Ling'en Dian ★**, an immense hall in which the interior columns and brackets have been left unpainted, creating an eye-catching contrast with the green ceiling panels. Slightly wider than the Hall of Supreme Harmony, Ling'en Dian contains a three-tiered platform and building materials that are superior to those of the Forbidden City.

The 1,195-sq.-m (12,863-sq.-ft.) **Underground Palace** at **Ding Ling** (summer ¥60, winter ¥40; 8:30am–6pm), rediscovered in 1956, was the burial place of the Wanli emperor (reign 1572–1620), his wife, and his favorite concubine. Construction of the burial chamber commenced before the emperor was 20 years old, making him "the living ancestor" in the words of Ray Huang, author of *1587, A Year of No Significance*. The "palace" is a vast marble vault, buried 27m (89 ft.) underground and divided into five large chambers. It's all a bit disappointing. The corpses have been removed, their red coffins replaced with cheap replicas, and burial objects moved to aboveground display rooms. The original marble thrones are still there, now covered in a small fortune of Renminbi notes tossed by Chinese visitors hoping to bribe the emperor's ghost. Outside, behind the ticket office, is the respectable **Shisan Ling Bowuguan (Ming Tombs Museum),** with short biographies of all the entombed emperors; several reproduced artifacts; a detailed, wood reproduction of the Ling'en Dian; and a 1954 photo of Mao reclining and reading a newspaper on a half-buried marble incense burner at Chang Ling.

3 EASTERN QING TOMBS (QING DONG LING; 清东陵) ★★

125km (78 miles) E of Beijing

The **Qing Dong Ling** have been open for more than 20 years but are still little visited despite offering considerably more to visitors than tombs of the Ming. Altogether 5 emperors, 15 empresses, 136 concubines, 3 princes, and 2 princesses are buried in 15 tombs here. The first to be buried was Shunzhi—the first Qing emperor to reign from Beijing—in 1663, and the last was an imperial concubine in 1935. The tomb chambers of four imperial tombs, the **Xiao Ling** (the Shunzhi emperor), **Jing Ling** (Kangxi), **Yu Ling** (Qianlong), and **Ding Ling** (Xianfeng), are open, as well as the twin **Ding Dong Ling** tombs (Dowager Empress Cixi and Empress Ci'an). Others of interest include a group site for the Qianlong emperor's concubines.

ESSENTIALS

VISITOR INFORMATION The tombs are in Zunhua County, Hebei Province (daily 8am–5:30pm summer, 9am–4:30pm winter). The *tong piao,* which offers access to all the tombs, costs ¥120.

GETTING THERE A special Qing Dong Ling **tourist** *(you)* **bus** departs from northeast of the Xuanwu Men metro stop (departures 6:30am–8am; ¥170, includes admission); this gives you about 3 hours at the site. From Qianmen, you can take **tourist** *(you)* **bus no. 13.**

WHERE TO STAY & DINE The **Yuyuan Shanzhuang (Imperial Gardens Mountain Villa;** © **0315/694-5348)** is a battered three-star set to the east of the tombs where the asking price for a twin room is ¥288, about twice what it's worth. Its best feature is the attached Manchurian restaurant, **Qing Yan Lou** (daily 11am–2pm and 6–9pm), which offers inexpensive game meats, and delicious green bean flour noodles *(culiu laozha).*

EXPLORING THE AREA

Although few others are as elaborate, the **Xiao Ling** was the first tomb on the site, and a model for others both here and at the Western Qing Tombs. As here, usually an approach road or **spirit way** may have guardian figures, and the entrance to the tomb itself is usually preceded by a large stele pavilion and marble bridges over a stream. To the right, the buildings used for preparation of sacrifices are now usually the residences of the staff, and hung with washing. Inside the gate, halls to the left and right were for enrobing and other preparations, and now house exhibitions, as usually does each **Hall of Eminent Favor,** at the rear, where ceremonies in honor of the deceased took place. Behind, if open, a doorway allows access past a stone altar to a steep ramp leading to the base of the **Soul Tower.** Through a passageway beneath, stairs to either side lead to a walkway encircling the mound, giving views across the countryside. If the tomb chamber is open, a ramp from beneath the Soul Tower leads to a series of chambers.

The twin **Ding Dong Ling** ★★ tombs have nearly identical exteriors, but Cixi had hers rebuilt in 1895, 14 years after Ci'an's death (in which she is suspected of having had a hand), using far more expensive materials. The main hall contains reproductions of pictures produced in 1903 by Cixi's photo studio within the Summer Palace. Everywhere there are reminders of the Forbidden City, such as the terrace-corner spouts carved as water-loving dragons *(che).* The interior has motifs strikingly painted in gold on dark wood, recalling the buildings where she spent her last years. There are walls of carved and gilded brick, and superbly fearsome wooden dragons writhe down the columns. After this, the other tombs seem gaudy.

The enclosure of the **Yu Fei Yuan Qin (Garden of Rest)** contains moss-covered tumuli for 35 of the Qianlong emperor's concubines. Another is buried in a proper tomb chamber, along with an empress whom Qianlong had grown to dislike.

The **Jing Ling** is the tomb of Qianlong's grandfather, the Kangxi emperor, and is surprisingly modest given that he was possibly the greatest emperor the Chinese ever had, but that's in keeping with what is known of his character. The spirit way leading to the tomb has an elegant five-arch bridge; the guardian figures are placed on an unusual curve quite close to the tomb itself, and are more decorated than those at earlier tombs. The **Yu Ling** ★★★ has the finest tomb chamber, a series of rooms separated by solid marble doors, with its walls and arched ceilings engraved with Buddha figures and more than 30,000 words of Tibetan scripture. The 3-ton doors themselves have reliefs of bodhisattvas and the four protective kings usually found at temple entrances. This tomb is worth the trip in its own right.

4 WESTERN QING TOMBS (QING XI LING; 清西陵) ★

140km (87 miles) SW of Beijing

The Yongzheng emperor broke with tradition and constructed his tomb here, away from his father (the Kangxi emperor). His son, the Qianlong emperor, decided to be buried near his grandfather and that thereafter burials should alternate between the eastern (see above) and western sites, although this was not followed consistently. The first tomb, the **Tai Ling,** was completed in 1737, 2 years after the Yongzheng reign. The last imperial interment was in 1998, when the ashes of Aisin Gioro Henry Puyi, the last emperor, were moved to a commercial cemetery here. He and 2 consorts were added to 4 emperors, 4 empresses, 4 princes, 2 princesses, and 57 concubines. The site is rural, more densely forested than the Qing Dong Ling, overlapped by orchards and agriculture, and with chickens, goats, and the odd rabbit to be encountered.

The **Chang Ling** (tomb of the Jiaqing emperor) and **Chong Ling** (tomb of the Guangxu emperor) are also open, as well as the **Chang Xi Ling** with the extraordinary sonic effects of its **Huiyin Bi**—an echo wall where, as the only visitor, you can try out the special effects available only in theory at the Temple of Heaven (p. 125).

ESSENTIALS

VISITOR INFORMATION   The ticket office is open from 8am to 5pm; a *tong piao* (for access to all the tombs) costs ¥120 and is good for 2 days.

GETTING THERE   The best way to get here is by taxi, which costs around ¥500. It's possible to visit **Marco Polo Bridge (Lu Gou Qiao)** on the way.

There's no access by tourist bus—part of the appeal for most visitors. Take a **bus** to Yixian from the Lize Qiao long-distance bus station (daily 6:50am–5pm, every 15 min.; 3-hr. trip; ¥20; last bus returns at 4pm), and then switch to a minivan *(miandi)* for the 15km (9⅓-mile) ride to the tombs (around ¥20; ¥100 to visit all the tombs), or turn right as you exit the bus station to find bus no. 9 waiting on the first corner (every hour; ¥3).

WHERE TO STAY   The modest, Manchu-themed **Ba Jiao Lou Manzu Zhuangyuan** lies just east of Tai Ling (© 0312/826-0828; ¥100 standard room). **Xing Gong Binguan,** near Yongfu Si on the eastern side of the tomb complex (© 0312/471-0038; standard room ¥150 after discount), was where Manchu rulers stayed when they came to pay their respects. The room constructed in 1748 to house the Qianlong emperor is now rented as two suites for ¥4,000—though the 1980s decor is criminal.

EXPLORING THE AREA

The **Da Bei Lou,** a pavilion containing two vast stelae, is on the curved route to the **Tai Ling.** The general plan of the major tombs follows that of the eastern tombs and, in fact, the **Chang Ling,** slightly to the west, is almost identical, brick for brick, to the Tai Ling, with the addition of a purple-tinged marble floor. The Jiaqing empress is buried just to the west on a far smaller scale in the **Chang Xi Ling,** the tomb mound a brick drum. But the perfectly semicircular rear wall offers the whispering-gallery effects found at some domed European cathedrals, and clapping while standing on various marked stones in the center of the site produces a variety of multiple echoes, while speech is amazingly amplified. The empress can't get much peace.

Jiaqing's son, the Daoguang emperor, was meant to be buried at Qing Dong Ling, but his tomb there was flooded. The relocated **Mu Ling** appears much more modest than those of his predecessors. There's no stele pavilion or spirit way, it's largely unpainted, and the tomb mound is a modest brick-wall drum, but this is the most expensive tomb: Wood used to construct the exquisite main hall is fragrant *nanmu*, sourced from as far away as Myanmar. The Guangxu emperor was the last to complete his reign (although Cixi, who died the next day, is again suspected of shortening it), and his **Chong Ling,** which has the only tomb chamber that is open, uses more modern materials than other tombs. It wasn't completed until 1915, well after the last emperor's abdication.

Several other rather battered tombs are open, and more are being opened, including the **Tai Ling Fei Yuan Qin,** a group of concubine tumuli, individually labeled with the years in which the concubines entered the Yongzheng emperor's service and their grades in the complex harem hierarchy.

The ashes of **Puyi** (properly known as the Xuantong emperor) lie buried on the eastern end of the site, up a slope behind a brand-new Qing-style memorial arch *(pailou),* and behind a shoddy, modern carved balustrade.

5 TANZHE SI 潭柘寺 & JIETAI SI 戒台寺 ★

Tanzhe Si 48km (30 miles) W of Beijing; Jietai Si 35km (22 miles) W of Beijing

Buried in the hills west of Beijing, **Tanzhe Si (Temple of the Pool and Wild Mulberry)** and **Jietai Si (Temple of the Ordination Platform)** are the tranquil kinds of Chinese temples visitors imagine before they actually come to China. These temples were unusual because they received imperial support (Qing rulers preferred Tibetan Buddhism), and both have long been popular with local pilgrims. They were also loved by early Western residents, who rented out halls inside the temples.

ESSENTIALS

VISITOR INFORMATION   Admission to **Tanzhe Si** (© 010/6086-2505) is ¥40; the ticket office is open from 8am to 5pm. Admission to **Jietai Si** (© 010/6980-6611) is ¥35; the ticket office is open Monday through Friday from 8am to 5:30pm.

GETTING THERE   Both temples are easily accessible by taking **bus no. 931** from the Pingguo Yuan metro stop to **Tanzhe Si** (daily 7am–5:30pm, about every 30 min.; 1-hr. trip; ¥2.50). At the far western end of Line 1 at the Pingguo Yuan metro stop, take a right and continue straight a few minutes to the bus station (be sure to take the plain red-and-beige, rather than the red-and-yellow *zhi* version of the bus). At Tanzhe Si, the last stop on this line, hike up the stone path at the end of the parking lot. From there, take **bus no. 931** east 13km (8 miles) to **Jietai Si,** where you reach the site by walking uphill from the bus stop. On weekends, the **tourist *(you)* bus no. 7** runs from the northeast corner of Qian Men (Sat–Sun 7–8:30am, every 30 min.; ¥60), but it regrettably includes a stop at the garish Shihua Caves. Round-trip by **taxi** costs less than ¥500, driver's fee for wait time included.

WHERE TO STAY   At both temples, basic but acceptable accommodations are available for those who want (or need) to spend more time in quietude.

EXPLORING THE AREA

Tanzhe Si ★★, set in peaceful forested grounds, dates back to the Western Jin dynasty (265–316), well before Beijing was founded. In the main courtyard on the central axis is a pair of 30m (98-ft.) ginkgo trees, supposedly planted in the Tang dynasty (618–907), as well as several apricot trees, cypresses, peonies, and purple jade orchids. The complex is extensive, and is said to have provided a model for the layout of the Forbidden City. Above and to the right of the main courtyard lies a rare **stupa yard** *(ta yuan),* stone monuments built in different styles over a period of several centuries and housing the remains of eminent monks. The **Guanyin Dian,** at the top of the western axis, was favored by Princess Miao Yan, a daughter of Kublai Khan; she is said to have prayed so fervently here that she left footprints in one of the floor stones (now stored in a box to the left). The main object of interest to local visitors is the **stone fish** *(shi yu)* to the left and behind this hall. Rubbing the relevant part of the fish is said to cure the corresponding malady. Everyone seems to rub its stomach.

The **ordination platform** *(jietai)* at **Jietai Si** ★, China's largest, is a three-tiered structure with 113 statues of the God of Ordination placed in niches around the base; it's located in the **Jie Tan Dian (Hall of the Altar of Ordination)** in the far-right (northwest) corner of the temple. It looks, as novelist Ann Bridge put it, "like a very high four-poster bed." Ceremonies conducted on this platform to commemorate the ascension of a devotee to full monkhood required permission from the emperor. Often referred to as the "Beida [Peking University, nominally the best university in China] of Buddhism" for its ability to attract the most promising monastic scholars, along with temples in Quanzhou and Hangzhou, it has been the most significant site for the ordination of Buddhist monks for 900 years. Surrounding courtyards have ancient, twisted pines (as venerable as the temple itself) and fragrant peony gardens.

6 CUAN DI XIA 爨低下

100km (62 miles) W of Beijing

Originally called **Cuan Di Xia (Under the Stove),** this tiny village of around 100 is an ideal 2-day trip for those with a passion for Chinese vernacular architecture or keen to experience life in rural China. Set in a narrow valley off the old trade route to Shanxi, Cuan Di Xia has the best-preserved *siheyuan* **(courtyard houses)** in the Beijing region. Opened to tourism in 1997, more than 70 dwellings are said to be here.

The impressive dwellings were designed by scholar-officials from the Ming who fled to this remote village toward the end of the dynasty. There they lived out one of the most pervasive legends in Chinese literature, that of the Peach Sanctuary (Taohua Yuan). Inhabitants live peacefully in a hidden rural Arcadia, preserving the traditions of an earlier era. Corn dangles from the eaves of the ancient dwellings, donkeys plow the fields, and the hills are alive with wildflowers.

ESSENTIALS

VISITOR INFORMATION   The ticket office (✆ **010/6981-8988**) is open 24 hours. Admission to the village costs ¥35.

GETTING THERE   From the Pingguo Yuan metro stop, turn right out of the southeast exit and continue for a few minutes to the **bus no. 929 *zhixian* stop** (the last sign) for the bus to Zhaitang (daily 7am–5pm, every hour; 2½-hr. trip). While traveling from the city, you'll leave behind the smokestacks of Shou Gang (Capital Iron and Steel Works, Beijing's number one polluter). From Zhaitang, **minivans** *(miandi)* (¥10) travel to Cuan Di Xia. The last bus returns from Zhaitang at 4:10pm. A *miandi* from Pingguo Yuan costs ¥130 one-way. A **taxi** from Beijing costs ¥400 round-trip.

WHERE TO STAY   For those staying overnight, most lodgings offer basic accommodations (no shower) for ¥50 for a two-person bed, or one bed for ¥15. We recommend the friendly and freshly renovated **Lao Meng Kezhan,** no. 23 in the lower part of the village (✆ **010/6981-9788**). Their restaurant, which adjoins the rather quiet main road, is an agreeable spot for alfresco dining.

The area is a magnet for artists, poets, and period-drama camera crews; many local tourists are mystified by the lack of karaoke bars and duck boats. One Beijinger asked in frustration, "Is there anything at all to do here?" A local, not much caring for his tone, deadpanned, "Absolutely nothing. You'd better go home."

Wander through the narrow lanes, their walls still showing faded slogans from the 1966–76 Cultural Revolution, including LONG LIVE CHAIRMAN MAO, WORKERS OF THE WORLD UNITE, and USE MAO ZEDONG THOUGHT TO ARM YOUR MINDS. Beyond the village, the path continues to rise, passing an intriguing open-air grain mill before entering groves of peach trees. The next village, **Baiyu Cun,** is around 6km (3¾ miles) northwest. The dwellings of this larger settlement are arranged in the more plebeian *pingfang* (bungalow) style.

7 CHENGDE 承德 ★★

Hebei Province, 233km (145 miles) NE of Beijing

If you can do only one overnight side trip from Beijing, make it Chengde—the summer camp of the Qing emperors. Here, in a walled enclosure containing numerous palaces, pavilions, and pagodas, as well as a vast hunting park, the emperors escaped Beijing's blazing summer temperatures, entertained delegations from home and abroad, and practiced the mounted military skills which had originally gained them their empire. The design of the resort, built between 1703 and 1794, was shaped by its varied diplomatic functions. Some buildings are plain and undecorated to show visiting tribesmen that the emperors had not lost touch with their roots or been too softened by luxury; others were copies of some of China's most famous and elegant buildings; and some were giant edifices with hints of minority architecture, intended both to show the emperor's sympathy for the traditions of tributary and border-dwelling peoples, and to overawe their emissaries.

In 1794 Britain's Lord Macartney arrived on a mission from George III, and not finding the Qianlong emperor at home in Beijing, followed him up to Chengde. He was impressed by the resort's vast scale, and was shown around by people who anticipated modern guides' hyperbole by telling him that the gilded bronze roof tiles of the Potala Temple were of solid gold.

The Jiaqing emperor died here in 1820, as did the Xianfeng emperor in 1861, having signed the "unequal" treaties which marked the close of the Second Opium War. The place came to be viewed as unlucky, and was already decaying by the fall of the Qing in 1911. But the **Mountain Retreat for Escaping the Heat,** along with the remaining **Eight Outer Temples** around its perimeter, still form one of the greatest concentrations of ancient buildings in China. It's an 18th-century version of a "Splendid China" theme park (as seen in Florida and Shenzhen), but with oversize buildings rather than the miniatures offered there.

Ordinary Beijingren now follow imperial tradition by flocking here to escape the baking summer heat. You can hurry around the main sights by spending a night here, but you might want to spend 2 nights.

ESSENTIALS

GETTING THERE Chengde has no airport, and although it's an easy side trip from Beijing, it's not well connected to anywhere else except the Northeast. A convenient morning all-seater **train** from Beijing Zhan, the K7711, departs at 6:30am, arriving in Chengde at 10:48am. It returns to Beijing as the K7712, leaving Chengde at 1:30pm, arriving in Beijing at 5:48pm. Soft seat costs ¥61, hard seat ¥41. The railway station is just south of the city center, and bus no. 5 from outside to your right runs to several hotels and to the Mountain Resort. The ticket office (up the stairs and to the right) is open from 5am to 10:30pm with brief breaks. There are also limited services to Shenyang (nine high-speed D-series trains daily) and Shijiazhuang (four trains daily, one D-series train at 5:14pm).

The soft-seat waiting room is through a door at the far left-hand end of the main hall as you enter, while luggage storage is on the right-hand side. On the train both to and from Beijing, enterprising staff sell tea for ¥3, instant coffee for ¥5, maps, and hotel reservations (do *not* book with them). About 1¼ hours after you leave Beijing, you'll see a crumbling stretch of the Great Wall.

At least until construction of a new road/rail interchange station at Dongzhi Men is complete, **bus** departures for Chengde from Beijing are more frequent from Liu Li Qiao Changtu Qiche Keyun Zhan (© 010/8383-1717 or 010/8383-1720, southwest of the Liu Li Qiao bridge). The 233km (145-mile) trip costs ¥73 for an Iveco or similar, with departures about every 30 minutes from 5:40am to 6:40pm. The current journey takes about 5 hours. At the moment it's possible to alight and see the Great Wall at Jin Shan Ling en route, and subsequently flag down a passing bus to finish the trip. Express buses from Beijing run to and from the forecourt of Chengde railway station. Escape the pestering of touts by dodging into a branch of the Sichuan restaurant Dongpo Fanzhuang, opposite and to the left (south) where you alight, and if you're ready for a quick lunch, have it here. The main long-distance bus station has been demolished to make way for an extension of the Sheng Hua Dajiudian, and most buses now depart from the **Qiche Dong Zhan** (© 0314/212-3588), a ¥20 taxi ride south, or take bus no. 118, which passes Yingzi Dajie and the Mountain Resort. The ticket office is open from 5:30am to 5pm. There are two services to Shijiazhuang (7am, 9am, 11am, and 2pm; 10 hr.; ¥121), with seven buses connecting with Qinhuangdao (6:30am, 7:30am, 8:05am, 8:30am, 10am, 1pm, and 5pm; 4 hr.; ¥97). Buses to Beijing run every 20 minutes, but it's easier to flag an Iveco from outside the railway station.

GETTING AROUND **Taxi** meters are generally not used. The fare is ¥5 in town, or ¥10 to the outer temples. If the meter is started, the ¥5 flag fall includes 1km; then it's ¥1.40 per kilometer, jumping 50% after 8km (5 miles). **Buses** usually charge ¥1.

VISITOR INFORMATION For tourist complaints, call © 0314/202-4549.

Fast Facts

Banks, Foreign Exchange & ATMs The main foreign exchange branch of the **Bank of China** (9am–5pm) is at the junction of Dong Dajie and Lizheng Men Dajie. Another convenient branch is at Lizheng Men Dajie 19, just east of the Mountain Villa Hotel. Both have ATMs that accept foreign cards, as does a branch on the corner of Nan Yingzi Dajie and Xinhua Lu.

Internet Access Internet cafes are few and mostly far from the usual visitor areas. Follow Nan Yingzi Dajie south until you cross the railway line, and turn right into Shanxi Ying to find a cluster of Internet bars (8am–midnight) on the first corner, which charge ¥1.50 per hour.

Post Office The post office is on Yingzi Dajie at its junction with Dong Dajie. It's open from 8am to 6pm (to 5pm in winter).

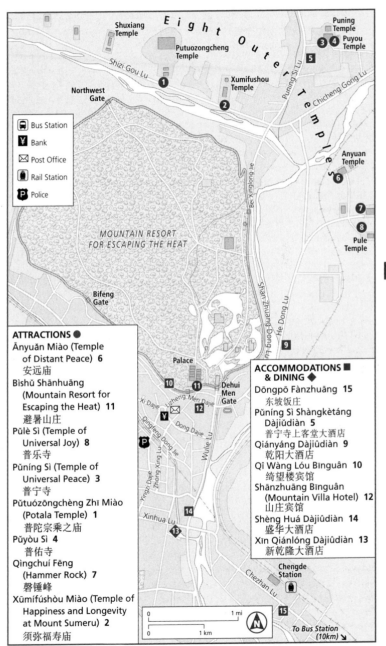

THE GREAT WALL & OTHER SIDE TRIPS

11

CHENGDE

Map labels:

Eight Outer Temples

Shuxiang Temple
Putuozongcheng Temple
Puning Temple
Puyou Temple
Shizi Gou Lu
Xumifushou Temple
Puning Si Lu
Chicheng Gong Lu
Northwest Gate
Anyuan Temple
Bei Xinglong Jie

Legend:
- Bus Station
- ¥ Bank
- ✉ Post Office
- Rail Station
- P Police

MOUNTAIN RESORT FOR ESCAPING THE HEAT

Pule Temple
Shan Zhuang He Dong Lu
Bifeng Gate

Palace
Dehui Men Gate
Lizheng Men Dajie
Xi Dajie
Qingfeng Dong Jie
Dong Dajie
Wulie Lu
Yingzi Dajie
Zhong Xing Lu
Xinhua Lu
Chezhan Lu
Chengde Station

0   1 mi
0   1 km

To Bus Station (10km) ↘

ATTRACTIONS ●

Ānyuǎn Miào (Temple of Distant Peace) **6**
安远庙

Bìshǔ Shānzhuāng (Mountain Resort for Escaping the Heat) **11**
避暑山庄

Pǔlè Sì (Temple of Universal Joy) **8**
普乐寺

Pǔníng Sì (Temple of Universal Peace) **3**
普宁寺

Pǔtuózōngchèng Zhī Miào (Potala Temple) **1**
普陀宗乘之庙

Pǔyòu Sì **4**
普佑寺

Qìngchuí Fēng (Hammer Rock) **7**
磬锤峰

Xūmífúshòu Miào (Temple of Happiness and Longevity at Mount Sumeru) **2**
须弥福寿庙

ACCOMMODATIONS ■ & DINING ◆

Dōngpō Fànzhuāng **15**
东坡饭庄

Pǔníng Sì Shàngkètáng Dàjiǔdiàn **5**
普宁寺上客堂大酒店

Qiányáng Dàjiǔdiàn **9**
乾阳大酒店

Qǐ Wàng Lóu Bīnguǎn **10**
绮望楼宾馆

Shānzhuāng Bīnguǎn (Mountain Villa Hotel) **12**
山庄宾馆

Shèng Huá Dàjiǔdiàn **14**
盛华大酒店

Xīn Qiánlóng Dàjiǔdiàn **13**
新乾隆大酒店

Visa Extensions   Walking south along Nan Yingzi Dajie, turn right after the Xinhua Bookstore into Xiao Tong Gou Jie, and then take the first left. Next to a branch of CITS you'll find a sign that reads ALIENS EXIT-ENTRY DEPARTMENT. Open Monday to Friday 8:30am to noon; 2:30 to 5:30pm in summer (1:30–5:30pm in winter).

RELAXING WITH THE EMPERORS

Bishu Shanzhuang (Mountain Resort for Escaping the Heat) ★

While the "Winter Palace," as Beijing's Forbidden City was sometimes called, was the creation of the indigenous Ming dynasty, the summer palace at Chengde was entirely the creation of the Manchu Qing, and lay beyond the Great Wall in the direction of their homelands. Here the emperor and nobility would play at the equestrian and military talents that won them China in the first place, with formal contests in archery and hunting in the well-stocked park. The lakes and their pavilions, stuffed with treasures, provided the emperor and his consorts with more refined diversions.

There's a half-day of wandering here, although many of the buildings shown as lying within the park have long since vanished. The most important remaining is the **Zheng Gong (Main Palace).** The message here is one of simplicity and frugality (the beams and columns are very plain, although actually made of hardwoods brought long distances at great expense), with a pleasing elegance in great contrast to the usual Qing gaudiness. The palace now serves as a museum, displaying ancient military equipment in the front rooms and period furnishings and antiquities at the rear.

Straight north, up the west side of lakes dotted with pavilions and crossed by many bridges, lies the **Wenjin Ge (Pavilion of Literary Delight),** a ripple-roofed southern-style building reached through a rockery, which is a copy of a famous library building from Ningbo.

A little farther northeast, the handsome **Liu He Ta (Pagoda of the Six Harmonies)** is the most striking building in the park. Its nine brick stories have green- or yellow-tiled eaves hung with bells and topped by a golden knob.

The pagoda is near the east entrance of the park, close to which the retired and unemployed can be found enjoying a game of croquet. If you've already examined the gaudy pavilions around the lakes, it's possible to leave this way to walk or catch a bus to the Eight Outer Temples.

Main entrance (Zheng Men) in Lizheng Men Dajie. ✆ **0314/207-6089.** Admission ¥90, ¥60 in winter. 6am–6pm.

WAI BA MIAO (EIGHT OUTER TEMPLES; 外八庙) ★★

There were originally 12 temples, built between 1713 and 1780, and not all of those that remain are open to the public. Summer hours are May 1 to October 15; outside these times, some lesser temples may be shut. Several temples have features unique to Chengde. Most are extremely grand and suitably impressive (their purpose, after all), with successive halls on rising ground.

Tip: Puning Si and the other northern temples are on morning itineraries for tour groups, followed by Pule Si and the eastern temples in the afternoon. If you're traveling independently, work the other way around. You can also buy a *tao piao* (all-inclusive) for ¥80, which includes entry to Xumifushou Miao, the Potala Temple, Pule Si, and Anyuan Miao.

Bus no. 118, from Yingzi Dajie or the Mountain Resort main entrance, will take you to the northern group of temples.

Anyuan Miao (Temple of Distant Peace)   Built in 1764, this is another example of architectural diplomacy, built in imitation of a temple (now long-vanished) in Yining on China's remote western borders to please Mongol tribes that were resettled around Chengde. You'll almost certainly be the only visitor.

Ⓒ **0314/205-7809.** Admission ¥10. Summer only 8:30am–5pm. A 15-min. walk north of Pule Si.

Pule Si (Temple of Universal Joy)   Tibetan advisors were employed in the design of this temple, built to receive annual tributary visits from defeated Mongol tribes. But the most striking element is the copy at the rear of the circular Hall of Prayer for Good Harvests from the Temple of Heaven. Shady benches around the quiet courtyards make perfect picnic stops.

Off Hedong Lu. Ⓒ **0314/205-7557.** Admission summer ¥30, winter ¥20. 8am–5:30pm (winter 8:30am–4:30pm). Bus: no. 10 from Wulie Lu to terminus. Taxi: a short ride from Puning Si.

Puning Si (Temple of Universal Peace)   The main Hall of Mahayana is impressive—story upon story of red walls and yellow roofs, topped with a gold knob surrounded by four minipagoda-like points. More impressive still is its contents, a giant copper-colored wooden Guanyin figure more than 22m (72 ft.) high, the largest of its kind in the world. It's possible to climb three levels of interior galleries to look the figure in the eye, as she sits in dusty gloom. While other sights in Chengde are managed by the sleepy local tourism bureau, this temple is run by an entrepreneurial group of monks: The temple now sports a hotel (see below) and a tacky but entertaining re-creation of a Qing market, and offers an evening show promising blessings and exorcisms by "real Tibetan lamas."

Off Puning Si Lu. Ⓒ **0314/205-8203.** Admission ¥50–¥10 to climb the Hall of Mahayana. 7:30am–6pm (winter 8:30am–5pm). Bus: no. 6 or 118 to Puning Si.

Putuozongcheng Zhi Miao (Potala Temple)   Five minutes' walk west, the Potala Temple, its tapering windows and slab-sided walls obviously influenced by Tibet, is in no way "a copy of the Potala Temple in Lhasa," as local guides like to say. Many windows are blind, and several outbuildings are solid, just intended to add to the massy splendor of the whole. Items on display in the surrounding galleries include two nine-story sandalwood pagodas climbing through holes cut in the floors, young girls' skulls fused with silver and once used as drinking vessels, and anatomically detailed esoteric statuary of sexual acts.

Shizi Gou Lu. Ⓒ **0314/216-3072.** Admission summer ¥40, winter ¥30. 7:30am–6pm (winter 8:30am–5pm). Bus: no. 118 to Putuozongcheng Zhi Miao.

Puyou Si   Next door to Puning Si, this temple was closed for renovations when I last visited. The point of entering is to see the remainder of a collection of statues of the 500 arhats (the first followers of the Sakyamuni Buddha). Many of these were destroyed in 1937 during the Japanese occupation, but the remainder have a lively jollity, and are hung with scarves placed by respectful devotees.

Ⓒ **0314/216-0935.** Admission ¥20. 8am–5:30pm (winter 8:30am–4:30pm).

Qingchui Feng (Hammer Rock)   Bus no. 10's terminus is actually the cableway to Hammer Rock. The characters specifically mean a kind of hammer for striking a Buddhist musical instrument, but the shape of this clublike column will inevitably remind all who see it of something completely different. It reminds the Chinese of that, too—they're just being polite. Pleasant strolls across the hills and sweeping views of the valley await those who ascend.

C 0314/205-7135. Admission ¥25. 24 hr. Cable car ¥27 one-way; ¥42 round-trip. Runs Apr 1–Oct 30 7:30am–5:30pm.

Xumifushou Miao (Temple of Happiness and Longevity at Mount Sumeru)
Partly inspired by Tashilhunpo in Tibet, this temple was constructed to make the Panchen Lama, number two in the Tibetan religious hierarchy, feel at home during a visit in 1780.

Shizi Gou Lu. *C* 0314/216-2972. Admission summer ¥30, winter ¥20. 7:30am–6pm (8:30am–5pm in winter). Bus: no. 118 to Xumifushou Zhi Miao.

SHOPPING

A lively **market** takes over the upper part of Yingzi Dajie at night, interesting for its color rather than for what's on sale. The street also has several department stores with ground-floor supermarkets. Toward the post office are a couple of bakeries where you can pick up snacks for the onward journey.

WHERE TO STAY

From the first week of May to the first week of October the town is busy, weekends particularly so, but only during the weeklong national holidays should it be difficult to find a room. Otherwise, the town has an excess of accommodations and, even in peak season, all hotels will have 20% discounts, rising to as much as 70% in the off season for the gently persuasive bargainer who just shows up. A 50% discount is taken for granted; you work down from there.

Expensive

Puning Si Shangketang Dajiudian ★★ (Finds   Run by the market-savvy monks of Puning Si, this newly opened hotel offers cozy accommodations within the west wing of the temple. Rooms are tastefully decorated with dark wood furniture and handmade paper lamps and are set around eight tranquil courtyards, which have rock gardens and ponds. Buddhist touches are in evidence: There's a large (if overpriced) vegetarian selection in the main restaurant, the proscription against soft beds is enforced, and there's little chance of sleeping in—the temple bells peal at 7:30am.

Puning Si. *C* 0314/205-8888. 100 units. ¥680 standard room. 30% summer discounts offered. No credit cards. **Amenities:** 2 restaurants; exercise room; large game room; indoor pool. *In room:* A/C, TV, fridge.

Sheng Hua Dajiudian   Opened in 2003, the four-star Sheng Hua is Chengde's best hotel in terms of furnishings. Rooms are spacious; luxury twin (standard) rooms even come equipped with their own computer. Bathrooms are well outfitted and come with elaborate massage-jet showers. A new wing, located on the site of the old bus station, opened in 2006. It houses a pool and fitness center. Staff is helpful with inquiries, and speaks English and French.

Wulie Lu 22. *C* 0314/227-1188. Fax 0314/227-1112. 114 units. ¥700–¥780 standard room; ¥1,500–¥1,800 suite. 30%–40% summer discounts offered. AE, MC, V. **Amenities:** 2 restaurants; forex; teahouse. *In room:* A/C, TV, fridge, hair dryer, Internet.

Moderate

Qi Wang Lou Binguan ★   Once good enough for the Qianlong emperor, it's now good enough for party luminaries, though it's less expensive than this would suggest. Standard hotel interiors have been recently renovated, and there are yet higher standards in a building opened in 2004. Inexpensive bike rental is offered, an excellent way to explore the town. Avoid the diabolical Western breakfast.

Bi Feng Men Dong Lu Bei 1 (a narrow street running up the west side of the park). ℭ **0314/202-4385.** Fax 0314/202-1904. 84 units. ¥500–¥800 standard room; from ¥480 3-bed basement room in newer building; ¥1,800–¥6,000 suite. Typical 50% discount off season. AE, MC, V. Bus: no. 5 from railway station to Bishu Shanzhuang. **Amenities:** Restaurant; bar; bike rental ¥50 per day; teahouse. *In room:* A/C, TV.

Shanzhuang Binguan (Mountain Villa Hotel) Once the only hotel in town, this six-building monster directly opposite the Mountain Resort underwent a full renovation in 2005. Unfortunately, the hotel recently eliminated a variety of simpler, cheaper rooms with common bathrooms for budget travelers, but the standard rooms are still a good deal. Usually these longer-standing hotels should be your last choice, but here a real effort has been made to stay in competition with the newer hotels.

Xiao Nan Men Jie 11 (opposite main entrance to Mountain Resort). ℭ **0314/209-1188.** Fax 0314/203-4143. mvhotel@cs-user.he.cninfo.net. 370 units. ¥580–¥680 standard room; ¥880–¥2,000 suite. 20% discount in summer. AE, DC, MC, V. Bus: no. 5 from railway station to Bishu Shanzhuang. **Amenities:** 2 restaurants; bike rental ¥60 per day; fitness room; forex. *In room:* A/C, TV, hair dryer, Internet (upon request).

WHERE TO DINE

The **nightmarket** on Yingzi Dajie runs through the heart of town. Stalls sell kabobs for ¥1 and other Chinese fast food, eaten at tables behind each stall.

As befits a former hunting ground, Chengde's specialty is game. The town is almost like a remote outpost of Guangdong, of whose residents other Chinese say, "They eat anything with legs except a table, and anything with wings except an airplane." Donkey, dog, and scorpion are on menus. But so are deer, *shan ji* ("mountain chicken," or pheasant), and wild boar—often as unfamiliar ingredients cooked in familiar styles. Stir-frying makes venison tough, but wild boar softens up nicely while retaining its gamy flavor.

The best restaurants are in larger hotels such as the **Qianyang Dajiudian.** Try *lurou chao zhenmo* (venison stir-fried with hazel mushrooms) and *quechao shanji pian* ("Sparrow's nest" pheasant slices). The **Xin Qianlong Dajiudian,** just south of the Sheng Hua Dajiudian on Xinhua Lu (ℭ **0314/207-2222**), open from 10am to 9pm, has attentive service, good portions, and a picture menu. Plump dumplings stuffed with donkey meat and onions are called *lurou dacong shuijiao;* 200 grams or four *liang (si liang)* should be enough per person. *Cong shao yezhurou* (wild boar cooked with onions) and *zhenmo shanji ding* (nuggets of pheasant with local mushrooms) are both good. As long as you don't venture into scorpion or roe deer backbone marrow, a meal costs around ¥80 for two. There's an older branch at Zhong Xing Lu 2. **Dongpo Fanzhuang** offers authentic Sichuan cuisine, and now runs four outlets, all staffed with natives of Chengdu. Convenient branches are located opposite the railway station and at Xiao Nan Men (ℭ **0314/210-6315**), a 5-minute walk east from the main entrance to the Mountain Resort. Open 10:30am to 9pm, no English menu, but the duty manager will do his best to translate for you.

12

Fast Facts

1 FAST FACTS: BEIJING

AREA CODES   The local code for Beijing is **010**.

BANKS & ATMS   Larger branches of the **Bank of China** typically exchange cash and traveler's checks on weekdays only, from 9am to 4pm, occasionally with a break for lunch (11:30am–1:30pm). Most central is the branch at the bottom of Wangfujing Dajie, next to the Oriental Plaza. Other useful branches include those at Fucheng Men Nei Dajie 410; on Jianguo Men Wai Dajie, west of the Scitech Building; in the Lufthansa Center, next to the Kempinski Hotel; and in Tower 1 of the China World Trade Center. Outside the airport, Bank of China **ATMs** accepting international cards 24 hours a day are now widespread, and include those outside the Wangfujing Dajie branch mentioned above. Others exist farther north on Wangfujing Dajie, outside the Xin (Sun) Dong An Plaza; on the left just inside the Pacific Century Plaza on Gongti Bei Lu east of Sanlitun (only 9am–9pm); and adjacent to the Bank of China branch next to the Scitech Building (see above; also 24 hr.). The Citibank ATM east of the International Hotel, and the Hongkong and Shanghai Bank (HSBC) machine at the entrance to COFCO Plaza, roughly opposite each other on Jianguo Men Nei Dajie, are Beijing's most reliable. There are also six ATMs at the airport. See "Money & Costs," in chapter 3, for further details on using ATMs.

BUSINESS HOURS   Offices are generally open 9am to 6pm, but closed Saturday and Sunday. All shops, sights, restaurants, and transport systems offer the same service 7 days a week. Shops are typically open at least 8am to 8pm. Bank opening hours vary (see "Banks & ATMs," above).

DRINKING LAWS   With the exception of some minor local regulations, there are no liquor laws in Beijing. Alcohol can be bought in any convenience store, supermarket, restaurant, bar, hotel, or club, 7 days a week, and may be drunk anywhere you feel like drinking it. If the shop is open 24 hours, then the alcohol is available 24 hours, too. Closing times for bars and clubs vary according to demand, but typically it's all over by 3am.

ELECTRICITY   The electricity used in all parts of China is 220 volts, alternating current (AC), 50 cycles. Most devices from North America, therefore, cannot be used without a transformer. The most common outlet takes the North American two-flat-pin plug (but not the three-pin version, or those with one pin broader than the other). Nearly as common are outlets for the two-round-pin plugs common in Europe. Outlets for the three-flat-pin (two pins at an angle) used in Australia, for instance, are also frequently seen. Most hotel rooms have all three, and indeed many outlets are designed to take all three plugs. Adapters are available for only ¥8 to ¥17 in department stores. Shaver sockets are common in bathrooms of hotels from three stars upward. British-style three-chunky-pin plugs also often occur in mainland joint-venture hotels built with

Hong Kong assistance, but hotels of this caliber will have adapters available.

EMBASSIES & CONSULATES Beijing has three main embassy areas—one surrounding Ritan Gongyuan north of Jianguo Men Wai Dajie, another in Sanlitun north of Gongti Bei Lu, and the newest one, home of the new U.S. Embassy, next to Liangma Qiao and just outside the north section of the East Third Ring Road. Embassies are typically open Monday through Friday from 9am to between 4 and 5pm, with a lunch break from noon to 1:30pm. The **Australian Embassy** is in Sanlitun at Dong Zhi Men Wai Dajie 21 (✆ **010/5140-4111;** fax 010/6532-4605). The **British Embassy** consular section is in Ri Tan at Floor 21, North Tower, Kerry Centre, Guanghua Lu 1 (✆ **010/8529-6600,** ext. 3363; fax 010/8529-6081). The **Canadian Embassy** is at Dong Zhi Men Wai Dajie 19 (✆ **010/5139-4000;** bejing-cs@international.gc.ca). The **New Zealand Embassy** is in Ri Tan at Dong Er Jie 1 (✆ **010/8532-7000;** fax 010/6532-4317). The **U.S. Embassy** is at 55 An Jia Lou Lu (✆ **010/8531-3000** or, after hours, 010/6532-1910; fax 010/8531-4000).

EMERGENCIES No one speaks English on emergency numbers in China, although your best bet will be ✆ **110.** Find help nearer at hand.

HOSPITALS For comprehensive care, the best choice is **Beijing United Family Hospital (Hemujia Yiyuan;** ✆ **010/6433-3960)** at Jiangtai Lu (2 blocks southeast of the Holiday Inn Lido); it is open 24 hours, is staffed with foreign-trained doctors, and has a pharmacy, a dental clinic, in- and out-patient care, and ambulance service. They are equipped to perform surgeries and deliver babies. Other reputable health-service providers, both with 24-hour ambulance services, are the **International Medical Center** (✆ **010/6465-1561),** inside the Lufthansa Center; and the **International SOS Clinic and Alarm Center** (✆ **010/6462-9112),** at suite 105, wing 1, Kunsha Building, 16 Xinyuanli. You can usually schedule a consultation within 24 hours and they have an emergency ward onsite.

INSURANCE Unless you have comprehensive private medical insurance, traveler's insurance is a must in Beijing. If you find yourself in the unhappy situation of needing medical care, comprehensive services come with high price tags. X-rays for a broken bone will set you back several hundred dollars, and more serious care, such as an emergency surgery, could easily cost thousands of dollars. For China, purchase travel insurance that includes an air ambulance or scheduled airline repatriation. Be clear on the terms and conditions—is repatriation limited to life-threatening illnesses, for instance? While there are advanced facilities staffed by foreign doctors in Beijing, regular Chinese hospitals are to be avoided. They may charge you a substantial bill, which you must pay in cash before you're allowed to leave. If this happens to you, you'll have to wait until you return home to submit your claim, so make sure you have adequate proof of payment.

For information on traveler's insurance, trip-cancellation insurance, and medical insurance while traveling, please visit www.frommers.com/planning.

LANGUAGE English is rare in Beijing. If you're staying at a reputable five-star hotel, use their well-trained, English-speaking staff to help you with phone calls and bookings. Almost no information, booking, complaint, or emergency lines in Beijing have anyone who speaks English.

LEGAL AID If you get on the wrong side of what passes for the law in China, contact your consulate immediately.

MAIL Sending mail from China is remarkably reliable, although sending it to private addresses within China is not. Take the mail to post offices rather than dropping it in a mailbox. Some larger hotels have postal services on-site. It helps if mail sent out of the country has its country of destination written in characters, but this is not essential. Hotel staff will often help. Letters and cards written in red ink will occasionally be rejected, as this carries very negative overtones. Costs are as follows. Overseas mail: **postcards** ¥4.20, **letters under 10g** ¥5.40, **letters under 20g** ¥6.50. EMS (**express parcels** under 500g): to Australia ¥160 to ¥210; to Europe ¥220 to ¥280; to the U.S. ¥180 to ¥240. **Normal parcels** up to 1kg: to Australia by air ¥70 to ¥144, by sea ¥15 to ¥89; to the U.K. by air ¥77 to ¥162, by sea ¥22 to ¥108 to the U.S. by air ¥95 to ¥159, by sea ¥20 to ¥84. Letters and parcels can be registered for a small extra charge. Registration forms and Customs declaration forms are in Chinese and French.

NEWSPAPERS & MAGAZINES Sino-foreign joint-venture hotels in the bigger cities have a selection of foreign newspapers and magazines available, but these are not otherwise on sale. The government distributes a propaganda sheet called *China Daily,* usually free at hotels. For the most current information on life in Beijing, particularly restaurants and nightlife, see the intermittently accurate listings in the free English-language expat-produced monthlies *The Beijinger* or *Time Out,* available in hotel lobbies and at bars in the major drinking districts (see chapter 10 for these). Online, *City Weekend* (www.city weekend.com.cn) manages to update its website with fair regularity, and *Local Noodles* (www.localnoodles.com) offers user-generated reviews on restaurants and bars around town.

POLICE Known to foreigners as the **PSB (Public Security Bureau,** *gong'an ju*), this is only one of several different bureaus in mainland China. The police (*jingcha*) are quite simply best avoided—honestly, they are looking to avoid doing

any work. Ideally, any interaction with the police should be limited to visa extensions. If you must see them for some reason, approach your hotel for assistance first, and visit the office listed under "Visa Extensions," under "Entry Requirements" in chapter 3, where you are likely to find an English speaker of sorts.

SMOKING The government of China is the world's biggest cigarette manufacturer. China is home to 20% of the world's population but 30% of the world's cigarettes. About one million people a year in China die of smoking-related illnesses. Nonsmoking tables in restaurants are almost unheard of, and NO SMOKING signs are favorite places beneath which to smoke, especially in elevators. Smokers are generally sent to the spaces between the carriages on trains, but they won't bother to go there if no one protests. You'll find the same attitude on air-conditioned buses.

TAXES Service charges mostly appear only in Sino-foreign joint-venture hotels, and range from 10% to 15%. Airport departure taxes are now included in the cost of your ticket.

TIME The whole of China is on Beijing time—8 hours ahead of GMT (and therefore of London), 13 hours ahead of New York, 14 hours ahead of Chicago, and 16 hours ahead of Los Angeles. There's no daylight saving time (summer time), so subtract 1 hour in the summer.

TIPPING In mainland China, as in many other countries, there is *no tipping,* despite what tour companies may tell you (although if you have a tour leader who accompanies you from home, home rules apply). Until recently, tipping was expressly forbidden, and some hotels still carry signs requesting you not to tip. Foreigners are overcharged at every turn, and it bemuses Chinese that they hand out free money in addition. Chinese never do it themselves, and indeed if a bellhop or another hotel employee hints that a tip would be welcome, he or she may be fired. Waitresses may run out of restaurants after you to give you change, and all but the most corrupt of taxi drivers will insist on returning it, too. In China, the listed price or the price bargained for is the price you pay, and that's that.

TOILETS Street-level public toilets in China are common, many detectable with the nose before they are seen. Ladies, always carry a pack of tissues with you, as free toilet paper in public bathrooms is rare. Entrance fees have been abolished in Beijing, but someone may still try to charge you for toilet paper, ¥.20. In many cases you merely squat over a trough. Use the standard Western equipment in your hotel room, in department stores and malls, and in branches of foreign fast-food chains. This is the principal benefit of the presence of so many branches of McDonald's.

VISITOR INFORMATION The Beijing Tourism Administration maintains a 24-hour **tourist information hot line** at © **010/12301.** Staff actually speak some English, so it's unfortunate that they rarely have the answers to your questions, and

simply refer you to CITS. Hotel concierges and guest relations officers are at least close at hand, although they often have little knowledge of the city, will be reluctant to work to find the answers if they can convince you to do something else instead, and, when they do find the answer to a question, do not note it down for the next time a guest asks. Beware of strong recommendations to visit dinner shows or other expensive entertainments, as they are often on a kickback.

You can also try the new BTA-managed **Beijing Tourist Information Centers (Beijing Shi Luyou Zixun Fuwu Zhongxin)** located in each district and all marked with the same aqua-blue signs. The most competent branch is in Chaoyang, on Gongti Bei Lu across from the City Hotel and next to KFC (© **010/ 6417-6627;** fax 010/6417-6656; daily 9am–5pm). Free maps are available at the door, and staff can sometimes be wheedled into making phone calls. Ignore the extortionist travel service.

WATER Tap water in mainland China is not drinkable. Use bottled water, widely available on every street, and provided for free in all the better hotels.

2 AIRLINE WEBSITES

Aeroflot
www.aeroflot.com

Air Canada
www.aircanada.com

Air China
www.airchina.com

Air France
www.airfrance.com

Air India
www.airindia.com

Air Asia (Malaysia)
www.airasia.com

Air New Zealand
www.airnewzealand.com

Alitalia
www.alitalia.com

All Nippon Airways
www.ana.co.jp

American Airlines
www.aa.com

Asiana Airlines
www.flyasiana.com

British Airways
www.british-airways.com

Cathay Pacific
www.cathaypacific.com

China Airlines
www.china-airlines.com

China Eastern
www.flychinaeastern.com

China Southern
www.flychinasouthern.com

Continental Airlines
www.continental.com

Delta Air Lines
www.delta.com

Egypt Air
www.egyptair.com

El Al Airlines
www.elal.co.il

Emirates Airlines
www.emirates.com

Finnair
www.finnair.com

Israir Airlines
www.israirairlines.com

Japan Airlines
www.jal.co.jp

KLM Royal Dutch Airlines
www.klm.com

Korean Air
www.koreanair.com

Lufthansa
www.lufthansa.com

Malaysia Airlines
www.malaysiaairlines.com

North American Airlines
www.flynaa.com

Northwest Airlines
www.nwa.com

Qantas Airways
www.qantas.com

Pakistan International Airlines
www.piac.com.pk

Philippine Airlines
www.philippineairlines.com

Singapore Airlines
www.singaporeair.com

South African Airways
www.flysaa.com

Swiss Air
www.swiss.com

Tarom Romanian Air Transport
www.tarom.ro

Thai Airways International
www.thaiair.com

Turkish Airlines
www.thy.com

United Airlines
www.united.com

US Airways
www.usairways.com

Vietnam Airlines
www.vietnamairlines.com

The Chinese Language

Chinese is not as difficult a language to learn as it may first appear to be—at least not once you've decided what kind of Chinese to learn. There are six major languages called Chinese. Speakers of each are unintelligible to each other, and there are, in addition, a host of dialects. The Chinese you are likely to hear spoken in your local Chinatown or Chinese restaurant, or used by your friends of Chinese descent when they speak to their parents, is more than likely to be Cantonese, which is the version of Chinese used in Hong Kong and in much of southern China. But the official national language of China is **Mandarin** (**Pǔtōnghuà**—"common speech"), sometimes called Modern Standard Chinese, and viewed in mainland China as the language of administration, of the classics, and of the educated. While throughout much of mainland China people speak their own local flavor of Chinese for everyday communication, they've all been educated in Mandarin, which, in general terms, is the language of Beijing and the north. Mandarin is less well known in Hong Kong and Macau, but it is also spoken in Taiwan and Singapore, and among growing communities of recent immigrants to North America and Europe.

Chinese grammar is considerably more straightforward than that of English or other European languages, even Spanish or Italian. There are no genders, so there is no need to remember long lists of endings for adjectives and to make them agree, with variations according to case. There are no equivalents for the definite and indefinite articles ("the," "a," "an"), so there is no need to make those agree either. Singular and plural nouns are the same.

Best of all, verbs cannot be declined. The verb "to be" is *shì*. The same sound also covers "am," "are," "is," "was," "will be," and so on, since there are also no tenses. Instead of past, present, and future, Chinese is more concerned with whether an action is continuing or has been completed, and with the order in which events take place. To make matters of time clear, Chinese depends on simple expressions such as "yesterday," "before," "originally," "next year," and the like. "Tomorrow I go New York," is clear enough, as is "Yesterday I go New York." It's a little more complicated than these brief notes can suggest, but not much.

There are a few sounds in Mandarin that are not used in English (see the rough pronunciation guide below), but the main difficulty for foreigners lies in tones. Most sounds in Mandarin begin with a consonant and end in a vowel (or -n, or -ng), which leaves the language with very few distinct noises compared to English. Originally, one sound equaled one idea and one word. Even now, each of these monosyllables is represented by a single character, but often words have been made by putting two characters together, sometimes both with the same meaning, thus reinforcing one another. The solution to this phonetic poverty is to multiply the available sounds by making them tonal—speaking them at different pitches, thereby giving them different meanings. *Mā* spoken on a high level tone (first tone) offers a set of possible meanings different from those of *má* spoken with a rising tone (second tone), *mǎ* with a dipping and then rising tone (third tone), or *mà* with an abruptly falling tone (fourth tone). There's also a different meaning for the neutral, toneless *ma*.

In the average sentence, context is your friend (there are not many occasions in which the third-tone *mǎ* or "horse" might be mistaken for the fourth-tone *mà* or "grasshopper," for instance), but without tone, there is essentially no meaning. The novice had better sing his or her Mandarin very clearly, as Chinese children do—a chanted singsong can be heard emerging from the windows of primary schools across China. With experience, the student learns to give particular emphasis to the tones on words essential to a sentence's meaning, and to treat the others more lightly. Sadly, most books using modern Romanized Chinese, called *Hànyǔ pīnyīn* ("Hàn language spell-the-sounds"), do not mark the tones, nor do these appear on **pīnyīn** signs in China.

Cantonese has *eight* tones plus the neutral, but its grammatical structure is largely the same as Mandarin, as is that of all versions of Chinese. Even Chinese people who can barely understand each other's speech can at least write to each other, since written forms are similar. Mainland China, with the aim of increasing literacy (or perhaps of distancing the supposedly now thoroughly modern and socialist population from its Confucian heritage), instituted a ham-fisted simplification program in the 1950s, which reduced some characters originally taking 14 strokes of the brush, for instance, to as few as 3 strokes. Hong Kong, separated from the mainland and under British control until 1997, went its own way, kept the original full-form characters, and invented lots of new ones too. Nevertheless, many characters remain the same, and some of the simplified forms are merely familiar shorthands for the full-form ones. But however many different meanings for each tone of *ma* there may be, for each meaning there's a different character. This makes the written form a far more successful communication medium than the spoken one, which leads to misunderstandings even between native speakers, who can often be seen sketching

characters on their palms during conversation to confirm which one is meant.

The thought of learning 3,000 to 5,000 individual characters (at least 2,500 are needed to read a newspaper) also daunts many beginners. But look carefully at the ones below, and you'll notice many common elements. In fact, a rather limited number of smaller shapes are combined in different ways, much as we combine letters to make words. Admittedly, the characters offer only general hints as to their pronunciation, and that's often misleading—the system is not a phonetic one, so each new Mandarin word has to be learned as both a sound and a shape (or a group of them). But soon it's the similarities among the characters, not their differences, which begin to bother the student. English, a far more subtle language with a far larger vocabulary, and with so many pointless inconsistencies and exceptions to what are laughingly called its rules, is much more of a struggle for the Chinese than Mandarin should be for us.

But no knowledge of the language is needed to get around China, and it's almost of assistance that Chinese take it for granted that outlandish foreigners (that's you and me unless of Chinese descent) can speak not a word (poor things) and must use whatever other limited means we have to communicate—this book and a phrase book, for instance. For help with navigation to sights, simply point to the characters in this book's map keys. When leaving your hotel, take one of its cards with you, and show it to the taxi driver when you want to return. In section 2, below, is a limited list of useful words and phrases that is best supplemented with a proper phrase book. If you have a Mandarin-speaking friend from the north (Cantonese speakers who know Mandarin as a second language tend to have fairly heavy accents), ask him or her to pronounce the greetings and words of thanks from the list below so that you can repeat and practice. While you are as likely to be laughed *at* as *with* in China, such efforts are always appreciated.

1 A GUIDE TO PĪNYĪN PRONUNCIATION

Letters in pīnyīn mostly have the values any English speaker would expect, with the following exceptions:

c *ts* as in bi*ts*

q *ch* as in *ch*in, but much harder and more forward, made with tongue and teeth

r has no true equivalent in English, but the *r* of *r*eed is close, although the tip of the tongue should be near the top of the mouth, and the teeth together

x also has no true equivalent, but is nearest to the *sh* of *sh*eep, although the tongue should be parallel to the roof of the mouth and the teeth together

zh is a soft j, like the *dge* in ju*dge*

The vowels are pronounced roughly as follows:

a as in f*a*ther

e as in *e*rr (*leng* is pronounced as English "lung")

i is pronounced *ee* after most consonants, but after c, ch, r, s, sh, z, and zh is a buzz at the front of the mouth behind closed teeth

o as in s*o*ng

u as in t*oo*

ü is the purer, lips-pursed u of French t*u* and German *ü*. Confusingly, **u** after j, x, q, and y is always ü, but in these cases the accent over ü does not appear.

ai sounds like *eye*

ao as in *ou*ch

ei as in h*ay*

ia as in *ya*k

ian sounds like *yen*

iang sounds like *yang*

iu sounds like *you*

ou as in t*oe*

ua as in g*ua*va

ui sounds like *way*

uo sounds like *or,* but is more abrupt

Note that when two or more third-tone "ˇ" sounds follow one another, they should all, except the last, be pronounced as second-tone "ˊ."

2 MANDARIN BARE ESSENTIALS

GREETINGS & INTRODUCTIONS

English	Pinyin	Chinese
Hello	Nǐ hǎo	你好
How are you?	Nǐ hǎo ma?	你好吗?
Fine. And you?	Wǒ hěn hǎo. Nǐ ne?	我很好，你呢?
I'm not too well/things aren't going well	Bù hǎo	不好

English	Pinyin	Chinese
What is your name? (very polite)	Nín guì xìng?	您贵姓?
My (family) name is . . .	Wǒ xìng . . .	我姓 . . . . . .
I'm known as (family, then given name)	Wǒ jiào . . .	我叫 . . . . . .
I'm [American]	Wǒ shì [Měiguó] rén	我是美国人
[Australian]	[Àodàlìyà]	澳大利亚人
[British]	[Yīngguó]	英国人
[Canadian]	[Jiānádà]	加拿大人
[Irish]	[Àiěrlán]	爱尔兰人
[New Zealander]	[Xīnxīlán]	新西兰人
I'm from [America]	Wǒ shì cóng [Měiguó] lái de	我是从美国来的
Excuse me/I'm sorry	Duìbùqǐ	对不起
I don't understand	Wǒ tīng bù dǒng	我听不懂
Thank you	Xièxie nǐ	谢谢你
Correct (yes)	Duì	对
Not correct	Bú duì	不对
No, I don't want	Wǒ bú yào	我不要
Not acceptable	Bù xíng	不行

BASIC QUESTIONS & PROBLEMS

English	Pinyin	Chinese
Excuse me/I'd like to ask	Qǐng wènyíxià	请问一下
Where is . . . ?	. . . zài nǎr?	. . . . . . 在哪儿?
How much is . . . ?	. . . duōshǎo qián?	. . . 多少钱?
. . . this one?	Zhèi/Zhè ge . . .	这个 . . .
. . . that one?	Nèi/Nà ge . . .	那个 . . .
Do you have . . . ?	Nǐ yǒu méi yǒu . . . ?	你有没有 . . . ?
What time does/is . . . ?	. . . jǐ diǎn?	. . . 几点?
What time is it now?	Xiànzài jǐ diǎn?	现在几点?
When is . . . ?	. . . shénme shíhou?	. . . 什么时候?
Why?	Wèishénme?	为什么?
Who?	Shéi?	谁?
Is that okay?	Xíng bù xíng?	行不行?
I'm feeling ill	Wǒ shēng bìng le	我生病了

NUMBERS

Note that more complicated forms of numbers are often used on official documents and receipts to prevent fraud—see how easily 1 can be changed to 2, 3, or even 10. Familiar Arabic numerals appear on bank notes, most signs, taxi meters, and other places. Be particularly careful with *four* and *ten,* which sound very alike in many regions—hold up fingers to make sure. Note, too, that *yī,* meaning "one," tends to change its tone all the time depending on what it precedes. Don't worry about this—once you've started talking about money, almost any kind of squeak for "one" will do. Finally note that "two" alters when being used with expressions of quantity.

English	Pinyin	Chinese
zero	líng	零
one	yī	一
two	èr	二
two (of them)	liǎng ge	两个
three	sān	三
four	sì	四
five	wǔ	五
six	liù	六
seven	qī	七
eight	bā	八
nine	jiǔ	九
10	shí	十
11	shí yī	十一
12	shí èr	十二
21	èr shí yī	二十一
22	èr shí èr	二十二
51	wǔ shí yī	五十一
100	yì bǎi	一百
101	yì bǎi líng yī	一百零一
110	yì bǎi yī (shí)	一百一（十）
111	yì bǎi yī shí yī	一百一十一
1,000	yì qiān	一千
1,500	yì qiān wǔ (bǎi)	一千五百
5,678	wǔ qiān liù bǎi qī shí bāi	五千六百七十八
10,000	yí wàn	一万

MONEY

The word *yuan* (¥) is rarely spoken, nor is *jiǎo,* the written form for one-tenth of a *yuan,* equivalent to 10 *fēn* (there are 100 *fēn* in a *yuan*). Instead, the Chinese speak of "pieces of money," *kuài qián,* usually abbreviated just to *kuài,* and they speak of *máo* for one-tenth of a *kuài. Fēn* have been overtaken by inflation and are almost useless. Often all zeros after the last whole number are simply omitted, along with *kuài qián,* which is taken as read, especially in direct reply to the question *duōshǎo qián*—"How much?"

English	Pinyin	Chinese
¥.30	sān máo qián	三毛钱
¥1	yí kuài qián	一块钱
¥2	liǎng kuài qián	两块钱
¥5.05	wǔ kuài líng wǔ fēn	五块零五分
¥5.50	wǔ kuài wǔ	五块五
¥550	wǔ bǎi wǔ shí kuài	五百五十块
¥5,500	wǔ qiān wǔ bǎi kuài	五千五百块
Small change	língqián	零钱

English	Pinyin	Chinese
I want to change money (foreign exchange)	Wǒ xiǎng huàn qián	我想换钱
credit card	Xìnyòngkǎ	信用卡
traveler's check	lǚxíng zhīpiào	旅行支票
department store	bǎihuò shāngdiàn	百货商店
or	gòuwù zhōngxīn	购物中心
convenience store	xiǎomàibù	小卖部
market	shìchǎng	市场
May I have a look?	Wǒ Kànyíxia, hǎo ma?	我看一下，好吗?
I want to buy . . .	Wǒ xiǎng mǎi . . .	我想买 . . .
How many do you want?	Nǐ yào jǐ ge?	你要几个?
Two of them	liǎng ge	两个
Three of them	sān ge	三个
1 kilo	yì gōngjīn	一公斤
Half a kilo	yì jīn	一斤
or	bàn gōngjīn	半公斤
1m	yì mǐ	一米
Too expensive!	Tài guì le!	太贵了
Do you have change?	Yǒu língqián ma?	有零钱吗?

TIME

morning	shàngwǔ	上午
afternoon	xiàwǔ	下午
evening	wǎnshang	晚上
8:20am	shàngwǔ bā diǎn èr shí fēn	上午八点二十分
9:30am	shàngwǔ jiǔ diǎn bàn	上午九点半
noon	zhōngwǔ	中午
4:15pm	xiàwǔ sì diǎn yí kè	下午四点一刻
midnight	wǔ yè	午夜
1 hour	yí ge xiǎoshí	一个小时
8 hours	bā ge xiǎoshí	八个小时
today	jīntiān	今天
yesterday	zuótiān	昨天
tomorrow	míngtiān	明天
Monday	Xīngqī yī	星期一
Tuesday	Xīngqī èr	星期二
Wednesday	Xīngqī sān	星期三
Thursday	Xīngqī sì	星期四

English	Pinyin	Chinese
Friday	Xīngqī wǔ	星期五
Saturday	Xīngqī liù	星期六
Sunday	Xīngqī tiān	星期天

TRANSPORT & TRAVEL

English	Pinyin	Chinese
I want to take . . .	Wǒ xiǎng qù . . .	我想去乘 . . .
plane	fēijī	飞机
train	huǒchē	火车
bus	gōnggòng qìchē	公共汽车
long-distance bus	chángtú qìchē	长途汽车
taxi	chūzū chē	出租车
airport	fēijīchǎng	飞机场
stop or station (bus or train)	zhàn	站
(plane/train/bus) ticket	piào	票
luxury (bus, hotel rooms)	háohuá	豪华
high-speed (buses, expressways)	gāosù	高速
air-conditioned	kōngtiáo	空调
I want to go to . . .	Wǒ xiǎng qù . . .	我想去 . . .
When's the last bus?	Mòbānchē jīdiǎn kāi?	末班车几点开?

NAVIGATION

English	Pinyin	Chinese
north	Běi	北
south	Nán	南
east	Dōng	东
west	Xī	西
Turn left	zuǒ guǎi	左拐
Turn right	yòu guǎi	右拐
Go straight on	yìzhí zǒu	一直走
crossroads	shízì lùkǒu	十字路口
10km	shí gōnglǐ	十公里
I'm lost	Wǒ diū le	我迷路了

HOTEL

English	Pinyin	Chinese
How many days?	Zhù jǐ tiān?	住几天?
standard room (twin or double with private bathroom)	biāozhǔn jiān	标准间
passport	hùzhào	护照
deposit	yājīn	押金
I want to check out	Wǒ tuì fáng	我退房

Here's a list of common signs and notices to help you identify what you are looking for, from restaurants to condiments, and to help you choose the right door at the public toilets. These are the simplified characters in everyday use in China, but note that it's increasingly fashionable for larger businesses and for those with a long history to use more complicated traditional characters, so not all may match what's below. Also, very old restaurants and temples across China tend to write their signs from right to left.

English	Pinyin	Chinese
hotel	bīnguǎn	宾馆
	dàjiǔdiàn	大酒店
	jiǔdiàn	酒店
	fàndiàn	饭店
restaurant	fànguǎn	饭馆
	jiǔdiàn	酒店
	jiǔjiā	酒家
bar	jiǔbā	酒吧
Internet bar	wǎngbā	网吧
cafe	kāfēiguǎn	咖啡馆
teahouse	cháguǎn	茶馆
department store	bǎihuò shāngdiàn	百货商店
shopping mall	gòuwù zhōngxīn	购物中心
market	shìchǎng	市场
bookstore	shūdiàn	书店
police (Public Security Bureau)	gōng'ānjú	公安局
Bank of China	Zhōngguó Yínháng	中国银行
public telephone	gōngyòng diànhuà	公用电话
public restroom	gōngyòng cèsuǒ	公用厕所
male	nán	男
female	nǚ	女
entrance	rùkǒu	入口
exit	chūkǒu	出口
bus stop/station	qìchē zhàn	汽车站
up (get on bus)	shang	上
down (get off bus)	xia	下
long-distance bus station	chángtú qìchē zhàn	长途汽车站
luxury	háohuá	豪华
highway	gāosù	高速公路

English	Pinyin	Chinese
railway station	huǒchēzhàn	火车站
hard seat	yìng zuò	硬座
soft seat	ruǎn zuò	软座
hard sleeper	yìng wò	硬卧
soft sleeper	ruǎn wò	软卧
direct (through) train	zhídá	直达车
express train	tèkuài	特快
metro/subway station	dìtiězhàn	地铁站
airport	feījīchǎng	飞机场
dock/wharf	mǎtóu	码头
passenger terminal (bus, boat, and so on)	kèyùn zhàn	客运站
ticket hall	shòupiào tīng	售票厅
ticket office	shòupiào chù	售票处
left-luggage office	xíngli jìcún chù	行李寄存处
temple	sì	寺
or	miào	庙
museum	bówùguǎn	博物馆
memorial hall	jìniànguǎn	纪念馆
park	gōngyuán	公园
hospital	yīyuàn	医院
clinic	zhěnsuǒ	诊所
pharmacy	yàofáng/yàodiàn	药房/药店
travel agency	lǚxíngshè	旅行社

THE CHINESE LANGUAGE

13

MANDARIN BARE ESSENTIALS

14

The Beijing Menu

One of the best things about any visit to China is the food, at least for the independent traveler. Tour groups are often treated to a relentless series of cheap, bland dishes designed to cause no complaints and to keep the costs down for the Chinese operator, so do everything you can to escape and order some of the specialties we've described for you in chapter 6. Here they are again, in alphabetical order and with characters you can show to the waitress.

Widely available dishes and snacks are grouped in the first list; you can order most of them in any mainstream or *jiachang cai* ("home-style") restaurant. Some dishes recommended in this guidebook's reviews of individual restaurants are commonly available enough to be on this first list. Note that some of the specialty dishes in the second list are available only in the restaurants reviewed, or in restaurants offering a particular region's cuisine.

Supplement these lists with the bilingual menu from your local Chinese restaurant at home. The characters will not be quite the same as those used in Beijing (more similar to those used in Hong Kong and Macau), but they will be understood. Don't expect the dishes to be the same, however. Expect them to be *better*.

Any mainstream nonspecialty restaurant can and will make any common Chinese dish, whether it's on the menu or not. But don't expect Beijing cooks to manage the subtler flavors of Cantonese cooking, for instance, unless the restaurant advertises itself as a southern-food specialist.

A surprising number of restaurants now have English menus. In the past, this was a warning of inflated prices, but now an English menu is often used to brand a restaurant as "classy" in the eyes of the locals.

Dishes often arrive in haphazard order, but menus generally open with *liang cai* (cold dishes). Except in top-class Sino-foreign joint-venture restaurants, you are strongly advised to avoid these for hygiene reasons. The restaurant's specialties also come early in the menu: They have significantly higher prices and if you dither, the waitress will recommend them, saying, "I hear this one's good." Waitresses always recommend ¥180 dishes, never ¥8 ones. Some of these dishes may occasionally be made from creatures you would regard as pets or zoo creatures (or best in the wild), and parts of them you may consider inedible or odd, like swallow saliva (the main ingredient of bird's nest soup, a rather bland Cantonese delicacy).

Main dishes come next; various meats and fish are followed by vegetables and *doufu* (tofu). Drinks come at the end. You'll rarely find desserts outside of restaurants that largely cater to foreigners. A few watermelon slices may appear, but it's best to forgo them.

Soup is usually eaten last. Outside Guangdong Province, Hong Kong, and Macau, rice also usually arrives at the end; if you want it with your meal, you must ask (point to the characters for rice, below, when the first dish arrives).

There is no tipping. Tea, chopsticks, and napkins should be free (although if a wrapped packet of tissues arrives you may pay a small fee); service charges do not exist outside of major hotels; and there are no cover charges or taxes. If asked what tea you would like, know that you are going to receive something above average and will be charged for it. Exercise caution—some varieties cost more than the meal!

Most Chinese food is not designed to be eaten solo, but if you do find yourself on your own, ask for small portions *(xiao pan,* 小盘*),* usually about 70% of the size of a full dish and about 70% of the price. This allows you to sample the menu properly without too much waste.

1 ORDERING

COMMON DISHES & SNACKS

Pinyin	English	Chinese
bābǎo zhōu	rice porridge with nuts and berries	八宝粥
bǎnlì shāo chìzhōng	soy chicken wings with chestnuts	板栗烧翅中
bāozi	stuffed steamed buns	包子
běijīng kǎoyā	Peking duck	北京烤鸭
bīngqílín	ice cream	冰淇淋
chǎofàn	fried rice	炒饭
chǎomiàn	fried noodles	炒面
cōng bào niúròu	quick-fried beef and green onions	葱爆牛肉
dāndān miàn	noodles in spicy broth	担担面
diǎnxin	dim sum (snacks)	点心
dì sān xiān	braised eggplant with potatoes and spicy green peppers	地三鲜
dòu zhī	fermented bean purée	豆汁
gānbiān sìjìdòu	sautéed string beans	干煸四季豆
gōngbào jīdīng	spicy diced chicken with cashews/peanuts	宫保鸡丁
guōtiē	fried dumplings/pot stickers	锅贴
hóngshāo fǔzhú	braised tofu	红烧豆腐
hóngshāo huángyú	braised yellow fish	红烧黄鱼
huíguō ròu	twice-cooked pork	回锅肉
huǒguō	hot pot	火锅
jiānbing	large crepe folded around fried dough with plum and hot sauces	煎饼
jiǎozi	dumplings/Chinese ravioli	饺子
jīngjiàng ròu sī	shredded pork in soy sauce	京酱肉丝
má dòufu	mashed soy bean	麻豆腐
mápó dòufu	spicy tofu with chopped meat	麻婆豆腐

Pinyin	English	Chinese
miàntiáo	noodles	面条
mǐfàn	rice	米饭
mù xū ròu	sliced pork with fungus (mu shu pork)	木须肉
niúròu miàn	beef noodles	牛肉面
ròu chuàn	kabobs	肉串
sānxiān	"three flavors" (usually prawn, mushroom, pork)	三鲜
shuǐjiǎo	boiled dumplings	水饺
suānlà báicài	hot-and-sour cabbage	酸辣白菜
suānlà tāng	hot-and-sour soup	酸辣汤
sù miàn	vegetarian noodles	素面
sù shíjǐn	mixed vegetables	素什锦
tángcù lǐji	sweet-and-sour pork tenderloin	糖醋里脊
tǔdòu dùn niúròu	stewed beef and potato	土豆炖牛肉
xiàn bǐng	pork- or vegetable-stuffed fried pancake	(肉或素) 馅饼
xīhóngshì chǎo jīdàn	tomatoes with eggs	西红柿炒鸡蛋
yángròu chuān	barbecued lamb skewers with ground cumin and chili powder	羊肉串
yóutiáo	fried salty doughnut	油条
yúxiāng qiézi	eggplant in garlic sauce	鱼香茄子
yúxiāng ròusī	shredded pork in garlic sauce	鱼香肉丝
zhēngjiǎo	steamed dumplings	蒸饺
zhōu	rice porridge	粥

THE HOT POT MENU

Huǒguō	Types of Hot Pot	火锅种类
yuānyang huǒguō	half spicy, half regular soup	鸳鸯火锅
qīngtāng huǒguō	chicken soup hot pot	鸡汤火锅
hóngwèi huǒguō	only spicy hot pot	红味火锅
yútóu huǒguō	fish-head soup	鱼头火锅

Shūcài lèi	Vegetables	蔬菜类
tǔdòu	potato	土豆
dòufu	tofu	豆腐
dòufu pí	tofu skin	豆腐皮
dòng dòufu	cold tofu	冻豆腐
dōngguā	Chinese winter melon	冬瓜
qīngsǔn	lettuce shoots	青笋
bái luób	fresh white radish	白罗卜
ǒupiàn	sliced lotus	藕片

Pinyin	English	Chinese
fěnsī	glass noodles	粉丝
huángdòuyá	soy bean sprouts	黄豆芽
bōcài	green spinach	菠菜
xiāngcài	caraway seeds	香菜
dōngsǔn	bamboo shoots	笋
mùěr	black agaric mushroom	黑木耳
pínggū	flat mushrooms	平菇
jīnzhēngū	needle mushrooms	金针菇
xiānggū	straw mushrooms	草菇
niángāo	Chinese rice cake	年糕

Ròu leì — Meats — 肉类

Pinyin	English	Chinese
zhūròu piàn	sliced pork	猪肉片
niúròu piàn	sliced beef	牛肉片
jīròu piàn	sliced chicken	鸡肉片
féi niú	fatty beef	肥牛
féi yáng	lamb	肥羊
huǒtuǐ	ham	火腿
niúròu wán	beef balls	牛肉丸
ròu wánzi	meatballs	肉丸子
xiajiao	shrimp dumplings	虾饺
dànjiǎo	egg dumplings	蛋饺
ānchun dàn	quail's eggs	鹌鹑蛋
yā cháng	duck's intestines	鸭肠
yā xuě	duck's blood	鸭血
yú tóu	fish head	鱼头
shànyú piàn	sliced eel	鳝鱼片
níqiu	loach	泥鳅
zhū nǎo	pig brains	猪脑

Hǎixiān — Seafood — 海鲜

Pinyin	English	Chinese
xiā	shrimps	虾
yú piàn	sliced fish	鱼片
yú wán	fish balls	鱼丸
mòyú piàn	black carp strips	墨鱼片
yóuyú piàn	cuttlefish strips	鱿鱼片

Tiáoliào — Seasoning — 可选调料

Pinyin	English	Chinese
làjiāo jiàng	chili hot sauce	辣椒酱
làyóu	chili oil	辣油
là	spicy	辣
búlà	not spicy	不辣
xiāngyóu	sesame oil	香油
huāshēng jiàng	peanut paste	花生酱

Pinyin	English	Chinese
shāchá jiàng	barbecue sauce	沙茶酱
zhīma jiàng	sesame paste	芝麻酱
dà suàn	garlic	大蒜
xiāngcài	cilantro	香菜
cù	vinegar	醋
búyào cù	without vinegar	不要醋
jiàngyóu	soy sauce	酱油

Miscellaneous

xiǎo wǎn	small bowl	小碗
dà wǎn	large bowl	大碗
píjiǔ	beer	啤酒
kāfēi	coffee	咖啡
kuàngquán shuǐ	mineral water	矿泉水
cháshuǐ	tea	茶水

Useful Phrases

Qǐng lái yī bēi bīng píjiǔ?	May I have a cold beer, please?	请来一杯冰啤酒?
Qǐng bǎ huǒ guān xiǎo yīdiǎn?	Could you turn the fire down a little, please?	请把火关小一点?
Qǐng bǎ huǒ kāi dà yīdiǎn?	Could you turn the fire up a little, please?	请把火开大一点?
Qǐng bāng wǒmen jiā yīdiǎn tāng?	Could you add some more soup, please?	请 帮我们加一点汤?

RESTAURANT

Jǐ wèi?	How many people?	几位
fúwùyuán	waiter/waitress	服务员
càidān	menu	菜单
Wǒ shì chī sù de	I'm vegetarian.	我是吃素的
Qǐng bù fàng wèijīng	Don't add MSG.	请不放味精
Yǒu méi yǒu . . . ?	Do you have . . . ?	有没有 . . . ?
Qǐng lái yí fènr . . .	Please bring a portion of . . .	请来一份儿 . . .
Wǒ chībǎo le	I'm full.	我吃饱了
Jiézhàng	Bill, please.	结帐

2 DISHES RECOMMENDED IN RESTAURANT REVIEWS

Pinyin	English	Chinese
bābǎo làjiàng	gingko, nuts, and pork in sweet chili sauce	八宝辣酱
bōluó fàn	pineapple rice	菠萝饭

Pinyin	English	Chinese	235
cháshùgū bāo lǎojī	chicken with tea-mushroom soup	茶树菇煲老鸡	
chénpí lǎoyā shānzhēn bāo	duck, dried tangerine peel, and mushroom potage	陈皮老鸭山珍煲	
cuìpí qiézi	sweet-and-sour battered eggplant	脆皮茄子	
cùngū shāo	deep-fried pork with medicinal herbs	寸骨烧	
Dǎizú xiāngmáocǎo kǎo yú	Dǎi grilled lemon grass fish	傣族香茅草烤鱼	
dà lāpí	cold rice noodles in sesame and vinegar sauce	大拉皮	
dà pán jī	diced chicken and noodles in tomato sauce	大盘鸡面	
Dōngběi fēngwèi dàpái	northeast-style braised ribs	东北风味大排	
Dōngpō ròu	braised fatty pork in small clay pot	东坡肉	
é'gān juǎn	goose-liver rolls with hoisin sauce	鹅肝卷	
gǒubùlǐ bāozi	pork-stuffed bread dumplings	狗不理包子	
guōbā ròu piān	pork with crispy fried rice	锅巴肉片	
guòqiáo mǐxiàn	crossing-the-bridge rice noodles	过桥米线	
huángdì sǔn shāo wánzi	Imperial bamboo shoots and vegetarian meatballs	皇帝笋烧素丸子	
huángjiǔ	"yellow" rice wine	黄酒	
huángqiáo ròu sūbǐng	shredded-pork rolls	黄桥肉酥饼	
huíxiāng dòu	aniseed-flavored beans	茴香豆	
jiāoliū wánzi	crisp-fried pork balls	焦熘丸子	
jīngjiàng ròusī	shredded pork with green onion rolled in tofu skin	腐皮肉丝卷	
jīnpái tiáoliào	"gold label" sesame sauce (for Mongolian hot pot)	金牌调料	
jīròu sèlā	deep-fried chicken pieces with herb dipping sauce	炸鸡肉色拉	
jiǔxiāng yúgān	dried fish in wine sauce	酒香鱼干	
juébā chǎo làròu	bacon stir-fried with brake leaves	蕨粑炒腊肉	
kǎo yángròu	roast mutton	烤羊肉	
làbā cù	garlic-infused vinegar	腊八醋	
láncài sìjìdòu	green beans stir-fried with salty vegetables	榄菜四季豆	
lǎogānmā shāojī	spicy diced chicken with bamboo and ginger	老干妈烧鸡	

Pinyin	English	Chinese
làròu dòuyá juǎnbǐng	spicy bacon and bean sprouts in pancakes	腊肉豆芽卷饼
làwèi huájī bāozǎi fàn	chicken and preserved sausage on rice in clay pot	腊味滑鸡煲仔饭
liángbàn zǐ lúsǔn	purple asparagus salad	凉拌紫芦笋
luóbo sī sūbǐng	shredded-daikon shortcake	萝卜丝酥饼
málà lóngxiā	spicy crawfish	麻辣小龙虾
málà tiánluó	field snails stewed in chili and Sìchuān pepper	麻辣田螺
mǎtí niúliǔ	stir-fried beef with broccoli, water chestnuts, and tofu rolls	马蹄牛柳
mìzhì zhǐbāo lúyú	paper-wrapped perch and onions on sizzling iron plate	秘制纸包鲈鱼
náng bāo ròu	lamb and vegetable stew served on flat wheat bread	馕包羊肉
náng chǎo yángròu	stir-fried lamb with bread	囊炒羊肉
nánrǔ kòuròu	braised pork in red fermented bean curd gravy	南乳扣肉
niúròu wán shuǐjiǎo	beef-ball dumplings	牛肉丸水饺
nóngjiā shāo jiān jī	farmhouse spicy sautéed chicken filet	农家烧煎鸡
nóngjiā xiǎochǎo	farmhouse soybeans, green onion, Chinese chives, and green pepper in a clay pot	农家素小炒
qiáo miàn māo ěrduo	"cat's-ear shaped" buckwheat pasta with chopped meat	荞面猫耳朵
ròudīng báicài xiànbǐng	meat cabbage pie	肉丁白菜馅饼
rúyì hǎitái juǎn	"as one wishes" seaweed rolls	如意海苔卷
sān bēi jī	chicken reduced in rice wine, sesame oil, and soy sauce	三杯鸡
sānxiān làohé	seafood and garlic chive buns	三鲜烙合
sè shāo niúròu	foil-wrapped beef marinated in mountain herbs	色烧牛肉
shāchá niúròu	beef sautéed with Taiwanese BBQ sauce	沙茶牛肉
shānyao gēng	yam broth with mushrooms	山药羹
shānyao húlu	red-bean rolls with mountain herbs	山药豆沙卷
shēngjiān bāozi	pork-stuffed fried bread dumplings	生煎包子
shǒubá fàn	rice with lamb and raisins	手扒饭
shǒuzhuā fàn	Uighur-style rice with carrot and mutton	手抓羊肉饭

Pinyin	English	Chinese
shǒuzhuā yáng pái	lamb chops roasted with cumin and chili	手抓羊排
shuǐzhǔ yú	boiled fish in spicy broth with numbing peppercorns	水煮鱼
suāncài tǔdòu	vinegared potato slices	酸菜土豆
suànxiāng jīchì	garlic paper-wrapped chicken wings	蒜香鸡翅
sǔngān lǎoyā bāo	stewed duck with dried bamboo shoots	笋干老鸭煲
Táiwān dòfu bāo	Taiwanese tofu and vegetables clay pot	台湾豆腐煲
tiānfú shāokǎo yángtuǐ	roasted leg of mutton with cumin and chili powder	天福烧烤羊腿
tiēbǐngzi	corn pancakes cooked on a griddle	贴玉米饼子
tǔdòu qiú	deep-fried potato balls with chili sauce	土豆球
tǔtāng shícài	clear soup with seasonal leafy greens	土汤时菜
xiāngcǎo cuìlà yú	whole fried fish with hot peppers and lemon grass	香草脆辣鱼
xiǎolóng bāozi	pork-stuffed steamed bread dumplings	小笼包子
Xībèi dà bàncài	Xībèi salad	西贝大拌菜
xièfěn dòufu	crabmeat tofu	蟹粉豆腐
xièsānxiān shuǐjiǎo	boiled crab dumplings with shrimp and mushrooms	蟹三鲜水饺
yángròu chuàn	spicy mutton skewers with cumin	羊肉串
yángyóu má dòufu	mashed soybeans with lamb oil	羊油麻豆腐
yán jú xiā	shrimp skewers in rock salt	盐局虾
yè niúròu juǎn	grilled la lop leaf beef	叶牛肉卷
yì bǎ zhuā	fried wheat cakes	一把抓
yóumiàn wōwo	steamed oatmeal noodles	莜面窝窝
yóutiáo niúròu	sliced beef with fried dough in savory sauce	油条牛肉
yǔjī shūcài	organic vegetables	有机蔬菜
zhá guàncháng	taro chips with garlic sauce	炸灌肠
zhájiàng miàn	wheat noodles with black bean mince	炸酱面
zhāngchá yā	crispy smoked duck with plum sauce	樟茶鸭
zhá qiéhé	pork-stuffed deep-fried eggplant	炸茄合

Pinyin	English	Chinese
zhá xiāngjiāo	deep-fried banana	炸香蕉
zhēnzhū nǎichá	pearl milk tea	珍珠奶茶
zhǐbāo lúyú	paper-wrapped perch in sweet sauce	纸包鲈鱼
zhījīcǎo kǎo niúpái	lotus-leaf-wrapped roast beef with mountain herbs	枳机草烤牛排
zhūròu báicài bāozi	steamed bun stuffed with pork and cabbage	猪肉白菜包子
zhúsūn qìguō jī	mushroom and mountain herbs chicken soup	竹荪气锅鸡
zhútǒng jī	chicken soup in bamboo vessel	竹筒鸡
zhútǒng páigǔ	spicy stewed pork in bamboo vessel with mint	竹筒排骨
zhútǒng zhūròu	steamed pork in bamboo vessel with coriander	竹筒猪肉
zuì jī	chicken marinated in rice wine	醉鸡
zuì xiā	live shrimp in wine	醉虾

INDEX